THE HUMAN RIGHT TO A HEALTHY ENVIRONMENT

The absence of a globally recognized right to a healthy environment has not prevented the development of human rights norms relating to the environment. Indeed, one of the most noteworthy aspects of human rights law over the last twenty years is that UN treaty bodies, regional tribunals, special rapporteurs, and other human rights mechanisms have applied human rights law to environmental issues even without a stand-alone, justiciable human right to a healthy environment. In *The Human Right to a Healthy Environment*, a diverse set of scholars and practitioners, all of whom have been instrumental in defining the relationship between human rights and the environment, provide their thoughts on what is, or should be, the role of an international human right to a healthy environment. The right to a healthy environment could be a capstone to this field of law, could help to provide structure to it, or could move it in new directions.

John H. Knox is Henry C. Lauerman Professor of International Law at Wake Forest University, North Carolina, and has written extensively on human rights and environmental issues. The first UN Special Rapporteur on human rights and the environment, he has led the effort to understand and promote the application of human rights to environmental issues. He won the Francis Deák Prize for scholarship in 2003. Between 1999 and 2005, he chaired a national advisory committee to the US Environmental Protection Agency, and from 2008 to 2012 he was of counsel to the Center for International Environmental Law.

Ramin Pejan is a staff attorney at Earthjustice's International Program, based in San Francisco. He is also an adjunct clinical professor at the University of California, Irvine, School of Law, in its International Justice Clinic. Prior to Earthjustice, Ramin worked for the United Nations Office of the High Commissioner for Human Rights and the United Nations Environment Programme on the links between human rights and environmental issues. From 2010 to 2012, Ramin worked in Bushbuckridge, South Africa, as legal counsel for the Association for Water and Rural Development, a non-profit organization focusing on water resource management issues in rural South Africa.

The Human Right to a Healthy Environment

Edited by

JOHN H. KNOX
Wake Forest University

RAMIN PEJAN
Earthjustice

CAMBRIDGE
UNIVERSITY PRESS

CAMBRIDGE
UNIVERSITY PRESS

University Printing House, Cambridge CB2 8BS, United Kingdom

One Liberty Plaza, 20th Floor, New York, NY 10006, USA

477 Williamstown Road, Port Melbourne, VIC 3207, Australia

314-321, 3rd Floor, Plot 3, Splendor Forum, Jasola District Centre, New Delhi - 110025, India

79 Anson Road, #06-04/06, Singapore 079906

Cambridge University Press is part of the University of Cambridge.

It furthers the University's mission by disseminating knowledge in the pursuit of education, learning and research at the highest international levels of excellence.

www.cambridge.org
Information on this title: www.cambridge.org/9781108421195
DOI: 10.1017/9781108367530

First published 2018

A catalogue record for this publication is available from the British Library

Library of Congress Cataloging in Publication data
NAMES: Knox, John H., editor. | Pejan, Ramin, editor.
TITLE: The human right to a healthy environment / edited by John H. Knox, Ramin Pejan.
DESCRIPTION: New York : Cambridge University Press, 2018.
IDENTIFIERS: LCCN 2018006529 | ISBN 9781108421195 (hardback) | ISBN 9781108431583 (paperback)
SUBJECTS: LCSH: Environmental law, International. | Human rights–Environmental aspects.
CLASSIFICATION: LCC K3585 .H853 2018 | DDC 344.04/6–dc23
LC record available at https://lccn.loc.gov/2018006529

ISBN 978-1-108-42119-5 Hardback
ISBN 978-1-108-43158-3 Paperback

Contents

Contributors

Sumudu Atapattu University of Wisconsin

David R. Boyd University of British Colombia, Vancouver

Rebecca M. Bratspies Center for Environmental Reform, City University of New York School of Law

Lilian Chenwi University of Witwatersrand, Johannesburg

Erin Daly Widener University School of Law, Delaware

Louis J. Kotzé North-West University, South Africa; University of Lincoln, UK

Marc Limon Universal Rights Group, Geneva

Daniel Magraw Johns Hopkins University, Baltimore

James R. May Widener University School of Law, Delaware

Marcos Orellana Human Rights Watch, USA

Ole W. Pedersen Newcastle Law School, Newcastle University, UK

Lavanya Rajamani Centre for Policy Research, New Delhi

César Rodríguez-Garavito University of Los Andes, Colombia

Dinah Shelton George Washington University, Washington, DC

Kristina Wienhöfer International Justice Initiative

Table of Cases

Acción de tutela instaurada por Orlando José Morales Ramos, contra la Sociedad Drummond Ltda, Decision No. T-154 – 2013 (Constitutional Court of Colombia, Sixth Chamber of Appeals, 2013).
Advocate Prakash Mani Sharma *v.* Cabinet Secretariat, No. 3027/2059 (Supreme Court of Nepal, 1997).
African Commission on Human and Peoples' Rights *v.* Kenya, Judgment, Application 006/2012, Judgment (African Court of Human and Peoples' Rights, 2017).
African Commission on Human and Peoples' Rights *v.* Kenya, Application No. 006/2012, Order of Provisional Measures (ACHPR, 2013).
Anglo Norwegian Fisheries Case (United Kingdom *v.* Norway), [1951] ICJ Rep. 116.
Anjum Irfan *v.* LDA, PLD 2002 Lahore 555 (Pakistan, 2002).
Appeal No. 575.998, Minas Gervais (Brazil Supreme Court of Justice, 2004).
Appeal No. 70011759842, Rio Grande do Sul (Brazil Supreme Court of Justice, 2005).
Appeal No. 70012091278, Rio Grande do Sul (Brazil Supreme Court of Justice, 2006).
Asghar Leghari *v.* Pakistan, No. 25501/2015 (Lahore High Court Green Bench, 2015).
Ashworth and Others *v.* United Kingdom, No. 39561/98 (European Court of Human Rights, 2004).
Askew *v.* Game & Fresh Water Fish Comm'n, 336 So. 2d 556 (Fla. 1976).
Asociación Interamericana para la Defensa del Ambiente y otros (Costa Rican Constitutional Court, 2009).
Asylum Case (Colombia *v.* Peru), [1950] ICJ Rep. 266.
Atanasov *v.* Bulgaria, No. 12853/03 (European Court of Human Rights, 2011).

Baba Dam Case, No. 1212–2007-RA (Constitutional Court of Ecuador, 2008).
Bankovic and Others *v.* Belgium and Others (Admissibility), No. 52207/99 (European Court of Human Rights, 2001).
Barcelona Traction, Light and Power Company Ltd (Belgium *v.* Spain), Second Phase, [1970] ICJ Rep. 32.
Beatriz Silvia Mendoza *v.* Argentina, M. 1569 (Supreme Court of Argentina, 2008).

Beatriz Silvia Mendoza *v.* National Government and Others (Federal Court of Morón, 2015).
Bordes and Temeharo *v.* France, No. 645/1995, CCPR/C/57/D/645/1995 (1996).
Brânduşe *v.* Romania, No. 6586/03 (European Court of Human Rights, 2009).
Budayeva and Others *v.* Russia, Nos. 15339/02, 21166/02, 20058/02, 11673/02 and 15343/02 (European Court of Human Rights, 2008).
Bulankulama and Six Others *v.* Ministry of Industrial Development and Seven Others, S.C. Application No 884/99 (F.R) (Supreme Court of the Democratic Socialist Republica of Sri Lanka).

Cambridge Water Co Ltd *v.* Eastern Counties Leather plc, [1994] 2AC 264, [1993] UKHL.
Canada – Continued Suspension of Obligations in the EC – Hormones Dispute, WT/DS320 (2008).
Centre for Minority Rights Development (Kenya) and Minority Rights Group International on behalf of Endorois Welfare Council *v.* Kenya, Communication 276/2003 (ACHPR, 2009).
Centre for Minority Rights Development – Kenya and Minority Rights Group International (on behalf of the Ogiek Community of the MauForest) *v.* Kenya, Communication 381/09.
Certification of the Constitution of the Republic of South Africa, 1996 (CCT 23/96) [1996].
City of Elgin *v.* County of Cook, 660 N.E.2d 875 (Ill. 1995).
Clean Air Foundation Limited & Gordon David Oldham *v.* Government of the Hong Kong Special Administrative Region, HCAL 35/2007 (Court of First Instance, Constitutional and Administrative Law List, Hong Kong, 2007).
Community of La Oroya, Peru, Inter-Am. Comm'n H.R, Case 12.718, Admissibility Report No. 76/09, OAS/Ser/L/V/II.135, doc. 23 (2009).
Concerned Residents of Manila Bay et al. *v.* Metropolitan Manila Development Authority and Others, Nos. 171947–8 (Supreme Court of the Philippines, 1998).
Concerned Residents of Manila Bay et al. *v.* Metropolitan Manila Development Authority and Others, Nos. 171947–8 (Supreme Court of the Philippines, 2008).
Constitutional Court of Colombia, sentencia no. C-443/09 (2009).
Constitutional Court of Colombia, sentencia no. T-291/06, 96 (2009).
Mary and Carrie Dann *v.* United States, Inter-Am. Comm'n H.R, Case 11.140, Report No. 75/02, Doc. 5 rev. 1 (2002).

Daubert *v.* Merrell Dow Pharmaceuticals, Inc., 509 U.S. 579, 590 (1993).
Daubert *v.* Merrell Dow Pharmaceuticals, Inc. *(Daubert II)*, 43 F.3d 131, 1316 (9th Cir. 1995).
Delia Saldias de Lopez *v.* Uruguay, Comm. No. 52/1979, UN Doc. CCPR/C/OP/1 (Human Rights Committee, 1984).
Demir and Baykara *v.* Turkey, No. 34503/97 (European Court of Human Rights, 2008).
Democratic Republic of Congo *v.* Burundi, Rwanda and Uganda, Communication No. 227/1999 (African Commission on Human and Peoples' Rights, 2003).
Di Sarno *v.* Italy, No. 30765/08 (European Court of Human Rights, 2012).
Dubetska and Others *v.* Ukraine, No. 30499/03 (European Court of Human Rights, 2011).

EC Measures concerning Meat and Meat Products (Hormones), WT/DS 26/AB/R and WT/DS 48/AB/R (WTO Appellate Body, 1998).
Ethyl Corp. *v.* EPA, 541 F2d 1 (D.C. Cir. 1976).
Expediente D-8019 (Colombia Constitutional Court, 2010).

Fadeyeva *v.* Russia, No. 55723/00 (European Court of Human Rights, 2005).
Fägerskiöld *v.* Sweden, No. 37664/04 (admissibility), (European Court of Human Rights, 2008).
Farooque *v.* Government of Bangladesh, (2002) WP 891 of 1994 (Supreme Court of Bangladesh).
Fredin *v.* Sweden, No. 12033/86 (European Court of Human Rights, 1991).
Fuel Retailers Association of Southern Africa *v.* Director-General Environmental Management, Department of Agriculture, Conservation and Environment, Mpumalanga Province and Others, Case No. CCT 67/06 (South Africa, 2007).
Fundepublico *v.* Mayor of Bugalagrande and Others, Interlocutorio No. 032, Tulua (Juzgado Primero Superior, Colombia, 1991).

Gabčíkovo-Nagymaros Case (Hungary *v.* Slovakia), [1997] ICJ Rep. 7.
Giacomelli *v.* Italy, No. 59909/00 (European Court of Human Rights, 2007).
Glisson *v.* City of Marion, 720 N.E.2d 1034, 1041 (Ill. 1999).
Golder *v.* United Kingdom, No. 4451/70 (European Court of Human Rights, 1975).
Greenwatch *v.* Attorney General and National Environmental Management Authority, Miscellaneous Application 140 (Uganda, 2002).

Hardy and Maile *v.* United Kingdom, No. 31965/07 (European Court of Human Rights, 2012).
Harrison *v.* Day, 200 Va. 439, 106 S.E. 2d 636 (1959).
Hatton and Others *v.* United Kingdom, No. 36022/97 (European Court of Human Rights, 2003).
H. M. Henares, Jr. et al. *v.* Land Transportation Franchising and Regulatory Board et al., G.R. No. 158290 (Supreme Court of Philippines, 2006).

Inter-American Court of Human Rights, Advisory Opinion OC-23-17 of November 15, 2017, para. 62.
Irazu Margarita *v.* Copetro S.A. (Camara Civil y Comercial de la Plata, Buenos Aires, Argentina, 1993).
Issa and Others *v.* Turkey, No. 31821/96 (European Court of Human Rights, 2004).

Jacobs *v.* Flemish Region, No. 80.018 (Belgium, Council of State, 1999).
Japan – Measures Affecting the Importation of Apples, Complaint by the United States, WT/DS245, Report of the Panel DSR 2003:IX.
James *v.* Bessemer Processing Co., 155 N.J. 279 (Supreme Court of New Jersey 1998).
Judgment 28, V. 20 AB (Constitutional Court of Hungary, 1994), p. 1919.

Kattan *v.* National Government, 1983-D (Argentina, 1983).
Kawas-Fernández *v.* Honduras, Inter-Am. Ct. H.R. (Ser. C) No. 196 (2009).
Kichwa Indigenous People of Sarayaku *v.* Ecuador, Inter-Am. Ct. H.R. (ser. C) No. 245 (2012).

Kiobel *v.* Royal Dutch Petroleum, 133 S. Ct. 1659 (U.S. Supreme Court, 2013).
Kyrtatos *v.* Greece, No. 4666/98 (European Court of Human Rights, 2003).

Lalanath de Silva *v.* Minister of Forestry and Environment, Fundamental Rights Application 569/98 (Supreme Court of Sri Lanka, 1998).
Ledyayeva, Dobrokhotova, Zolotareva and Romashina *v.* Russia, Nos. 53157/99, 53247/99, 53695/00 and 56850/00 (European Court of Human Rights, 2006).
Legality of the Threat or Use of Nuclear Weapons, Advisory Opinion, [1996] ICJ Rep. 226.
Liberian Eastern Timber Corporation (LETCO) *v.* Liberia, ARB 83/2, Award (ICSID, 1986).
Lohrmann *v.* Pittsburgh Corning Corp., 782 F.2d 1156 (4th Cir. 1986).
Loizidou *v.* Turkey, No. 15318/89 (European Court of Human Rights, 1996).
Case of the S.S. Lotus (France *v.* Turkey), [1927] P.C.I.J. (ser. A) No. 10.

Matsipane Mosetlhanyane and Others *v.* Attorney-General of Botswana, No. CALB–074–10 (Botswana Court of Appeal, 2011).
Matthews *v.* United Kingdom, No. 24833/94 (European Court of Human Rights, 1999).
Mayagna (Sumo) Awas Tingni Community *v.* Nicaragua, Inter-Am. Ct. H.R. (ser. C) No. 79 (2001).
Maya Indigenous Communities of the Toledo Dist. *v.* Belize, Inter-Am. Comm'n H.R., Case 12.053, Merits Report No. 40/04, OEA/Ser.L/V/II.122 doc. 5, rev. 1 (2004).
M. M. Levy y Asociacion Ecologista Limonense *v.* Ministerio del Ambiente y Energia, No. 2001–13295 (Costa Rica, 2001).
M. C. Mehta *v.* Union of India, No. 2002 (4) SCC 356 (India).
M. C. Mehta *v.* Union of India, No. AIR 1988 SC 1115 (India).
M. C. Mehta *v.* Union of India, No. AIR 1988 SC 1031 (Supreme Court of India).
M. C. Mehta *v.* Union of India (1991) SCR 86 1991 SCC (2) 353 (India).
Metropolitan Nature Reserve *v.* Panama, Inter-Am. Comm'n H.R, Case 11.533, Admissibility Report No. 88/03, Inter-Am. C.H.R., OEA/Ser.L/V/II.118 Doc. 70 rev. 2 at 524 (2003).
Military and Paramilitary Activities in and Against Nicaragua (Nicaragua *v.* United States of America), *Merits*, [1986] ICJ Rep. 14.
Minors Oposa *v.* Secretary of the Department of Environmental and Natural Resources, 33 ILM 173 (Supreme Court of the Philippines, 1993).
Missouri *v.* Illinois, 200 U.S. 496 (1906).
Case of the Moiwana Community (Suriname), Inter-Am Ct H.R. (ser. C) No. 124 (2005).
Montana Environmental Information Center *v.* Department of Environmental Quality, 296 Mont. 207, 988 P. 2d 1236 (1999).
Moreno Gomes *v.* Spain, No. 4143/02 (European Court of Human Rights, 2005).
Murli S. Deora *v.* Union of India, 8 SCC 765 (Supreme Court of India, 2001).

New York *v.* New Jersey, 256 U.S. 296 (1921).
North Sea Continental Shelf Cases (Federal Republic of Germany/Denmark/Netherlands), [1969] ICJ Rep. 3, 44.

Okyay et al. *v.* Turkey, No. 36220/97 (European Court of Human Rights, 2005).
Oneryildiz *v.* Turkey, No. 48939/99 (European Court of Human Rights, 2004).
Opinion C-2/13 of the Court on Accession of the European Union to the European Convention for the Protection of Human Rights and Fundamental Freedoms (European Court of Justice, 2014).

Pablo Miguel Fabián Martínez and Others *v.* Minister of Health and Director General of Environmental Health, Exp. No. 2002–2006-PC/TC (Constitutional Court, 2006).
The Paquete Habana, 175 U.S. 677 (1900).
Pavel Ocepek, Breg pri Komendi, No. Up-344/96 (Slovenia Constitutional Court, 1999).
Powell and Rayner *v.* United Kingdom, No. 9310/81 (European Court of Human Rights, 1990).
Presidente de la sociedad Marlene S.A. *v.* Municipalidad de Tibas, No. 6918/94 (Constitutional Chamber of Supreme Court, Costa Rica, 1994).
Prosecutor *v.* Anto Furundžija, Case No. IT-95–17/1-T (International Criminal Tribunal for the former Yugoslavia, 1998).
Pulp Mills on the River Uruguay (Argentina *v.* Uruguay), [2010] ICJ Rep. 83.

R *v.* Turner, QB 834 (England, 1975).
Reserve Mining *v.* EPA, 514 F.2d 492 (8th Cir. 1975).
Robb *v.* Shockoe Slip Found., 324 S.E.2d 674, 676 (Va. 1985).
Robertson *v.* Methow Valley Citizens Council, 490 U.S. 332, 351 (1989).
Robinson Township *v.* Pennsylvania, 83 A.3d 901, 975–6 (Pa. 2013).

S. A. R. L. Benvenuti & Bonfant *v.* Congo, ARB 77/2, Award (ICSID, 1981).
Sala Constitucional de Costa Rica, resolución no. 2003–04654 (2003); Sala Constitucional de Costa Rica, resolución no. 2007–02154 (2007).
Salim *v.* State of Uttarakhand and Others (High Court of Uttarakhand at Nainital, Writ Petition (PIL) No. 126 of 2014) (2017).
Saramaka People *v.* Suriname, 2007 Inter-Am. Ct. H.R. (ser. C) No. 172 (2007).
Sawhoyamaxa Indigenous Community *v.* Paraguay, Inter-Am.Ct. H.R. (ser. C) No. 146 (2006).
Seadade Industries, Inc. *v.* Florida Power & Light Co., 245 So. 2d 209 (Fla. 1971).
Sentencia No. 166–15-SEP-CC (Constitutional Court of Ecuador) (2015).
Scattering Fork Drainage Dist. *v.* Ogilvie, 311 N.E.2d 203, 210 (Ill. App. Ct. 1974).
Shehla Zia *v.* WAPDA, PLD 1994 SC 693 (Supreme Court of Pakistan, 1994).
Social and Economic Rights Action Centre (SERAC) and the Centre for Economic and Social Rights (CESR) *v.* Nigeria, Communication No. 155/96 (ACHPR, 2001).
South-West Africa Cases (Ethiopia *v.* South Africa; Liberia *v.* South Africa), Second Phase, Judgment [1966] ICJ Rep. 298.
Southern Bluefin Tuna Cases (New Zealand *v.* Japan; Australia *v.* Japan), *Provisional Measures*, ITLOS Rep. 1999, 280–336 (ITLOS, 1999).
State Highway Comm'n *v.* Vanderkloot, US-24, 220 N.W. 2d 416 (Mich. 1974).
Suray Prasad Sharma Dhungel *v.* Godavari Marble Industries and Others, WP 35/1991 (Supreme Court of Nepal, 1995).

Taşkin and Others *v.* Turkey, No. 46117/99 (European Court of Human Rights, 2006).
Tătar *v.* Romania, No. 67021/01 (European Court of Human Rights, 2009).
T. N. Godavarman Tirumulpad *v.* Union of India, No. AIR 1999 SC 43 (India).
Trail Smelter Arbitration (U.S./Canada), Arbitral Trib., 3 U.N. Rep. Int'l Arb. Awards 1905 (1941).
Tyrer *v.* United Kingdom, No. 5856/72 (European Court of Human Rights, 1978).

United States – Import Prohibition of Certain Shrimp and Shrimp Products, WT/DS58/AB/R (World Trade Organization Appellate Body, 1998).

Vellore Citizens' Welfare Forum *v.* Union of India, Writ. Pet. No. 914 of 1991 (Supreme Court of India, 1996).
Venter, No. 82.130 (Belgium, Council of State, 1999).

P.K. Waweru *v.* Republic of Kenya (2006). High Court of Kenya, Misc. Civil Application no. 118 of 2004, 2 March 2006. KLR (Environment and Land) 1 (2006) 677.
Whaling in the Antarctic (Australia *v.* Japan; *New Zealand intervening*), [2014] ICJ Rep. 226.
Wheeler *v.* Director de la Procuraduria General Del Estado de Loja Juicio, No. 11121–2011–10 (Provincial Court of Justice of Ecuador, 2011).

Xakmok Kasek Indigenous Community *v.* Paraguay, Merits, Reparations, and Costs, Inter-Am Ct. H.R. (ser. C) No. 214 (2010).

Yakye Axa *v.* Paraguay, Merits, Reparations and Costs, Inter-Am. Ct. H.R. (ser. C) No. 125 (2005).

T. V. Zlotnikova, K. E. Lebedeva et al. *v.* Russian Federation, No. GPKI 97–249 (Supreme Court of Russia, 1998).

Table of Treaties and Other International Instruments

Aarhus Convention on Access to Information, Public Participation in Decision-Making and Access to Justice in Environmental Matters, June 25, 1998, in force October 21, 2001, 2161 UNTS 447.

African Charter on Human and Peoples' Rights, June 27, 1981, in force October 21, 1986, 1520 UNTS 217.

Protocol on Amendments to the Protocol on the Statute of the African Court of Justice and Human Rights, June 27, 2014, not in force.

Protocol to the African Charter on Human and Peoples' Rights on the Establishment of an African Court on Human and Peoples' Rights, July 10, 1998, in force January 25, 2004, OAU Doc. OAU/LEG/EXP/AFCHPR/PROT (III).

Protocol to the African Charter on Human and Peoples' Rights on the Rights of Women in Africa, September 13, 2000, in force November 25, 2005, AU Doc. CAB/LEG/66.6.

Additional Protocol to the American Convention on Human Rights in the Area of Economic, Social and Cultural Rights: Protocol of San Salvador, November 17, 1988, in force November 16, 1999, 28 ILM 161.

African Charter on the Rights and Welfare of the Child, July 1, 1990, in force November 29, 1999, OAU Doc. CAB/LEG/24.9/49.

African Convention on the Conservation of Nature and Natural Resources, September 25, 1968, in force June 16, 1969, OAU Doc. CAB/LEG/24.1.

African Convention on the Conservation of Nature and Natural Resources (Revised Version), July 11, 2003, not in force.

American Convention on Human Rights, November 22, 1969, in force July 18, 1978, 1114 UNTS 123, art. 29.

Arab Charter on Human Rights, May 22, 2004, in force March 15, 2008, 12 IHRR 893 (2005).

Association of Southeast Asian Nations (ASEAN) Human Rights Declaration, November 18, 2012.

Bamako Convention on the Ban of Import into Africa and the Control of Transboundary Movement and Management of Hazardous Waste within Africa, January 30, 1991, in force April 22, 1998.

Charter of the United Nations, June 26, 1945, in force October 24, 1945, 1 UNTS 16.
Constitutive Act of the African Union, July 11, 2000, in force May 26, 2001, OAU Doc. CAB/LEG/23.15.
Convention on the Preservation of Wild Animals, Birds, and Fish in Africa, May 19, 1900, not in force.
Convention Relative to the Preservation of Fauna and Flora in their Natural State, November 8, 1933, in force January 14, 1936.
Council of Europe Parliamentary Assembly, Environment and Human Rights, 24th Sess., Rec. 1614 (2003).

Declaration of the UN Conference on the Human Environment, UN Doc. A/Conf.48/14/Rev.1 (June 5–16, 1972).
Declaration on the Right to Development, UN Doc. A/RES/41/128 (December 4, 1986).

Espoo Convention on Environmental Impact Assessment in a Transboundary Context, February 25, 1991, in force September 10, 1997, 1989 UNTS 310.
European Convention for the Protection of Human Rights and Fundamental Freedoms, November 4, 1950, in force September 3, 1953, 213 UNTS 221, art. 17.

International Covenant on Civil and Political Rights, December 16, 1966, in force March 23, 1976, 999 UNTS 171.
International Covenant on Economic, Social and Cultural Rights, December 16, 1966, in force January 3, 1976, 993 UNTS 3.
International Labour Organization, Convention Concerning Indigenous and Tribal Peoples in Independent Countries (C 169), June 27, 1989, in force September 5, 1991, 28 I.L.M. 1382.

Johannesburg Declaration on Sustainable Development, UN Doc. A/CONF.199/20 (2002).

Kyoto Protocol to the United Nations Framework Convention on Climate Change, December 11, 1997, in force February 16, 2005, 2303 UNTS 148.

Malé Declaration on the Human Dimension of Global Climate Change, November 14, 2007.

Optional Protocol to the International Covenant on Economic, Social and Cultural Rights, December 10, 2008, in force May 5, 2013, UN Doc. A/RES/63/117.

Paris Agreement, December 12, 2015, in force November 4, 2016, UN Doc. FCCC/CP/2015/19.

Rio Declaration on Environment and Development, UN Doc. A/CONF.151/26/Rev.1, annex I (June 14, 1992).

Statute of the International Court of Justice, June 26, 1945, 33 UNTS 993.

1

Introduction

John H. Knox and Ramin Pejan

Two of the great achievements of international law have been to define the human rights integral to a life of dignity, freedom, and equality, and to develop rules and institutions that protect the global environment. Because these two areas of the law developed separately and at different times, the relationship between them was at first unclear. In the last two decades, however, it has become more and more evident that human rights and environmental protection have a fundamental interdependence: A healthy environment is necessary for the full enjoyment of human rights and, conversely, the exercise of rights (including rights to information, participation, and remedy) is critical to environmental protection.

This relationship has been recognized at every level of the world's legal systems, from domestic courts to multilateral treaties. Perhaps the highest-profile acknowledgment of the linkage is the Paris Agreement on climate change, adopted in December 2015, which includes in its preamble the statement: "Parties should, when taking action to address climate change, respect, promote and consider their respective obligations on human rights, the right to health, the rights of indigenous peoples, local communities, migrants, children, persons with disabilities and people in vulnerable situations and the right to development, as well as gender equality, empowerment of women and intergenerational equity."[1]

Although many aspects of the relationship of human rights and the environment have become clear, some important issues remain unresolved, including the status of a globally recognized human right to a healthy environment.[2] Most countries, and almost all regional human rights systems, have endorsed the right to a healthy environment, but it has never been adopted in a universal human rights treaty

[1] Paris Agreement, December 12, 2015, in force November 4, 2016, UN Doc. FCCC/CP/2015/19.

[2] Throughout this book, unless otherwise indicated, references to the "right to a healthy environment" should be read generally to include alternative versions such as a right to a "satisfactory," or "clean," or "sustainable" environment. Several chapters explore the possible legal consequences of different formulations of the right.

or declaration. Its absence from the seminal human rights instruments can be explained by timing: The modern environmental movement began in the late 1960s, after the adoption of the Universal Declaration of Human Rights and the two International Covenants.[3] It is remarkable, however, that fifty years later, after most of the countries of the world have recognized the right in their national constitutions or regional human rights instruments, or both, the United Nations has still not endorsed it.

The 1972 Stockholm Declaration, adopted by the first UN conference on the environment, came closest, stating in its first principle that "man has the fundamental right to freedom, equality and adequate conditions of life, in an environment of a quality that permits a life of dignity and well-being."[4] Over the next several decades, however, as most states have highlighted the importance of environmental protection by including the right in national law and regional treaties, the United Nations has declined invitations to strengthen the Stockholm language. In 1992, the UN Conference on Environment and Development in Rio de Janeiro avoided using "rights" language, instead stating, in the first principle of the Rio Declaration, that human beings "*are entitled to* a healthy and productive life in harmony with nature."[5] Three years later, the UN Commission on Human Rights, then the principal UN human rights body, rejected a proposal by its expert sub-commission to consider a draft declaration on human rights and the environment that recognized the right. Nor was the right mentioned by the later international conferences on sustainable development, in Johannesburg in 2002 and Rio de Janeiro in 2012.

Nevertheless, the absence of a globally recognized right to a healthy environment has not prevented the development of human rights norms relating to the environment. Indeed, one of the most noteworthy aspects of human rights law over the last twenty years is that UN treaty bodies, regional tribunals, special rapporteurs, and other human rights mechanisms have applied human rights law to environmental issues even without a stand-alone, justiciable human right to a healthy environment. They have done so by "greening" other human rights – that is, applying already-recognized rights, such as rights to life and health, to environmental problems. Human rights bodies have identified how environmental harm interferes with the full enjoyment of human rights, and they have concluded that states have obligations under human rights law to protect human rights from environmental harm.

3 Universal Declaration of Human Rights, General Assembly res. 217A (III), UN Doc. A/810 (1948); International Covenant on Civil and Political Rights, December 16, 1966, in force March 23, 1976, 999 UNTS 171; International Covenant on Economic, Social and Cultural Rights, December 16, 1966, in force January 3, 1976, 993 UNTS 3.

4 Declaration of the UN Conference on the Human Environment, UN Doc. A/Conf.48/14/Rev.1 (June 5–16, 1972).

5 Rio Declaration on Environment and Development, UN Doc. A/CONF.151/26/Rev.1, annex I (June 14, 1992) (emphasis added). See Dinah Shelton, "What Happened in Rio to Human Rights?" *Yearbook of International Environmental Law* 3(1) (1993), pp. 75–93.

The editors of this volume have been privileged to witness this blossoming field of human rights law from front-row seats. In 2012, the Human Rights Council – the successor to the Commission on Human Rights – decided to inform itself and the public of the developments in this area by appointing an independent expert to a three-year term to "study the human rights obligations relating to the enjoyment of a safe, clean, healthy and sustainable environment," to identify best practices in their use, and to issue public reports to the Council.[6] One of the editors (John Knox) had the honor of being appointed as the independent expert; the other (Ramin Pejan) was the human rights officer at the Office of the High Commissioner for Human Rights (OHCHR) assigned to support the new mandate.

Over the first eighteen months of the mandate, we held consultations in every UN region and, with the help of attorneys and academics working on a *pro bono* basis, examined virtually every statement made by a human rights body on environmental issues, with the goal of "mapping" the human rights norms relating to the environment. Human rights bodies had, by this time, examined hundreds of environmental situations. We described their statements in eleven reports, one for each source or set of sources. For example, individual reports covered the decisions of the Human Rights Committee interpreting the International Covenant on Civil and Political Rights and four other treaty bodies; statements of the General Assembly and the Human Rights Council; reports of UN special rapporteurs; and the regional human rights systems. Another three reports addressed environmental instruments.[7]

The mapping review revealed that this wide variety of bodies had reached very similar conclusions. At a general level, they agreed that environmental harm can and often does interfere with the full enjoyment of many human rights, including rights to life and health, and that states have obligations to protect against such interference. More specifically, they agreed that states have procedural and substantive obligations, as well as obligations relating to the protection of those who are particularly vulnerable to environmental harm. These conclusions were summarized in a report presented to the Human Rights Council in March 2014.[8] Four years

6 Human Rights Council res. 19/10 (March 12, 2012).

7 The reports, which total more than 750 pages, are available at http://srenvironment.org/mapping-report-2014–2/ and at www.ohchr.org/EN/Issues/Environment/SREnvironment/Pages/MappingReport.aspx.

8 John H. Knox, *Report of the Independent Expert on the Issue of Human Rights Obligations Relating to the Enjoyment of a Safe, Clean, Healthy and Sustainable Environment: Mapping Report*, UN Doc. A/HRC/25/53 (December 30, 2013). Later reports have identified good practices in the use of these obligations, proposed methods of implementing the obligations, and applied them to specific environmental issues, including climate change and biodiversity. John H. Knox, *Report of the Independent Expert on the Issue of Human Rights Obligations Relating to the Enjoyment of a Safe, Clean, Healthy and Sustainable Environment: Compilation of good practices*, UN Doc. A/HRC/28/61 (February 3, 2015); *Report of the Special Rapporteur on the Issue of Human Rights Obligations Relating to the Enjoyment of a Safe, Clean, Healthy and Sustainable Environment: Implementation Report*, UN Doc. A/HRC/31/53 (December 28, 2015); *Report of the Special Rapporteur on the Issue of Human Rights*

later, the final report of John Knox to the Council presented Framework Principles on Human Rights and the Environment that set out these obligations in detail.[9]

The procedural obligations of states include duties: (a) to assess environmental impacts and make environmental information public; (b) to facilitate public participation in environmental decision making, including by protecting the rights of freedom of expression and association; and (c) to provide access to remedies for harm. With respect to substantive obligations, human rights bodies have agreed that states have duties to adopt and implement legal frameworks to protect against environmental harm that may infringe on enjoyment of human rights, and that these laws should regulate private actors as well as government agencies. While states have discretion in deciding the appropriate level of environmental protection in light of their economic situation, they should take into account international and national standards for health and safety, ensure that their environmental standards are non-retrogressive, and implement them effectively.

In adopting and implementing environmental standards, procedural or substantive, states should never discriminate on prohibited grounds. Moreover, human rights bodies have emphasized that states may owe heightened duties to those who are particularly vulnerable to environmental degradation. Although these duties require further elaboration, the norms are already quite detailed in some areas. For example, the rights of indigenous peoples in relation to the environment have been clarified in international instruments and by human rights bodies.[10]

Against this backdrop of an extensive set of human rights obligations relating to the environment, what is, or should be, the role of the human right to a healthy environment? Normally, of course, the international recognition of a right precedes the development of obligations under human rights law. Most famously, the Universal Declaration of Human Rights, which listed fundamental rights recognized by the international community, was followed by treaties that elaborated corresponding obligations on states and established institutions to promote compliance. If the right to a healthy environment were following this template, its international recognition would establish it as a new cornerstone in the human rights framework, on which detailed obligations could be built.

Obligations Relating to the Enjoyment of a Safe, Clean, Healthy and Sustainable Environment: Climate Change Report, UN Doc. A/HRC/31/52 (February 1, 2016); *Report of the Special Rapporteur on the Issue of Human Rights Obligations Relating to the Enjoyment of a Safe, Clean, Healthy and Sustainable Environment: Biodiversity Report*, UN Doc. A/HRC/34/49 (January 19, 2017).

9 John Knox, *Report of the Special Rapporteur on the Issue of Human Rights Obligations Relating to the Enjoyment of a Safe, Clean, Healthy and Sustainable Environment*, UN Doc. A/HRC/37/59 (January 24, 2018).

10 See, e.g., United Nations Declaration on the Rights of Indigenous Peoples, UN Doc. A/RES/61/295 (September 13, 2007); James Anaya, *Report of the Special Rapporteur on the Rights of Indigenous Peoples: Extractive Industries Operating within or Near Indigenous Territories*, UN Doc. A/HRC/18/35 (July 11, 2011).

While this approach has been taken, to differing degrees, in the countries that have adopted a constitutional right to a healthy environment, at the international level the body of norms described earlier has already evolved on the basis of an interlocking web of rights. That does not mean that recognition of the human right to a healthy environment would be meaningless. On the contrary, it could have important advantages: Adoption or endorsement of the right at the global level could raise the visibility of these norms and give them greater coherence and clarity. In this sense, a "new" human right to a healthy environment would be a capstone: a marker that reflects the maturity of this body of law.

At the same time, many believe that the existing international norms on human rights and the environment do not go far enough. For example, the developing international jurisprudence has had little to say about future generations or intrinsic "rights of nature," even though they are addressed in some national constitutions.[11] More prosaically, not all countries recognize the already identified rights-based environmental norms to the same extent, since the norms have been derived from a wide variety of human rights instruments by a wide variety of human rights bodies, none of whose authority is recognized as universally binding. In either respect, the global recognition of a human right to a healthy environment could act as a cornerstone for the development of these obligations, by filling in gaps in the evolving jurisprudence or by providing a basis for entirely new sets of obligations. Whether and how the right could serve this function would depend greatly on how it is recognized, as well as on how it is interpreted going forward.

Of course, these two roles are not mutually exclusive. In law (if not in architecture), a norm may be a capstone and a cornerstone at the same time. Global recognition of the right to a healthy environment could both provide a reference point for the norms as they have developed so far, and help to provide a basis for further development of norms in the future. However, the distinction between capstones and cornerstones does have implications for the method of recognition of the norm. To the degree that the recognition of a right to a healthy environment is treated as a capstone without independent legal effects, formal approval by an intergovernmental body would not be necessary. However, the higher the expectation that the right would provide a foundation for further norm development, the more important some sort of intergovernmental approval would be.

The consideration of these questions led us to invite a diverse set of scholars and practitioners, all of whom have been instrumental in defining the relationship

[11] International tribunals may be starting to break their relative silence on these issues. As this book was being prepared for publication, the Inter-American Court of Human Rights issued a pathbreaking advisory opinion on human rights and the environment that reviews and clarifies their interdependence. Among other things, the opinion relates the human right to a healthy environment to the protection of components of the environment such as forests and rivers, even in the absence of harm to humans. See Inter-American Court of Human Rights, Advisory Opinion OC-23-17 of November 15, 2017, para. 62.

between human rights and the environment, to provide their thoughts on the right to a healthy environment. We are very fortunate that they accepted our invitation to contribute chapters to this book.

Their contributions examine many different facets of the right to a healthy environment, categorized in roughly the following order. (We say "roughly" because many of the authors address more than one of these issues, as well as others not listed here.)

1. Where the right to a healthy environment already exists, at the national and regional levels, how has it been interpreted and applied? What lessons does that experience have for the recognition of the right at the international level?
2. Is the right to a healthy environment already part of customary international law, or even *jus cogens*?
3. Is adoption or recognition of a "new" human right to a healthy environment in an international instrument justified on ethical and/or legal grounds?
4. How could the right be recognized at the international level by the UN General Assembly or the Human Rights Council?
5. What role can the right to a healthy environment and other human rights play in addressing climate change, which has been called both the greatest environmental challenge of our time and the greatest threat to human rights of the twenty-first century?

NATIONAL AND REGIONAL EXPERIENCE WITH THE RIGHT TO A HEALTHY ENVIRONMENT

At the outset of any consideration of the right to a healthy environment at the global level, it is important to bear in mind that the right has already been incorporated into the laws of most of the countries of the world. Chapters 2 and 3, by David Boyd and by Erin Daly and James May, respectively, each draw lessons from the experience with constitutional environmental rights. Boyd notes that the right now enjoys direct constitutional protection in 100 countries, and he points out that this figure actually understates its acceptance, since the courts in at least another dozen countries have interpreted the right as an essential part of the constitutional right to life, and others have ratified regional treaties that include a version of the right to a healthy environment. In all, he finds that the governments of at least 155 nations have recognized the right.

Drawing on his own empirical research, Boyd argues that the adoption of constitutional rights to a healthy environment has led to stronger environmental laws and to judicial decisions requiring environmental protection. Other benefits include increasing the public role in environmental governance, because the right has been consistently interpreted to include the procedural rights of access to information, public participation, and access to justice. Conversely, he concludes that few of the potential downsides of the right have materialized. Environmental rights have not been construed to trump all other rights; instead, legislators and judges have opted for careful balancing of environmental and other interests. It is true that in some countries, formal adoption of the right has had little effect, often because countries that lack effective legal institutions fail to implement most or all of their human rights commitments, including those related to environmental protection. On the whole, however, he concludes that the effects of the widespread adoption of the right at the national level have been overwhelmingly beneficial, and that it should be recognized as expeditiously as possible at the global level as well.

Daly and May state that domestic environmental constitutionalism provides several lessons for the meaning, scope, and enforcement of a global environmental right. They explain that a very wide variety of formulations are used, including references to the right to a "clean," "harmonious," and "balanced" environment. Some provisions are explicitly anthropocentric, others are ecocentric, and some include both perspectives. The constitution of Ecuador, for example, recognizes both the "right to a healthy and ecologically balanced environment" with a chapter dedicated to rights of nature. Different legal consequences can result from such different legal texts. The authors also show that constitutions differ greatly in how clearly they link the right to other rights, and in the creation of effective enforcement mechanisms. They conclude that the drafters of an instrument recognizing the right at the global level should "clarify as much as possible which elements of the environment should be protected and why," link the right explicitly to other human rights, and create effective mechanisms for vindicating the right.

As noted earlier, the right to a healthy environment has also been adopted in many regional instruments. In most of these instruments, however, the right is non-justiciable. The San Salvador Protocol to the American Convention on Human Rights, for example, states that "[e]veryone shall have the right to live in a healthy environment," but does not include the right in the short list of economic, social, and cultural rights whose violation may be the subject of a claim to the Inter-American Commission on Human Rights.[12] The Arab Charter on Human Rights and the ASEAN Human Rights Declaration each include the right to a "healthy" (Arab Charter) or "safe, clean and sustainable" (ASEAN Declaration) environment as an element of the right to an adequate standard of living, but neither instrument

[12] Additional Protocol to the American Convention on Human Rights in the Area of Economic, Social and Cultural Rights: Protocol of San Salvador, November 17, 1988, in force November 16, 1999, 28 ILM 161, arts. 11(1), 19(6).

establishes oversight mechanisms that can receive complaints of violation of the right.[13] Similarly, the Aarhus Convention, which was negotiated under the auspices of the UN Economic Commission for Europe, states that its parties are required to guarantee the rights of access to information, public participation in decision making, and access to justice in environmental matters "[i]n order to contribute to the protection of the right of every person of present and future generations to live in an environment adequate to his or her health and well-being,"[14] but its compliance mechanism reviews alleged violations only of the procedural access rights, not of the general environmental right that they support.

Exceptionally, the African Charter not only provides that "[a]ll peoples shall have the right to a general satisfactory environment favourable to their development," but also makes the provision subject to review by both the African Commission on Human and Peoples' Rights and the African Court on Human and Peoples' Rights.[15] In Chapter 4, Lilian Chenwi places the Charter's language in its historical and textual context, analyzes its potential tension with the right to development, which the Charter also recognizes, and explains in detail how the right has been interpreted and applied by the African Commission and the African Court. Her contribution includes one of the very first scholarly treatments of the May 2017 decision by the Court on the rights of the indigenous Ogiek people, who face eviction from their ancestral home in the Mau Forest in Kenya.[16] She concludes that the experience of the African human rights bodies "authenticate[s] the view that such a right can be made effective and accentuate[s] the role that indigenous communities play in this regard." Her chapter also highlights the importance of construing the right in light of its linkages with other rights.

The absence of a judiciable right to a healthy environment has not prevented other regional tribunals from contributing to the development of human rights norms relating to the environment. The Inter-American Commission and Court, for example, have issued many important decisions, chiefly on the rights of indigenous and tribal peoples to communal property in the face of rising development pressures.[17]

[13] Arab Charter on Human Rights, May 22, 2004, in force March 15, 2008, 12 IHRR 893 (2005), art. 38; Association of Southeast Asian Nations (ASEAN) Human Rights Declaration, November 18, 2012, art. 28(f).

[14] Aarhus Convention on Access to Information, Public Participation in Decision-Making and Access to Justice in Environmental Matters, June 25, 1998, in force October 21, 2001, 2161 UNTS 447, art. 1.

[15] African Charter on Human and Peoples' Rights, June 27, 1981, in force October 21, 1986, 1520 UNTS 217, art. 24.

[16] *African Commission on Human and Peoples' Rights* v. *Kenya, Judgment*, Application 006/2012 (African Court of Human and Peoples' Rights, 2017).

[17] See, e.g., *Kichwa Indigenous People of Sarayaku* v. *Ecuador*, Inter-Am. Ct. H.R. (ser. C) No. 245 (2012); *Saramaka People* v. *Suriname*, 2007 Inter-Am. Ct. H.R. (ser. C) No. 172 (2007); *Sawhoyamaxa Indigenous Community* v. *Paraguay*, Inter-Am. Ct. H.R. (ser. C) No. 146 (2006). They have also emphasized the importance of protecting the rights of

But the most active regional tribunal in this respect has been the European Court of Human Rights.

In Chapter 5, Ole Pedersen explains that despite the absence of an explicit environmental right in the European Convention on Human Rights, the European Court has managed to develop "an elaborate and extensive body of case law which all but in name provides for a right to a healthy environment." It has constructed this body of jurisprudence primarily on the basis of the rights to life and to respect for private and family life. Pedersen notes that the jurisprudence has a wide scope, ranging from noise pollution through industrial pollution to natural disasters and flooding, and that it addresses the risk of harm, not merely the *ex post* application of human rights norms to materialized harms. At the same time, the jurisprudence includes what Pedersen describes as more restrictive elements, including a focus on procedural protections (such as obligations to provide information and establish regulatory institutions) and on whether the government has followed its own environmental standards. If procedural safeguards are met and the government has met domestic standards, the Court affords states a wide "margin of appreciation," or area of discretion, in deciding what level of environmental protection to adopt.

As explained earlier, the jurisprudence of the African, European, and Inter-American human rights tribunals, similar decisions and statements by other human rights bodies (including UN treaty bodies and special rapporteurs), and decisions by national courts are creating a rights-based environmental jurisprudence. In Chapter 6, Dinah Shelton, who has broken ground in scholarship in this field for over twenty-five years, examines some of the key issues judges must face in cases involving allegations that governmental action or inaction has caused environmental harm that, in turn, infringes or threatens the full enjoyment of human rights. Drawing on cases from the International Court of Justice, regional tribunals, and domestic courts, her chapter addresses a range of overarching issues in cases concerning the environment and human rights, including challenges to the admissibility of claims, the impact of scientific uncertainty, the burden of proof, the degree of deference owed to the government, and the application of legal principles such as the precautionary principle. She makes clear that while there are valid reasons to support judicial deference to legislative decisions in environmental matters, a rights-based perspective emphasizes that judicial oversight is necessary to protect the rights of those in marginalized and minority communities, who often bear a disproportionate burden of environmental harm.

environmentalists to life and to freedom of association. See *Kawas-Fernández v. Honduras*, Inter-Am. Ct. H.R. (Ser. C) No. 196 (2009).

THE RIGHT AS A NORM OF CUSTOMARY INTERNATIONAL LAW, OR *JUS COGENS*

The widespread acceptance by so many countries of environmental rights, and of the right to a healthy environment in particular, raises the question whether the rights are already part of customary international law. In Chapter 7, Rebecca Bratspies points out that most inquiries into the existence of customary law either reason inductively to derive custom from the course of state-to-state interactions, or deductively from multilateral instruments. Either way, this analysis is top-down, looking at whether international conduct has crystallized into customary norms. Bratspies takes a different, bottom-up approach, looking at the obligations states have imposed on themselves through their own domestic laws. Focusing on the near-universal adoption of environmental impact assessment laws, she argues that some key components of a human rights-based approach to environmental protection have hardened into customary international law. Her analysis also shows how similar inquiries could be conducted for other elements of the right, including in particular procedural duties relating to public participation and access to remedies for environmental harm, which are reflected in many domestic and regional environmental laws.

In Chapter 8, Louis Kotzé addresses the next logical question: Can the right to a healthy environment be considered a *jus cogens* norm? *Jus cogens* norms are peremptory – that is, they bind all states regardless of their consent, overriding inconsistent international agreements. Kotzé concludes that international environmental instruments such as the Stockholm and Rio Declarations support the right to a healthy environment only as "soft law" that provides non-binding guidance to states. Nevertheless, he argues that it is worthwhile to continue the debate on the emergence of the right in international law for several reasons, including that such a high-level recognition of the right could be critically important to establish regulatory priorities in global environmental governance, and that it could provide a basis for international compliance and enforcement mechanisms to hold states accountable for their environment-related actions. Kotzé also describes the potential allure of *jus cogens* status for establishing a peremptory norm against environmental harm that affects the sustainability of the Earth's ecosystems. While existing law provides only a slim basis for concluding that environmental norms already are *jus cogens*, he argues that the urgency of the present crisis and the recognition of the need for international cooperation support the development of such norms. He suggests that building blocks could include the widely accepted no-harm rule (*sic utere tuo ut alienum non laedas*), as well as fundamental human rights norms such as the prohibition of racial discrimination where such discrimination is directly linked to environmental harm.

THE ETHICAL AND LEGAL JUSTIFICATIONS FOR ADOPTING THE RIGHT IN INTERNATIONAL LAW

César Rodríguez-Garavito, in Chapter 9, analyzes the potential benefits and costs of formally codifying the right to a healthy environment into international positive law. He begins by challenging what might be considered the assumption underlying this issue: That is, that the status of the right to a healthy environment as a human right depends on its incorporation in a legal instrument. He points out first that, as Amartya Sen has argued, human rights are fundamentally *ethical* claims about the intrinsic worth of every human being, which can and typically do precede their legal codification.[18] And he notes that the right to a healthy environment would appear, at least, to meet the threshold conditions Sen has proposed for recognition of a human right, including that it has wide recognition in the public sphere and that its realization depends to a large degree on the decisions of others. Rodríguez-Garavito also continues the analysis of previous chapters on the right as a customary norm, arguing that state practice and *opinio juris* both provide evidence of such a status.

Nevertheless, he acknowledges that the lack of an explicit recognition of the right in positive international law "undoubtedly limits its impact," and he argues that the adoption of the right would have several benefits, including the greater certainty, precision, and coercive power that a new legal instrument would provide to advocates and victims. He notes that formal recognition of the right could have costs as well, such as atomizing demands for justice into individual claims, and strengthening the dominance of professional organizations rather than affected communities – problems that are relevant to human rights generally, not just in the environmental context. He also points out the potential costs of obtaining the recognition of the right in international law, which could demand considerable political and institutional effort.

In Chapter 10, Marcos Orellana continues the consideration of the legal justification for the right to a healthy environment in light of the General Assembly's guidelines for the development of instruments in the field of human rights, which set out substantive standards that the recognition of "new" human rights should meet.[19] He finds that the right to a healthy environment meets these standards. For example, it is "consistent with the existing body of international human rights law," it is "of fundamental character and derive[s] from the inherent dignity and worth of the human person," and it is "sufficiently precise to give rise to identifiable and practicable rights and obligations." In addition to these substantive standards, Orellana distills several procedural safeguards from Philip Alston's 1984 proposal for

[18] See Amartya Sen, "Elements of a Theory of Human Rights," *Philosophy and Public Affairs* 32(4) (2004).

[19] General Assembly res. 41/120 (December 4, 1986).

greater "quality control" with respect to the recognition of new rights.[20] For example, before rights are accepted at the international level, they should go through an "incubation" phase in which they are recognized in national constitutions and legislation; there should be prior discussion and analysis of the implications of international recognition; and governments and other stakeholders should have opportunities to express their opinions on the proposals. Here, too, Orellana shows that these procedural steps have been fulfilled: The right has been widely adopted at the national level, and the relationship between human rights and environmental protection has been widely discussed by governments as well as by judges, scholars, and practitioners.

THE ROLE OF THE GENERAL ASSEMBLY AND THE HUMAN RIGHTS COUNCIL

A right to a healthy environment could be adopted in the form of a new treaty or as a protocol to an existing one. Pedersen states that a logical vehicle could be a protocol to the International Covenant on Economic, Social and Cultural Rights, but he notes that this path would be politically difficult, if not impossible. Boyd suggests that a resolution from the UN General Assembly might be the path of least resistance for maximum reward. Orellana explains that the General Assembly has played the preeminent role, historically, in proclaiming rights, but he argues that the Human Rights Council can do more than simply advise the General Assembly: The Council may itself recognize new rights, at least when the new rights are based on existing rights. Still more clearly, the Council may engage in a fresh debate concerning the right to a healthy environment, as a basis either for proclaiming the right itself or recommending its proclamation to the General Assembly.

The role of the Human Rights Council in this respect is examined in more detail by Marc Limon, in Chapter 11. Limon notes that its predecessor, the Commission on Human Rights, began to consider the relationship of human rights and the environment in the mid-1990s, but truncated its discussion without reaching agreement on any lasting conclusions or institutional reforms. However, soon after the Council was created in 2006, it began afresh with a different initiative, on human rights and climate change. Prompted by the 2007 Malé Declaration on the Human Dimension of Global Climate Change, the Council adopted a resolution in 2008 stating explicitly for the first time that climate change has implications for the full enjoyment of human rights, and requesting the Office of the High Commission for Human Rights to prepare a study on human rights and climate change.[21] Although that study led to greater attention to the issue in the Council and beyond,

[20] Philip Alston, "Conjuring Up New Human Rights: A Proposal for Quality Control," *American Journal of International Law* 78(3) (1984).

[21] Human Rights Council res. 7/23 (March 28, 2008).

the Council did not agree on whether or how it should continue to examine the relationship between climate change and human rights.

As a result, some countries, led by Costa Rica, the Maldives, and Switzerland, decided to pursue a less politically divisive initiative, seeking to clarify how human rights norms could apply to environmental policy more generally. Although some countries would have preferred to continue to focus on climate change, the eventual result was a resolution adopted by consensus calling for the establishment of "an independent expert on the issue of human rights obligations relating to the enjoyment of a safe, clean, healthy and sustainable environment."[22] Limon, who at the time was a diplomat in the mission of the Maldives in Geneva, writes that it was the "unspoken hope" of the main sponsors that this norm-clarifying exercise would not only represent important progress in itself, but that it would also open the door to discussion of the merits of declaring a universal right to a clean and healthy environment. He concludes by describing the resolution on human rights and the environment adopted by the Council in March 2016, which illustrates how far the Council has come in understanding and setting such norms.[23] He points out that much of its text could provide substantive content for a future right to a healthy environment.

HUMAN RIGHTS AND CLIMATE CHANGE

The Malé Declaration, as Limon notes, is a seminal document in the effort to bring human rights to bear on climate change: It was the first international instrument to state explicitly that "climate change has clear and immediate implications for the full enjoyment of human rights," and it called on the UN human rights system to address the issue. The Declaration is also significant for its recognition of the right to a healthy environment, which it describes as "the fundamental right to an environment capable of supporting human society and the full enjoyment of human rights."[24] In Chapter 12, Daniel Magraw and Kristina Wienhöfer place the Malé Declaration in its historical context and analyze its formulation of an overarching environmental right. They emphasize its broad scope: it links to the right to other human rights; it addresses the human being both individually and in society; and it encompasses the entire range of threats to the environment. They point out that the Malé formulation also avoids some of the problems of other terms. References to a "healthy" environment, for example, may be problematic because the natural environment is not always healthy for humans, and because the emphasis on health ignores issues that are of central importance to human rights but do not directly implicate health, such as the right

[22] Human Rights Council res. 19/10 (March 12, 2012).
[23] Human Rights Council res. 31/8 (March 23, 2016).
[24] Malé Declaration on the Human Dimension of Global Climate Change, November 14, 2007.

to enjoy culture. It may also be ambiguous whether the term "healthy" extends beyond human health to include health of ecosystems.

Magraw and Wienhöfer point out that the Declaration was intended to "put a human face on climate change," and that it helped to catalyze action not only in the Human Rights Council, but also in the climate negotiations. In particular, it was the founding document of the Climate Vulnerable Forum, the organization of states that are most vulnerable to climate change, which played an important role in the negotiations culminating in the Paris Agreement adopted in December 2015. As noted at the beginning of this introduction, the Paris Agreement is the first multilateral environmental agreement to include an explicit reference to human rights in its preamble. Lavanya Rajamani, in Chapter 13, explains that the Agreement also recognizes special interests and vulnerabilities, and that it is "implicitly attentive to the need to create enabling socioeconomic conditions for the effective protection of human rights." At the same time, she emphasizes that the Agreement stops short of recognizing a right to a healthy environment or a stable climate.

Rajamani describes the history of the reference to human rights in the Paris Agreement, highlighting the statement in the 2010 Cancun decisions by the Conference of the Parties that parties should "fully respect human rights" in all climate-related actions. She notes that in the negotiation leading up to Paris, many parties and NGOs argued for the inclusion of references to human rights to life, food, shelter, and health, which would be adversely affected by climate impacts. In February 2015, eighteen countries voluntarily pledged to enable meaningful collaboration between their human rights representatives and their climate negotiators, and many states pushed for an explicit human reference in what became Article 2 of the Paris Agreement, which identifies the purpose of the agreement. As Rajamani explains, however, this effort met with resistance from other states, and in the end, the reference was only included in the preamble in carefully limited language that focuses on the human rights aspects of response measures rather than climate change itself. Nevertheless, she concludes that the inclusion of an explicit reference signals greater receptivity to rights concerns, which may suggest that the right to a healthy environment is closer to acknowledgment at the international level.

In the final chapter, Sumudu Atapattu examines whether the right to a healthy environment would help or hinder action in relation to climate change. She reviews the development of detailed jurisprudence applying human rights norms to environmental issues generally, and explains that some aspects of that jurisprudence apply to climate change without difficulty – in particular, it is no longer seriously debated that climate change will lead to the infringement of many protected rights. The nature of states' climate obligations under human rights law, however, remains controversial. While the Paris Agreement's preambular reference to human rights, as well as its support for procedural rights such as education and transparency, is an important step forward, much remains to be done to bring human rights norms to bear on mitigation and adaptation. In particular, the disastrous effects of climate change on the most vulnerable communities, who have contributed little or nothing to the problem, raise profound issues of justice.

She argues that even if adopted, the right to a healthy environment would not be a panacea. It would continue to be constrained by the limitations inherent in the human rights framework, especially the difficulties in applying human rights extraterritorially. Still, she states that "the recognition of a stand-alone right to a healthy environment would send a clear signal to the international community that environmental rights are important, that such rights are justiciable, and that other protected rights could be jeopardized if a right to a healthy environment is not respected." Above all, the right would give additional avenues to victims of environmental abuses to seek redress through international as well as national mechanisms. Finally, she concludes with reference to a theme emphasized throughout the book: Even in the absence of a clear, stand-alone right, states still have human rights obligations that they are required to fulfill in taking action in relation to environmental issues.

* * *

This review of the contributions to this book makes clear that recognition of a global right to a healthy environment would have real benefits, both as a capstone symbolizing the growing maturity of this area of the law, and as a cornerstone for further legal developments. As a capstone, it would provide a more coherent framework for human rights norms related to environmental protection. In Orellana's words: "The normative content of human rights in respect of the environment would thus no longer be dispersed or fragmented across a range of rights, but would come together under a single normative frame." May and Daly further explain that a stand-alone right "would confirm the interdependence and the indivisibility of human and environmental rights."

At the same time, the right could lead to the greater acceptance and further development of the norms in this area. As several of the contributors point out, global recognition of the right to a healthy environment could push countries that have not yet recognized a constitutional right to do so, and it might open new legal remedies at the national as well as the international level. Global recognition of the right would also strengthen regional efforts, and Pedersen says that it could have that effect even in the regional tribunal that has been the most active in linking human rights and the environment: the European Court of Human Rights. Rajamani and Atapattu each highlight ways that the growing receptivity to rights concerns in the climate context is leading to development of more specific obligations.

One of the simplest and most compelling arguments for recognition of the right is that it would make clear that environmental concerns are on the same level as other fundamental human interests recognized as human rights. Boyd states that a human right to a healthy environment would level the playing field with competing social and economic rights. Rodríguez-Garavito agrees that the right could serve as a "source of countervailing arguments and power vis-à-vis other legally protected goals, such as the exigencies of economic development." Perhaps because human dependence on the environment is so fundamental, it has often been taken for granted, and even ignored, as we have pursued other goals of economic and social development. But if we have learned anything about the environment over the last forty years, it is that a healthy environment cannot be assumed, and that unsustainable development puts all of our rights at risk. It seems clear that it is past time to codify this recognition in the form of a human right to a healthy environment, on the same level as the other rights that are integral to human lives of dignity, freedom, and equality.

We close this introduction by thanking our contributors again for their thoughtful, thought-provoking analyses. The following chapters shed light on many of the questions concerning the right to a healthy environment, but we do not pretend that they are, or should be, the final word. In the continuing conversation on the relationship between human rights and the environment, this volume is not a capstone but, perhaps, a cornerstone that can provide a basis for the further exploration and development of these fundamentally important issues.

2

Catalyst for Change

Evaluating Forty Years of Experience in Implementing the Right to a Healthy Environment

*David R. Boyd**

For decades, there has been a lively debate among scholars in the fields of human rights and environmental law about whether explicit legal recognition of the right to a healthy environment would provide tangible benefits.[1] Proponents have asserted that recognition of this right would contribute to a variety of positive procedural and substantive outcomes ranging from increased public participation in environmental management to cleaner air and water. Critics argued that no such right existed and nor should it because it suffered from fatal flaws, duplicated existing rights, and would ultimately prove ineffective. An evaluation of the empirical evidence regarding these conflicting positions is long overdue, especially in light of the remarkable extent to which the right to a healthy environment has become legally established.

Despite its relatively recent provenance, the right to a healthy environment enjoys widespread legal recognition across the world, both internationally and nationally. Although environmental rights and responsibilities have deep roots in many indigenous cultures, the first formal acknowledgment of the human right to live in a healthy environment appeared in the 1972 Stockholm Declaration.[2] Despite its soft law status, the Stockholm Declaration has had profound impacts on environmental law, constitutional law, and human rights law. Although not yet recognized in a legally binding global instrument, the right to a healthy

* Associate Professor, University of British Columbia Institute for Resources, Environment, and Sustainability.

1 See David R. Boyd, *The Environmental Rights Revolution: A Global Study of Constitutions, Human Rights, and the Environment* (University of British Columbia Press, 2012).

2 Declaration of the UN Conference on the Human Environment, UN Doc. A/Conf.48/14/ Rev.1 (1972).

environment is explicitly included in the African (Banjul) Charter on Human and People's Rights, the San Salvador Protocol, the Aarhus Convention, and the Arab Charter on Human Rights.[3] Collectively, these regional treaties have been ratified by 120 nations (see Table 1).

At the national level, the right to a healthy environment enjoys direct constitutional protection in 100 countries (see Table 1). A typical example is Article 112 of Norway's Constitution, which states: "Every person has a right to an environment that is conducive to health and to natural surroundings whose productivity and diversity are preserved. Natural resources should be made use of on the basis of comprehensive long-term considerations whereby this right will be safeguarded for future generations as well."[4]

No other social or economic right has spread as quickly through the world's constitutions.[5] There are at least twelve additional countries where courts have ruled that the right to a healthy environment is an implicit but essential element of the right to life, and therefore is an enforceable right that merits constitutional protection.[6] The right to a healthy environment also is explicitly incorporated in legislation in more than 100 countries (see Table 1). In total, governments of at least 155 nations have recognized the right to a healthy environment in legally binding instruments, at the national and/or the international level.[7] Many other countries have signed non-binding soft law declarations that include the right to a healthy environment, such as the Male' Declaration (2007) and the Association of Southeast Asian Nations Human Rights Declaration (2012).

[3] African Charter on Human and Peoples' Rights, June 27, 1981, in force October 21, 1986, 1520 UNTS 217; Additional Protocol to the American Convention on Human Rights in the Area of Economic, Social and Cultural Rights: Protocol of San Salvador, November 17, 1988, in force November 16, 1999, 28 ILM 161; Arab Charter on Human Rights, May 22, 2004, in force March 15, 2008, 12 IHRR 893 (2005); Aarhus Convention on Access to Information, Public Participation in Decision-Making and Access to Justice in Environmental Matters, June 25, 1998, in force October 21, 2001, 2161 UNTS 447.

[4] Constitution of Norway, art. 112 (2015) in Google Constitute, www.constituteproject.org.

[5] David S. Law and Mila Versteeg, "The Evolution and Ideology of Global Constitutionalism," *California Law Review* 99(5) (2011), pp. 1163–257.

[6] David R. Boyd, "The Implicit Constitutional Right to a Healthy Environment," *Review of European Community and International Environmental Law* 20(2) (2011), pp. 171–9.

[7] The thirty-eight UN member nations that do not recognize the right to a healthy environment in national constitutions, legislation, or regional treaties are: Afghanistan, Antigua and Barbuda, Australia, Bahamas, Barbados, Belize, Brunei Darussalam, Cambodia, Canada, China, Dominica, Japan, Kiribati, Kuwait, Laos, Lebanon, Liechtenstein, Marshall Islands, Micronesia, Monaco, Myanmar, Nauru, New Zealand, North Korea, Oman, Papua New Guinea, Saint Kitts and Nevis, Saint Lucia, Saint Vincent and the Grenadines, Samoa, San Marino, Singapore, Solomon Islands, Tonga, Trinidad and Tobago, Tuvalu, United States, and Vanuatu.

TABLE 1. *Legal recognition of the right to a healthy environment in UN nations*

	National Constitution	International Convention*	National Legislation
Afghanistan	N	N	N
Albania	Y	Y	Y
Algeria	N	Y	N
Andorra	Y	N	Y
Angola	Y	Y	Y
Antigua and Barbuda	N	N	N
Argentina	Y	Y	Y
Armenia	Y	Y	Y
Australia	N	N	N
Austria	N	Y	N
Azerbaijan	Y	Y	Y
Bahamas	N	N	N
Bahrain	N	Y	N
Bangladesh	Yi	N	N
Barbados	N	N	N
Belarus	Y	Y	Y
Belgium	Y	Y	Y
Belize	N	N	N
Benin	Y	Y	Y
Bhutan	N	N	Y
Bolivia	Y	Y	Y
Bosnia and Herzegovina	N	Y	Y
Botswana	N	Y	N
Brazil	Y	Y	Y
Brunei Darussalam	N	N	N
Bulgaria	Y	Y	Y
Burkina Faso	Y	Y	Y
Burundi	Y	Y	Y
Cambodia	N	N	N
Cameroon	Y	Y	Y
Canada	N	N	N
Cape Verde	Y	Y	Y
Central African Republic	Y	Y	Y
Chad	Y	Y	Y
Chile	Y	N	Y
China	N	N	N
Colombia	Y	Y	Y
Comoros	Y	Y	Y
Congo-Brazzaville	Y	Y	N
Congo-Democratic Republic of	Y	Y	Y
Costa Rica	Y	Y	Y

(*continued*)

Table 1. (*continued*)

	National Constitution	International Convention*	National Legislation
Cote d'Ivoire	Y	Y	Y
Croatia	Y	Y	Y
Cuba	N	N	Y
Cyprus	N	Y	N
Czech Republic	Y	Y	Y
Denmark	N	Y	N
Djibouti	N	Y	Y
Dominica	N	N	N
Dominican Republic	Y	N	Y
East Timor	Y	N	Y
Ecuador	Y	Y	Y
Egypt	Y	Y	N
El Salvador	Y	Y	Y
Equatorial Guinea	N	Y	N
Eritrea	N	Y	Y
Estonia	Yi	Y	N
Ethiopia	Y	Y	Y
Fiji	Y	N	N
Finland	Y	Y	Y
France	Y	Y	Y
Gabon	Y	Y	Y
Gambia	N	Y	Y
Georgia	Y	Y	Y
Germany	N	Y	N
Ghana	N	Y	N
Greece	Y	Y	Y
Grenada	Y	N	N
Guatemala	Yi	Y	N
Guinea	Y	Y	N
Guinea-Bissau	N	Y	N
Guyana	Y	N	N
Haiti	N	N	Y
Honduras	Y	Y	Y
Hungary	Y	Y	Y
Iceland	Y	Y	N
India	Yi	N	Y
Indonesia	Y	N	Y
Iran	Y	N	?
Iraq	Y	N	Y
Ireland	N	Y	N
Israel	Yi	N	N
Italy	Yi	Y	N
Jamaica	Y	N	N
Japan	N	N	N

	National Constitution	International Convention*	National Legislation
Jordan	N	Y	N
Kazakhstan	N	Y	Y
Kenya	Y	Y	Y
Kiribati	N	N	N
Korea, North	N	N	N
Korea, South	Y	N	Y
Kuwait	N	N	?
Kyrgyzstan	Y	Y	Y
Laos	N	N	N
Latvia	Y	Y	Y
Lebanon	N	N	?
Lesotho	N	Y	Y
Liberia	N	Y	Y
Libya	N	Y	?
Liechtenstein	N	N	N
Lithuania	N	Y	Y
Luxembourg	N	Y	N
Macedonia	Y	Y	Y
Madagascar	Y	Y	N
Malawi	Y	Y	Y
Malaysia	Yi	N	N
Maldives	Y	N	N
Mali	Y	Y	Y
Malta	N	Y	N
Marshall Islands	N	N	N
Mauritania	Y	Y	Y
Mauritius	N	Y	N
Mexico	Y	Y	Y
Micronesia	N	N	N
Moldova	Y	Y	Y
Monaco	N	N	N
Mongolia	Y	N	Y
Montenegro	Y	Y	Y
Morocco	Y	N	Y
Mozambique	Y	Y	Y
Myanmar	N	N	N
Namibia	N	Y	N
Nauru	N	N	N
Nepal	Y	N	Y
Netherlands	Y	Y	N
New Zealand	N	N	N
Nicaragua	Y	Y	Y
Niger	Y	Y	Y
Nigeria	Yi	Y	N

(continued)

Table 1. (*continued*)

	National Constitution	International Convention*	National Legislation
Norway	Y	Y	Y
Oman	N	N	N
Pakistan	Yi	N	N
Palau	N	N	Y
Panama	Y	Y	Y
Papua New Guinea	N	N	N
Paraguay	Y	Y	Y
Peru	Y	Y	Y
Philippines	Y	N	Y
Poland	Y	Y	Y
Portugal	Y	Y	Y
Qatar	N	Y	N
Romania	Y	Y	Y
Russia	Y	N	Y
Rwanda	Y	Y	Y
Saint Kitts and Nevis	N	N	N
Saint Lucia	N	N	N
Saint Vincent and the Grenadines	N	N	N
Samoa	N	N	N
San Marino	N	N	N
Sao Tome and Principe	Y	Y	Y
Saudi Arabia	N	Y	N
Senegal	Y	Y	Y
Serbia	Y	Y	Y
Seychelles	Y	Y	N
Sierra Leone	N	Y	N
Singapore	N	N	N
Slovakia	Y	Y	Y
Slovenia	Y	Y	Y
Solomon Islands	N	N	N
Somalia	Y	Y	N
South Africa	Y	Y	Y
South Sudan	Y	N	N
Spain	Y	Y	Y
Sri Lanka	Yi	N	N
Sudan	Y	Y	?
Suriname	N	Y	N
Swaziland	N	Y	N
Sweden	N	Y	N
Switzerland	N	Y	N
Syrian Arab Republic	N	Y	N
Tajikistan	N	Y	Y
Tanzania	Yi	Y	Y

	National Constitution	International Convention*	National Legislation
Thailand	Y	N	Y
Togo	Y	Y	Y
Tonga	N	N	N
Trinidad and Tobago	N	N	N
Tunisia	Y	Y	Y
Turkey	Y	N	Y
Turkmenistan	Y	Y	Y
Tuvalu	N	N	N
Uganda	Y	Y	Y
Ukraine	Y	Y	Y
United Arab Emirates	N	Y	N
United Kingdom	N	Y	N
United States	N	N	N
Uruguay	Yi	Y	Y
Uzbekistan	N	N	Y
Vanuatu	N	N	N
Venezuela	Y	N	Y
Vietnam	Y	N	Y
Yemen	N	Y	Y
Zambia	Y	Y	Y
Zimbabwe	Y	Y	Y
	112	**121**	**103**

Y = Yes, Yi = implicit, N = No
* Includes African Charter, San Salvador Protocol, Aarhus Convention, and Arab Charter

EXAMINING THE EFFECTS OF THE RIGHT TO A HEALTHY ENVIRONMENT AT THE INTERNATIONAL LEVEL

There are two primary pathways through which international recognition of the right to a healthy environment can lead to improved environmental outcomes and a decline in adverse effects on human and ecosystem health. The first pathway is through the direct application of this human right in cases brought before international courts and tribunals. There is a growing body of jurisprudence – from the Inter-American Court of Human Rights, the Inter-American Commission on Human Rights, the European Court of Human Rights, the European Committee of Social Rights, and the African Commission on Human and Peoples' Rights – in cases involving violations of the right to a healthy environment. The connections between environmental degradation and human rights have influenced international tribunal rulings in cases that involve countries from Nigeria and Peru to Russia and Turkey. Air pollution, water pollution, noise pollution, exposure to toxic substances, and the failure to enact and enforce environmental laws have all been identified as violations of various human rights, including the right to a healthy environment.

However, there are significant concerns about the effectiveness of these international processes, as is the case for many other realms of human rights. Relatively few cases reach these regional bodies, the processes are reactive and extremely lengthy, remedies thus far have been limited, and on-the-ground implementation of decisions has been modest at best and in some cases, completely nonexistent. A well-known example is the *SERAC* case, in which the African Commission issued a highly regarded decision about the devastating impacts of oil and gas development on the people of Nigeria.[8] Widespread oil pollution was clearly identified as a violation of the right to live in a healthy environment. Despite praise for the legal precedent established by the Commission's ruling, there has been little or no change in the actual environmental conditions endured by communities in oil-producing regions. However, there are ongoing efforts to kick-start the cleanup process, including a UN report emphasizing the urgent need and assessing the likely cost as being several billion dollars.[9]

The second pathway is through the indirect influence of international human rights law on national constitutional, environmental, and human rights law. International recognition of the right to a healthy environment has affected national constitutions, legislation, and jurisprudence. The Stockholm Declaration is often cited as an inspiration by nations that subsequently rewrote constitutions and legislation to include environmental rights and responsibilities.[10] Similarly, there are many instances of international law influencing decisions about the right to a healthy environment in national court systems. For example, the Stockholm Declaration influenced decisions of the Supreme Court of India protecting the implicit constitutional right to a healthy environment.[11] The right to a healthy environment in the African Charter led Kenyan and Nigerian courts to make important rulings finding the right to be an essential part of the constitutional right to life, although not explicitly articulated as such in either the Kenyan or Nigerian constitutions.[12]

8 *Social and Economic Rights Action Centre (SERAC) and the Centre for Economic and Social Rights (CESR)* v. *Nigeria*, Communication No 155/96 (2001). See Danwood Mzikenge Chirwa, "A Fresh Commitment to Implementing Economic, Social, and Cultural Rights in Africa: Social and Economic Rights Action Center (SERAC) and the Center for Economic and Social Rights v. Nigeria," *ESR Review* 3(2) (2002), pp. 19–21.

9 United Nations Environment Programme, *Environmental Assessment of Ogoniland* (2011).

10 See Marc Pallemaerts, "The Human Right to the Environment as a Substantive Right," in Maguelonne Dejeant-Pons and Marc Pallemaerts (eds.), *Human Rights and the Environment: Compendium of Instruments and Other International Texts on Individual and Collective Rights Relating to the Environment in the International and European Framework* (Council of Europe, 2002).

11 Vasanthi Nimushakavi, *Constitutional Policy and Environmental Jurisprudence in India* (Macmillan India, 2006), pp. 23, 156–7.

12 *P.K. Waweru* v. *Republic of Kenya* (2006). High Court of Kenya, Misc. Civil Application no. 118 of 2004, 2 March 2006. KLR (Environment and Land) 1 (2006) 677.

Costa Rican and Colombian courts have cited the San Salvador Protocol in cases involving the right to a healthy environment.[13]

Given that both of these pathways are producing legal and environmental benefits, there is a prima facie case that further international recognition of the right to a healthy environment would provide additional benefits of a similar nature. However, it is widely acknowledged that recognition of the right to a healthy environment at the national level has had more important legal implications as well as tangible consequences for human and ecosystem health.

EXAMINING THE EFFECTS OF THE RIGHT TO A HEALTHY ENVIRONMENT AT THE NATIONAL LEVEL

Despite its rapid spread across the world, until recently, little research had been conducted to evaluate the impacts of legally entrenching the right to a healthy environment. For decades, proponents have argued that the potential benefits of recognizing the right to a healthy environment include:

- stronger environmental laws and policies;
- improved implementation and enforcement;
- greater citizen participation in environmental decision making;
- increased accountability;
- reduction in environmental injustices;
- a level playing field with social and economic rights; and
- better environmental performance.

Critics, on the other hand, argued that the right to a healthy environment is:

- too vague to be useful;
- redundant because of existing human rights and environmental laws;
- a threat to democracy, because it shifts power from elected legislators to judges;
- not enforceable;
- likely to cause a flood of litigation; and
- likely to be ineffective.

Is the right to live in a healthy environment merely a paper tiger with few practical consequences? Or is this right a powerful catalyst for accelerating progress toward a sustainable future? To date, the only comprehensive efforts to answer these questions have focused on the experiences of the 100-plus nations where this right enjoys constitutional status. This recent research demonstrates that the incorporation of the

[13] Sala Constitucional de Costa Rica, resolución no. 2003–04654 (2003); Sala Constitucional de Costa Rica, resolución no. 2007–02154 (2007); Constitutional Court of Colombia, sentencia no. C-443/09 (2009).

right to a healthy environment in a country's constitution leads directly to two important legal outcomes: stronger environmental laws, and court decisions defending the right from violations.[14] Evidence indicates that the other anticipated benefits of constitutional environmental rights also are being realized, while the potential drawbacks are not materializing. Perhaps most importantly, empirical evidence also indicates that environmental rights contribute to stronger environmental performance, including cleaner air, safer drinking water, and smaller ecological footprints. Unfortunately, there is not yet any comparable research that attempts to quantify the effects of recognizing the right to a healthy environment in regional treaties or in national legislation.

Strengthening Environmental Laws

In at least eighty nations, environmental laws were strengthened after the right to a healthy environment gained constitutional status. Laws were amended to focus on environmental rights, as well as access to environmental information, public participation in decision making, and access to justice. This includes almost all of the nations with constitutional environmental rights in Eastern and Western Europe, Latin America and the Caribbean, and Asia; and a clear majority of such nations in Africa.[15] To cite just one example, Spain's recognition of a constitutional right to a healthy environment more than three decades ago, in 1978, continues to exert a major influence on the development of environmental legislation. Spain's Environmental Responsibility Law and its Law on Natural Heritage and Biodiversity, both enacted in 2007, make repeated reference to Article 45 of the constitution, which sets out the right to a healthy environment.[16]

Among the small number of nations where no constitutional influence on environmental laws is discernible are countries where the constitutional changes are very recent (e.g., Fiji 2013, Vietnam 2013, Tunisia 2014, Grenada 2015) and countries wracked by civil war and other overriding social, economic, or political crises (e.g. Democratic Republic of the Congo). The majority of the nations where there is no evidence that constitutional recognition of the right to a healthy environment has influenced environmental laws are in Africa.

In some nations, the constitutional right to a healthy environment has exerted an influence upon the entire body of environmental law and policy. This is clearly the case in Argentina, where the reform of the constitution in 1994 to include the right to a healthy environment "triggered the need for a new generation of environmental

[14] Boyd, *The Environmental Rights Revolution*.

[15] Ibid., chapters 6–10.

[16] Environmental Responsibility Law (2007); Law on Natural Heritage and Biodiversity (2007). See also Law 27/2006, which deals with procedural environmental rights.

legislation."[17] After 1994, Argentina passed a new comprehensive environmental law which "sought to make the constitution a reality," a law governing access to environmental information, and minimum standard laws on issues ranging from industrial waste to clean water.[18] The national constitution also caused a cascade effect, as provincial constitutions were amended to incorporate the right to a healthy environment, and provincial environmental laws altered to identify the right as a guiding principle.[19] The constitutional right to a healthy environment also had a comprehensive effect on environmental law in other countries including Portugal, Costa Rica, Brazil, Colombia, South Africa, and the Philippines.[20] A similar transformation is underway in France following the enactment of its Charter for the Environment in 2005.[21]

Constitutional recognition of the right to a healthy environment is clearly not the only factor contributing to improved environmental laws. For example, the European Union's accession process had a major influence on environmental legislation in Eastern Europe. Other key factors include public pressure, the migration of ideas and legislative approaches from other jurisdictions, and international assistance from agencies such as the UN Environment Programme and the International Union for the Conservation of Nature.

Improving Implementation and Enforcement

Recognition of the constitutional right to a healthy environment can facilitate increased implementation and enforcement of environmental laws. Citizens, communities, and non-governmental organizations (NGOs) in Europe, Latin America, and Asia have supplemented the enforcement efforts of the state, drawn attention to violations, and provided an impetus for the allocation of additional resources to environmental monitoring and protection. A leading example is the cooperative approach taken in Brazil, where the public and NGOs can report alleged violations of constitutional rights and environmental laws to the independent Ministerio

[17] Juan Rodrigo Walsh, "Argentina's Constitution and General Environmental Law as the Framework for Comprehensive Land Use Regulation," in Nathalie J. Chalifour et al. (eds.), *Land Use Law for Sustainable Development* (Cambridge University Press, 2007), pp. 503–25 at 505.

[18] See Daniel A. Sabsay, "Constitution and Environment in Relation to Sustainable Development," in Maria Di Paola (ed.), *Symposium of Judges and Prosecutors of Latin America: Environmental Compliance and Enforcement* (Fundacion Ambiente y Recursos Naturales, 2003), pp. 33–43.

[19] An example of a provincial law that incorporates the right to a healthy environment as a guiding principle is Rio Negro's *Environmental Impact Assessment Law*. Rio Negro Law No. 3266, 16 December 1998.

[20] Boyd, *The Environmental Rights Revolution*, chapter 11.

[21] David Marrani, "The Second Anniversary of the Constitutionalisation of the French Charter for the Environment: Constitutional and Environmental Implications," *Environmental Law Review* 10(1) (2008), pp. 9–27 at 25.

Publico, which conducts investigations, civil actions, and prosecutions. The constitutional changes in 1988 that empowered the Ministerio Publico to enforce constitutional environmental rights have resulted in a dramatic increase in enforcement of environmental laws.[22] A Brazilian judge wrote that "hundreds of pages would be needed to mention all the precedents" set by Brazilian courts in recent years dealing with constitutional protection for the environment.[23] In the state of Sao Paolo alone, between 1984 and 2004, the Ministerio Publico filed over 4,000 public civil actions in environmental cases addressing issues ranging from deforestation to air pollution.[24] There are now agencies similar to the Ministerio Publico in the majority of Latin American nations.[25]

Increasing Accountability

Government and corporate accountability are increased by more rigorous implementation and enforcement of environmental laws. One measurable indicator of the influence of the constitutional right to a healthy environment on accountability is court decisions based on this right. Court decisions defending the right to a healthy environment have been made in more than fifty nations and are increasing in frequency and importance. This includes most nations in Western Europe, most nations in Latin America, the Caribbean and Eastern Europe, a minority of nations in Asia, but only a few nations in Africa.[26]

The number of reported cases per nation ranges from one (e.g., Malawi, the Seychelles) to hundreds in some Latin American, Asian, and European nations. Language barriers hinder recognition and understanding of this enormous body of jurisprudence. Nevertheless, in total, there are thousands of reported cases on the right to a healthy environment, led by Colombia, Costa Rica, Brazil, Argentina, India, the Philippines, Belgium, and Greece. The recent adoption of environmental rights provisions in some constitutions, combined with difficulties in accessing the jurisprudence of some nations, mean that these statistics likely underestimate the full extent of litigation based on the right to a healthy environment.[27]

[22] Lesley K. McAllister, *Making Law Matter: Environmental Protection and Legal Institutions in Brazil* (Stanford University Press, 2008).

[23] Vladimir Passos de Freitas, "The Importance of Environmental Judicial Decisions: The Brazilian Experience," in M. E. Di Paola (ed.), *Symposium of Judges and Prosecutors of Latin America: Environmental Compliance and Enforcement*, pp. 59–64 at 62.

[24] McAllister, *Making Law Matter*, p. 99.

[25] See generally Rosaly Ledezma (ed.), *Ministerios Públicos en America Latina* (Asamblea Legislativa Plurinacional de Bolivia Cámara de Diputados, 2011).

[26] See Boyd, *The Environmental Rights Revolution*, chapters 6–10.

[27] See Stephen Stec, "Environmental Justice through Courts in Countries in Economic Transition," in Jonas Ebbesson and Phoebe Okowa (eds.), *Environmental Law and Justice in Context* (Cambridge University Press, 2009), pp. 158–75.

Data from Latin America, Europe, and India indicate that the majority of lawsuits based on the constitutional right to a healthy environment are successful.[28] In Brazil, environmental public civil actions are successful in 67.5 percent of cases.[29] In Colombia, the applicants were successful in 53 percent of the cases based on the right to a healthy environment brought between 1991 and 2008.[30] In Costa Rica, roughly 66 percent of cases asserting violations of the right to a healthy environment are successful.[31] Jariwala estimated that nearly 80 percent of environmental cases brought in India up until 1999 were successful.[32] These statistics should assuage concerns that environmental activists will attempt to block economic development by filing frivolous lawsuits.

Courts have ruled that the constitutional right to a healthy environment imposes four types of duties upon government: to respect the right by not infringing it through state action; to protect the right from infringement by third parties (which may require regulations, implementation, and enforcement); to take actions to fulfill the right (e.g., by providing services including clean water, sanitation, and waste management); and to promote the right (through public education or mass media). In addition, courts have consistently held that laws, regulations, and administrative actions that violate the constitutional right to a healthy environment will be struck down. While the precise nature of what constitutes a "healthy environment" varies from country to country, depending on a variety of context-specific circumstances, the emphasis is always on securing improved environmental conditions.

It is rare for courts to decide that the right to a healthy environment is not directly enforceable, although this has occurred in South Korea, Spain, the Czech Republic, Slovakia, and Paraguay. In these nations, the courts are constrained by constitutional language specifying that the right can only be enforced pursuant to enabling legislation. Overall, constitutional principles related to the right to a healthy environment "have created the right conditions for courts of law . . . to begin to play a more prominent role in protecting the environment."[33]

28 See Nicolas de Sadeleer, Gerhard Roller, and Miriam Dross, *Access to Justice in Environmental Matters and the Role of NGOs: Empirical Findings and Legal Appraisal* (Europa Law Publishing, 2005).

29 Kathryn Hochstetler and Margaret E. Keck, *Greening Brazil: Environmental Activism in State and Society* (Duke University Press, 2007), p. 55.

30 Defensoria del Pueblo, *Diagnostic del cumplimiento del derecho humano al agua en Colombia* (Defensoria del Pueblo, 2009).

31 Boyd, *The Environmental Rights Revolution*, p. 136, n. 104.

32 C. M. Jariwala, "The Directions of Environmental Justice: An Overview," in S. K. Verma and K. Kusum (eds.), *Fifty Years of the Supreme Court of India: Its Grasp and Reach* (Oxford University Press, 2000), pp. 469–94.

33 United Nations Economic Commission for Latin America and the Caribbean, *The Sustainability of Development in Latin America and the Caribbean: Challenges and Opportunities* (United Nations, 2002), p. 163.

Increasing Public Involvement

Constitutional environmental provisions have substantially increased the public's role in environmental governance. The right to a healthy environment has been interpreted consistently as including procedural environmental rights: access to information, participation in decision making, and access to justice. Citizens, in ever-increasing numbers, are using these rights. Other major factors contributing to the growing public role in environmental governance include the enhanced importance of civil society, advances in communications technology (particularly the internet), and in many nations the transition from closed, authoritarian types of government to open, participatory democracy. In many nations that recognize the right to a healthy environment, administrative processes and courthouse doors are now open to citizens who lack a traditional economic or personal interest but seek to protect society's collective interest in a healthy environment.[34]

Several Latin American nations – Costa Rica, Colombia, Argentina, and Brazil – are global leaders in terms of enhancing access to justice. The Philippines, with its special procedural rules for environmental litigation, is moving in the same direction.[35] Procedural innovations have radically increased the ability of citizens, communities, and environmental non-governmental organizations (ENGOs) to seek judicial protection of their constitutional rights, including the right to a healthy environment.[36] These innovations reduce costs, decrease delays, and minimize risks previously associated with pursuing judicial remedies.

Advance Screening of New Laws and Regulations

Constitutional recognition of the right to a healthy environment generally requires that all proposed laws and regulations be screened to ensure that they are consistent with the government's duty to respect, protect, promote, and fulfill the right. In some nations, this is a formal process. For example, in France, the Constitutional Council reviews proposed legislation prior to its enactment. In other nations, the screening process is informal. For example, in Colombia, the close scrutiny of the Constitutional Court has compelled legislators to consider constitutional case law when drafting the content of new legislation.[37]

[34] Boyd, *The Environmental Rights Revolution*, chapters 5–10.

[35] See Supreme Court of the Philippines, Resolution A.M. No. 09–6–8-SC, Rules of Procedure for Environmental Cases (2010).

[36] Boyd, *The Environmental Rights Revolution*, chapter 6.

[37] Manuel José Cepeda Espinosa, "The Judicialization of Politics in Colombia: The Old and the New," in Rachel Sieder, Line Schjolden, and Alan Angell (eds.), *The Judicialization of Politics in Latin America* (Palgrave Macmillan, 2005), pp. 67–104.

Providing a Safety Net

In some countries, the constitutional right to a healthy environment has been used to close gaps in environmental law. Costa Rica and Nepal offer examples of courts ordering governments to enact legislation or regulations (to protect fisheries and reduce air pollution, respectively).[38] The courts did not spell out the details of the laws but merely clarified that certain legislation is an essential element of fulfilling the government's environmental responsibilities. In other nations, courts issued carefully crafted judgments that did not compel but rather influenced states to take action (e.g., legislation governing plastic bags in Uganda, public smoking in India, and air quality standards in Sri Lanka).[39]

Courts are not always willing to fill legislative or regulatory gaps, often justifying their refusal on the basis of respect for the separation of powers. For example, the Supreme Court of the Philippines, despite agreeing that air pollution from motor vehicles was a threat to health, declined to order the government to convert all of its vehicles to compressed natural gas because it believed this would have interfered with legislative and executive responsibilities.[40]

Preventing Rollbacks

Another legal advantage flowing from constitutional recognition of the right to a healthy environment is that it may prevent the future weakening of environmental laws and policies (commonly referred to as rollbacks). Courts have articulated the principle, based on the right to a healthy environment, that current environmental laws and policies represent a baseline that can be improved but not weakened.[41] This concept is called the standstill principle in Belgium and is also recognized in France, Hungary, South Africa, and many nations in Latin America. In France, it is known as the "ratchet effect" or the "non-regression" principle.[42] Belgian authorities

[38] *Suray Prasad Sharma Dhungel* v. *Godavari Marble Industries and Others*, WP 35/1991 (Supreme Court of Nepal, 1995); *Asociación Interamericana para la Defensa del Ambiente y otros* (Costa Rican Constitutional Court, 2009).

[39] *Lalanath de Silva* v. *Minister of Forestry and Environment*, Fundamental Rights Application 569/98 (Supreme Court of Sri Lanka, 1998); *Greenwatch* v. *Attorney General and National Environmental Management Authority*, Miscellaneous Application 140 (Uganda, 2002); *Murli S. Deora* v. *Union of India*, 8 SCC 765 (Supreme Court of India, 2001).

[40] *H. M. Henares, Jr. et al.* v. *Land Transportation Franchising and Regulatory Board et al.*, G.R. No. 158290 (Supreme Court of Philippines, 2006). See also *Anjum Irfan* v. *LDA*, PLD 2002 Lahore 555 (Pakistan, 2002).

[41] Luc Lavrysen, "Presentation of Aarhus-Related Cases of the Belgian Constitutional Court," *Environmental Law Network International Review* 2 (2007), pp. 5–8.

[42] Michel Prieur, "De l'Urgente Nécessité de Reconnaitre le Principe de Non Regression en Droit de l'Environnement," *IUCN Academy of Environmental Law E-Journal* 1 (2011), pp. 26–45.

are precluded from weakening levels of environmental protection except in limited circumstances where there is a compelling public interest.[43] For example, a proposal to accommodate motor racing by weakening standards for air and noise pollution was rejected.[44] Similarly, Hungary's Constitutional Court rejected an attempt to privatize publicly owned forests because weaker environmental standards governed private land.[45] The standstill principle recognizes that in society's quest for sustainable development, the only viable direction is toward stronger environmental laws and policies.

Addressing Environmental Justice

The constitutional right to a healthy environment should promote environmental justice by ensuring a minimum standard of environmental quality for all members of society. Some politically weak and marginalized communities have enjoyed success in the courts in enforcing their right to a healthy environment. Many cases, particularly in Latin America, deal with the provision of clean water, sewage treatment, and adequate waste management – environmental concerns more likely to confront the poor than middle or upper classes. Millions of people enjoy clean drinking water today because the constitutional right to a healthy environment compelled governments to strengthen laws, invest in infrastructure, and protect water supplies.

There are many examples of courts addressing environmental injustices by defending peoples' right to live in a healthy environment. Citizens in countries as diverse as Russia, Romania, Chile, and Turkey brought lawsuits based on their right to a healthy environment and received compensation for damage to their health caused by industrial pollution.[46] For example, because of litigation based on their constitutional environmental rights, people in the Peruvian village of La Oroya finally received medical treatment for their long-term exposure to lead and other heavy metals emitted by a nearby smelter.[47]

There are some situations where systemic changes are being produced by constitutions, legislation, and litigation. In Brazil, litigation based on the constitutional right to a healthy environment resulted in a new government policy that all citizens have the right to a core minimum of essential services including clean water,

[43] Lavrysen, "Presentation of Aarhus-Related Cases," pp. 5–8.

[44] *Jacobs* v. *Flemish Region*, No. 80.018 (Belgium, Council of State, 1999); *Venter*, No. 82.130 (Belgium, Council of State, 1999).

[45] *Judgment* 28, V. 20 AB (Constitutional Court of Hungary, 1994), p. 1919.

[46] *Tătar* v. *Romania*, No. 67021/01 (European Court of Human Rights, 2009); *Fadeyeva* v. *Russia*, No. 55723/00 (European Court of Human Rights, 2005); *Okyay et al.* v. *Turkey*, No. 36220/97 (European Court of Human Rights, 2005). In Chile, see "Defensa de los Derechos Humanos: Caso Contaminación en Arica," in *Fiscalía del Medio Ambiente* (2012), at www.fima.cl.

[47] *Pablo Miguel Fabián Martínez and Others* v. *Minister of Health and Director General of Environmental Health*, Exp. No. 2002–2006-PC/TC (Constitutional Court, 2006).

adequate sanitation, and proper waste management.[48] The comprehensive court-ordered cleanup and restoration of the Matanza-Riachuelo watershed in Argentina has spurred better living conditions for millions of economically marginalized people. In 2008, the Argentine Supreme Court issued a comprehensive decision based on the constitutional right to a healthy environment in which it ordered:

- regular inspections of all polluting enterprises and implementation of wastewater treatment plans;
- closure of all illegal dumps, redevelopment of landfills, and cleanup of the riverbanks;
- improvement of the drinking water, sewage treatment, and storm-water discharge infrastructure in the river basin;
- development of a regional environmental health plan, including contingencies for possible emergencies;
- supervision, by the federal Auditor General, of the budget allocation for implementation of the restoration plan;
- ongoing judicial oversight of the implementation of the plan, with a federal court judge empowered to resolve any disputes related to the Court's decision; and
- notice that any violations of the timelines established by the Court would result in daily fines against responsible politicians.[49]

These remedies are intended to restore past damage as well as prevent future degradation of the river system. Substantial on-the-ground progress has already been made. The World Bank approved $US 2 billion in financing for the Matanza-Riachuelo Basin Sustainable Development Project.[50] The Argentine government established a new watershed authority (ACUMAR) which must (i) implement a comprehensive action plan, (ii) coordinate and harmonize activities, and (iii) control and monitor environmental compliance.[51] The number of environmental inspectors in the region increased from three to 250.[52] Progress to date includes three new drinking water treatment plants serving millions of people, eight new or upgraded sewage treatment systems serving millions of people, hundreds of polluting companies and illegal garbage dumps closed, thousands of people relocated from riverside slums to social housing, hundreds of kilometers of riverbank restored,

48 Appeal No. 575.998, Minas Gervais (Supreme Court of Justice, 2004); Appeal No. 70011759842, Rio Grande do Sul (Supreme Court of Justice, 2005); Appeal No. 70012091278, Rio Grande do Sul (Supreme Court of Justice, 2006).

49 *Beatriz Silvia Mendoza* v. *Argentina*, M. 1569 (Supreme Court of Argentina, 2008).

50 Project Appraisal Document on a Proposed Adaptable Loan Program in the Amount of $US840 Million to the Argentine Republic for the Matanza-Riachuelo Basin Sustainable Development Project, Phase 1, Report No. 48443-AR (World Bank, 2009).

51 *Law on the Matanza-Riachuelo Watershed*, Law No. 26.168 (B.O. 15 November 2006).

52 Tseming Yang and Robert V. Percival, "The Emergence of Global Environmental Law," *Ecology Law Quarterly* 36(3) (2009), pp. 615–64.

dozens of new parks, playgrounds, plazas, and other public spaces, and the creation of 200 monitoring stations to measure water, air, and soil quality.[53] The Supreme Court continues to hold quarterly public hearings in which it questions the federal Environment Minister and the head of ACUMAR on progress toward fulfilling the Court's order. International scholars have hailed the litigation for its "remarkable policy impact" and benefits for marginalized communities.[54] As the World Bank observed, there have been previous pledges to restore the Matanza-Riachuelo watershed, but the Supreme Court ruling ensures an unprecedented degree of political and legal accountability.[55] In 2015, an Argentine court ordered the federal, provincial, and municipal governments to create a comprehensive plan for the next phase of the Riachuelo clean-up effort.[56]

On the other hand, it may be difficult for the communities most affected by environmental degradation to influence law and policy-making processes or take advantage of their constitutional right to a healthy environment. Barriers include limited awareness of their rights, lack of financial resources, lack of access to legal assistance, and distrust of the judicial system. Some critics claim that environmental litigation brought by middle class litigants to enforce their right to a healthy environment worsens the plight of the poor. For example, the closure or relocation of polluting factories in India is alleged to have displaced workers and caused adverse socioeconomic effects.[57] More broadly, there are unresolved questions about leakage, wherein legislation, litigation, or other societal forces displace environmentally harmful activities from relatively wealthy nations to poorer nations or regions.[58]

Leveling the Playing Field

Another advantage of the constitutional right to a healthy environment is the prospect of a level playing field with competing social and economic rights. Environmental laws often constrain the exercise of property rights, recognizing that there are circumstances in which the public interest should take precedence over private interests. In many nations where environmental rights are articulated in constitutions, courts have rejected challenges in which plaintiffs alleged that their

[53] Matanza-Riachuelo Watershed Authority, *Pisa 2012 Actualizado* (ACUMAR, 2013), at www.acumar.gov.ar.

[54] Kristi Staveland-Saeter, *Litigating the Right to a Healthy Environment: Assessing the Policy Impact of the Mendoza Case* (Michelson Institute, 2011), p. 48.

[55] Report No. 48443-AR (World Bank, 2009), p. 15.

[56] *Beatriz Silvia Mendoza* v. *National Government and Others* (Federal Court of Morón, 2015).

[57] Kelly D. Alley and Daniel Meadows, "Workers' Rights and Pollution Control in Delhi," *Human Rights Dialogue* 2(11) (2004), pp. 15–17.

[58] David Asher Ghertner and Matthias Fripp, "Trading Away Damage: Quantifying Environmental Leakage through Consumption-Based Life-Cycle Analysis," *Ecological Economics* 63(2/3) (2006), pp. 563–77.

property rights were violated by environmental laws or policies. For example, Slovenia's Constitutional Court upheld a tax on water pollution based on the constitutional interest in environmental protection.[59] In Belgium, "courts are no longer inclined when facing conflicting interests, to automatically sacrifice environmental interests in favor of economic interests."[60]

Governments and courts go to great efforts to balance competing rights and conflicting social priorities. For example, in a Turkish case involving air pollution from coal-fired power plants, the courts ordered the installation of pollution abatement equipment instead of requiring the plants to be closed.[61] Some would argue that courts have not gone far enough to level the playing field and defend constitutional environmental rights, particularly in cases involving powerful economic interests, such as the Sardar Sarovar Dam in India, the Camisea natural gas project in Peru, the Belo Monte hydroelectric project in Brazil, or French controversies involving genetically modified crops.[62] On the other hand, the constitutional right to a healthy environment played an instrumental role in the Greek Council of State's repeated decisions to strike down approvals for the Acheloos water diversion project, Colombia's repeated refusal to permit the Eco Oro gold mine to proceed in an ecosystem that provides drinking water for millions of people, the Finnish Supreme Administrative Court's decision blocking the Vuotos hydroelectric project, Costa Rican court decisions blocking offshore oil and gas development, the Ecuadorian Constitutional Court's rejection of the Baba Dam, Hungarian and Russian court decisions preventing the privatization of public forests, and the Thai Supreme Court's decision to block dozens of petrochemical projects.[63] These cases involved powerful actors and major economic consequences, yet courts took bold decisions based on the right to a healthy environment. At a minimum, constitutional provisions requiring environmental protection should ensure a better balancing of competing interests than has been the case in the past.

[59] *Pavel Ocepek, Breg pri Komendi*, No. Up-344/96 (Constitutional Court, 1999).

[60] Luc Lavrysen, "Belgium," in Louis J. Kotze and Alexander R. Paterson (eds.), *The Role of the Judiciary in Environmental Governance: Comparative Perspectives* (Kluwer Law International, 2009), pp. 85–122 at 114.

[61] *Okyay et al.* v. *Turkey*, No. 36220/97 (European Court of Human Rights, 2005).

[62] Philippe Cullet, *The Sardar Sarovar Dam Project* (Ashgate, 2009); Stephen J. Turner, *A Substantive Environmental Right: An Examination of the Legal Obligations of Decision-Makers towards the Environment* (Kluwer Law, 2009).

[63] Greece Council of State, Nos. 2759/1994, 2760/1994, 3478/2000; Timo Koivurova, "The Case of Vuotos: Interplay between International, Community, and National Law," *Review of European Community and International Environmental Law* 13(1) (2004), pp. 47–60; *M. M. Levy y Asociacion Ecologista Limonense* v. *Ministerio del Ambiente y Energia*, No. 2001–13295 (Costa Rica, 2001); *Baba Dam Case*, No. 1212–2007-RA (Constitutional Court of Ecuador, 2008); *T. V. Zlotnikova, K.E. Lebedeva et al.* v. *Russian Federation*, No. GPKI 97–249 (Russia Supreme Court of Russia, 1998); Kochakorn Boonlai and Pisit Changplayngam, "Thai Court Halts Many New Plants in Big Industrial Zone," *Reuters*, December 3, 2009.

Leading to Environmental Education

Recognition of the right to a healthy environment has been a catalyst for national laws related to environmental education in nations including the Philippines, Armenia, South Korea, and Brazil.[64] Cases involving the right to a healthy environment have spurred courts in India, Argentina, and the Philippines to issue creative orders requiring governments to develop and implement environmental education programs.[65] The French Charter for the Environment has revitalized environmental education in France.[66] In addition, extensive efforts have been made by international agencies to educate judges, enforcement agencies, prosecutors, and other groups involved in the implementation and enforcement of environmental laws about the right to a healthy environment.[67]

The Impact on Environmental Performance

While the foregoing developments are impressive, the ultimate test of the right to a healthy environment is whether it contributes to healthier people and healthier ecosystems. The evidence in this regard is strikingly positive. One study concluded that nations with the right to a healthy environment in their constitutions have smaller ecological footprints, rank higher on comprehensive indices of environmental indicators, are more likely to ratify international environmental agreements, and have made faster progress in reducing emissions of sulfur dioxide, nitrogen oxides, and greenhouse gases than nations without such provisions. For example, between 1980 and 2005, wealthy industrialized nations recognizing environmental rights reduced sulfur dioxide emissions by 84.8 percent. In comparison, wealthy industrialized nations that did not recognize the right to a healthy environment reduced emissions by just 52.8 percent during the same time period.[68]

A second, and more sophisticated, quantitative analysis of the effects of constitutional environmental rights on environmental performance, published in 2016, reached the same conclusion. An examination of the influence of constitutional environmental rights on the outcomes of the Yale Center for Environmental Law and Policy's Environmental Performance Index (based on a wide range of environmental indicators) concluded: "Ultimately we find evidence that

64 Environmental Education Promotion Act (South Korea, 2008); National Environmental Awareness and Education Act of 2008 (Philippines); Law on Ecological Education of the Population (Armenia, 2001); National Environmental Education Policy Act (Brazil, 1999).

65 *Beatriz Silvia Mendoza and Others* v. *National Government and Others* (2008) *(Damages stemming from contamination of the Matanza-Riachuelo River)*, M. 1569 (Supreme Court of Argentina, 2008); *Concerned Residents of Manila Bay et al.* v. *Metropolitan Manila Development Authority and Others*, Nos. 171947–48 (Supreme Court of the Philippines, 1998); *M. C. Mehta* v. *Union of India*, No. AIR 1988 SC 1031 (Supreme Court of India).

66 Marrani, "The Second Anniversary of the Constitutionalisation of the French Charter."

67 Boyd, *The Environmental Rights Revolution.*

68 Ibid., chapter 12.

constitutions do indeed matter."[69] A similar study, also published in 2016, found that constitutional environmental rights are positively related to increases in the proportion of populations with access to safe drinking water.[70]

Constitutional recognition of the right to a healthy environment has been consistently linked to stronger environmental legislation, increasing enforcement of environmental laws, and superior environmental performance. Most importantly, these constitutional provisions are making a substantial contribution to improving people's lives and well-being. Benefits include improved access to safe drinking water, cleaner air, more effective sanitation and waste management practices, more sustainable approaches to managing natural resources, and healthier ecosystems.

THE POTENTIAL DISADVANTAGES

Few of the potential downsides of the right to a healthy environment have materialized. The widespread reliance on this right by citizens, legislatures, and courts demonstrates that it is neither too vague to be implemented nor merely duplicates the protections offered by existing human rights and environmental laws. Environmental rights have not been used systematically to trump other rights, with legislators and judges opting instead for careful balancing. There has been no flood of frivolous litigation, as lawsuits based on the right to a healthy environment represent a small fraction of the total number of cases in any given nation and enjoy a high success rate.

Two critiques have some degree of validity. First, there are some countries where even constitutionally guaranteed environmental rights have had minimal impact. Problems such as the absence of the rule of law and effective legal institutions (including an independent judiciary), widespread poverty, civil wars, or authoritarian governments can pose daunting obstacles to progress in realizing most or all human rights, including the right to a healthy environment. The majority of the nations where environmental rights have not yet had a discernible effect are in sub-Saharan Africa, where political, legal, economic, and social problems are pervasive.

Second, excessive judicial activism can undermine democracy by shifting power from elected politicians to unelected judges. The most prominent example is the Supreme Court of India, which has been accused of exceeding its reach in several high-profile cases, involving motor vehicles in Delhi, pollution of the Ganges River,

[69] Christopher Jeffords and Lanse Minkler, "Do Constitutions Matter? The Effects of Constitutional Environmental Rights Provisions on Environmental Performance," *Kyklos* 69(2) (2016), pp. 295–334 at 296.

[70] Christopher Jeffords, "On the Temporal Effects of Static Constitutional Environmental Rights Provisions on Access to Improved Sanitation Facilities and Water Sources," *Journal of Human Rights and the Environment* 7(1) (2016), pp. 74–110.

and forest conservation.[71] The Indian Supreme Court's actions can be defended as responding to government's persistent failure to implement and enforce its environmental laws, as mandated by the constitution. In general, however, excessive judicial activism is rare.

THE NEED FOR A GLOBAL INSTRUMENT

Despite the remarkable progress in recognizing and implementing the right to a healthy environment at the national level, there is still no legally binding global instrument that includes this fundamental right. The main global human rights agreements were negotiated at a time when the pace and magnitude of human-induced environmental degradation were not widely recognized. Thus, it is not surprising that the Universal Declaration of Human Rights, the International Covenant on Civil and Political Rights, and the International Covenant on Economic, Social, and Cultural Rights make no mention of the right to a healthy environment. As Kennedy Cuomo noted, the drafters of these documents could not be expected to "foresee the enormity of ecological degradation and the consequent necessity for human rights norms to encompass environmental considerations."[72]

In light of the clear empirical evidence that the right to a healthy environment is delivering substantial benefits at the national level, it should be a priority to pursue recognition of this vital human right in a new global instrument. Three of the most prominent options include a resolution of the UN General Assembly, a new Protocol to the International Covenant on Economic, Social, and Cultural Rights, and a new stand-alone instrument.

It is unclear whether the political appetite exists today for a new global human rights instrument that is legally binding and focused explicitly on the environment, although such an accord could prove to be incredibly influential. While more recent regional human rights regimes spanning Africa, Europe, Latin America, and the Middle East have incorporated the right to a healthy environment, past attempts to create a stand-alone global environmental rights treaty have failed. The UN Sub-Commission for the Prevention of Discrimination and Protection of Minorities appointed one of its members, Fatma Zohra Ksentini, as a Special Rapporteur on Human Rights and the Environment in 1990. With the assistance of sixteen experts, Ksentini developed "Draft Principles on Human Rights and the Environment" that she hoped would form the basis of a legally binding UN treaty.[73] However, the Draft Principles failed to gain the requisite political support to move forward.

71 *M. C. Mehta* v. *Union of India*, No. 2002 (4) SCC 356 (Delhi motor vehicle pollution); *M. C. Mehta* v. *Union of India*, No. AIR 1988 SC 1115 (Ganges pollution); *T. N. Godavarman Tirumulpad* v. *Union of India*, No. AIR 1999 SC 43 (forest conservation).

72 Kerry Kennedy Cuomo, "Human Rights and the Environment: Common Ground," *Yale Journal of International Law* 18(1) (1993), pp. 227–33.

73 Fatma Zohra Ksentini, *Final Report*, UN Doc. E/CN.4/Sub.2/1994/9, annex III (July 6, 1994).

UN General Assembly resolutions related to human rights and the environment have been made in the past, but were weakly worded. For example, in 1990, a resolution was passed stating: "All individuals are entitled to live in an environment adequate for their health and well-being."[74] A similar resolution in 2000 referred to "the entitlement of every person and all peoples to a healthy environment."[75] In both cases, the word "right" is conspicuous by its absence. A stronger resolution, similar to the General Assembly's clear and compelling resolution on the right to water and sanitation (adopted in 2010), would be more likely to have the desired effect.[76] That resolution recognized "the right to safe and clean drinking water and sanitation as a human right that is essential for the full enjoyment of life and all human rights." Most new or amended national constitutions since the General Assembly resolution in 2010 have included an explicit reference to the right to water, and domestic court decisions dealing with the right to water have cited the resolution.[77] This option offers the advantage of expediency, as a resolution could be drafted and approved in relatively short order, while crafting agreements and securing the necessary ratifications are much more time-consuming. A disadvantage is that it would not provide a forum or mechanism for the resolution of individual complaints related to violations of the right, although as mentioned earlier, these mechanisms have been largely ineffective.

Creating a new Optional Protocol to the International Covenant on Economic, Social, and Cultural Rights (ICESCR) represents a potential middle ground between a new global treaty dedicated specifically to environmental rights and a General Assembly resolution. It would be a logical choice, as many national constitutions incorporate the right to a healthy environment in the same chapter as economic, social, and cultural rights. A second Optional Protocol recognizing the right to a healthy environment, as an issue-specific instrument, would be comparable to the Second Optional Protocol to the International Covenant on Civil and Political Rights aiming at the abolition of the death penalty. The recent Optional Protocol to the ICESCR that created an individual complaints mechanism illustrates the political viability of pursuing this approach, and would provide a forum for addressing alleged human rights violations. However, it is sobering to note that this Optional Protocol took eighteen years to negotiate, an additional five years to secure the necessary ratifications, and, although it came into force in 2013, binds only twenty-two state parties as of February 2017.

[74] General Assembly res. 45/94 (December 14, 1990).

[75] General Assembly res. 55/107 (December 4, 2000).

[76] General Assembly res. 64/292 (July 28, 2010).

[77] Ten states that have recently adopted or amended their constitutions to include the right to water are: Dominican Republic, Egypt, Fiji, Kenya, Mexico, Morocco, Nepal, Somalia, Tunisia, and Zimbabwe. An example of a case citing the General Assembly resolution is *Matsipane Mosetlhanyane & Others* v. *Attorney-General of Botswana*, No. CALB–074–10 (Botswana Court of Appeal, 2011).

Given the long timelines and political obstacles to either a new global treaty or a second Optional Protocol to the ICESCR, seeking a General Assembly resolution on the right to a healthy environment seems like the path of least resistance for maximum reward. In whichever form, a new global instrument would: acknowledge that the right to a healthy environment must be universally protected (rather than subject to today's patchwork quilt of protection); serve as an impetus for more nations to incorporate this right in their constitutions and legislation; and potentially provide a mechanism for increased accountability where national governments violate or fail to protect this vital human right. Global recognition of the right to a healthy environment would also result in new reporting requirements (e.g., as part of the UN Human Rights Council's Universal Periodic Review) that would further raise the profile of this issue both politically and publically. In the past, opponents of global recognition of the right to a healthy environment have argued that the content of this right and the associated duties are not known with sufficient precision. The experiences of many countries in recognizing and implementing this right through domestic law and the outstanding work of the UN Special Rapporteur on Human Rights and the Environment, John Knox, in comprehensively cataloguing the procedural and substantive elements of this right, along with government's corresponding obligations, should help to overcome this uncertainty.[78]

CONCLUSION

The right to live in a healthy environment is now a firmly established legal principle throughout most countries in Africa, Latin America, and Europe. It is emerging in Asia, the Caribbean, Oceania, and the Middle East. The right to a healthy environment enjoys constitutional recognition in at least 100 nations, is included in more than 100 nations' environmental legislation, and is part of regional treaties ratified by more than 120 nations (see Table 1). This right has been the subject of thousands of court decisions spanning more than fifty countries over the past four decades. New or amended constitutions incorporating the right to a healthy environment were enacted in Jamaica, Morocco, and South Sudan in 2011; Somalia in 2012; Fiji, Vietnam, and Zimbabwe in 2013; Tunisia in 2014; and Grenada in 2015. Draft constitutions in Algeria, Tanzania, and Zambia also include environmental rights and responsibilities. It is now unusual for new constitutions to fail to include environmental rights and responsibilities.

There are still some countries that have not yet recognized the right to a healthy environment, including the United States, Canada, China, Japan, Australia, and New Zealand. However, in some of these countries, governments at the sub-national level recognize environmental rights. In the United States, the right to a healthy

[78] Reports of the Special Rapporteur are at www.srenvironment.org and www.ohchr.org/EN/Issues/Environment/SREnvironment/Pages/SRenvironmentIndex.aspx.

environment is found in six state constitutions, including Hawaii, Illinois, Massachusetts, Montana, Pennsylvania, and Rhode Island, as well as in ordinances passed by dozens of local governments. In Canada, environmental rights are legislated in two provinces (Quebec and Ontario) and three territories (Yukon, Northwest Territories, and Nunavut), as well as more than 130 municipal resolutions. There are also promising signs among some of these laggards. In the United Kingdom, a joint committee of the House of Commons and the House of Lords recommended that the right to a healthy environment be included in a proposed UK Bill of Rights.[79] Similar proposals have been advanced to include the right to a healthy environment in a new bill of rights for New Zealand.[80] Canada came close to legislating an environmental bill of rights in 2011, and efforts to pass this type of law are ongoing.[81]

With the 50th anniversary of the landmark Stockholm Declaration rapidly approaching (2022), the time is ripe for the establishment of a global instrument that recognizes the right of all citizens in all countries to live in a healthy environment. Given the substantial positive effects of recognizing this right at the national level, the severe environmental challenges that continue to face humanity, and the enormity of the associated rights violations, this should be a global priority. A General Assembly resolution that clearly and forcefully articulates the right to a healthy environment is likely the most expedient and effective approach, following the successful precedent set by the 2010 resolution on the right to water and sanitation.

In the meantime, all nations with a genuine interest in protecting human and ecosystem health and well-being should move expeditiously to incorporate the right to a healthy environment into their constitutional and legal frameworks. This is particularly true in the case of small island states, which are particularly vulnerable to climate change, yet lag behind other nations in providing legal recognition of the right to a healthy environment.[82] Given the importance of clean air, safe drinking water, healthy ecosystems, and a stable climate to the future of humanity, recognizing environmental rights should be regarded as an urgent moral obligation, not a mere policy option.

[79] UK House of Commons and House of Lords Joint Committee on Human Rights, *Twenty-ninth Report* (House of Lords, 2008).

[80] New Zealand Constitutional Advisory Panel, *New Zealand's Constitution: A Report on a Conversation* (2013).

[81] Canadian Environmental Bill of Rights, Bill C-469, 40th Parliament, 3rd Session. Bill C-469 passed second reading in the House of Commons but was not enacted prior to the dissolution of Parliament for the spring election in 2011. In 2016, Bill C-202 was introduced during the 1st Session of the 42nd Parliament.

[82] Of the 38 UN nations that do not recognize the right to a healthy environment in their constitutions, environmental legislation, or through ratification of an international treaty, more than half are small island states: Antigua and Barbuda, Bahamas, Barbados, Brunei Darussalam, Dominica, Kiribati, Marshall Islands, Micronesia, Nauru, Papua New Guinea, Saint Kitts and Nevis, Saint Lucia, Saint Vincent and the Grenadines, Samoa, Singapore, Solomon Islands, Tonga, Trinidad and Tobago, Tuvalu, and Vanuatu.

3

Learning from Constitutional Environmental Rights

*Erin Daly and James R. May**

INTRODUCTION

This chapter examines how national environmental constitutionalism can contribute to the development of an international human right to a healthful environment. We suggest that the lessons learned in forty years of domestic environmental constitutionalism can inspire and inform considerations concerning an international environmental right's meaning, scope, and enforceability.

More than one-half of the countries in the world have incorporated environmental rights constitutionally, leading to thoughtful consideration about what environmental rights mean and how to enhance their effectiveness. In addition to these substantive environmental rights, constitutions also guarantee procedural requirements, establish reciprocal duties of public and private actors to protect the environment, and announce policy objectives and fundamental values relating to environmental protection.

Given the existing environmental human rights obligations on states, the question is whether an international human right to a healthful environment is warranted. We believe that such a right has the potential to advance environmental protection for two principal reasons. First, as a legal matter, a human right to a healthy environment would impose supra-national obligations on states to observe or protect rights that otherwise may not be reflected in domestic law or in regional instruments.[1] As a normative matter, establishing such a right would confirm the interdependence and the indivisibility of human and environmental rights.

* Erin Daly is Professor of Law and James R. May is Distinguished Professor of Law, both at Widener University Delaware Law School, where they co-direct the Dignity Rights Project.

[1] See generally Philip Allott, "The Emerging Universal Legal System," in Janne Nijman and Andre Nollkemper (eds.), *New Perspectives on the Divide between National and International Law* (Oxford University Press, 2007), pp. 63–83.

Environmental rights *are* human rights: They exist for the benefit of humans, and the harms caused by environmental degradation are violations of well-recognized human rights, such as the right to life, to health, and to dignity. This is reflected in human experience throughout the world, in all natural and social settings: For example, illegal dumping of toxic waste endangers the surrounding ecosystems, as it contaminates drinking water, arable soils, and habitable land, and otherwise threatens people's right to life, health, or dignity. Likewise, mining, deforestation, and environmental degradation brought about by climate change threaten both environmental and human interests and needs. As John Knox has written: "Human rights are grounded in respect for fundamental human attributes such as dignity, equality and liberty. The realization of these attributes depends on an environment that allows them to flourish. … Human rights and environmental protection are inherently interdependent."[2]

The clearest and most pervasive legal manifestation of the linking of environmental and human rights is in the constitutions of most of the world's nations. Consequently, courts have reviewed, construed, and enforced many of these provisions, providing a constitutional framework for environmental protection and associated human rights and well-being around the globe. Domestic environmental constitutionalism has also informed policy making and improved environmental performance in almost every country where it has taken hold. With this decades-old, evolving, and geographically extensive experience, domestic environmental constitutionalism has much to contribute to the development of an international human right to a healthy environment.

This chapter explores some of the lessons that the international effort can glean from experiences at the domestic constitutional level. Part One briefly surveys the emergence and growth of global environmental constitutionalism. Part Two describes some of the principal contrapuntal features of international environmental law. Part Three describes ways that the lines between the international and national legal regimes respecting environmental rights already blur, providing content and clarity to both areas of law. In the final part, we identify some lessons learned from the domestic constitutionalization of environmental rights that could advance the development of an international environmental human right. We conclude that there are abundant opportunities for the experiences of domestic environmental

[2] John H. Knox, *Report of the Independent Expert on the Issue of Human Rights Obligations Relating to the Enjoyment of a Safe, Clean, Healthy and Sustainable Environment: Preliminary Report*, UN Doc. A/HRC/22/43 (December 24, 2012), para. 10. See also Daniel J. Whelan, *Indivisible Human Rights: A History* (University of Pennsylvania Press, 2010); Erin Daly, "Environmental Human Rights: Paradigm of Indivisibility" (2011), available at http://works.bepress.com/erin_daly/24 ("The constitutional right to a healthy environment is perhaps the paradigmatic example of the indivisibility claim. Environmental rights are inseparable from many other rights, including (depending on the factual nature of the claim) the right to life, to health, to dignity, to subsistence, to employment, to property and so on.").

constitutionalism to contribute to the development of a comparable right at the international level, especially concerning its meaning, scope, and enforcement.

GLOBAL ENVIRONMENTAL CONSTITUTIONALISM

Environmental rights and values are a common feature of modern constitutionalism. About half of the world's constitutions guarantee a substantive right to a clean or quality or healthy environment explicitly or implicitly, and about half of those also guarantee procedural rights to information, participation, or access to justice in environmental matters.[3] Nearly seventy constitutions specify that individuals have responsibilities or duties to protect the environment[4] and others include directive principles of state policy. A few constitutions address specific environmental endowments including water, flora, and fauna, while others define the environment in certain ways, including as a public trust or in terms of sustainable development.[5] Moreover, some state constitutions in federal systems – including Germany, Brazil, and the United States – include environmental provisions, some of which are even more elaborate than their counterparts at the national level.[6]

Environmental constitutionalism has resulted from several global political and legal trends that have gathered strength in the last few decades. First, the spread of constitutionalism in the post-colonial period of the 1960s and 1970s, and

3 See generally James R. May and Erin Daly, *Global Environmental Constitutionalism* (Cambridge University Press, 2015); James R. May and Erin Daly, *Environmental Constitutionalism: A Research Compendium* (Edward Elgar, 2016); "Symposium on Global Environmental Constitutionalism: An Introduction and Overview," *Widener Law Review* 21 (2015); James R. May and Erin Daly, "*Robinson Township* v. *Pennsylvania*: A Model for Environmental Constitutionalism," *Widener Law Review* 21 (2015), p. 151; Erin Daly and James R. May, "Comparative Environmental Constitutionalism," *Jindal Global Law Review* 6(1) (2015); James R. May, "Constitutional Directions in Procedural Environmental Rights," *Journal of Environmental Law and Litigation* 28 (2014), p. 101; James R. May and Erin Daly, "Environmental Rights and Liabilities," *European Journal of Environmental Liability* 3 (2012), p. 75; James R. May and Erin Daly, "New Directions in Earth Rights, Environmental Rights and Human Rights: Six Facets of Constitutionally Embedded Environmental Rights Worldwide," *IUCN Academy of Environmental Law E-Journal* 1 (2011). See also David R. Boyd, *The Environmental Rights Revolution: A Global Study of Constitutions, Human Rights, and the Environment* (University of British Columbia Press, 2012); David R. Boyd, *The Right to a Healthy Environment: Revitalizing Canada's Constitution* (University of British Columbia Press, 2012), p. 65; Richard P. Hiskes, *The Human Right to a Green Future: Environmental Rights and Intergenerational Justice* (Cambridge University Press, 2008); Tim Hayward, *Constitutional Environmental Rights* (Oxford University Press, 2005).

4 See, e.g., Benin Constitution, art. 27 ("Every person has the right to a healthy, satisfying, and lasting environment, and has the duty to defend it."); Cameroon Constitution, art. 55 ("Everyone is obliged to preserve nature and prevent damages, as well as to be careful with removing natural riches."); India Constitution, art. 51A(g): "It shall be the duty of every citizen of India . . . to protect and improve the natural environment including forests, lakes, rivers and wild life, and to have compassion for living creatures."

5 May and Daly, *Global Environmental Constitutionalism*, chapters 7–10.

6 Ibid., chapter 8.

then in the post-communist period in the 1980s and 1990s, created a global norm of constitution-making. In the new millennium, the practice of adopting and amending constitutions has continued apace, spreading most recently throughout the Arab world.[7] As a result, legal traditions in all regions of the world have seen new or dramatically amended constitutions adopted in the last few decades. For the most part, this has produced longer constitutions with more elaborate provisions, drawing from both civil and political and socioeconomic lists of rights, often in intermingled and undifferentiated ways.

At the same time, growing global consciousness of environmentalism in tandem with increasing threats to social and environmental sustainability have contributed to the greening of constitutions. The frequent high-profile global summits on environmental matters in Stockholm (1972), Rio (1992), Kyoto (1997), Rio again (2012), and Paris (2015), among dozens of others, seem to have influenced drafters of domestic constitutions, who have included sustainable development, climate change, biodiversity, protection of waters, and other environmental matters within their constitutional texts.

Environmental constitutionalism benefits from several attributes that distinguish it from other legal forms of environmental protection, whether at the international, regional, or local levels.

First, constitutionalism originates in a particular historical moment in a nation's history, when the government and the people have focused their attention on the new structures, symbols, and relations that will govern the country for the next generation.[8] This process often culminates in public ratification of the new or revised constitutional text that, at least potentially, engages the populace throughout the territory of the state. Sometimes, it can involve the constitutional court, where there is judicial power to confirm the constitutionality of the new text.[9]

Although not all constitutional revisions arise out of or culminate in populist movements, constitutions are amenable to popular engagement in a way that international law is not. Many international accords are negotiated in locations disconnected from those most affected by the environmental concern under discussion. For instance, the most recent mega-conference, held in Paris in 2015 and focusing on global climate change, was one of the most well-attended events of its kind, attracting nearly 38,000 participants.[10] Still, the number of participants in these conferences – though global in representation – pales in comparison to the number of individuals in any given state engaged in drafting, advocating for or against, and

7 Andrea Pin, *The Arab Road to Dignity: The Goal of the Arab Spring* (Kellogg Institute for International Studies, 2016).

8 See James R. May, "Constituting Fundamental Environmental Rights Worldwide," *Pace Environmental Law Review* 23 (2005/2006), pp. 113–29.

9 See, e.g., *Certification of the Constitution of the Republic of South Africa*, CCT 23/96 (1996).

10 See www.cop21.gouv.fr/en/cop21-at-le-bourget-in-figures (indicating that 37,878 badges were issued).

ratifying a national constitution.[11] This kind of widespread and concentrated public engagement invests in the constitutional moment a populist ethos that can remain forceful over time. To be sure, fifty constitutions embody this ethos by including the phrase "we the people."[12]

The structure of environmental constitutionalism also distinguishes it from international protection for the environment because constitutions include lists of rights, whether independent or interrelated. Including environmental rights on these lists guarantees that environmental rights will be read in tandem with other rights and values recognized in each constitutional culture. Thus, environmental rights can be advanced in conjunction with rights to health, water, dignity, and life, among others.

And while some constitutional systems protect the rights *of* nature itself, or permit standing on behalf of non-human entities, environmental constitutionalism tends to be anthropocentric. Indeed, notwithstanding some provisions in directive principles or preambles to responsibilities and duties, environmental constitutionalism is typically rights-based: It assumes that a healthy environment can be assured or at least advanced by guaranteeing individuals the right to assert claims for violations against governmental (and sometimes private) actors.

Environmental constitutionalism also comes with its own enforcement mechanisms: judicial tribunals with the power to decide cases, draft influential opinions, and sometimes make binding precedents. These mechanisms can animate provisions to keep them relevant. And this, in turn, has produced a common law of judicial interpretation and application that can influence political and legal developments in one country and influence constitutionalism elsewhere. Constitutional environmental cases are on the rise throughout the world, not only in civil law systems (namely in Western Europe) but also in common law countries (namely in India and its neighbors) and in countries with mixed legal systems (such as Latin American democracies) – in marked contrast to international law, which has limited and underutilized enforcement mechanisms that are, in any case, difficult for individuals to access and invoke.

[11] Although voter turnout was only 32 percent in the 2012 referendum on the Egyptian constitution, more than 17 million cast a vote, nearly two-thirds voting in favor. "Egypt's constitution passes with 63.8 percent approval rate," *Egypt Independent*, December 25, 2012. In 2010, 8 million people voted in Kenya's constitutional referendum, with 68 percent voting in favor. African Elections Database: Elections in Kenya, http://africanelections.tripod.com/ke.html#2010_Constitutional_Referendum. In 2008, more than 7 million Ecuadorians – or 75 percent of the electorate – voted (with more than a two-thirds majority) for radical changes to the constitution, including environmental rights and rights of nature. See www.sudd.ch/event.php?lang=de&id=ec012008. Even at the subnational level, the extent of popular commitment can be impressive: In 1971, the Environmental Rights Amendment of the Pennsylvania Constitution was approved by a 4 to 1 margin, receiving more votes than any candidate for statewide office.

[12] See www.constituteproject.org/search?lang=en&q=%22we%20the%20people%22 (visited March 24, 2017).

INTERNATIONAL LAW AND ENVIRONMENTAL RIGHTS

An abundance of international treaties and agreements customs already define and describe norms, relationships, and responses among and between states to meet the many global ecological challenges.[13] Indeed, there are more than 1150 multilateral environmental agreements on topics as diverse as energy, freshwater resources, habitat protection, nature, oceans, pollution and wastes, species protection, weapons, and climate change.[14] Despite the multitude of environmental agreements, few mention the negative impact of environmental degradation on human rights or the positive impact of environmental protection on the enjoyment of human rights and the quality of life.[15] For example, the 2015 Paris Agreement on climate change mentions human beings only three times, all in the preamble to the agreement.[16] Thus, domestic environmental rights have an important and strategic role to play in achieving human rights.

International environmental law is notoriously difficult to enforce by individuals or states, given entrenched principles of state sovereignty and limited enforcement mechanisms that individuals can access. The Aarhus Convention stands as a counterexample, guaranteeing procedural environmental rights standing on three pillars: the right to information, the right to participation, and access to justice.[17] And while its Compliance Committee has resolved only forty-seven complaints, three-fifths have found non-compliance.[18]

Recently, supranational law at the regional level has begun to give attention to environmental human rights by providing protection – and enforcement mechanisms – for environmental rights within the package of human rights. Such provisions are

[13] See generally Philippe Sands, *Principles of International Environmental Law*, 2d ed. (Cambridge University Press, 2003).

[14] International Environmental Agreements Database Project, at http://iea.uoregon.edu/page.php?query=summarize_by_year&yearstart=1950&yearend=2012&inclusion=MEA (visited March 25, 2017), counts 1159 MEAs between 1959 and 2012.

[15] Alexandre Kiss, "The Legal Ordering of Environmental Protection," in Nicholas Tsagourias (ed.), *Toward World Constitutionalism: Issues in the Legal Ordering of the World Community* (Martinus Nijhoff Publishers, 2005), pp. 567–84.

[16] Paris Agreement, December 12, 2015, in force November 4, 2016, UN Doc. FCCC/CP/2015/l9 ("Recognizing that climate change represents an urgent and potentially irreversible threat to human societies and the planet and thus requires the widest possible cooperation by all countries, and their participation in an effective and appropriate international response, with a view to accelerating the reduction of global greenhouse gas emissions," and "Acknowledging that climate change is a common concern of humankind, Parties should, when taking action to address climate change, respect, promote and consider their respective obligations on human rights, the right to health, the rights of indigenous peoples, local communities, migrants, children, persons with disabilities and people in vulnerable situations and the right to development, as well as gender equality, empowerment of women and intergenerational equity").

[17] [Aarhus] Convention on Access to Information, Public Participation in Decision-Making and Access to Justice in Environmental Matters, June 25, 1998, in force October 21, 2001, 2161 UNTS 447.

[18] See www.unece.org/index.php?id=35294 (visited May 27, 2016).

included in the African Charter on Human and Peoples' Rights,[19] the Protocol on Economic, Social and Cultural Rights to the American Convention on Human Rights,[20] the Association of Southeast Asian Nations Human Rights Declaration,[21] and the Arab Charter.[22] And while the European Convention on Human Rights does not explicitly provide for a right to a healthy environment, provisions within it have been interpreted as affording environmental rights.[23] International human rights institutions and treaty bodies have also made strong connections between human rights and environmental outcomes.[24]

THE RELATIONSHIP BETWEEN INTERNATIONAL AND NATIONAL LAW

International and national governance domains regularly converge, connect, and overlap, exerting both downward and upward pressure on each other in environmental arenas, as elsewhere. Sometimes, norms and values develop in syncopated synchronicity, examples of which include species protection, waste minimization, and pollution prevention – as constitutionalism and internationalism borrow from each other in iterative steps.

The downward pressure, from the international to the national level, can be seen in direct and wholesale ways as well as in more subtle and incremental ways. Some constitutions, such as Spain's, explicitly provide that international law is a source of law for purposes of constitutional interpretation.[25] South Africa's constitution goes further by requiring consideration of international law.[26] Like many other constitutions, these two also include specific rights whose origins lie in international law, foremost among which is the right to human dignity.[27]

[19] African Charter on Human and Peoples' Rights, June 27, 1981, in force October 21, 1986, 1520 UNTS 217, art. 24. See Lilian Chenwi, Chapter 4.

[20] Additional Protocol to the American Convention on Human Rights in the Area of Economic, Social and Cultural Rights: Protocol of San Salvador, November 17, 1988, in force November 16, 1999, 28 ILM 161, art. 11.

[21] Association of Southeast Asian Nations Human Rights Declaration, November 18, 2012, art. 28(f).

[22] Arab Charter on Human Rights, May 22, 2004, in force March 15, 2008, 12 IHRR 893 (2005), art. 38.

[23] See Ole Pedersen, Chapter 5.

[24] See generally John H. Knox, *Report of the Independent Expert on the Issue of Human Rights Obligations Relating to the Enjoyment of a Safe, Clean, Healthy and Sustainable Environment; Mapping Report*, UN Doc. A/HRC/25/53 (December 30, 2013).

[25] Constitution of Spain, art. 10.2.

[26] South Africa Constitution, art. 39 ("When interpreting the Bill of Rights, a court, tribunal or forum: a. must promote the values that underlie an open and democratic society based on human dignity, equality and freedom; b. must consider international law; and, c. may consider foreign law.").

[27] The right to dignity, for instance, derives from the Universal Declaration of Human Rights and the two international covenants that form the so-called International Bill of Rights.

Constitutions have also adopted certain rules or principles of international environmental law, bringing them into the domestic constitutional sphere. Approximately three dozen constitutions – many of these outside Europe – provide for the rights to information, participation, and access to justice in environmental matters, which mirror the provisions of international instruments such as Principle 10 of the Rio Declaration and the Aarhus Convention. In addition, at least seventeen constitutions refer to sustainable development,[28] a principle primarily advanced in international law.

Even without an explicit textual mandate, many courts have incorporated international and foreign law into their own domestic constitutional jurisprudence, including some well-established principles of environmental law. For instance, the precautionary principle, which reflects customary international law and has been codified in numerous international instruments,[29] has informed constitutional environmental law in several cases. One example is from Sri Lanka, where the court ordered an environmental impact statement for a mining enterprise on the basis of the precautionary principle.[30]

The fluidity between national and supra-national law can also be seen at the regional level. In Europe, national constitutions routinely borrow not only from each other but also from international documents including the International Bill of Rights and European human rights instruments from 1950 onward. In turn, the European Union Charter of Fundamental Rights found its inspiration in the constitutions of the European states.[31] Similarly, many post-colonial constitutions

International Covenant on Civil and Political Rights, December 16, 1966, in force March 23, 1976, 999 UNTS 171; International Covenant on Economic, Social and Cultural Rights, December 16, 1966, in force January 3, 1976, 993 UNTS 3. The right to dignity is now recognized in most of the world's constitutions, including: Germany Basic Law, art. 1: "Human dignity shall be inviolable. To respect and protect it shall be the duty of all state authority."; Egypt Constitution, art. 51: "Dignity is a right for every person that may not be infringed upon. The state shall respect, guarantee and protect it." Colombia Constitution, art. 21: "The right to dignity is guaranteed. An Act shall provide the manner in which it shall be upheld."

28 See, e.g., Constitution of Colombia, chapter 3, art. 80 ("The State shall plan the handling and use of the natural resources in order to guarantee their sustainable development, their conservation, restoration, or substitution"); Constitution of Eritrea, chapter 2, art. 8(2) ("The State shall work to bring about a balanced and sustainable development throughout the country, and shall use all available means to enable all citizens to improve their livelihood in a sustainable manner, through their participation."); Constitution of Greece, art. 24(1) ("The State is bound to adopt special preventive or repressive measures for the preservation of the environment in the context of the principle of sustainable development."). See generally May and Daly, *Global Environmental Constitutionalism*, chapter 9 and appendix E.

29 See, e.g., Rio Declaration, Principle 15.

30 *Bulankulama and Six Others* v. *Ministry of Industrial Development and Seven Others*, S.C. Application No 884/99 (Supreme Court of Sri Lanka); see also *Vellore Citizens' Welfare Forum* v. *Union of India*, Writ. Pet. No. 914 of 1991 (Supreme Court of India, 1996); *Shehla Zia* v. *WAPDA*, PLD 1994 SC 693 (Supreme Court of Pakistan, 1994). See also *Expediente D-8019* (Colombia Constitutional Court, 2010).

31 See Catherine Dupré, *The Age of Dignity* (Hart, 2015), pp. 70–1.

throughout Africa have borrowed heavily from the 1963 Charter of the Organization of African Unity and the 1981 African Charter on Human and People's Rights.[32] In the Americas, the Organization of American States has been no less influential on the domestic sphere, particularly in national constitutional reform efforts.[33] The result is a porous and interconnected constitutional system that stretches throughout the continents and permeates both the texts of instruments (charters, treaties, constitutions, and laws), and the caselaw that has developed around those texts.

Examples of domestic law asserting upward pressure so as to influence international norms and rights include marine conservation, and, outside the environmental realm, human rights in respect of cruel and unusual punishment, child labor, and gender equality, implying "a transnational way of thinking about institutional arrangements that traditionally were conceived in a strictly national manner."[34] Perhaps the most significant example of this influence is the slow but steady turn toward a rights-based approach to international environmental protection. As we have seen, for more than four decades, constitutions have included in their lists of rights a human right to a quality or healthy environment, as well as other rights and obligations relating to environmental protection; this rights-based approach is now coming to the attention of the international community.

LESSONS FOR AN INTERNATIONAL HUMAN RIGHT TO A HEALTHY ENVIRONMENT

Should the movement toward international recognition of a human right to a healthy environment be successful, drafters will likely consider the global textual commitment in constitutions, as well as their interpretations and applications by national constitutional tribunals. In forty years of evolving environmental constitutionalism, progress has been made in understanding ways to optimize the effectiveness of textual commitments to environmental human rights. We suggest here some lessons from the domestic sphere that could be applied to advance an international human right to a healthy environment, concerning meaning, scope, and enforcement.

[32] See Mildred Aristide, "A Historical and Dignity-Centred Perspective on Haiti's Struggle for Justice," *International Journal of African Renaissance Studies* 1 (2006), pp. 265, 266; African Commission on Human and Peoples' Rights, "Impact of the African Charter on Domestic Human Rights in Africa," www.achpr.org/instruments/achpr/impact-on-domestic-human-rights (visited March 25, 2017).

[33] See Organization of American States, *Meeting the Challenges: The Role of the OAS in the Americas, 2005–2010* (2010), www.oas.org/documents/eng/quinquenio_2010_ENG.pdf (visited March 25, 2017) (noting participation in constitutional processes in Bolivia, Ecuador, Guatemala).

[34] Klaus Bosselmann, "Global Environmental Constitutionalism: Mapping the Terrain," *Widener Law Review* 21 (2015), p. 171.

Meaning

The first lesson that domestic environmental constitutionalism lends to an international human right to a healthful environment is that meaning matters: Because textual clarity is critical, the right should economically set forth its nature, scope, and application.

Some constitutional provisions assert responsibilities or duties of the state or private interests, while other provisions demarcate national territorial sovereignty[35] or attribute ownership.[36] But, typically, environmental constitutionalism is rights-based: It assumes that a healthy environment can be assured or at least advanced by guaranteeing individuals the right to assert claims for violations against governmental (and sometimes private) actors. Thus, it is fundamentally a human-centered endeavor.

Perhaps syntactically the most straightforward conception of "environment" is the *natural* environment, including air, water, land, and biodiversity. And yet the adjectives – whether quality, clean, healthy, harmonious, or balanced – can suggest a tilt toward human interests. Some provisions are explicitly anthropocentric,[37] while others are ecocentric; indeed, domestic constitutions provide a warren of examples of ecologically-based conceptions of the environment, including those from Cape Verde, Jamaica, Laos, South Africa, South Sudan, and Sudan,[38] each of which purports to protect ecological aims. Still others can be read either anthro- or bio-centrically if they simply protect the right to a healthy environment without making clear whether the quality of health is meant to apply to the environment or to the persons who live in it. Kenya's constitution, for instance, provides that "every person has the right to a clean and healthy environment."[39] Attributing the right to every person suggests that environmental cleanliness and health are intended to protect the human experience. Whatever the language or intent of the drafters, these provisions tend toward anthropocentrism in application because the rights they guarantee are invariably asserted by humans.

35 E.g., Mexico Constitution, art. 42 ("The national territory comprises: I. The integral parts of the Federation; II. The islands' including the reefs and keys in adjacent seas; III. The islands of Guadalupe and the Revillagigedos situated in the Pacific Ocean; IV. The continental shelf and the submarine shelf of the islands' keys, and reefs; V. The waters of the territorial seas to the extent and under terms fixed by international law and domestic maritime law; VI. The space located above the national territory to the extent and according to rules established by international law on the subject.").

36 E.g., Ghana Constitution, art. 257 "All public lands in Ghana shall be vested in the President on behalf of, and in trust for, the people of Ghana.").

37 E.g., Constitution of Democratic Republic of Congo, art. 53 ("All persons have the right to a healthy environment that is favorable to their development.").

38 Constitution of Cape Verde, part II, title III, art. 72(1); Jamaica Constitution, art. 3(1); Laos Constitution, chapter 2, art. 17; South Africa Constitution, section 24; South Sudan Constitution, art. 41(3); Sudan Constitution, chapter 11(1).

39 Kenya Constitution, art. 42.

Ecuador's constitution is unique in complementing the now-familiar "right to a healthy and ecologically balanced environment"[40] with a chapter dedicated to rights *of* nature.[41] Adopted amid constitutional reform in 2008, this provision is likely to gain increasing attention, galvanized by a 2015 Constitutional Court opinion finding that a lower court's failure to consider the rights of nature violated due process. In a case involving the property interests of a shrimp farmer against the natural rights of the mangroves ecosystem, the Court explained:

> The rights of nature constitute one of the most important innovations of the present constitution, as it moves us away from a conception of nature-as-object, that considers nature as property and focuses its protection exclusively pursuant to the right to enjoy a healthy natural environment, toward a notion that recognizes the rights of nature itself. The novelty consists in the change in paradigms on the basis of which nature, being a living thing, is considered a holder of rights.[42]

Other nations have also contemplated the possibility of protecting the rights of nature, and Bolivia has adopted this approach in its framework legislation.[43] A high court in India has recently recognized the status of the River Ganges and Yamana as juridical persons.[44]

The text of the right should also identify the intended forms of enforcement. Constitutions recognize rights that are individualized, collective, or asserted on behalf of lives yet to come. Among these, individualized rights are most common, expressly recognized in at least seventy-six constitutions worldwide, along with a concomitant duty to protect them.[45] Examples of collective rights (e.g., "Environmental protection is the collective responsibility of the state and the community at large") are less common, although not rare.[46] And more than three dozen countries recognize the rights of future generations.[47] Such provisions may be useful not only

40 Constitution of the Republic of Ecuador, art. 14 ("The right of the population to live in a healthy and ecologically balanced environment that guarantees sustainability and the good way of living (sumak kawsay), is recognized.").

41 Ibid., arts. 71–4.

42 *Sentencia No. 166–15-SEP-CC* (Constitutional Court of Ecuador, 2015), pp. 9–10. The Court continued: "In this sense, it is important to reiterate that the Constitution of the Republic consecrates a double dimension to nature and the environment in general, considering it not only based on the traditional paradigm as the object of rights, but also as an independent subject with its own specific rights. This reflects that within the juridical relationship between nature and humanity, there is a biocentric vision in which nature is prioritized, in counterpoint to the classical anthropocentric conception in which the human being is at the center and nature is surrounded by nature which was considered merely the supplier of resources."

43 Bolivia, Law of the Rights of Mother Earth (Law 071 of the Plurinational State), 2010.

44 *Salim* v. *State of Uttarakhand and Others* (High Court of Uttarakhand at Nainital, Writ Petition (PIL) No. 126 of 2014) (2017).

45 See, e.g., Yemen Constitution, art. 35 ("Each individual shall have a religious and national duty to protect the environment.").

46 May and Daly, *Global Environmental Constitutionalism*, pp. 82–4.

47 See generally May and Daly, *Global Environmental Constitutionalism*, chapter 9 and appendix E.

for ontological reasons, but also to establish the scope of enforceability and to ensure that resources are "safeguarded" "in the interests not only of the present generation but also of future generations."[48]

A good practice, which is seen far more often in the breach in constitution drafting, is to include some explanation or interpretive guidance. Where this is done – as it was in the adoption of the rights of nature provision in Ecuador – it can be of enormous utility and persuasive authority for a court seeking to interpret the constitutional text.[49]

Scope

Whereas international agreements typically isolate one particular aspect of the environment – whether it be biodiversity, marine life, hazardous wastes, or climate change – environmental provisions in national constitutions can effectively reinforce their relevance and extend their scope through connections with associated rights in a holistic bill or charter of rights. For example, the Colombian Constitutional Court saw that the right to a healthy environment and the independent rights of nature mutually reinforced each other.[50]

Environmental rights can be found side by side with civil and political rights such as voting, association, and speech rights and with social and economic rights such as rights to housing, healthcare, education, and water. For example, about thirty constitutions recognize rights to clean, safe, or potable water as a basic human or environmental right.[51] The value of clean water can therefore be augmented by being protected once as a human right and once as an environmental right.

Some constitutions strengthen the environmental right by expressly connecting it to other constitutional or international rights within the provision itself. For example, Indonesia's provides that "Each person has a right to a life of well-being in body and mind, to a place to dwell, to enjoy a good and healthy environment,

48 Papua New Guinea Constitution, chapter 1, pmbl.

49 The lower court in the Ecuadorian rights of nature case quoted at length from the speech of Alberto Acosta, President of the Constituent Assembly, to understand more fully the purpose of constitutionalizing the rights of nature. See *Wheeler* v. *Director de la Procuraduria General Del Estado de Loja Juicio*, No. 11121–2011–10 (Provincial Court of Justice, 2011).

50 Sentencia No. 166–15-SEP-CC at 14.

51 These include the constitutions of Bolivia (art. 16(I)), Colombia (art. 366), the Democratic Republic of Congo (art. 48), Ecuador (art. 12), Ethiopia (art. 90(1)), Gambia (art. 216(4)), the Maldives (art. 23), Panama (arts. 110, 118), South Africa (art. 27(1); Swaziland (art. 215), Switzerland (art. 76), Uganda (arts. 14(b), 21), Uruguay (art. 47), Venezuela (arts. 127, 304), and Zambia (art. 112(d)). See May and Daly, *Global Environmental Constitutionalism*, chapter 6 and appendix I; Boyd, *The Right to a Healthy Environment*, p. 85.

and to receive medical care," whereas Greece gives every person a right to the "protection of the natural and cultural environment."[52]

In this way, environmental rights are of a piece and on a par with both individual and collective rights, with negative liberties and positive rights, with substantive as well as procedural rights. Indeed, they are the archetypical indivisible rights because they cut across and partake of nearly all other sets of rights.[53] Moreover, although constitutional provisions are open to application in a wide variety of settings, they tend to be temporally and geographically bounded to a particular territory or geographic feature, unlike provisions in international law.[54]

Enforcement

Perhaps the most important difference between constitutional provisions and international law is that the former are intended to be enforced against states, most commonly by individuals or ad hoc collectivities taking action to defend or advance recognized rights on behalf of themselves or the general public. This contrasts dramatically with all forms of international agreements and law, which are built around the immunizing principle of national sovereignty.

Even at the constitutional level, however, environmental rights can resist effective enforcement. Of the more than 100 countries that have recognized an express or implied environmental right, many lack independent judiciaries to enforce them. And only a portion of those independent judiciaries have standing provisions that would invite constitutional challenges seeking vindication of constitutional rights. And even where such opportunities exist on paper, lawyers rarely have the experience to bring significant environmental rights claims and clients rarely have the resources to fund them. Even when strong cases are brought, judges face myriad interpretive, practical, and political obstacles: How are the amorphous terms to be interpreted? Will the government comply with an adverse ruling, and will the judge be subject to professional or personal sanctions? How can the order be enforced if the government ignores it? How will compliance be monitored, and who will pay for it? How should fees and costs be allocated? And so on.

[52] Indonesia Constitution, section 10A, art. 28H(1); Greece Constitution, part II, art. 24(1). See also Georgia Constitution, chapter 2, art. 37(3) (guaranteeing the right to "live in a healthy environment and enjoy natural and cultural surroundings.").

[53] Daly, "Environmental Human Rights: Paradigm of Indivisibility." See generally Whelan, *Indivisible Human Rights.*

[54] See *Robinson Township* v. *Pennsylvania*, 83 A.3d 901, 975–6 (Commonwealth Court of Pennsylvania, 2013) (plurality opinion) ("Pennsylvania's past is the necessary prologue here: the reserved rights, and the concomitant duties and constraints, embraced by the Environmental Rights Amendment, are a product of our unique history."). See also *Salim* v. *State of Uttarakhand*, supra. n. 44 (holding that the Rivers Ganga and Yamuna have juristic personality).

Several lessons from environmental constitutionalism inform enforcement of an international right. The first is to put words into action. Any environmental right – whether at the local, national, regional, or international level – should be established in conjunction with a tribunal with political independence, sufficient funding, and the full scope of remedial authority. Because environmental rights are transversal – applying independently or in connection with both civil and political rights and with social, economic, and cultural rights – they are subject sometimes to immediate remediation and other times to progressive realization.[55] Hence, a tribunal implementing environmental rights may sometimes need to order the immediate rectification of a situation, such as when an environmental rights defender is silenced, and sometimes may need to maintain continuing jurisdiction to ensure compliance with a judicial order over time. This may happen, for instance, if a government is under an obligation to act (e.g., to create a climate change plan[56]), or whether other remedial measures that take time are required. The details of the structure and authority of such a tribunal are beyond the scope of this chapter; suffice it to say here that *some* kind of dispute resolution body should be dedicated to enforcing such international rights, and that the experience at the national level with domestic tribunals (whether of general jurisdiction, constitutional jurisdiction, or specifically environmental jurisdiction) furnishes abundant examples to follow or avoid.

The second lesson is to think big. Each remedial action is effective only insofar as it coordinates the response to the environmental problem with other branches of government and, increasingly, with elements within the private for-profit and not-for-profit sectors. For example, when the Supreme Tribunal of Argentina ordered the clean-up of the Matanza-Riachuelo River, that country's most polluted river basin, public and private defendants were directed to work together; in response, the government established an intergovernmental river basin authority to implement, manage, and monitor the clean-up.[57] Courts in the Philippines, in India, and in Bangladesh and Pakistan have also been thoughtful and assertive in their design of remedial orders to ensure a broad-based partnership to take responsibility for environmental protection. Courts have ordered establishment of national environmental policies,[58] school curricular reform,[59] public education campaigns,[60] the

[55] See, e.g., Maldives Constitution, chapter 2 ("the State undertakes to achieve the progressive realisation of these rights by reasonable measures within its ability and resources: [including] . . . a healthy and ecologically balanced environment.").

[56] *Asghar Leghari* v. *Pakistan*, No. 25501/2015 (Lahore High Court Green Bench, 2015).

[57] *Beatriz Silvia Mendoza* v. *Argentina*, M. 1569 (Supreme Court of Argentina, 2008).

[58] *Asghar Leghari* v. *Pakistan*; *Advocate Prakash Mani Sharma* v. *Cabinet Secretariat*, No. 3027/2059 (Supreme Court of Nepal, 1997).

[59] *Concerned Residents of Manila Bay et al.* v. *Metropolitan Manila Development Authority*, Nos. 171947–48 (Supreme Court of the Philippines, 2008).

[60] *Farooque* v. *Government of Bangladesh*, WP 891 of 1994 (Supreme Court of Bangladesh, 2002).

reallocation of lands,[61] and ongoing reporting obligations.[62] Some courts have ordered the establishment of new governmental authorities, while others have compelled private entities[63] or public-private partnerships[64] to manage implementation of remedial orders. Tribunals enforcing an international right to a quality environment should have, and be comfortable exercising, the full range of remedial powers. One further step would be to authorize a tribunal to work in dialogue with governments to establish comprehensive yet tailored remedial measures subject to immediate implementation with ongoing mandate.

The third lesson is to think about others. Because environmental endowments are invariably shared among segments of the population, cases vindicating environmental rights tend to benefit not only the plaintiffs, but the public as well.[65] An international human right to a quality environment should be available for individuals and collectives, advancing claims on behalf of themselves and future generations. Guidance could be taken from the Argentina river case,[66] and the decision of the Philippine Supreme Court to order the clean-up of Manila Bay.[67] Other procedural rules that function as barriers to implementation should also be avoided: This would require attention to costs, burdens of proof, and evidentiary requirements, among other things. The Philippines and Argentina both provide good examples here, too. In the Philippines, the Supreme Court has developed rules of procedure for environmental cases that encourage the vindication of environmental rights in extraordinary ways, including on behalf of nature itself.[68] In Argentina, summary proceedings in environmental matters (among other things) are provided for directly in the Constitution.[69]

The fourth lesson is to think about process by explicitly promoting access to information, participation, and justice. The constitutions of about three dozen countries guarantee access to information, participation, and remedy specifically in environmental matters.[70] Some constitutions explicitly provide that environmental

61 *M.C. Mehta* v. *Union of India*, SCR 86 1991 SCC (2) 353 (Supreme Court of India, 1991).
62 *Farooque* v. *Bangladesh*.
63 *Shehla Zia* v. *WAPDA*.
64 Constitutional Court of Colombia, sentencia no. T-291/06, 96 (2009).
65 See generally James R. May and Erin Daly, "Vindicating Fundamental Environmental Rights Worldwide," *Oregon Review of International Law* 11 (2010), p. 365.
66 *Beatriz Silvia Mendoza* v. *Argentina*.
67 *Concerned Residents of Manila Bay et al.* v. *Metropolitan Manila Development Authority*.
68 The Philippine rules provide for consideration of cases brought on behalf of nature, known as the "writ of kalikasan." Such a writ can be pursued on behalf "of persons whose constitutional right to a balanced and healthful ecology is violated, or threatened" by a public official or private entity, "involving environmental damage of such magnitude as to prejudice the life, health or property of inhabitants in two or more cities or provinces." Philippines Supreme Court, Rules of Procedure for Environmental Cases, A.M. No. 09–6–8-SC (2010), Rule 7(1).
69 Argentina Constitution, section 43.
70 See May and Daly, *Global Environmental Constitutionalism*, chapter 8, appendix I.

information must be timely and complete or full.[71] Other constitutions explicitly provide for or impose a duty on the state to provide for public participation in environmental decision making, sometimes even expressing the purpose of such right: "Public authorities shall support the activities of citizens to protect and improve the quality of the environment."[72] Still others are focused on access to justice. The Azerbaijan constitution provides for "the right ... to get compensation for damage rendered to the health and property due to the violation of ecological rights."[73]

The development of an international right to a healthy environment is not as simple as it sounds. The right should be expressed in such a way as to make clear its meaning, its scope, the procedural or substantive rights with which it is associated and meant to be supported by, and the enforcement mechanisms that will ensure its effectiveness. Lessons from the experience at the national level can be informative and influential for those considering whether an international right is beneficial, and if so, why and how.

CONCLUSION

An international human right to a healthy environment would be a valuable complement to the regime of constitutional environmental rights that is flourishing within nation-states throughout the world. An international right would bind nations to environmental norms and would create a worldwide standard for environmental protection that would recognize the indivisible connection between human rights and the natural environment.

There are already abundant and growing axes of communication between international and national legal domains: The two types of law have been engaging with and learning from each other for so long, in so many contexts, that developments at one level necessarily engage the experiences and insights at the other. This is especially true in the environmental context, where decades of international protection of almost all aspects of the natural environment have influenced and are now being influenced by domestic environmental constitutionalism.

We suggest three areas in particular where domestic environmental constitutionalism might be instructive for the architects of an international human right to a healthy environment. Drafters of the international right should consider the language that is used in environmental protection, clearly establishing a human right to a quality environment and, at the same time, clarifying as much as possible which elements of the environment should be protected and why. Second, efforts should be made to link environmental rights to other human rights, including especially

[71] See, e.g., Czech Republic Charter of Fundamental Rights and Freedoms, art. 35(2); Russian Federation Constitution, art. 42; Serbia Constitution, art. 74.

[72] Poland Constitution, chapter 2, art. 74 (4).

[73] Azerbaijan Constitution, part II, chapter 3, art. 39(11).

water, health, life, and dignity. Ideally, substantive rights should be buttressed by procedural rights to information, participation in environmental decision making, and access to justice. And third, attention should be paid to creating an effective mechanism for vindicating environmental rights, with sensitivity to costs and burdens and other procedural hurdles, and to facilitate invocation of the right by individuals and communities for present and future generations, and perhaps even on behalf of nature itself.

4

The Right to a Satisfactory, Healthy, and Sustainable Environment in the African Regional Human Rights System

*Lilian Chenwi**

The protection of the environment has been an essential part of Africans' social, cultural, and religious life for many generations.[1] It is also an essential part of human rights protection in Africa. As observed by the African Commission on Human and Peoples' Rights (African Commission), "collective rights, *environmental rights*, and economic and social rights are essential elements of human rights in Africa."[2] It is thus of significance that, at the African regional level, environmental rights are recognized as explicit treaty norms, with normative unity with other rights and corresponding obligations.

However, Africa continues to be characterized by, among other problems, resource exploitation, water pollution, loss of biodiversity, and continuous degradation of the environment,[3] with the latter having negative effects on human rights.[4] Climate change, globalization, and increased urbanization are among the key factors contributing to Africa's environmental challenges.[5] Although Africa depends

* Associate Professor, School of Law, University of the Witwatersrand, South Africa.

[1] Emeka Polycarp Amechi, "Enhancing Environmental Protection and Socio-Economic Development in Africa: A Fresh Look at the Right to a General Satisfactory Environment under the African Charter on Human and Peoples' Rights," *Law, Environment and Development Journal* 5(1) (2009), pp. 58–72, 62.

[2] *Social and Economic Rights Action Centre and the Centre for Economic and Social Rights* v. *Nigeria*, Communication No. 155/96 (2001) (*SERAC* case or *SERAC* v. *Nigeria*), para. 68 (emphasis added).

[3] Werner Scholtz, "Human Rights and the Environment in the African Union Context," in Anna Grear and Louis J. Kotzé (eds.), *Research Handbook on Human Rights and the Environment* (Edward Elgar Publishing, 2015), p. 401; Achim Steiner, *An Introduction to the African Convention on the Conservation of Nature and Natural Resources* (International Union for Conservation of Nature Environmental Law Centre, 2004), p. 1.

[4] Scholtz, "Human Rights and the Environment," p. 401.

[5] New Partnership for Africa's Development (NEPAD), *Review of the Implementation of the Action Plan of the AU/NEPAD Environment* (2012), p. 10.

on the extraction of natural resources to foster economic growth, achieve sustainable development, and reduce poverty, extractive activities also contribute to environmental damage in the continent.[6] As observed by the African Commission, "the increasing rate of the destruction of the African environment and ecosystem by extractive industrial activities with impunity" is an issue of concern.[7] Hence, the Commission has elevated attention to the impact of extractive activities on environmental protection and environmental rights with the establishment of the Working Group on Extractive Industries, Environment and Human Rights Violations.[8]

In both national and regional priorities, concerns relating to the environment continue to rank highly.[9] For example, the African Union (AU) has identified environmental protection as one of the areas of common interest to African states.[10] It has gone further to develop various policy responses aimed at addressing Africa's environmental concerns.[11] One of these policy responses is the environment initiative of the New Partnership for Africa's Development, which addresses the links between economic, development, poverty, health, and the environment at the national and sub-regional levels as well as the regional level.[12] Its effectiveness has, however, been limited by both institutional and implementation challenges.[13]

This chapter provides an overview of the right to a satisfactory, healthy, and sustainable environment in the African regional human rights system, focusing on: its normative development; its nature and content, including its normative unity with other rights; the correlating obligations; and enforcement in cases of violations. In particular, the chapter considers its enforcement by the African Commission and

6 Joe Asamoah, "The Management of Strategic Resources: The Oil and Gas Find in Ghana," in Timothy Afful-Koomson and Kwabena Awusu Asubonteng (eds.), *Collaborative Governance in Extractive Industries in Africa* (United Nations University Institute for Natural Resources in Africa, 2013), p. 184.

7 African Commission on Human and Peoples' Rights res. 321 (November 18, 2015), pmbl.

8 African Commission on Human and Peoples' Rights res. 148 (November 25, 2009).

9 See Steiner, *Introduction to the African Convention*, p. 1; see also the Revised African Convention on the Conservation of Nature and Natural Resources, July 11, 2003, in force April 6, 2017 (Revised African Convention), pmbl. (affirming that "the conservation of the African environment [is] a primary concern of all Africans."). As at January 29, 2018, the Revised African Convention had been ratified by sixteen African states: Angola, Benin, Burkina Faso, Burundi, Chad, Côte d'Ivoire, Comoros, Congo, Ghana, Libya, Lesotho, Liberia, Mali, Niger, Rwanda, and South Africa (see ratification/accession status list (updated June 15, 2017) available at www.au.int/web/sites/default/files/treaties/7782-sl-revised_african_convention_on_the_conservation_of_nature_and_natural_re.pdf).

10 Constitutive Act of the African Union, July 11, 2000, in force May 26, 2001, OAU Doc. CAB/LEG/23.15, art 13(1). As at January 29, 2018, all fifty-five African states have ratified/acceded to the Constitutive Act (see ratification/accession status list (updated June 15, 2017) available at www.au.int/web/sites/default/files/treaties/7758-sl-constitutive_act_of_the_african_union_2.pdf).

11 The limited scope of this chapter does not allow for a consideration of AU's policy responses, beyond the AU treaties and standards mentioned in the chapter.

12 New Partnership for Africa's Development, *Review of the Implementation of the Action Plan of the AU/NEPAD Environment*, pp. 7–8.

13 Ibid., p. 12.

the African Court on Human and Peoples' Rights (African Court). The chapter also explores the possibility for ensuring accountability for violation of the right, through prosecution, within the African Court of Justice and Human Rights.

NORMATIVE DEVELOPMENT

This section reviews selected key instruments at the regional level (excluding sub-regional levels) and aims to show how environmental protection evolved in the instruments as time progressed, moving from a non-rights-based approach to a rights-based approach.

The development of standards at the African regional level can be traced as far back as the colonial period, when the colonial powers initiated conventions that focused on conserving nature and natural resources, with utilitarian objectives. Two conventions were adopted in this regard. First, the Convention on the Preservation of Wild Animals, Birds, and Fish in Africa (the 1900 Convention), adopted by the colonial powers, was aimed at preventing "indiscriminate slaughter" and ensuring "the preservation throughout their possessions in Africa of the various forms of animal life existing in a wild state which are either useful to man or are harmless."[14] Second, the Convention Relative to the Preservation of Fauna and Flora in their Natural State (the 1933 Convention), was aimed at preserving fauna and flora, including limiting or prohibiting their collection or destruction, as they were in danger "of extinction or permanent injury."[15]

Post-colonialism, due to the need for a treaty on the protection of nature that takes into consideration the specific interests of Africans, the Organization of African Unity (OAU) adopted in 1968 the African Convention on the Conservation of Nature and Natural Resources (the African Convention).[16] The Convention dealt with a range of aspects relating to the protection of the environment, and has been described as a "modern approach to the conservation of nature" in that it is not limited to utilitarian objectives, but introduces new approaches to nature conservation such as perceiving environmental management as a common responsibility of

[14] Convention on the Preservation of Wild Animals, Birds, and Fish in Africa, May 19, 1900, not in force, pmbl.

[15] Convention Relative to the Preservation of Fauna and Flora in Their Natural State, adopted on November 8, 1933, in force January 14, 1936, pmbl.

[16] African Convention on the Conservation of Nature and Natural Resources, September 25, 1968, in force June 16, 1969, OAU Doc. CAB/LEG/24.1. As at January 29, 2018, the African Convention had been ratified/acceded to by thirty-two African states: Algeria, Burkina Faso, Cameroon, Central Africa Republic, Côte d'Ivoire, Comoros, Congo, Djibouti, Democratic Republic of the Congo, Egypt, Gabon, Ghana, Guinea, Kenya, Liberia, Madagascar, Mali, Malawi, Morocco, Mozambique, Nigeria, Niger, Rwanda, Senegal, Seychelles, Sudan, Swaziland, Tanzania, Togo, Tunisia, Uganda, and Zambia (see ratification/accession status list (updated June 15, 2017) available at www.au.int/web/sites/default/files/treaties/7763-sl-african_convention_on_the_conservation_of_nature_and_natural_resources_.pdf).

African states (in addition to individual state action).[17] The Convention (which has subsequently been revised, as indicated later) was, however, limited in that it did not make provision for institutional structures for its effective implementation.[18] It was also silent on environmental protection as a human right.

However, this changed in 1981 with the adoption by the OAU of the African Charter on Human and Peoples' Rights (African Charter).[19] It is the first treaty, internationally, to recognize the right of peoples to "a general *satisfactory* environment favourable to their development."[20] The inclusion of this right was not a controversial issue during the drafting of the Charter.[21] The relevant provision reflects an acknowledgment that a satisfactory environment is important to economic, social, and cultural development and the realization of other human rights in Africa.[22] Two other provisions in the African Charter relevant to environmental protection are also worthy of note: the right of peoples to "freely dispose of their wealth and natural resources," to "be exercised in the exclusive interest of the people,[23] and the right of peoples to economic, social, and cultural development, with regard to "their freedom and identity" and "the equal enjoyment of the common heritage of mankind."[24] The African Charter does not suffer from an institutional defect, as the African Commission was established to promote, protect, and interpret the rights in the Charter.[25] The enforcement mechanism was subsequently strengthened with the establishment of the African Court, which has jurisdiction over cases and disputes concerning the interpretation and application of the Charter and other relevant human rights treaties.[26]

[17] IUCN Environmental Law Programme, *An Introduction to the African Convention on the Conservation of Nature and Natural Resources*, IUCN Environmental Policy and Law Paper No. 56 (2004), p. 4.

[18] Philippe Sands and Jacqueline Peel, *Principles of International Environmental Law*, 3d ed. (Cambridge University Press, 2012), p. 25; Steiner, *Introduction to the African Commission*, p. 4.

[19] African Charter on Human and Peoples' Rights, June 27, 1981, in force October 21, 1986, 1520 UNTS 217. As at January 29, 2018, all African states (with the exception of Morocco) – i.e., fifty-four in total – have ratified/acceded to the African Charter (see ratification/accession status list (updated June 15, 2017) available at www.au.int/web/sites/default/files/treaties/7770-sl-african_charter_on_human_and_peoples_rights_2.pdf).

[20] African Charter, art. 24.

[21] Amechi, "Enhancing Environmental Protection," p. 63 (emphasis added).

[22] Ibid., p. 62.

[23] African Charter, art 21.

[24] Ibid., art. 22.

[25] Ibid., art. 45.

[26] Protocol to the African Charter on Human and Peoples' Rights on the Establishment of an African Court on Human and Peoples' Rights, July 10, 1998, in force January 25, 2004, OAU Doc. OAU/LEG/EXP/AFCHPR/PROT (III) ("African Court Protocol"), art. 3. As at January 29, 2018, the African Court Protocol had been ratified by thirty African states – Algeria, Benin, Burkina Faso, Burundi, Cameroon, Chad, Côte d'Ivoire, Comoros, Congo, Gabon, Gambia, Ghana, Kenya, Libya, Lesotho, Mali, Malawi, Mozambique, Mauritania, Mauritius, Nigeria, Niger, Rwanda, South Africa, Sahrawi Arab Democratic Republic, Senegal, Tanzania, Togo, Tunisia, and Uganda (see ratification/accession status list (updated June 15, 2017) available at

In 1990, the OAU adopted the African Charter on the Rights and Welfare of the Child (African Children's Charter), which does not contain a provision on the right to a satisfactory or healthy environment. However, it requires "the development of respect for the environment and natural resources" through education.[27]

In 1991, the need to address the dumping of hazardous and toxic waste in Africa resulted in the OAU adopting the Bamako Convention on the Ban of Import into Africa and the Control of Transboundary Movement and Management of Hazardous Waste within Africa (Bamako Convention).[28] It recognizes that hazardous wastes and their transboundary movement are a threat to the environment, and that "the reduction of their generation to a minimum in terms of quantity and/or hazard potential" is an effective way of protecting the environment.[29] The Convention has been seen to have "raised the bar in international environmental regulation of transboundary movement of hazardous wastes."[30] Although the Bamako Convention does not refer to environmental protection as a right, it recalls the African Charter, which as stated earlier provides for this right.[31]

In 2003, the institutional limitation in the African Convention on the Conservation of Nature, coupled with developments in the field of international environmental law and policy, resulted in the revision of the African Convention and the adoption by the African Union – the successor to the OAU – of the Revised African Convention on the Conservation of Nature and Natural Resources, which explicitly

www.au.int/web/sites/default/files/treaties/7778-sl-protocol_to_the_african_charter_on_human_and_peoplesrights_on_the_estab.pdf).

27 African Charter on the Rights and Welfare of the Child, July 1, 1990, in force November 29, 1999, OAU Doc. CAB/LEG/24.9/49 (African Children's Charter), art. 11(2)(g). As at January 29, 2018, the African Children's Charter had been ratified/acceded to by forty-eight African states (the exceptions being Democratic Republic of Congo, Sahrawi Arab Democratic Republic, Somalia, South Sudan, Sao Tome and Principe, and Tunisia that have signed but not yet ratified the treaty (see ratification/accession status list (updated June 15, 2017) available at www.au.int/web/sites/default/files/treaties/7773-sl-african_charter_on_the_rights_and_welfare_of_the_child_1.pdf).

28 Bamako Convention on the Ban of Import into Africa and the Control of Transboundary Movement and Management of Hazardous Waste within Africa, January 30, 1991, in force April 22, 1998. As at January 29, 2018, the Bamako Convention had been ratified/acceded to by twenty-seven African states: Angola, Benin, Burkina Faso, Burundi, Cameroon, Chad, Côte d'Ivoire, Comoros, Congo, Democratic Republic of Congo, Egypt, Ethiopia, Gabon, Gambia, Libya, Liberia, Mali, Mozambique, Mauritius, Niger, Senegal, Sudan, Tanzania, Togo, Tunisia, Uganda, and Zimbabwe (see ratification/accession status list (updated June 15, 2017) available at www.au.int/web/sites/default/files/treaties/7774-sl-bamako_convention_on_the_ban_of_the_import_into_africa_and_the_control_0.pdf).

29 Ibid., pmbl.

30 Adebola Ogunlade, "Can the Bamako Convention Adequately Safeguard Africa's Environment in the Context of Transboundary Movement of Hazardous Wastes?" *University of Dundee* (2010), p. 19.

31 Bamako Convention, pmbl.

accentuates the right to a satisfactory environment in the African Charter as a key principle.[32] The Revised African Convention is aimed at enhancing protection of the environment, fostering "conservation and sustainable use of natural resources," and harmonizing and coordinating environmental policies "with a view to achieving ecologically rational, economically sound and socially acceptable development policies and programmes."[33] Actions taken by states have to be guided by three key principles: (1) "the right of all peoples to a satisfactory environment favourable to their development"; (2) "the duty of States, individually and collectively to ensure the enjoyment of the right to development"; and (3) "the duty of States to ensure that developmental and environmental needs are met in a sustainable, fair and equitable manner."[34]

In the same year, the African Union adopted the Protocol to the African Charter on Human and Peoples' Rights on the Rights of Women in Africa (African Women's Protocol), which recognizes the right of women to "a *healthy* and *sustainable* environment."[35]

NATURE AND CONTENT

The right to a satisfactory environment is provided for in the African Charter as a collective right. It is a right to be claimed by "peoples." The Charter fails to define "peoples." This has been seen as a deliberate omission by the drafters so as to allow for flexibility in its application and interpretation.[36] Based on the African Commission's jurisprudence, "peoples" may be demarcated by factors other than

[32] African Convention on the Conservation of Nature and Natural Resources (Revised Version).

[33] Ibid., art. 2.

[34] Ibid., art. 3. Article 16 of the Convention requires the parties to adopt measures necessary to ensure dissemination of, and public access to, environmental information; public participation in decision making with a potentially significant impact on the environment, and access to justice in environmental matters. Article 17 addresses traditional rights and intellectual property rights of local communities.

[35] Protocol to the African Charter on Human and Peoples' Rights on the Rights of Women in Africa, September 13, 2000, in force November 25, 2005, AU Doc. CAB/LEG/66.6, art. 18 (emphasis added). As at January 29, 2018, the African Women's Protocol had been ratified/acceded to by thirty-eight African states – Algeria, Angola, Benin, Burkina Faso, Cameroon, Cape Verde, Côte d'Ivoire, Comoros, Congo, Djibouti, Democratic Republic of Congo, Equatorial Guinea, Gabon, Gambia, Ghana, Guinea-Bissau, Kenya, Libya, Lesotho, Liberia, Mali, Mozambique, Mauritania, Namibia, Nigeria, Rwanda, South Africa, Senegal, Seychelles, Sierra Leone, Swaziland, Tanzania, Togo, Tunisia, Uganda, Zambia, and Zimbabwe (see ratification/accession status list (updated June 15, 2017) available at www.au.int/web/sites/default/files/treaties/7783-sl-protocol_to_the_african_charter_on_human_and_peoples_rights_on_the_righ.pdf).

[36] *African Commission on Human and Peoples' Rights* v. *Kenya*, Application 006/2012, Judgment (African Court of Human and Peoples' Rights, 2017) (*Ogiek* case or *ACHPR* v. *Kenya* (Judgment)), para. 196.

territorial boundaries or nationality.[37] The term can imply the whole population of a country, or a part of the population bound together by cultural, linguistic, ethnic, or other factors.[38] The Commission has held that in relation to the collective rights guaranteed under Articles 19 to 24 of the African Charter, which include the right to a satisfactory environment, for "a collective of individuals" to be recognized as "peoples," they should manifest "a common historical tradition, racial or ethnic identity, cultural homogeneity, linguistic unity, religious and ideological affinities, territorial connection, and a common economic life or other bonds, identities and affinities they collectively enjoy."[39] A collective of individuals can also be recognized as "peoples" if they "suffer collectively from the deprivation of such rights."[40] The African Court, in relation to the understanding of "peoples" as used in the African Charter, has held that, "in the context of the struggle against foreign domination in all its forms, the Charter primarily targets the peoples comprising the populations of the countries struggling to attain independence and national sovereignty."[41] On whether the rights recognized for "peoples" in the Charter extend beyond "the population as the constituent elements of the State" to "ethnic groups or communities" within the state (i.e., "sub-state ethnic groups and communities that are part of that population"), the Court answered in the affirmative, provided that they are not calling into question the state's sovereignty and territorial integrity without its consent.[42] It went further to state that "nothing prevents peoples' rights, such as the right to development (Article 22), the right to peace and security (Article 23) or the right to a healthy environment (Article 24) from being recognised, where necessary, specifically for the ethnic groups and communities that constitute the population of a State."[43]

Notwithstanding the provision of the right to a satisfactory environment as a collective right in the African Charter, its nature "is relatively uncontested in that it is a right to which individuals, communities and the public at large can be beneficiaries of."[44] It is worth noting that the right to a *healthy* and *sustainable*

37 Frans Viljoen, *International Human Rights Law in Africa* (Oxford University Press, 2012), pp. 221–2.

38 Christof Heyns and Magnus Killander, "Africa," in Daniel Moeckli, Sangeeta Shah, and Sandesh Sivakumaran (eds.), *International Human Rights Law* (Oxford University Press, 2014), p. 445; Scholtz, "Human Rights and the Environment," p. 407.

39 *Centre for Minority Rights Development (Kenya) and Minority Rights Group International on behalf of Endorois Welfare Council* v. *Kenya*, Communication 276/2003 (African Commission, 2009) (*Endorois* case or *Endorois Welfare Council* v. *Kenya*), para. 151.

40 Ibid.

41 *ACHPR* v. *Kenya* (Judgment), para. 197.

42 Ibid., paras. 198–9.

43 Ibid., para. 199.

44 Morné van der Linde and Lirette Louw, "Considering the Interpretation and Implementation of Article 24 of the African Charter on Human and Peoples' Rights in Light of the *SERAC* Communication," *African Human Rights Law Journal* 3 (2003), p. 174.

environment in the African Women's Protocol is guaranteed to "women" as the Protocol's scope is limited to women.

The right is also provided for as a composite right: It refers to protection of the environment as well as promotion of development in Africa. As the African Commission puts it, the right to a satisfactory environment is important in improving the quality of life and safety of individuals and in promoting development.[45] Article 24 of the African Charter thus reinforces the principle of interdependency of rights, which is a key principle in the Charter,[46] reflecting normative unity between the right to satisfactory environment and development. This relationship has been seen as challenging in that environmental degradation often results from aspects relating to development, and measures adopted to address environmental degradation are related to development processes.[47] Also, a key question is whether the right to a satisfactory environment can be claimed even if it violates socioeconomic development requirements, or whether the claiming of the right should be limited only to instances where it does not violate socioeconomic development requirements.[48] This question seems to denote some sort of a tension between the right to a satisfactory environment and the right to development, which is evident in the wording of Article 24 of the African Charter itself. This tension lies beneath the *SERAC* case discussed subsequently, as the Nigerian government, in pursuing development and short-term benefits, allowed oil companies to engage in activities that violated environmental and other human rights.

The tension between development and environmental rights is, however, not insurmountable. For example, Scholtz has argued that the notion of sustainable development, which is an objective of the African Union, is useful in reconciling any tension in a way that responds to the specific needs of Africans.[49] However, he cautions that sustainable development does not provide "an exact account of how developmental and environmental needs should be balanced," especially in situations "where there are trade-offs between environmental and economic considerations."[50] Although economic interests have often trumped environmental considerations in Africa, the African regional human rights framework seeks to ensure that a reconciliation is achieved between economic development and environmental concerns by providing for a justiciable right to a satisfactory environment coupled

[45] *SERAC* v. *Nigeria*, para. 51.

[46] See African Charter, pmbl. ("civil and political rights cannot be dissociated from economic, social and cultural rights").

[47] Morné van der Linde, "African Responses to Environmental Protection," *Comparative and International Law Journal of Southern Africa* 35(1) (2002), p. 106.

[48] Amechi, "Enhancing Environmental Protection," p. 60.

[49] Scholtz, "Human Rights and the Environment," pp. 402, 411–415.

[50] Ibid., p. 412.

with the guarantee of other derivative environmental rights (identified later in this chapter) as well as a justiciable right to development, whose substantive elements such as well-being "cannot be achieved if environmental concerns are negated."[51] Viljoen has also seen the African regional human rights framework as a tool to ease this tension between environmental rights and the right to development, arguing that the framework is "more favourable to the individual, and more restrictive to the developmentalist state."[52]

The normative unity of the right to a satisfactory environment with other rights goes beyond development to include the right to health and the right to life, amongst others. The normative unity between the right to life and the right to a satisfactory environment is evident from the African Commission's broad interpretation of the responsibilities of states to protect life to include taking "preventive steps to preserve and protect the natural environment."[53] The Commission has also interpreted the positive obligation on states to protect the life of all detained persons and provide conditions necessary for a dignified life, to include "an environment free from disease."[54] Furthermore, the African Commission's finding of a violation of the right to life on the basis of environmental degradation and the destruction of sources of livelihood of people is reflective of a normative unity between the right to life and the right to a satisfactory environment.[55]

The right to a general satisfactory environment and the right to health, as stated by the African Commission, are also interlinked and mutually dependent. In the Commission's view, an environment that is not clean and safe affects not only Article 24, but also Article 16 of the African Charter.[56] Also, "a clean and safe environment," as the Commission notes, "is closely linked to economic and social rights insofar as the environment affects the quality of life and safety of the individual."[57] The normative unity between the right to a satisfactory environment and the right to education is recognized in the African Children's Charter as noted in the preceding section of this chapter. The African Commission is also of the view that the right to education has a vital role in environmental protection.[58] Also, the right to a satisfactory environment is one of the rights from which the right to water and

[51] Ibid., p. 415.
[52] Viljoen, *Human Rights Law in Africa*, p. 272.
[53] African Commission on Human and Peoples' Rights, General Comment No. 3 (2015), paras. 3, 41.
[54] Ibid., para. 36.
[55] *SERAC* v. *Nigeria*, para. 67.
[56] Ibid., paras. 51–2.
[57] Ibid., para. 51.
[58] African Commission on Human and Peoples' Rights, *Principles and Guidelines on the Implementation of Economic, Social and Cultural Rights in the African Charter on Human and Peoples' Rights* (2011), para. 69.

sanitation is derived.[59] Sanitation thus has to be at a level of adequacy and safety that is conducive to protection of the environment.[60]

With regard to whether the right is of such a nature that it is subject to limitations, it should be noted that the African Charter does not explicitly subject the rights in it to progressive realization and resource availability. However, as the African Commission has indicated, these limitations are implicit in the Charter by virtue of Articles 60 and 61 of the Charter, requiring inspiration to be drawn from international law and standards on human and peoples' rights, African practices consistent with these norms, general principles of law recognized by African states, and legal doctrine and precedents.[61] Further, the Charter includes a general limitation clause, requiring that rights in the Charter "be exercised with due regard to the rights of others, collective security, morality and common interest."[62] It should, however, be noted, as seen from the African Court's jurisprudence, that a "mere assertion by a State Party of the existence of a common interest warranting interference with [a] right is not sufficient to allow the restriction of the right or sweep away the essence of the right in its entirety."[63] Adequate substantiation of the genuineness of the interference in order to protect a common interest is required.[64] Another condition to be met in relation to the limitation of rights in the African Charter is that of necessity and proportionality. As stated by the African Court, "any interference with the rights and freedoms guaranteed in the Charter shall be necessary and proportional to the legitimate interest sought to be attained by such interference."[65]

It has also been argued that the right to satisfactory environment in the African Charter is capable of extraterritorial application, as the Charter does not have a jurisdiction clause.[66] The extraterritorial reach of the African Charter – on the basis of its lack of a jurisdiction clause – has been noted by various writers. Milanovic, for example, observes in relation to treaties with no jurisdiction clause, citing the African Charter as one of the examples, that their application, "at least at first

[59] Ibid., para. 87 ("While the African Charter does not directly protect the right to water and sanitation, it is implied in the protections of a number of rights, including but not, limited to the rights to life, dignity, work, food, health, economic, social and cultural development and *to a satisfactory environment*.") (emphasis added).

[60] Ibid., para. 91.

[61] Ibid., para. 13.

[62] African Charter, art. 27(2).

[63] *ACHPR* v. *Kenya* (Judgment), para. 188 (speaking in relation to the right to culture, which would also be applicable if Article 27(2) is applied in relation to the right to a healthy environment, since the Court was considering the right in the context of environmental concerns raised as justification by the state).

[64] Ibid.

[65] Ibid.

[66] Scholtz, "Human Rights and the Environment," p. 403.

glance, is consequently neither confined to the territory of a state party nor to the territories or persons over which the state party has jurisdiction."[67]

Despite being described as "the most explicit normative statement of an environmental right in any binding human rights instrument,"[68] the right to a satisfactory environment in the African Charter is vaguely phrased in that it does not provide any indication of what the right entails beyond the promotion of (socioeconomic) development, resulting in difficulties in understanding its exact content by looking at the relevant provision itself. However, such difficulties have, to some extent, been clarified by the African Commission, which has recognized substantive and procedural aspects of the right. The content of the right includes the prevention of "pollution and ecological destruction," the promotion of conservation, securing "an ecologically sustainable development and use of natural resources," and the "monitoring of threatened environments."[69] Notwithstanding this clarification, "the kind of conservation envisaged by the right" and the extent of permissible or non-permissible environmental degradation and pollution remain unclear.[70] Taking into consideration the African Charter's requirement of an environment of a quality that is favorable to development, it has been argued that "the environmental conservation envisaged under the right is the type that will enhance the well-being of Africans by securing for them an ecologically sustainable development and use of natural resources," and that "the pollution and environmental degradation" to be prevented "must be of such significant level, severity or persistence as to render impossible the enjoyment of an environment that is favourable to human health and well-being."[71]

The vague provision (in terms of phrasing) in the African Charter can be contrasted with the provision in the African Women's Protocol, which is more elaborate in spelling out the content of the right to a *healthy* and *sustainable* environment. The Protocol explicitly requires sustainable use of natural resources and preservation of the environment, "new and renewable energy sources," "development of women's indigenous knowledge systems," regulation of "the management, processing, storage and disposal of domestic waste," and "the storage, transportation and disposal of toxic waste."[72]

OBLIGATIONS OF STATES AND NON-STATE ACTORS

Both states and non-state actors have obligations in relation to the right to a satisfactory or healthy and sustainable environment.

[67] Marko Milanovic, *Extraterritorial Application of Human Rights Treaties: Law, Principles, and Policy* (Oxford University Press, 2011), p. 17.
[68] Scholtz, "Human Rights and the Environment," p. 405.
[69] *SERAC* v. *Nigeria*, paras. 52, 53.
[70] Amechi, "Enhancing Environmental Protection," p. 65.
[71] Ibid., pp. 65, 68.
[72] African Women's Protocol, art. 18(2).

States undertake under the African Charter "to adopt legislative or other measures to give effect to" the rights in the Charter.[73] Despite the use of "or," adoption of legislative measures alone would be insufficient to comply with this obligation, especially if certain groups still suffer rights deprivation.[74] In addition, this general obligation is not qualified by use of territory or jurisdiction; thus, it has extraterritorial reach. As Viljoen observes, in some instances the responsibility of states parties to the African Charter extends to extraterritorial incidents or events in cases where the state exercises *de facto* or effective control.[75]

States also have obligations to respect, protect, promote, and fulfill the right to a satisfactory environment. The African Commission has recognized that all rights generate these four levels of obligations.[76] The obligation to respect requires states to refrain from interfering with the enjoyment of the right. The obligation to protect requires them to protect people from the violation of their right by other parties, including the provision of effective remedies. States are required to promote the right, including ensuring that individuals enjoy the right. Generally, the obligations to respect, protect, and fulfill rights have also been seen to have extraterritorial reach.[77]

Lastly, states have to take "'reasonable and other measures" to ensure actual realization of the right. The African Commission further spells out the obligations on states parties in relation to the right to a satisfactory or healthy environment in the following words:

> The right to a general satisfactory environment, as guaranteed under article 24 of the African Charter or the right to a healthy environment, as it is widely known,

73 African Charter, art. 1.

74 In *ACHPR* v. *Kenya*, the African Court found the adoption of legislative measures to be insufficient, as the state failed to recognize the Ogieks as a distinct tribe, resulting in denial of access to their land and consequential violation of other rights to which they are entitled. In addition to the legislative measures, the state also had to demonstrate adoption of other measures to give effect to the rights violated. *ACHPR* v. *Kenya* (Judgment), para. 216.

75 See Frans Viljoen, "Admissibility under the African Charter," in Malcolm Evans and Rachel Murray (eds.), *The African Charter on Human and Peoples' Rights: The System in Practice, 1986–2000* (Cambridge University Press, 2002), p. 78; Frans Viljoen, "International Protection of Human Rights," in Hennie Strydom (ed.), *International Law* (Oxford University Press, 2016), p. 329.

76 *SERAC* v. *Nigeria*, para. 44.

77 The African Commission has recognized the extraterritorial obligations of states to "respect" rights in the African Charter in its decision in *Democratic Republic of Congo* v. *Burundi, Rwanda and Uganda*, Communication No. 227/1999 (2003). The extraterritorial reach of obligations to respect, protect, and fulfill rights has also been recognized in the Maastricht Principles on Extraterritorial Obligations of States in the area of Economic, Social and Cultural Rights, adopted September 28, 2011. Principle 3, for example, provides: "All States have obligations to respect, protect and fulfill human rights, including civil, cultural, economic, political and social rights, both within their territories and extraterritorially." These Principles can serve as a source of inspiration for the African regional system by virtue of Articles 60 and 61 of the African Charter.

therefore imposes clear obligations upon a government. It requires the state to *take reasonable and other measures* to prevent pollution and ecological degradation, to promote conservation, and to secure an ecologically sustainable development and use of natural resources.[78]

The Commission also notes that governments are required "to take necessary steps for the improvement of all aspects of environmental and industrial hygiene," and "to desist from directly threatening the health and environment of their citizens."[79]

States parties undertake under the African Women's Protocol "to adopt all necessary measures and in particular . . . provide budgetary and other resources for the full and effective implementation of the rights" in the Protocol.[80] States' obligations in relation to women's right to a healthy and sustainable environment include the obligation to "take all appropriate measures" to: ensure women's participation "in the planning, management and preservation of the environment and the sustainable use of natural resources at all levels"; promote "research and investment in new and renewable energy sources and appropriate technologies, including information technologies and facilitate women's access to, and participation in their control"; protect and facilitate "the development of women's indigenous knowledge systems"; regulate "the management, processing, storage and disposal of domestic waste"; and "ensure that proper standards are followed for the storage, transportation and disposal of toxic waste."[81]

The African Commission's Principles and Guidelines further elaborate on state obligations in relation to the right to a satisfactory or healthy environment:

> States parties should ensure the prior informed consent by indigenous populations/communities to any exploitation of the resources of their traditional lands and that they benefit accordingly. States parties should further ensure that indigenous communities/populations give prior consent to any activities aimed at accessing and using their traditional knowledge. States parties should ensure that both state and non-state actors respect the rights of peoples to a satisfactory environment.[82]

Since other human rights can be the basis for derivative environmental rights or can be useful in developing environmentally-responsive actions based on their linkage with the right to a satisfactory environment, the African Commission has

[78] *SERAC* v. *Nigeria*, para. 52 (emphasis added).

[79] Ibid.

[80] African Women's Protocol, art 26(2).

[81] Ibid., art 18(2).

[82] African Commission, Principles and Guidelines, para. 44. The Principles and Guidelines represent an authoritative interpretation of the relevant rights in the African Charter. Their purpose, as stipulated in the preamble, is "to assist State Parties to comply with their obligations under the African Charter." They were adopted pursuant to the African Commission's explicit mandate in Article 45(1)(b) of the African Charter "to formulate and lay down, principles and rules aimed at solving legal problems relating to human and peoples' rights and fundamental freedoms upon which African Governments may base their legislations."

also identified state obligations in relation to other rights that would promote the right to a satisfactory environment. For instance, states have to "[e]nsure that national development plans and programmes are designed towards the realisation of a healthy environment that is conducive to the right to health, for example in matters relating to water resources management and sanitation."[83] This is stated as one of the minimum core obligations of states in relation to the right to health. States have to "[p]rotect individuals and peoples against environmental ... hazards, preventing air, land and water pollution and alleviating the adverse effects of urban development, industrialisation, and global warming on ecosystems, livelihood and food security."[84] Education systems that are put in place should be directed at, *inter alia*, "the development of respect for the environment and natural resources."[85] This is stated as one of the obligations of states in relation to the right to education. State obligations in relation to the right to food include an obligation to "[e]nsure that all persons are able to feed themselves directly through environmentally ... sustainable methods."[86]

The Revised African Convention also outlines various state obligations. These include: the obligation to "adopt and implement all measures necessary" for environmental protection, including "preventive measures and the application of the precautionary principle, and with due regard to ethical and traditional values as well as scientific knowledge in the interest of present and future generations."[87] While recognizing the "sovereign right" of states "to exploit their own resources pursuant to their environmental and developmental policies," the Revised African Convention also reaffirms their "responsibility to ensure that activities within their jurisdiction or control do not cause damage to the environment of other states or of areas beyond the limits of national jurisdiction."[88] It further reaffirms African states' responsibility to protect and conserve "'their environment and natural resources" and use "them in a sustainable manner with the aim to satisfy human needs according to the carrying capacity of the environment."[89]

African states have to act individually or jointly in working toward the realization of the right to a satisfactory or healthy environment. The importance of international cooperation is recognized in the African Charter.[90] The Revised African Convention also recognizes the importance of international cooperation (cooperation between African states, within sub-regional arrangements as well as with other states)

83 Ibid., para. 67(q).
84 Ibid., para. 67(s).
85 Ibid., para. 71(f)(6).
86 Ibid., para. 86(g).
87 Revised African Convention, art. 4.
88 Ibid., pmbl.
89 Ibid.
90 African Charter, pmbl. (calling on states to "promote international co-operation, having due regard to the Charter of the United Nations and the Universal Declaration of Human Rights").

in achieving the objectives of the Convention.[91] Based on the obligation to act jointly or collectively, which is explicitly stated in relation to the right to development in the African Charter, it has been argued, in the context of environmental protection, that other states may have positive extraterritorial obligations toward African peoples.[92] Nevertheless, cooperation between states is relevant in addressing transboundary environmental consequences of state measures.[93]

In relation to non-state actors, although the African Charter does not explicitly recognize the duties of non-state actors specifically in relation to the right to a satisfactory environment, it does recognize the duties of individuals to the society to respect others without discrimination, and to have due regard for the rights of others and common interests.[94] The African Commission has recognized that non-state actors have to "respect the rights of peoples to a satisfactory environment."[95] However, the African Charter does not provide any enforcement mechanism for the stipulated duties. They can thus be enforced through the state's obligation to protect or through prosecution at the national or, if the relevant mechanisms come into force, African regional level.

ENFORCEMENT IN CASES OF VIOLATIONS

African Commission

The African Commission has the mandate to promote, protect, interpret, and monitor implementation of the right to a satisfactory or healthy environment provided for in the African Charter and the African Women's Protocol.[96] The mandate to promote, protect, interpret, and monitor children's right to education directed at the development of respect for the environment and natural resources rests with the African Committee of Experts on the Rights and Welfare of the Child (African Children's Committee).[97] Since the case law of the African Children's Committee, as at the time of writing, does not deal with environmental rights, the focus in this sub-section is limited to the case law of the African Commission dealing with or relevant to environmental rights and protection. It is through the

91 Revised African Convention, pmbl. and arts. 7(4) and 22.

92 Scholtz, "Human Rights and the Environment," p. 404.

93 Hennie Strydom, "Introduction to Regional Environmental Law of the African Union," in Werner Scholtz and Jonathan Verschuuren (eds.), *Regional Environmental Law: Transregional Cooperative Lessons in Pursuit of Sustainable Development* (Edward Elgar Publishing, 2015), p. 34.

94 African Charter, art. 27. On the duties of children to, *inter alia*, society, see African Children's Charter, art. 31.

95 African Commission, Principles and Guidelines, para. 44.

96 African Charter, art. 45; African Women's Protocol, arts. 26 and 27.

97 African Children's Charter, art. 42.

consideration of complaints that the African Commission's protective mandate is undertaken.[98] Its promotional mandate is mostly undertaken through the work of special mechanisms such as the Working Group discussed subsequently.

SERAC v. *Nigeria,* decided in 2001, is the first case in which the African Commission had an opportunity to elaborate on the content of Article 24 of the African Charter. The case concerned the alleged violation of, *inter alia,* the right to a satisfactory environment by the Nigerian government on the basis that it had failed to meet minimum duties in relation to the right.[99] It was argued that the government had directly participated "in the contamination of air, water and soil and thereby harm[ed] the health of the Ogoni population," had failed "to protect the Ogoni population from the harm caused by the NNPC [Nigerian National Petroleum Company] Shell Consortium but instead us[ed] its security forces to facilitate the damage," and had failed "to provide or permit studies of potential or actual environmental and health risks caused by the oil operations."[100]

After setting out the content of the right and the obligations of states as stated in the respective preceding sections of this chapter, the African Commission considered the conduct of the Nigerian government. While acknowledging the Nigerian government's "right to produce oil, the income from which will be used to fulfill the economic and social rights of Nigerians," the Commission observed that the government must comply with its duties so as to protect the right to a satisfactory environment.[101] It held that for the Nigerian government to comply with the right to a satisfactory environment, the government must "take reasonable and other measures to prevent pollution and ecological degradation, to promote conservation, and to secure an ecologically sustainable development and use of natural resources"; and it must order or at least permit "independent scientific monitoring of the threatened environments," require and publicize "environmental and social impact studies prior to any major industrial development," appropriately monitor and provide information to those affected, and provide "meaningful opportunities for individuals to be heard and to participate in development decisions affecting their communities."[102] The Commission found that the Nigerian government had not done this; instead, it attacked, burned, and destroyed villages and homes of the Ogoni people.[103] The Commission held that the government of Nigeria was in violation of Article 24, among other provisions, of the African Charter, for failing to prevent environmental pollution, regulate the oil companies, and hold them accountable

98 See African Charter, arts. 46–59.
99 *SERAC* v. *Nigeria,* para. 50.
100 Ibid.
101 Ibid., para. 54.
102 Ibid., paras. 52, 53.
103 Ibid., para. 54.

for the violations resulting from their operations. Thus, the Nigerian government "did not live up to the minimum expectations of the African Charter."[104]

Following the finding of a violation, the African Commission appealed to the Nigerian government "to ensure protection of the environment, health and livelihood of the people of Ogoniland." To achieve this, the government was required to: stop the attacks on them; investigate human rights violations that have occurred; prosecute those involved in the violations; adequately compensate the victims of violations, including relief and resettlement assistance; clean up lands and rivers that were damaged by oil operation; ensure that "appropriate environmental and social impact assessments are prepared for any future oil development and that the safe operation of any further oil development is guaranteed through effective and independent oversight bodies for the petroleum industry"; and provide "information on health and environmental risks and meaningful access to regulatory and decision-making bodies to communities likely to be affected by oil operations."[105]

Despite being praised for elaborating on the content – both substantive and procedural – of the right to a satisfactory environment, the decision has been criticized for, *inter alia*, not adequately clarifying the implications of the link between the right to a satisfactory environment and favorable development.[106] The African Commission also failed to elaborate on the concept of "peoples," merely implying that the "Ogonis" or "Ogoni Community as a whole" qualify as "peoples."

As mentioned previously, the African Commission has found that one of the obligations of the government stemming from the right to a satisfactory environment is the duty to "secure an ecologically sustainable development and use of natural resources."[107] This duty is closely related to peoples' right to "freely dispose of their wealth and natural resources" guaranteed in the African Charter, which must "be exercised in the exclusive interest of the people."[108] The Commission also found that the Nigerian government violated this right as it allowed private actors, particularly the oil companies, "to devastatingly affect the well-being of the Ogonis."[109]

In the *Endorois* case, decided in 2009, the African Commission subsequently dealt with the right of people to freely dispose of their natural resources and the right to development, which are both intrinsically linked to the right to a satisfactory environment.[110] This was the first case in which the Commission recognized the rights of indigenous peoples to own land and to development. The case is also important in the context of environmental protection, as the Kenyan government sought to remove the Endorois community from their ancestral land "for purposes of

[104] Ibid., para. 68.
[105] Ibid., para. 71.
[106] Scholtz, "Human Rights and the Environment," p. 407.
[107] *SERAC* v. *Nigeria*, para. 52.
[108] African Charter, art. 21.
[109] *SERAC* v. *Nigeria*, paras. 58, 70.
[110] *Endorois Welfare Council* v. *Kenya*.

conserving the environment and wildlife."[111] The Kenyan government thus advanced environmental protection as the basis for the eviction. The African Commission was, however, concerned that "no effective participation was allowed for the Endorois, nor has there been any reasonable benefit enjoyed by the community," and that "a prior environment and social impact assessment was not carried out."[112] It found the "failure to guarantee effective participation and to guarantee a reasonable share in the profits of the Game Reserve (or other adequate forms of compensation)," and the failure to provide for conditions favorable to the Endorois people's development, to amount to a violation of the right to economic, social, and cultural development.[113] The Commission also found the lack of adequate compensation or restitution of the land by the Kenyan government to be a violation of the right to freely dispose of natural resources.[114] The "pollution of the traditional environment" was also considered in its analysis in arriving at the finding of a violation of the right to economic, social, and cultural development.[115]

The decision places emphasis on better processes, empowerment, and improving the capabilities and choices of people in the realization of rights and respecting their agency. The African Commission found normative unity between the right to land, including the right to freely dispose of natural resources within the land, and the right to life,[116] as well as between the right to property and the right to freely dispose of natural resources.[117]

The African Commission's ability to play a significant role in driving the right to environment forward is, however, constrained by a number of challenges. These include limited resources, which hamper the Commission's ability, for instance, to conduct urgent missions that it considers appropriate and to respond to lack of or inadequate or delayed enforcement of its decisions. Also, considering the extent of violations of environmental and related rights resulting in the establishment of a special mechanism, the Commission needs to be proactive and to make effective use of its standing to submit cases to the African Court relating to violations of environmental rights. The Commission also should review its very minimalist approach in developing the notion of provisional measures. These measures have the potential to protect rights and prevent irreparable harm and could thus be useful in ensuring

[111] Ibid., para. 164.
[112] Ibid., para. 228.
[113] Ibid., paras. 228, 298.
[114] Ibid., para. 268.
[115] Ibid., para. 293. See also Faustin Ntoubandi and Roland Adjouvi, "A Wider Human Rights Spectrum to Fight Climate Change in Africa?," in Ottavio Quirico and Mouloud Boumghar (eds.), *Climate Change and Human Rights: An International and Comparative Law Perspective* (Routledge, 2016), p. 265.
[116] *Endorois Welfare Council* v. *Kenya*, paras. 21, 216.
[117] Ibid., para. 256.

respect for and protection of the environmental rights guaranteed in the African Charter.[118] However, the impact of such measures would depend on the extent of enforcement, as provisional measures in the African system have generally "been met with virtually universal disregard, thus inhibiting any positive impact or a proper assessment of their impact."[119]

African Court

The protective mandate of the African Commission is complemented by the African Court, which is vested with more concrete and binding judicial, including remedial, powers.[120] The African Court also complements the protective mandate of the African Children's Committee, though not explicitly mentioned in the African Court Protocol, as the Court can hear cases related to the rights in the African Children's Charter. Under Article 3 of the African Court Protocol, the African Court has jurisdiction over cases and disputes concerning the interpretation and application of the right to a satisfactory or healthy environment in the African Charter, African Women's Protocol, or other relevant human rights treaties. However, the restrictive standing accorded to individuals and non-governmental organizations (NGOs) limits their ability to bring cases before the Court, which in turn limits the opportunities that the Court has to take environmental rights forward through judicial enforcement.[121]

At the time of writing, the African Court has had the opportunity to make pronouncements in one case relating to alleged violations of African Charter rights for environmental purposes. This is the *Ogiek* case, in which the Court handed down its judgment on May 26, 2017.[122] The Court had previously issued a provisional measures order on March 15, 2013, so as to prevent irreparable harm to

[118] For further reading on the African Commission's use of provisional measures, see Lilian Chenwi, "Provisional Measures in Rights Protection in Africa: A Comparative Analysis," *South African Yearbook of International Law* 39 (2014), pp. 224, 226–33.

[119] Ibid., p. 243.

[120] African Court Protocol, art. 2 (stating that the African Court "shall … complement the protective mandate" of the African Commission) and arts. 27 and 30 (on the remedial powers of the Court and its binding nature, as states parties undertake to comply with its decisions).

[121] Access to the Court is limited for NGOs and individuals, as states are required to enter an Article 34(6) declaration recognizing the competence of the Court to receive cases under Article 5(3) submitted by NGOs with observer status before the African Commission and individuals. Of the thirty states parties to the African Court Protocol, only eight states – Burkina Faso, Malawi, Mali, Tanzania, Ghana, Côte d'Ivoire, Benin, and Tunisia – have entered such a declaration. See AU Executive Council, "Decision on the Mid-Term Activity Report of the African Court on Human and Peoples' Rights," Decision No. EX.CL/Dec.973(XXXI), Doc. EX.CL/1029(XXXI), Thirty-First Ordinary Session of the Executive Council, 27 June to 01 July 2017, at para. 7. It is thus crucial that other state parties review their position on the issue and enter the relevant declaration.

[122] *ACHPR* v. *Kenya* (Judgment).

the community and prejudice to the case while it was considering it.[123] The case was first brought before the African Commission, but due to the "serious or massive violations of human rights and non-compliance with Provisional Measures issued by the Commission" to Kenya, the Commission referred the case to the African Court.[124]

The *Ogiek* case concerned an indigenous minority ethnic group in the Mau Forest, in Kenya, who faced eviction from the government, without prior consultation or consideration of the importance of the Mau Forest for the Ogieks' survival, on the basis that the forest is "a reserved water catchment zone" and was part of government land.[125] The government thus advanced environmental protection as one of the bases for the eviction. The case is therefore similar in some respects to the *Endorois* case. The *Ogiek* case related to alleged violations – for purposes of preserving the natural environment – of the right to land (Article 14), the right to non-discrimination in the enjoyment of rights (Article 2), the right to life (Article 4), the right to freedom of religion (Article 8), the right to culture (Article 17(2) and (3)), the right to development (Article 21), and the right to freely dispose of wealth and natural resources (Article 22); as well as violation of the Kenyan government's general obligation under Article 1 of the Africa Charter.[126] Key questions in the case included what constitutes an indigenous group and whether the Kenyan government's alleged environmental concerns can justify non-compliance with its obligations toward these groups, or its interference with their rights, provided for under the African Charter.

In its provisional measures order, the African Court ordered the Kenyan government to immediately stop land transactions in the Mau Forest (i.e., to stop distributing land in the area) and to refrain from actions that would irreparably prejudice the case.[127] The African Court's provisional measures order was ground-breaking, as it was the Court's first intervention to protect the rights of an indigenous community.

In its judgment, the African Court began with a finding that the Ogieks were indeed "an indigenous population."[128] This was based on its consideration of various

[123] *African Commission on Human and Peoples' Rights* v. *Kenya*, Application No. 006/2012, Order of Provisional Measures (ACHPR, 2013) (*Ogiek* case or *ACHPR* v. *Kenya* (Provisional Measures Order)).

[124] *Centre for Minority Rights Development – Kenya and Minority Rights Group International (on behalf of the Ogiek Community of the MauForest)* v. *Kenya*, Communication 381/09; African Commission on Human and Peoples' Rights, "Press Release on the upcoming Public Hearing of Application 006/2012 – *African Commission on Human and Peoples' Rights* v. *The Republic of Kenya*, from 27 to 28 November 2014, in Addis Ababa, Ethiopia," www.achpr.org/press/2014/11/d235.

[125] *ACHPR* v. *Kenya* (Provisional Measures Order), para. 3; *ACHPR* v. *Kenya* (Judgment), paras. 6–8.

[126] *ACHPR* v. *Kenya* (Provisional Measures Order), para. 4; *ACHPR* v. *Kenya* (Judgment), paras. 10, 101.

[127] *ACHPR* v. *Kenya* (Provisional Measures Order), para. 25.

[128] *ACHPR* v. *Kenya* (Judgment), para. 112.

factors including the Ogieks' "strong attachment with nature, particularly, land and the natural environment," with their survival being dependent on "unhindered access to and use of their traditional land and the natural resources thereon."[129] It then went on to find a violation of the right to land, and "consequential violations" of the rights to non-discrimination, freedom of religion, culture, free disposal of wealth and natural resources, and economic, social, and cultural development, in the context of environmental concerns advanced by the Kenyan government as justifications for interferences with these rights.[130] The findings are elaborated subsequently.

The African Court held that Ogieks have the right to occupy, use, and enjoy their ancestral land.[131] But it had to consider whether this right can be restricted in the public interest and whether the restriction is necessary and proportional as stipulated in Article 14 of the African Charter, since the Kenyan government had advanced "the preservation of the natural ecosystem" as justification for evicting the Ogieks from the Mau Forest.[132] The Court established that the environmental degradation in the forest was not due to the Ogieks' presence in it (as no evidence was provided by the government to support this) but because of "encroachments upon the land by other groups and government excisions for settlements and ill-advised logging concessions."[133] Put differently, the government was in fact responsible for much of the environmental degradation. Hence, the eviction of the Ogieks was not a necessary and proportionate measure to preserve the natural ecosystem of the Mau Forest.[134] It held further that the need to preserve the natural ecosystem of the forest "cannot, by any standard, serve as a reasonable and objective justification for the lack of recognition of the Ogieks' indigenous or tribal status and denying them the associated rights derived from such status."[135]

[129] Ibid., paras. 105–11.

[130] The Court did not find a violation of the right to life as it was not convinced that the "the sole fact of eviction and deprivation of economic, social and cultural rights" resulted in violation of the right to life since, despite adverse effect of the evictions on the decent existence of the Ogieks, a "causal connection between the evictions of the Ogieks by the [government] and the deaths alleged to have occurred as a result" was not established. Ibid., paras. 153, 155–6. This finding was also influenced by the distinction the Court made between the right to life in the physical sense and its existential understanding (i.e., the right to a decent existence), pointing out that Article 4 of the African Charter relates to the former. Ibid., para. 154.

[131] Ibid., para. 128. This was based on a reading of Article 14 of the African Charter together with Article 26 of the United Nations Declaration on the Rights of Indigenous Peoples on the right of indigenous people to own, use, develop, and control land and resources that they have occupied, traditionally owned, or used or acquired. Ibid., para. 126. The Court also found Article 14 right to be of both an individual and a collective nature. Ibid., para. 123.

[132] Ibid., paras. 129–30.

[133] Ibid., para. 130.

[134] Ibid., paras. 130, 131.

[135] Ibid., para. 145.

Also, because other similar groups' status had been recognized and the forest had been allocated to other people in a manner not compatible with environmental preservation, the Ogieks' right to non-discrimination was also found to have been violated.[136]

The link between the environment and "the practice and profession of religion" was also highlighted by the Court, particularly "in the context of traditional societies, where formal religious institutions often do not exist."[137] It emphasized that access to the natural environment and land is necessary for indigenous societies to enjoy freedom of religion. Hence, "[a]ny impediment to, or interference with accessing the natural environment, including land, severely constrains their ability to conduct or engage in religious rituals with considerable repercussion on the enjoyment of their freedom of worship."[138] The Court found the eviction of the Ogieks and the requirement of paying for a license in order to access the Mau Forest to be an interference with their freedom of worship.[139] This limitation on the right could not be justified since less restrictive means existed such as sensitization campaigns aimed at ensuring public health and respect for law and order.[140]

The Court further found interference with the Ogieks' right to culture – a collective and an individual right – on the basis that, despite the Ogieks' ensuring maintenance of the environment within their clan boundaries while undertaking their cultural practices, restrictions on access to the Mau Forest and their eviction from it affected their ability to preserve their traditional activities.[141] The Court then had to consider whether such interference was justifiable since the government had argued that the right to culture has to be balanced with environmental conservation for future generations. In this regard, the government made the following contentions: First, the "cultural rights of indigenous people such as the Ogieks may encompass activities related to natural resources, such as fishing or hunting which could have a negative impact on the environment and these must be balanced against other public interests."[142] Second, "the Ogieks no longer live as hunters and gatherers, thus, they cannot be said to conserve the environment. They have adopted new and modern ways of living, including building permanent structures, livestock keeping and farming which would have a serious negative impact on the forest if they are allowed to reside there."[143]

136 Ibid., paras. 145, 146.
137 Ibid., para. 164.
138 Ibid.
139 Ibid., para. 166.
140 Ibid., para. 167.
141 Ibid., paras. 177, 183, 190.
142 Ibid., para. 174.
143 Ibid., para. 175.

Unlike Article 14, Article 17 of the African Charter contains no restrictions, hence the Court considered the limitations in Article 27(1) and (2) of the African Charter.[144] The Court found insufficient evidence to support the contention relating to the transformation of the Ogieks' lifestyle.[145] While it found the restriction on the Ogieks' right to culture in order to preserve the natural environment of the Mau Forest to be justifiable "in principle" so as to safeguard the "common interest," the Court held that the government must adequately substantiate the need to protect such common interest, which it failed to do in the present case.[146] For example, as stated by the Court, the government spoke generally of certain cultural activities that are detrimental to the environment, without going into specifics on the activities and how they degrade the environment.[147] The Court thus held that the reason for protecting the natural environment was not a legitimate justification for interference with the right to culture of the Ogieks.[148]

The Court did not go into a detailed discussion of the right to freely dispose of wealth and natural resources. After recognizing that the notion of "peoples" applies in this case,[149] it held that on the basis of its finding a violation of the right to land (specifically, "the right to use *(usus)* and the right to enjoy the produce of the land *(fructus)*, which presuppose the right of access to and occupation of the land"), the right to enjoy and freely dispose of natural resources was accordingly violated.[150] In particular, "the Ogieks have been deprived of the right to enjoy and freely dispose of the abundance of food produced by the ancestral land."[151]

On the right to economic, social, and cultural development, the Court again stated that the term "peoples" applies to the Ogieks; thus, they are entitled to enjoy this right.[152] It held that the right must be read in light of Article 23 of the United Nations Declaration on the Rights of Indigenous Peoples, which accentuates the right of indigenous people "to determine and develop priorities and strategies for exercising their right to development," particularly to participate in economic and social programs affecting them.[153] The Court found a violation of the right to economic, social, and cultural development on the basis that the Ogieks were

[144] Ibid., para. 187. As indicated previously, Article 27 provides for individual duties toward one's "family and society, the State and other legally recognised communities and the international community" as well as having "due regard to right of others, collective security, morality and common interest" when exercising one's right.

[145] Ibid., paras. 185–6.

[146] Ibid., para. 188.

[147] Ibid., para. 189.

[148] Ibid.

[149] Ibid., paras. 195–9.

[150] Ibid., para. 201.

[151] Ibid.

[152] Ibid., para. 208.

[153] Ibid., para. 209.

evicted without effective consultation, the evictions had adverse impact on their economic, social, and cultural development, and they were not "actively involved in developing and determining health, housing and other economic and social programmes affecting them."[154]

Based on the finding of violations of African Charter provisions, the Court also found that the government had not taken adequate legislative and other measures to give effect to the violated rights and, therefore, was also in violation of its general obligation under Article 1 of the Charter "to undertake to adopt legislative and other measures to give effect to" the rights, duties, and freedoms enshrined in the Charter.[155] The Court then reserved its decision on reparations, which would be made after the parties have made submissions on reparations.[156] At the time of writing, the reparations decision had not been issued. It is worth noting, however, that the African Commission has called "on the Court to order reparations in this case which are equitable, fair and take full account of the extent of the suffering experienced by the Victims, as well as to take follow up measures to ensure that this order is implemented."[157]

The *Ogiek* judgment is quite significant – a landmark and historic judgment – as it not only accentuates the duty of states to recognize and protect the rights of indigenous groups and vulnerable ethnic communities but also, crucially, recognizes the key role of indigenous peoples in Africa in conserving and protecting land, natural resources, and the environment. It is clear from the judgment that environmental conservation and development policies cannot be at the expense of rights realization and enjoyment for vulnerable groups and communities.

There is also potential for ensuring accountability for violation of the right to a satisfactory, healthy, and sustainable environment through prosecution at the African regional level. Following the integration of the initially separate courts – the African Court and the African Court of Justice – as the African Court of Justice and Human Rights, and the recent decision to create a criminal section within the joint court, accountability for violations of environmental rights resulting from trafficking in hazardous waste and illicit exploitation of natural resources can also be achieved through prosecution, once the Protocol on Amendments to the Protocol on the Statute of the African Court of Justice and Human Rights

[154] Ibid., paras. 210–211.
[155] Ibid., paras. 214–217.
[156] Ibid., paras. 222–3 and 227.
[157] African Commission on Human and Peoples' Rights, "Press Statement of the African Commission on Human and Peoples' Rights following the handing down of the judgement in Application 006/2012 by the African Court" (Arusha, Tanzania, May 26, 2017), available at www.achpr.org/press/2017/05/d358. The statement also addresses the complementary relationship between the African Court and the Commission.

(Amended African Court Protocol), as well as the joint court itself, comes into force/operation.[158] Trafficking in hazardous waste and illicit exploitation of natural resources are recognized as international crimes under the Amended African Court Protocol.[159] Further, the Amended African Court Protocol is not limited to individual criminal liability but also makes provision for corporate criminal liability where there is corporate intention, as shown from a corporation's policy, to do an act constituting an offense.[160]

Promotion Through Special Mechanisms: The Working Group on Extractive Industries, Environment and Human Rights Violations

The legal basis in the African Charter for the African Commission's establishment of special mechanisms for the promotion of rights is Article 46(1), which requires the Commission to promote human and people's rights through, *inter alia*, collecting documents, undertaking studies and researches, organizing conferences and seminars, disseminating information, and formulating and adopting principles and rules. The aspects provided for in Article 46(1) correspond with the mandate of special mechanisms. Rule 23(1) of the African Commission's Rules of Procedure further stipulates that "[t]he Commission may create subsidiary mechanisms such as special rapporteurs, committees, and *working groups*."

Of specific relevance to the present chapter is the Working Group on Extractive Industries, Environment and Human Rights Violations. Its establishment was informed by reported cases of violations of human rights by companies operating in the extractive industries in Africa.[161] The Group is thus mandated to, *inter alia*, monitor, conduct research, and report on the impact of extractive industries/activities on human rights in the African Charter.[162] It is also mandated to "[r]esearch specific issues pertaining to the right of all peoples to freely dispose of their wealth and natural resources and *to a general satisfactory environment favourable to their development*."[163]

The Working Group has been praised for the research it has conducted, its exchange of information with other stakeholders, its development of resources, and its contribution to an understanding of the rights to freely dispose of natural resources and to a general satisfactory environment.[164] It has also held regional

158 Protocol on Amendments to the Protocol on the Statute of the African Court of Justice and Human Rights, June 27, 2014, not in force.

159 Ibid., arts. 28L and 28L *bis*.

160 Ibid., art. 46C.

161 Miriam Azu, "A Review of the Work of the African Commission's Working Group on Extractive Industries, Environment and Human Rights Violations in Africa," *AfricLaw* (2016).

162 African Commission res. 148.

163 Ibid. (emphasis added).

164 Azu, "Review."

consultations to evaluate and strengthen the implementation of environmental and related rights. Through these actions, the Working Group has raised awareness of environmental and related rights and correlating state obligations as well as drawn attention to environmental challenges in Africa.

Furthermore, it has been reported that the Working Group has developed a draft toolkit on the right of African peoples to prevent development of their natural resources or development processes that affect their environment, lives, and/or livelihoods without their free, prior, and informed consent.[165] Simply put, it is an empowerment tool that accentuates the active involvement of African peoples in development processes that affect them. Through this, the Group has promoted due process (including consultation, participation, and informed consent) in relation to activities that could negatively impact environmental and human rights as an imperative.[166]

The Working Group has recently been tasked with the elaboration of reporting guidelines in relation to extractive industries that would adequately guide states parties on the information they should incorporate in their periodic reports to the African Commission.[167] This would enable the Commission to better monitor compliance by states parties with the standards in the African Charter, as the lack of such guidelines is seen to have undermined proper monitoring of compliance.[168]

The Working Group has, however, been criticized for: (a) failing "to inform the African Commission on the possible liability of non-state actors in certain instances of human rights abuses" (an example being the liability of mining companies that were implicated in the Marikana killings of miners by South African police in 2012); and (b) failing to report comprehensively on its work.[169] As with other regional institutions and mechanisms, the challenges of underfunding (thus limited resources), lack of cooperation of African states in relation to country visits, and conflicting schedules have hampered the Group's activities and ability to contribute more to the promotion of environmental rights.[170] Until these challenges as well as the reporting challenge are addressed, the impact of the activities of the Working Group will remain limited and distant.

CONCLUSION

The existing regional legal and institutional framework on environmental rights and protection and the explicit recognition of a right to a satisfactory or healthy environment in the African regional human rights system are powerful tools for addressing Africa's environmental concerns. Although the right to a satisfactory environment is

165 Ibid.
166 Ibid.
167 African Commission on Human and Peoples' Rights res. 364 (November 4, 2016).
168 Ibid.
169 Ibid.
170 Ibid.

vaguely phrased in the African Charter, the African Commission has sought to give content to this right, though to a limited extent, as it has not only had limited opportunities to elaborate on the right but has failed to make effective use (in relation to adequate content development of the right) of the limited opportunities. The decisions of the Commission linking environmental protection to human rights have focused on the rights of tribal or indigenous peoples whose environmental rights have been affected due to extractive activities or that have been affected by forced removals from their land for environmental purposes.

The practical usefulness of the African Commission's efforts to deal with environmental degradation and violations of rights for environmental purposes has been limited by the challenge of non-compliance (or delayed/partial compliance) with its decisions by African states and its limited regulatory powers.[171] However, this does not diminish the value of the Commission's decisions, as has been emphasized in relation to the *SERAC* case.[172]

Further, as shown in this chapter, there is potential within the judicial mechanisms at the African regional level to fortify African Commission's efforts. The African Court has accentuated the important role of indigenous communities in environmental protection and the conservation of land and natural resources. It has also shown in the *Ogiek* judgment that mere assertion of environmental degradation concerns (even if justifiable in principle) cannot be used as justification for violation of the rights of vulnerable communities.

Despite being limited, the African Commission's approach and the African Court's provisional measures order and judgment are progressive and could be useful in the development of the right to a clean, satisfactory, healthy, and sustainable environment at the international level, especially as they authenticate the view that such a right can be made effective and accentuate the role that indigenous communities can play in this regard. In developing an international standard on this right, it is clear from this chapter that the right to a satisfactory or healthy environment cannot be dealt with in isolation due to its normative unity with other rights. Also, environmental protection can be achieved either directly or indirectly through rights that are intrinsically linked to the right to a satisfactory or healthy environment. The African Commission's jurisprudence, for example, identifies some of these rights that are interlinked with environmental rights as explained earlier. It is important for such linkages to be explicitly recognized in an international framework on the right to a healthy or satisfactory environment. The earlier discussion has also identified components of the right and various related obligations, which can inform the framing of the right and correlating state obligations at the international level.

[171] Malgosia Fitzmaurice, "Environmental Degradation," in Daniel Moeckli, Sangeeta Shah, and Sandesh Sivakumaran (eds.), *International Human Rights Law* (2014), p. 593.

[172] See Kaniye S. A. Ebeku, "The Right to a Satisfactory Environment and the African Commission," *African Human Rights Law Journal* 3 (2003), p. 165.

5

The European Court of Human Rights and International Environmental Law

*Ole W. Pedersen**

INTRODUCTION

In the context of an increase in policy initiatives and scholarship focusing on environmental rights, one notable factor – most notable by its omission – stands out: the fact that international human rights law and international environmental law have very little to say explicitly about one such right. So far, the right to a healthy environment (in variable forms) is only unequivocally provided for in regional human rights and environmental instruments and in the domestic constitutions of countries. In this dearth of explicit international endorsement of the right to a healthy environment, the European Court of Human Rights is, however, often considered a positive outlier. The reasons for this are obvious, although at times overlooked. Notwithstanding the absence of any reference to the environment in the European Convention on Human Rights, the Court has nevertheless succeeded in carving out an elaborate and extensive body of case law that all but in name provides for a right to a healthy environment.[1]

The premise of this development rests, as do many of the doctrines developed in the decades since the Convention's inception, on the Court's plea that the Convention is to be interpreted as a living instrument in light of "present day conditions."[2] As early as 1991, the Court thus observed, in *Fredin*, that "in today's society the protection of the environment is an increasingly important consideration."[3]

* Reader of Environmental Law, Newcastle Law School.

[1] For a brief overview of the Court's case law, see Council of Europe, *Manual on Human Rights and the Environment* (2012).

[2] See, e.g., *Tyrer* v. *United Kingdom*, No. 5856/72 (European Court of Human Rights, 1978) and Alan Boyle, "Human Rights or Environmental Rights? A Reassessment," *Fordham Environmental Law Review* 18 (2007), pp. 471, 499 (noting that the Convention is perceived as an "exceptionally vibrant" instrument).

[3] *Fredin* v. *Sweden*, No. 12033/86 (European Court of Human Rights, 1991).

This point is now well beyond dispute – so much so that in the recent *Dubetska* v. *Ukraine* case, the Ukrainian government did not contest that it had obligations to address environmental problems under the Convention.[4] Accordingly, today the Court's case law thus expands to issues covering industrial pollution, noise, natural disasters, and flooding. Importantly, Convention responsibility may now be triggered on account of the presence of risk of harm as opposed to mere *ex post* application of the Convention to materialized harms. Such willingness to allow societal realities to influence its interpretation has won the Court many admirers in the epistemic communities surrounding international environmental law and human rights law.

The aspect of the Court's case law, however, that is at times overlooked relates to the fact that on closer reading it contains features that arguably serve to restrict the application of the otherwise progressive willingness to entertain environmental claims under the Convention. The first of these features is that the Court is significantly more likely to find against a state where the responding state has, one way or another, failed to implement, apply, or adhere to its own domestic environmental standards and rules. That is, the Court is more likely to uphold an environmental claim based on a "rule of law" type argument.[5] A second restricting feature relates to the fact that the Court is increasingly keen to stress that its jurisdiction is that of an international court, as opposed to a domestic tribunal hearing a full merits-based review of the relevant issue. Thus, the Court has made clear that by reference to its self-imposed doctrine of margin of appreciation, when it comes to environmental decision making, contracting states enjoy a wide degree of discretion.[6] Consequently, the Court's jurisdiction is primarily one of supervision. This deference is coupled with an argument that the most recent case law from the Court arguably signals a slight retreat in its otherwise progressive jurisprudence. This retreat is most notable from the recent decision of *Hardy and Maile* v. *United Kingdom*,[7] in which the Court explicitly refrained from expanding on the parts of its previous case law relating to the precautionary principle.[8]

In light of this dichotomy of, on the one hand, a progressive and in parts principled case law and, on the other hand, a recent retreat from this jurisprudence in certain respects, it becomes relevant to consider what impact the potential promulgation of a right to a healthy environment in international law might have

4 *Dubetska and Others* v. *Ukraine*, No. 30499/03 (European Court of Human Rights, 2011), p. 95.

5 Ole W. Pedersen, "The Ties that Bind: The Environment, the European Convention on Human Rights and the Rule of Law," *European Public Law* 16(4) (2009), p 571.

6 *Powell and Rayner* v. *United Kingdom*, No. 9310/81 (European Court of Human Rights, 1990), p. 44.

7 *Hardy and Maile* v. *United Kingdom*, No. 31965/07 (European Court of Human Rights, 2012). See also Ole W. Pedersen, "Environmental Risks, Rights and Black Swans," *Environmental Law Review* 15 (2003), p. 55.

8 In *Tătar* v. *Romania*, No. 67021/01 (European Court of Human Rights, 2009), the Court had specifically relied upon the precautionary principle when finding against Romania in incidents relating to the infamous mining projects in Baia Mare.

on the Court's case law. Such a consideration will necessarily have an element of speculation attached to it, but in light of the recent work of the United Nations Special Rapporteur on human rights and the environment – finding, among other things, that the relationship between human rights and the environment is in need of greater conceptual clarity – this is a price worth paying.[9] The chapter proceeds in the following way: The next section briefly discusses the main elements of the Court's case law and argues that the Court's emphasis on procedural environmental rights plays an important role. The chapter then goes on to consider the ways in which a right to a healthy environment could potentially be facilitated in international law, before discussing what the potential impacts of this development might be on the Court's case law.

THE ENVIRONMENT AND THE EUROPEAN COURT OF HUMAN RIGHTS

Instead of recapping in specific terms all of the Court's environmental case law, this section will examine a series of developments and principles developed in the Court's more recent jurisprudence.[10] As noted, the Court's environmental case law now establishes that where acts of physical pollution attain a certain level of severity, to the extent that there is an "actual interference with the applicant's private sphere,"[11] application of the Convention is triggered. For the most part, this tends to implicate Articles 2 (right to life) and 8 (right to respect for private and family life). It is worth noting that although the substantive scopes of these two provisions are materially different, the Court has held that "in the context of dangerous activities the scope of the positive obligations under Article 2 of the Convention largely overlap with those under Article 8."[12] This gives rise to an important element of the case law: Namely, that the Court's jurisprudence is not necessarily restricted to cases where the material harm has manifested itself but also to situations where there is a risk of exposure to such harm. One prominent example is *Brânduşe* v. *Romania*, where the applicant complained of the risk to which he was exposed as a result of being incarcerated in a prison placed in close proximity to a landfill site.[13] Despite

[9] John H. Knox, *Report of the Independent Expert on the Issue of Human Rights Obligations Relating to the Enjoyment of a Safe, Clean, Healthy and Sustainable Environment: Preliminary Report*, UN Doc. A/HRC/22/43 (December 24, 2012).

[10] For a review of older case law, see Ole W. Pedersen, "European Environmental Human Rights and Environmental Rights: A Long Time Coming?" *Georgetown International Environmental Law Review* 21 (2008), p. 73.

[11] *Fadeyeva* v. *Russia*, No. 55723/00 (European Court of Human Rights, 2005), pp. 69–70.

[12] *Budayeva and Others* v. *Russia*, Nos. 15339/02, 21166/02, 20058/02, 11673/02 and 15343/02 (European Court of Human Rights, 2008), p. 133.

[13] *Brânduşe* v. *Romania*, No. 6586/03 (European Court of Human Rights, 2009). See also *Di Sarno* v. *Italy*, No. 30765/08 (European Court of Human Rights, 2012), p. 108 ("Article 8 may be relied on even in the absence of any evidence of a serious danger to people's health").

his having suffered no physical harm, the Court held that the applicant was entitled to information allowing him to assess the specific environmental risks posed by the landfill site.

In subsequent cases, including *Tătar* v. *Romania*, the Court has held that where individuals are exposed to material risks (be it from pollution or natural hazards), the responding government is under a positive obligation to put in place regulatory initiatives that regulate the licensing, start-up, operation, and control of the hazardous activity, which must include appropriate public surveys and studies allowing the public to assess the risks and effects associated with the relevant activities.[14] This aspect is significant as it goes some way toward addressing the criticism that the application of human rights law to environmental problems is exclusively reactive. Further significance is derived from the fact that when deciding what activity or risk gives rise to the responsibility, the Court has found that the fact that an activity is subject to the requirement of an environmental impact assessment (EIA) in domestic law is enough to consider it a material risk.[15] In reaching this conclusion, the Court has found support, albeit only on one occasion, in the precautionary principle and its inherent emphasis on the desire to mitigate certain risks.[16] Importantly, however, this line of reasoning is restricted by two factors, one which is perhaps somewhat evident and the other which may well be a disappointment to those who think that the Court ought to expand its case law even further.

The first restrictive element relates to the fact that where a responding state has put in place a regulatory system designed to mitigate risks and where this system allows for the participation and making of representations of those exposed to the risk, the Court is less inclined to find a breach (except where, as noted, the state has entirely ignored this system of rules). While this may seem obvious, it suggests that although the Court is in part willing to expand the reach of its case law, it simultaneously sets a seemingly high threshold for the application of this law once a domestic response has been adopted. Consider, for example, the Court's decisions in *Hatton* v. *United Kingdom*[17] and *Hardy and Maile* v. *United Kingdom*.[18] The first case centered on complaints relating to a government-approved scheme for night flights at the biggest airport in the United Kingdom. In light of the opportunities afforded the applicants when it came to making representations regarding the scheme, the Court found that no violation of the Convention had taken place (although a robust dissent was issued by a minority of the Grand Chamber).

[14] *Tătar* v. *Romania*, p. 88.

[15] See *Taşkin and Others* v. *Turkey*, No. 46117/99 (European Court of Human Rights, 2006); Christopher Hilson, "Risk and the European Convention on Human Rights: Towards a New Approach," in Catherine Barnard and Oke Okudu (eds.), *Cambridge Yearbook of European Legal Studies 2008–9* (Hart Publishing, 2009).

[16] *Tătar* v. *Romania*.

[17] *Hatton and Others* v. *United Kingdom*, No. 36022/97 (European Court of Human Rights, 2003).

[18] *Hardy and Maile* v. *United Kingdom*.

Similarly, in *Hardy and Maile* the applicants sought to impress upon the Court the perceived failure of the UK government in properly managing a potential risk arising from activities relating to the shipping, docking, and loading of liquefied natural gas (LNG) tankers near their homes. In reaching the conclusion that no violation had taken place, the Court specifically took note of the very extensive regulatory framework in place in the United Kingdom (including several licensing regimes) governing facilities of the relevant type. Consequently, where a regulatory system is in place and designed to deal with a particular risk, it seems that the Court reverts to its default position of affording states a wide margin of appreciation, thereby relying on its supervisory jurisdiction. It must be said, however, that the specific characteristics of a given regulatory system are far from well defined, and the Court does not offer much in the way of detail regarding when such a system can be said to fulfill its *Tătar* minimum requirements.[19]

The second, perhaps more implied, restrictive element encountered upon closer reading of the Court's case law is the reluctance of the Court to develop further the precautionary emphasis first intimated in its *Tătar* decision. As will be discussed, the Court's reliance on the precautionary principle – notwithstanding its highly contingent nature[20] – could have added a potentially significant scope to the Court's jurisprudence. However, in *Hardy and Maile*, the Court simply ignored the principle, in spite of the explicit invitation by the applicants to interpret Article 8 in light thereof. From this it is hard to suppress a sense that the Court is retreating from the high-water mark of the *Tătar* decision and its precautionary tone. If this is the case (and only time can tell), it suggests that the Court's case law may well be at a standstill or, at the least, that the Court has reached the end point of how far it is willing to expand the Convention to cover environmental issues. In this light, might an internationally recognized right to a healthy environment offer scope for further developments?

Before embarking on a discussion of the potential impacts of such a recognition on the case law of the European Court of Human Rights, it is worth briefly considering how a right to a healthy environment could be promulgated.[21] The most obvious way to do so would be for the parties to one of the main international human rights treaties to adopt an additional protocol providing for a right to a healthy environment. This could, for example, take the form of an additional protocol to the International Covenant on Economic, Social and Cultural Rights (ICESCR). In light of the protocol to the Covenant adopted in 2008 (coming into force in 2013), which established an individual complaints mechanism, this approach is not as farfetched as perhaps it once was. Having said that, the lack of

[19] Pedersen, "Environmental Risks, Rights and Black Swans."

[20] Ole W. Pedersen, "From Abundance to Indeterminacy: The Precautionary Principle and Its Two Camps of Custom," *Transnational Environmental Law* 3 (2014), p. 323.

[21] See also Alan Boyle, "Human Rights and the Environment: Where Next?" *European Journal of International Law* 23(3) (2012), p. 631.

widespread support for the 2008 protocol arguably points to a situation where a new additional protocol on the right to a healthy environment is unlikely to receive extensive support.

Of course, another option would be for the UN General Assembly to adopt a declaration reaffirming the link between human rights and the environment. This could, for example, be modeled on the Declaration on the Rights of Indigenous Peoples adopted in 2007 or, less ambitiously, take the form of the resolution adopted in 2010, recognizing the human right to water and sanitation.[22] Notwithstanding the lack of lawmaking power of the General Assembly, the comparison with the Declaration on the Rights of Indigenous Peoples is particularly important, since it is well established that the Declaration contains provisions that seemingly represent customary law.[23] A UN General Assembly resolution could therefore serve to significantly underscore the right to a healthy environment.

Nevertheless, there are important reasons for assuming that the likelihood of any of the scenarios coming to fruition is low. The primary one is that there is little to suggest that the majority of states are necessarily interested in expressly facilitating (or taking formal steps toward defining) a right to a healthy environment, be it in binding or non-binding form. Support for such skepticism is found most recently in the negotiations surrounding the Paris Agreement, adopted at the 21st Conference of the Parties to the UN Framework Convention on Climate Change.[24] Initial attempts were made to secure the inclusion of a reference to the need for states to protect and respect human rights obligations when taking actions to address climate change in the substantive provisions of the Agreement. However, as a result of resistance, the reference to human rights obligations was moved to the Agreement's preamble.[25] Whether this relocation will have a substantive effect is beyond the point in this context. But suffice it to say that it evidently highlights the unease that some states still harbor when it comes to the attempt to formally and expressly link human rights and the environment.

Further support for the argument that the adoption of an international right to a healthy environment is unlikely is found in the experience gained from the attempts by the Council of Europe's Parliamentary Assembly to adopt an additional protocol providing for a right to a healthy environment.[26] Such attempts have been generally unsuccessful to date, having been rejected by the Committee of Ministers. The Aarhus Convention on Access to Information, Public Participation

[22] General Assembly res. 64/292 (July 28, 2010).

[23] S. James Anaya, *Indigenous Peoples in International Law*, 2d ed. (Oxford University Press, 2004), p. 61.

[24] Paris Agreement, December 12, 2015, in force November 4, 2016, UN Doc. FCCC/CP/2015/19.

[25] See Lavanya Rajamani, Chapter 13; Sumudu Atapattu, Chapter 14.

[26] See, e.g., Council of Europe Parliamentary Assembly, Environment and Human Rights, 24th sess., rec. 1614 (2003).

in Decision-Making and Access to Justice in Environmental Matters, adopted by the UN Economic Commission for Europe in 1998,[27] does refer to "the right of every person of present and future generations to live in an environment adequate to his or her health and well-being," but it characterizes this language as the "objective" of the agreement. Moreover, the UK government issued a statement upon signature that it understands the reference "to the 'right' of every person 'to live in an environment adequate to his or her health and well-being' to express an aspiration which motivated the negotiation of this Convention."

Having said that, the move toward adopting an international right to a healthy environment has found some success in regions other than Europe, including Africa and Latin America.[28] In addition, even where attempts to promulgate an explicit right have been defeated, this has not deterred judicial development of the right. On the contrary, in the European context, as already discussed, the European Court of Human Rights has not been inhibited from developing its case law in this respect. In fact, it may well be argued that the absence of an explicit and specific right to a healthy environment in international law has had very little negative impact on the jurisprudential development of such a right (at least in Europe). Instead, it seems that international courts and tribunals have so far contributed significantly more to the development of the environmental rights agenda than have international treaty organizations.

Notwithstanding the low likelihood of a right to a healthy environment being adopted in a global agreement, it is useful to consider what, if any, effect such a right might have on the European Court and its environmental rights jurisprudence. A possible glimpse of this is gained from examining the way in which the Court thus far has engaged with international law generally – and international environmental law, more specifically – in its environmental jurisprudence. From this, it quickly and unsurprisingly becomes evident that the Court does indeed rely on international law when interpreting the Convention. In *Loizidou* v. *Turkey*, the Court thus held that the "Convention must be interpreted in the light of the rules of interpretation [i.e.] the Vienna Convention [on the Law of Treaties]" and that this includes "any relevant rules of international law applicable in the relations between the parties."[29]

[27] Aarhus Convention on Access to Information, Public Participation in Decision Making and Access to Justice in Environmental Matters, June 25, 1998, in force October 21, 2001, 2161 UNTS 447.

[28] See African Charter on Human and Peoples' Rights, June 27, 1981, in force October 21, 1986, 1520 UNTS 217; Additional Protocol to the American Convention on Human Rights in the Area of Economic, Social and Cultural Rights: Protocol of San Salvador, November 17, 1988, in force November 16, 1999, 28 ILM 161. On the African experience, see Lilian Chenwi, Chapter 4.

[29] *Loizidou* v. *Turkey*, No. 15318/89 (European Court of Human Rights, 1996), p. 43. See also *Golder* v. *United Kingdom*, No. 4451/70 (European Court of Human Rights, 1975), in which the Court made the same argument notwithstanding the fact that the Vienna Convention was not yet in force at that point in time. Instead the Court noted that the relevant provisions of the Convention (Articles 31–3) "enunciate in essence generally accepted principles of international law." Ibid., p. 29.

What is more, when it comes to specific subsets of the Court's jurisprudence, there is evidence to suggest that the Court is particularly keen on utilizing international law as an interpretive background.[30] One specific subset of the Court's case law where this is particularly evident is that of its environmental jurisprudence.

For example, in *Taşkin* v. *Turkey*, the Court made explicit reference to both the 1992 Rio Declaration and the 1998 Aarhus Convention. This is significant for a number of reasons. First and most obvious, the Rio Declaration is not in itself a legally binding instrument. Second, Turkey is not a party to the Aarhus Convention and its relevance for a claim against Turkey is not therefore immediately evident, except to the extent that the Convention can be said to reflect general international law.[31] It certainly does not seem to reflect "international law [which is] applicable in relations between the parties."[32] Moreover, in other cases the Court has referred to the attempts by the Council of Europe's Parliamentary Assembly to adopt an additional protocol on environmental rights despite the fact that these were, as noted, unsuccessful.[33] The Court has since gone on to reaffirm its reliance on the Aarhus Convention in cases against parties as well as non-parties.[34]

Elsewhere, the Court has made extensive references to European Union law, which for all intents and purposes is international law from the point of view of the European Convention system. This is most striking in the *Tătar* decision, where the Court refers to the precautionary principle as found not just in the Rio Declaration but also in what is now the Treaty for the Functioning of the European Union's environmental chapter (i.e., forming part of the primary EU law that confers environmental competences on the Union).[35] Significantly, the Court also referred to an EU Commission Communication relating to the operation of safe mining, i.e., a policy document with no self-standing legal force.[36] The trend of relying on international environmental law or EU environmental law seemingly reached a peak in the *Di Sarno* decision, relating to the maladministration of waste management activities in the Campania region of Italy.[37] Here the Court relied extensively on European Union law (in the form of a series of directives on waste management) as well as the case law from the Court of Justice for the European Union (CJEU), which had found Italy in violation of its obligations under EU law. The European

30 See Magdalena Forowicz, *The Reception of International Law in the European Court of Human Rights* (Oxford University Press, 2010).

31 See Pedersen, "European Environmental Human Rights and Environmental Rights: A Long Time Coming?" for a discussion on whether the Convention's emphasis on procedural rights serves as a basis for a regional custom to emerge.

32 *Loizidou* v. *Turkey*, p. 43.

33 *Atanasov* v. *Bulgaria*, No. 12853/03 (European Court of Human Rights, 2011), pp. 55–7.

34 See *Demir and Baykara* v. *Turkey*, No. 34503/97 (European Court of Human Rights, 2008), p. 83; *Okyay et al.* v. *Turkey*, No. 36220/97 (European Court of Human Rights, 2005), p. 52; *Atanasov* v. *Bulgaria*, pp. 55–7.

35 *Tătar* v. *Romania*, p. 69.

36 Ibid.

37 *Di Sarno* v. *Italy*.

Court of Human Rights also, as now seems settled practice, relied on the Aarhus Convention as well as the Draft Articles of the International Law Commission on state responsibility (in the context of dismissing Italy's claim that its failures were justified by references to *force majeure*).[38]

What role the references and reliance on international law and EU instruments play is not, however, always easy to discern. Often these references are merely listed in the part of a particular judgment titled "relevant international materials" or "relevant international texts on the right to a healthy environment." At times, the Court's seemingly precise way of reasoning is not clear and there is very little to suggest that the Court engages in any in-depth analysis of the different international instruments and the responsibilities they impose on states. As noted, the Court rarely makes any explicit reference to the exact legal status of the international norms nor does it explain the relevance of these norms to the particular facts in a case. Presumably, the Court makes these references for two related though different reasons. First, one would assume that the references to international rules and EU law are made in the attempt to clarify the provisions of the European Convention and the Court's interpretation thereof. A second reason may well be that the references to developments in international and regional environmental law serve to aid the Court in accentuating the importance of certain norms (e.g., environmental rights). This latter point was prevalent in the robust dissenting opinion delivered by the minority in the Grand Chamber's decision in *Hatton*.[39]

As noted, however, this is not always evident from the case law itself. What is more, if indeed these assumptions are correct, it would suit the Court to develop its specific reasoning in more detail. As it stands, the Court's attempt to develop the Convention in light of other instruments, while admirable, rests on somewhat vague jurisprudential and doctrinal grounds. For example, it is not necessarily a given that the CJEU's findings relating to the EU's rather technical and detailed waste directives need be particularly persuasive when it comes to the interpretation of the European Convention. A CJEU decision – delivered in a regulatory framework and based on its own underlying reasons and assumptions favoring compliance from EU Member States – need not necessarily set a guiding threshold for the European Court of Human Rights, whose task it is to secure observance of fundamental human rights. (This is not to intimate that a right to a healthy environment ought not form part of the corpus on international human rights law, but merely to highlight that the two legal systems rest, in part, on different foundations.)[40] Similarly, it is not necessarily evident that the European Court needs to rely on the rules

[38] Ibid., pp. 111–12. In the end, the Court found Italy to be in violation of the substantive obligations of Article 8 but not the procedural obligations.

[39] *Hatton* v. *United Kingdom*.

[40] See also *Opinion C-2/13 of the Court on Accession of the European Union to the European Convention for the Protection of Human Rights and Fundamental Freedoms* (European Court of Justice, 2014).

on state liability and *force majeure*, as these are developed by the International Law Commission. For example, there may well be good reasons why the Court would want to interpret *force majeure* in the context of the European Convention in a narrower manner than the one provided for by the International Law Commission's Draft Articles (not that it did so in the *Di Sarno* case). The European Convention, after all, seeks to regulate the fundamental obligations owed by a contracting party to its citizens, whereas the Draft Articles confine themselves to the relationship between states in accordance with the principle of good neighborliness. What can persuasively be said to constitute *force majeure* in one context may not necessarily do so in the other. Thus, when simply applying these rules and norms (thereby ignoring their inherent contingency), the Court is arguably guilty of simplifying matters, resulting in its case law lacking doctrinal rigor.

Whatever the specific means of referring to and relying upon international, regional, and EU environmental law when interpreting the Convention, it is evident that the European Court of Human Rights is willing and keen to make use of external sources and authorities. In the context of the potential of a possible right to a healthy environment in international law, it therefore seems uncontentious to argue that such a right might well provide further interpretive background for the Court. On one reading, it may even provide an impetus to develop the Court's case law further in light of the slight retreat, as discussed. Similarly, it may not make much of a difference, from the Court's point of view, whether a right takes the form of a binding international legal instrument or non-binding declaration or resolution; the Court has shown willingness to rely on different types of international norms. On the other hand, it seems equally uncontentious to highlight that the explicit lack of one such right has not proved to be a hindrance for the Court. On the contrary. And, as a result, the potential low likelihood of the international community agreeing on a substantive right as part of an international legally binding agreement may, from the Court's point of view, not prove terribly important. This ambivalent dichotomy of, on the one hand, the ability of an international right to spur on the Court's case law, and, on the other, the fact that the lack thereof has not prevented the Court from developing its environmental jurisprudence, perhaps seems unsatisfactory for those favoring the adoption of a right in international law. For the Court's environmental rights case law succeeds in serving as an important reminder of the evident link between the enjoyment of basic environmental conditions and human rights, while, at the same time, highlighting that this case law has been developed against a background of international legal silence on the issue (at least in a positivist legal tradition). In doing so, the Court's case law serves to simultaneously inspire as well as frustrate.

CONCLUSION

In the context of the potential creation of a right to a healthy environment, this chapter has sought to establish what impact one such right might have on the case law of the European Court of Human Rights relating to the environment. Without doubt, the Court's case law represents a significant contribution to the development of environmental rights in international law. In carving out this distinct body of case law, the Court has, importantly, come to take inspiration from international and regional (mainly EU) environmental law. In this light, there may well be scope for a future right to a healthy environment under international law to further expand the Court's case law. This development would no doubt be welcomed by those favoring a stronger application of the human rights system to environmental problems – especially considering some of the Court's more recent cases which arguably suggest a slight retreat in its "progressive" environmental jurisprudence. On the other hand, it is hard to ignore the fact that the development of the Court's environmental jurisprudence in its present form has taken place without any explicit right to a healthy environment in international law, binding on European states. Irrespective of whether the right is adopted in international law and irrespective of which direction the Court decides to take its environmental jurisprudence, it would suit the Court to carefully consider the interpretive means and doctrines utilized when relying on international and regional environmental law instruments.

6

Complexities and Uncertainties in Matters of Human Rights and the Environment

Identifying the Judicial Role

*Dinah Shelton**

There are known knowns; there are things we know we know. We also know there are known unknowns; that is to say we know there are some things we do not know. But there are also unknown unknowns – the ones we don't know we don't know.

Donald Rumsfeld**

Ensuring a clean and healthy environment consistent with the enjoyment of human rights requires the adoption of laws and regulations to control pollution and limit the unsustainable exploitation of natural resources. To be legitimate and transparent, this process should be based on agreed and scientifically-based definitions of what constitutes "pollution" and "unsustainable" exploitation. Then, relevant agencies or other governing bodies should apply the law and evaluate each proposed project or activity within their jurisdiction to assess possible impacts on the environment and on persons who may be negatively affected. Legitimacy and transparency also require that the public and all those involved in the approval process be fully informed of the risks of harm and be able to make their voices heard before a decision is taken.

Some states lack the proper regulatory framework to prevent environmental harm that can infringe human rights. Other countries have enacted comprehensive environmental laws, including constitutional guarantees of environmental quality as a human right, but fail to enforce them. Inadequacies in either lawmaking or enforcement can endanger the natural environment and limit the ability of members of society to exercise and enjoy their human rights.[1] In addition to infringing the now widely

* Manatt/Ahn Professor of International Law Emeritus, George Washington University Law School.

** *Little Oxford Dictionary of Quotations*, 4th edn. (OUP, 2008), p. 212.

1 The Inter-American Commission on Human Rights has emphasized that each state has a duty to enforce its internal law and its international commitments in the field of environmental protection; although the right to development implies that the state is free to exploit its natural resources and grant concessions, the authorities must apply and enforce the legal provisions that protect the rights to life, health, and to live in a healthy environment. Lack of regulation,

guaranteed right to a satisfactory environmental quality, deficits in environmental law and policy may affect other rights, including the rights to life, health, adequate standard of living (including the right to safe drinking water and sanitation), information, public participation in decision making, property, privacy and home life, culture, access to justice and redress, and freedoms of association and religion.

Litigation is a common response to governance failures. In the context of human rights and the environment, cases may aim to prevent a project or activity from receiving approval, to challenge approval that has been given and thus enjoin initiation or continuation of a project, or to obtain redress when harm has occurred or is imminent. Some litigants may go further and challenge a particular law or regulation as contrary to human rights, rather than attacking the lack of proper application of the law or failings in enforcement. In hearing such matters, judges on national and international tribunals often face significant challenges and questions about their role in allowing matters to be litigated (e.g., issues of standing, private rights of action, and political questions), admitting and evaluating scientific evidence, establishing the appropriate standard of review, applying the precautionary and other environmental principles, and designing redress. Often cases pose sensitive questions of democratic governance that affect the degree of scrutiny or deference courts should afford when legislative or administrative decisions are challenged after they have been adopted through a properly-conducted process.

This chapter examines some of the key problems facing judges in cases where the applicant or plaintiff alleges that governmental action or inaction has resulted in environmental harm or risk that infringes or threatens the enjoyment of human rights. The discussion provides examples from national and international courts because many of the issues the judges face are similar, although jurisdictional limits are often more restrictive in international tribunals. The sections in this chapter follow the normal sequence of litigation, first considering challenges to the admissibility of claims, then issues of evidence, including the impact of scientific uncertainty and burden of proof. The discussion then turns to application of legal principles, such as the precautionary principle, questioning how it should impact cases involving the environment and human rights.

Throughout, the chapter considers the tension between judicial deference to democratic decision making and judicial scrutiny based on the need to protect the rights of those in the minority, who may be the subject of discrimination or exclusion, as well as the interests of those who bear a disproportionate burden when the environment is harmed for the gain of others, including society as a whole. To give one example, polluting industries that benefit society with jobs and help fulfill

inappropriate regulations or the lack of supervision in the application of the law can cause serious impacts on the environment, which thereafter translate into human rights violations. Inter-American Commission on Human Rights (IACHR), *Report on the Human Rights Situation in Ecuador*, OEA/Ser.L/V/II.96, Doc. 10 rev., (April 24, 1997), chapters 8–9.

economic rights may be placed deliberately, through zoning or other regulations, in predominantly minority communities, negatively affecting the rights to health and life of the residents, because the minority may not be informed and cannot outvote the majority or otherwise prevent the industry placement. Litigation alleging racial or other prohibited discrimination may be the only recourse.

WHEN SHOULD COURTS HEAR HUMAN RIGHTS CLAIMS BASED ON ENVIRONMENTAL RISK OR HARM?

Courts and tribunals are established to decide disputes that fall within their jurisdiction. The scope of that jurisdiction, however, is often a matter of disagreement. Governmental bodies have raised objections to national and international courts accepting to decide human rights cases related to underlying environmental conditions or activities posing risk of environmental harm. Indeed, there has been considerable backlash to some decisions related to economic development projects and environmental harm, with the government challenging the appropriateness of any judicial review of projects it deems important to the state's economy. It is also not unknown for litigators and judges to face pressure, even threats to their personal safety.

At the national level, efforts to litigate constitutional provisions on environmental protection raise issues of justiciability. South African courts have deemed the right to environment to be justiciable.[2] In Argentina, the right is deemed a subjective right entitling any person to initiate an action for environmental protection.[3] Colombia also recognizes the enforceability of the right to environment.[4] In Costa Rica, a court stated that enforcing the right to health and to the environment is necessary to ensure that the right to life is fully enjoyed.[5] Nonetheless, courts recognize that environmental harm is often the consequence of private action and that preventing deterioration requires affirmative management of resources, as well as regulations to ensure that private conduct is properly controlled. This means mandating state

[2] *Fuel Retailers Association of Southern Africa* v. *Director-General Environmental Management, Department of Agriculture, Conservation and Environment, Mpumalanga Province and Others*, Case No. CCT 67/06, (South Africa, 2007).

[3] *Kattan* v. *National Government*, No. 1983-D (Juzgado Nacional de la Instancia en lo Contencioso administrativo Federal No. 2, Argentina, 1983), p. 576; *Irazu Margarita* v. *Copetro S.A.* (Camara Civil y Comercial de la Plata, Buenos Aires, Argentina, 1993) ("The right to live in a healthy and balanced environment is a fundamental attribute of people. Any aggression to the environment ends up becoming a threat to life itself and to the psychological and physical integrity of the person.").

[4] *Fundepublico* v. *Mayor of Bugalagrande and Others*, Interlocutorio No. 032, Tulua (Juzgado Primero Superior, Colombia, 1991) ("It should be recognized that a healthy environment is a sina qua non condition for life itself and that no right could be exercised in a deeply altered environment.").

[5] *Presidente de la sociedad Marlene S.A.* v. *Municipalidad de Tibas*, No. 6918/94 (Constitutional Chamber of Supreme Court, Costa Rica, 1994).

action to interfere with uses of private property, which many courts see as more appropriate for political bodies, at least in the absence of clear regulatory standards the courts can apply.

In the United States, more than thirty of the fifty states have added constitutional provisions that refer to environmental or natural resource protection as a state constitutional right or, more often, as a governmental duty, with a direction to the state to enact appropriate measures.[6] The extent to which such provisions create a private right of action is contested,[7] but courts have struck down measures that directly contravene the constitutional mandate.[8] Judges evaluate the language and drafting history of the provision in deciding whether or not litigation may proceed, in particular, whether the legislature considered the issue of private enforcement or the creation of environmental rights; where legislative intent is clear one way or the other, the judiciary will defer.

It is easier to bring cases in those half a dozen U.S. states that expressly formulate a constitutional right rather than creating duties on the state to act as trustee of public property.[9] Such provisions have been interpreted to create enforceable rights and grant broad standing. In *Montana Environmental Information Center* v. *Department of Environmental Quality*,[10] for example, the state supreme court held that the fundamental right to a clean and healthy environment is implicated whenever water quality is impaired, without a requirement that plaintiffs show actual injury to health in order to challenge the government.

Litigants in other U.S. courts continue to be excluded from court based on strict standing requirements that bar claimants who cannot show personalized economic

6 Article 2(a) of Florida's constitution, for example, reads: "It shall be the policy of the state to conserve and protect its natural resources and scenic beauty. Adequate provision shall be made by law for the abatement of air and water pollution and of excessive and unnecessary noise." Fla. Const. art. 2, sec. 7(a). The Florida courts have held that they can refer to the section in deciding cases because it is an expression of the public interest in natural resources. See *Seadade Industries, Inc.* v. *Florida Power & Light Co.*, 245 So. 2d 209 (Fla. 1971); *Askew* v. *Game & Fresh Water Fish Comm'n*, 336 So. 2d 556 (Fla. 1976). New York's Constitution similarly declares the state's policy "to conserve and protect" its natural resources and scenic beauty. N.Y. Const., art. XIV, sec. 4. See also Ill. Const. art. XI, sec. 1.

7 Classic constitutional law texts assert that such statements have "only moral force." See Thomas McIntyre Cooley, *A Treatise on the Constitutional Limitations Which Rest Upon the Legislative Power of the State of the American Union*, Volume 1, 8th ed. (Little, Brown, and Co., 1927), p. 165.

8 See *Harrison* v. *Day*, 200 Va. 439, 106 S.E. 2d 636 (1959).

9 Note that commentators also view those provisions referring to the public trust doctrine as being "based on the notion that the public holds inviolable rights in certain lands and resources," with the state acting in trust for the public rights. Frank P. Grad, *Treatise on Environmental Law* (Matthew Bender, 1997), sec. 10.05[1]. For the seminal work on this topic, see Joseph L. Sax, "The Public Trust Doctrine in Natural Resource Law: Effective Judicial Intervention," *Michigan Law Review* 68(3) (1970), pp. 471–566.

10 *Montana Environmental Information Center* v. *Department of Environmental Quality*, 296 Mont. 207, 988 P. 2d 1236 (1999).

losses due to environmental harm. This is despite the fact that many of the constitutional provisions appear intended to liberalize standing rules, even creating *actio popularis* due to awareness that government officials may lack the will or capacity to maintain a clean and healthy environment.[11] An Illinois Court of Appeals, for example, held against a plaintiff's standing despite the state's constitutional[12] guarantee of a "right to a healthful environment" explicitly enforceable "against any party, governmental or private."[13] More than two decades later, the Illinois Supreme Court clarified that the constitutional right to a clean and healthful environment creates no new cause of action,[14] but it does give "standing to an individual to bring an environmental action for a grievance common to members of the public,"[15] even in cases where a resident may not be able to demonstrate the "particularized" harm that is normally required.

Some courts have erected a further barrier, interpreting constitutional provisions as non-self-executing.[16] Individuals thus will be barred from invoking constitutional provisions unless and until the legislature enacts measures to establish precise regulations and standards governing the topic.[17] Courts are particularly reluctant to enforce constitutional provisions that refer only generally to conservation of resources, because judges deem the vagueness of such language involves them in lawmaking in violation of their proper judicial function.

Judges' understanding of the proper judicial role may also preclude consideration of a case if the court feels that the subject matter of the dispute raises political rather than legal issues. In *Clean Air Foundation Limited & Gordon David Oldham* v. *Government of the Hong Kong Special Administrative Region*,[18] the applicants sought judicial review of the authorities' alleged failure to take the measures necessary to combat air pollution, which the applicants argued had reached levels that violated their right to health in breach of the Bill of Rights and various international human rights agreements, in particular Article 12 of the International Covenant on Economic, Social and Cultural Rights, which recognizes "the right of

[11] "Because the wrong here has reached crisis proportions and because it affects individuals in so fundamental a way, the Committee is of the view that the 'special injury' requirement for standing is particularly inappropriate and ought to be waived." Ill. Comp. Stat. Ann., Const. art. XI, sec. 2, *Constitutional Commentary*, p. 277 (West 1971).

[12] Ill. Const. art. II, sec. 2.

[13] *Scattering Fork Drainage Dist.* v. *Ogilvie*, 311 N.E.2d 203, 210 (Ill. App. Ct. 1974).

[14] *City of Elgin* v. *County of Cook*, 660 N.E.2d 875 (Ill. 1995).

[15] *Glisson* v. *City of Marion*, 720 N.E.2d 1034, 1041 (Ill. 1999).

[16] See, e.g., *Robb* v. *Shockoe Slip Found.*, 324 S.E.2d 674, 676 (Va. 1985).

[17] Michigan's Supreme Court has a three-part test that first examines the language, then the purpose and circumstances of the adoption, and finally the preference for constitutional over unconstitutional constructions. See *State Highway Comm'n* v. *Vanderkloot*, US-24, 220 N.W. 2d 416 (Mich. 1974).

[18] *Clean Air Foundation Limited & Gordon David Oldham* v. *Government of the Hong Kong Special Administrative Region*, HCAL 35/2007 (Court of First Instance, Constitutional and Administrative Law List, Hong Kong, 2007).

everyone to the enjoyment of the highest attainable standard of physical and mental health." The Court accepted that Article 12 imposes a duty on state authorities to combat air pollution, but nonetheless held that the issue of air quality standards was one of policy, not law and "that to interfere with the lawful discretion given to policy makers would amount to an abuse of the supervisory jurisdiction vested in the courts."[19] The applicants submitted that their aim was to determine whether the Government had met its obligations in law. The Court was unable to agree, finding that the real issues in the case were not issues of legality but went to the question of why the Government had not chosen to pursue certain policies. Other courts, by way of contrast, have allowed challenges to the lack of state action, relying on international standards, when the constitution itself contains the rights to health and a healthy environment as fundamental rights.[20]

International courts also must have regard for their jurisdictional limits in order to maintain their legitimacy. Human rights tribunals are created by and have jurisdiction in respect to a specific treaty or treaties, wherein the rights and obligations are set forth and indications given of the norms that the tribunal may apply.[21] These human rights bodies are created expressly "to ensure the observance of the engagements undertaken by the High Contracting Parties"[22] or they "have competence with respect to matters relating to the fulfillment of the commitments made by the States Parties" to the agreement.[23] The language of these mandates indicates that states parties intend the tribunals to undertake compliance monitoring of state obligations. They do so even when the underlying cause of the violation lies in environmental conditions. In general, these are pollution matters, not conflicts over depletion of natural resources. The main exception to this is cases concerning the ancestral lands of indigenous peoples, where their collective property rights extend to the natural resources on those lands.[24]

[19] Ibid.

[20] See, e.g., *Acción de tutela instaurada por Orlando José Morales Ramos, contra la Sociedad Drummond Ltda*, Decision T-154–2013 (Constitutional Court of Colombia, Sixth Chamber of Appeals, 2013). The action sought to enforce the violation of the right to life, to a healthy environment, to privacy, and to health of Mr. Orlando José Morales Ramos, his wife and his eleven children, most of them minors, near the Pribbenow mine located in La Loma, municipality of El Paso, Colombia.

[21] In some instances, human rights treaties give the commission or court an expansive list of normative sources they may apply in interpreting the guaranteed human rights. See, e.g., African Charter on Human and Peoples' Rights, June 27, 1981, in force October 21, 1986, 1520 UNTS 217, arts. 60, 61; American Convention on Human Rights, November 22, 1969, in force July 18, 1978, 1114 UNTS 123, art. 29.

[22] European Convention for the Protection of Human Rights and Fundamental Freedoms, November 4, 1950, in force September 3, 1953, 213 UNTS 221, art. 17.

[23] American Convention, art. 33.

[24] See, e.g., *Mayagna (Sumo) Awas Tingni Community* v. *Nicaragua*, Inter-Am. Ct. H.R. (ser. C) No. 79 (2001); *Maya Indigenous Communities of the Toledo Dist.* v. *Belize*, Inter-Am. Comm'n H.R., Case 12.053, Merits report No. 40/04, OEA/Ser.L/V/II.122 doc. 5, rev. 1 (2004); *Yakye Axa* v. *Paraguay*, Merits, Reparations and Costs, Inter-Am. Ct. H.R, (ser. C) No. 125 (2005); *Case of*

Apart from the African Commission and Court on Human and Peoples' Rights, no international human rights tribunal monitors compliance with a treaty-based "right to environment" provision, because no such right was written into UN human rights treaties or the European and American[25] Conventions. This alone may give rise to government objections that human rights tribunals are exceeding their jurisdiction in deciding cases related to the environment, but in fact UN treaty bodies and the Inter-American and European tribunals most often hear complaints about failures to enforce national environmental rights[26] or about environmental degradation that violates one or more of the guaranteed rights in the agreements over which they have jurisdiction.[27] In other words, human rights tribunals hear human rights cases – they do not hear environmental cases.

The cases presented in Europe and the Americas often center on issues of the rule of law because they are grounded in the failure of states to enforce their own constitutions, laws (including international obligations[28]), and judicial decisions.[29] These cases raise quintessential human rights issues.[30] The issue of compliance with domestic law is particularly important when there is a domestic constitutional right to environmental protection.[31] Domestic constitutional guarantees and other

the Moiwana Community (Suriname), Inter-Am Ct H.R. (ser. C) No. 124 (2005), para 131; *Sawhoyamaxa Indigenous Community* v. *Paraguay*, Inter-Am.Ct. H.R. (ser. C) No. 146 (2006); *Xakmok Kasek Indigenous Community* v. *Paraguay*, Merits, Reparations, and Costs, Inter-Am Ct. H.R. (ser. C) No. 214 (2010); *Kichwa Indigenous People of Sarayaku* v. *Ecuador*, Inter-Am. Ct. H.R. (ser. C) No. 245 (2012).

For treaty rights of indigenous peoples related to the environment, see International Labour Organization, Convention Concerning Indigenous and Tribal Peoples in Independent Countries (C 169), June 27, 1989, in force September 5, 1991, 28 I.L.M. 1382.

25 Article 17 of the Additional Protocol to the American Convention on Human Rights in the Area of Economic, Social and Cultural Rights: Protocol of San Salvador, November 17, 1988, in force November 16, 1999, 28 ILM 161, does contain environmental rights, but the article was not made justiciable.

26 In many of the cases discussed *infra* the applicants cite constitutional provisions guaranteeing the right to a safe and healthy or other quality environment. See, e.g., *Okyay et al.* v. *Turkey*, No. 36220/97 (European Court of Human Rights, 2005) and *Kyrtatos* v. *Greece*, No. 4666/98 (European Court of Human Rights, 2003), discussed *infra*.

27 Most commonly invoked are the rights to life, health, property, culture, information, privacy, and home life. See Dinah Shelton, "Developing Substantive Environmental Rights," *Journal of Human Rights and the Environment* 1(1) (2010), pp. 89–121.

28 *Oneryildiz* v. *Turkey*, No. 48939/99 (European Court of Human Rights, 2004); *Maya Indigenous Communities*. See also *Mary and Carrie Dann* v. *United States*, Inter-Am. Comm'n H.R, Case 11.140, Report No. 75/02, Doc. 5 rev. 1 (2002), paras. 127–131; *Report on Ecuador*, Ch. VIII, text following n. 42.

29 The European Court requires at a minimum that the state should have complied with its domestic environmental standards. See, e.g., *Ashworth and Others* v. *United Kingdom*, No. 39561/98 (European Court of Human Rights 2004); *Moreno Gomes* v. *Spain*, No. 4143/02 (European Court of Human Rights, 2005).

30 *Taşkin and Others* v. *Turkey*, No. 46117/99 (European Court of Human Rights, 2006).

31 *Okyay and Others* v. *Turkey*, para. 57; *Tătar* v. *Romania*, No. 67021/01 (European Court of Human Rights, 2009).

enactments are most important in cases where the applicants have no independent claim under the European Convention for severe pollution, but instead are seeking nature protection or protection of the environment more generally.[32]

Applications to human rights tribunals must fall within the personal, temporal, geographic, and subject matter jurisdiction of the particular body. This limits the cases that can be brought. In *Fadayeva* v. *Russia*,[33] the European Court noted that because "no right to nature preservation is as such included among the rights and freedoms guaranteed by the Convention," the adverse effects of environmental pollution must attain a certain minimum level if they are to fall within the subject matter of the Court under Article 8 (right to privacy and home life).

The requirement of sufficient harm also affects personal jurisdiction in most systems, because only the African Charter allows an *actio popularis*.[34] Elsewhere, the harm or risk to the application must be sufficiently imminent and proven to make the applicant a "victim" for purposes of admissibility.[35] This requirement makes it difficult to bring cases seeking nature protection not related to human well-being. In 2004, the Inter-American Commission declared inadmissible a petition from a Panamanian national contending that the government had violated the right to property of all Panamanians by authorizing construction of a public roadway through the Metropolitan Nature Reserve in Panama.[36] The Commission determined that no specific victims were identified or could be identified because all citizens of Panama were deemed to own the Reserve, thus the claim was inadmissible as an *actio popularis*.

Factors lending support to greater acceptance by courts of environmental cases linked to human rights include the fact that states often adopt constitutional provisions guaranteeing environmental quality due to public demand and pursuant to a referendum. The guarantees provided thus represent the collective will of society to place environmental rights among the highest normative values in the legal system. Courts should defer to that decision by accepting cases seeking to enforce the rights guaranteed. Moreover, it has become increasingly clear that discrimination, exclusion, and lack of democratic participation are often present in cases of environmental harm and require judicial review to protect the rights of the marginalized and disfavored. The role of courts as a check on government overreach is well established.

[32] *Kyrtatos* v. *Greece*.

[33] *Fadeyeva* v. *Russia*, No. 55723/00 (European Court of Human Rights, 2005).

[34] See *Social and Economic Rights Action Centre (SERAC) and the Centre for Economic and Social Rights (CESR)* v. *Nigeria*, No. 155/96 (ACHPR 2001).

[35] See *Bordes and Temeharo* v. *France*, No. 645/1995, CCPR/C/57/D/645/1995 (1996). The risk of harm from nuclear radiation due to nuclear testing by France in the South Pacific was deemed too remote for the victims to qualify as victims.

[36] *Metropolitan Nature Reserve* v. *Panama*, Inter-Am. Comm'n H.R., Case 11.533, Admissibility Report No. 88/03, OEA/Ser.L/V/II.118 Doc. 70 rev. 2 (2003), p. 524.

Counseling restraint, however, are concerns about issues of comity, acts of state, and deference to political decisions. National courts may have good reason to feel that cases involving transboundary environmental harm are best left to international tribunals or diplomacy. International human rights bodies may face innovative claims and efforts to expand jurisdiction well beyond what is conferred by the relevant legal instruments. Human rights treaties generally require each state to respect and ensure guaranteed rights "to all individuals within its territory and subject to its jurisdiction."[37] This geographic limitation reflects the reality that a state normally will have the power to protect or the possibility to violate human rights only of those within its territory and jurisdiction, absent exceptional circumstances. In contrast, pollution of coastal waters or the atmosphere may cause significant harm to individuals and the environment thousands of miles away. States emitting high levels of greenhouse gases or depleting their forests or other carbon sinks can contribute to climate change that threatens the global environment now and in the future. Courts must consider whether to accept cases from applicants challenging activities that cause transboundary harm[38] or on behalf of future generations.[39] Although litigation based on transboundary environmental harm exists in both national[40] and international tribunals,[41] jurisdictional requirements present considerable hurdles to the admissibility of these matters in human rights tribunals.

Finally, all courts, national and international, must consider issues of judicial administration. Human rights bodies, as well as many national courts, are facing rising caseloads and insufficient personnel and other resources to manage them. They may lack the ability to undertake extensive fact-finding or the funds to appoint independent experts that would provide scientific evidence or assess uncertainty. Courts may be concerned that applicants without a financial or other serious personal stake in litigation will be unable or unwilling to gather the evidence and present issues fully to the court. They must also consider that broad support for the challenged decision or activity may make it difficult to obtain compliance with an adverse judgment.

[37] International Covenant on Civil and Political Rights, art. 2(1). The European Court of Human Rights has several times indicated that jurisdiction in international law is "primarily territorial." *Bankovic and Others* v. *Belgium and Others* (Admissibility), No. 52207/99 (European Court of Human Rights, 2001), para. 59; *Issa and Others* v. *Turkey*, No. 31821/96 (European Court of Human Rights, 2004).

[38] For a discussion of the unsuccessful efforts of the Inuit to bring a case of climate change to the Inter-American Commission on Human Rights, see Juliette Niehuss, "Inuit Circumpolar Conference v. Bush Administration: Why the Arctic Peoples Claim the United States' Role in Climate Change Has Violated Their Fundamental Human Rights and Threatens Their Very Existence," *Sustainable Development Law and Policy* 5(2) (2005).

[39] *Minors Oposa* v. *Secretary of the Department of Environmental and Natural Resources*, 33 ILM 173 (Supreme Court of the Philippines, 1993).

[40] *Missouri* v. *Illinois*, 200 U.S. 496 (1906); *New York* v. *New Jersey*, 256 U.S. 296 (1921).

[41] *Trail Smelter Arbitration (U.S./Canada)*, Arbitral Trib., 3 U.N. Rep. Int'l Arb. Awards 1905 (1941).

FACT-FINDING: SCIENCE AND THE LAW

Some of the concerns about environmental rights litigation focus on evidentiary issues, including the evaluation of risk, causality, and proof of harm. A few commentators have questioned whether legally trained, non-technical judges are the appropriate arbiters of a clean and healthy environment and whether the judicial branch is the appropriate venue for resolving value-laden, science-based environmental decisions.[42] As the Hong Kong case cited earlier illustrates, a number of judges have themselves expressed concerns about the institutional capacity and propriety of court involvement in environmental decision making. To date, these issues have arisen mainly in national and international courts of general jurisdiction, like the International Court of Justice, and not in human rights tribunals, because most international human rights cases of this type are brought only after domestic remedies have thoroughly revealed the risks entailed or the harm produced by the challenged activity.

Judges and lawmakers rarely come from a scientific background and usually lack extensive training in epidemiology, biology, environmental sciences, or the scientific method generally. The legal system is designed such that evidence on these issues and the facts related to them are normally introduced by the party relying on them, often through the written and/or oral testimony of experts. Despite the limits of knowledge, scientific evidence plays a critical role in many cases concerned with environmental law and human rights. This puts the judge in the position of having to understand the basic scientific material presented and how the information should be appreciated in the case before the court.[43]

Scientific evidence is necessary to evaluate risks to the environment or natural resources. It is also important to cases alleging injury from pollution, and when environmental regulations are challenged as either a disproportionate infringement of rights or, in the international arena, as a disguised restriction on trade. Environmental science helps determine the causal links between the activities and the impacts, giving courts a set of data on which to base decisions about whether or not a proper balance of interests has been made. The substance of environmental rights involves evaluating ecological systems, determining the impacts that can be tolerated and what is needed to maintain and protect the natural base on which life depends. Environmental quality standards, precaution, and principles of sustainability can establish the limits of environmental decision making and continue to give specific content to environmental rights in law.

[42] See, e.g., Barton Thompson, Jr., "Constitutionalizing the Environment: The History and Future of Montana's Environmental Provisions," *Montana Law Review* 64(1) (2003), pp. 157–198, 158.

[43] For a comment on the difficulties of assessing scientific evidence at the ICJ, see *Gabčíkovo-Nagymaros Case (Hungary* v. *Slovakia)*, [1997] ICJ Rep. 91 (Sep. Op. of Judge Weeramantry), para. 118.

Science has been defined as "the intellectual and practical activity encompassing the systematic study of the structure and behavior of the physical and natural world through observation and experiment."[44] Based on observation, scientists formulate and test hypotheses through experiments. Controversy over whether opinions are truly based on science as so defined has come up in regard to subjects as diverse as climate change, evolution, appropriate levels for extraction of renewable and non-renewable natural resources, decisions over approval of projects and activities, and regulation of human reproduction. The scientific community has expressed concern about the impact of "pseudoscience" on individual rights, asserting that "decisions that impact fundamental constitutional rights must not be made on the basis of false, unreliable, pseudoscientific evidence."[45] Scientists seek the exclusion of unscientific opinions and support courts that refuse to grant deference to laws restricting human rights when those laws are enacted on the basis of unreliable scientific claims. The scrutiny required of new proposals and asserted scientific findings is one filter that can help separate the speculative from the validated hypothesis. Scientific validity means that knowledge has been derived by scientific method, and indicators of that include testability or falsifiability, error rate, peer review, publication, and acceptance of the opinion in the scientific community.[46]

The *Japanese Whaling Case*[47] required the ICJ to delve into these issues, as it presented a question of how to interpret Article VIII of the Whaling Convention, which allows states to whale "for purposes of scientific research."[48] Both Australia

[44] *Whole Woman's Health et al.* v. *Kirk Cole, Commissioner, Texas Department of State Health Services, et al.*, Brief Amici Curiae of Scientists, Science Educators, Skeptics, The Center for Inquiry, and the Richard Dawkins Foundation for Research and Science in Support of Petitioners, in the Supreme Court of the United States (January 4, 2016), p. 7, available at www.americanbar.org/content/dam/aba/publications/supreme_court_preview/briefs_2015_2016/15-274_amicus_pet_NationalAbortionFederationetal.authcheckdam.pdf.

[45] Ibid., p. 6. On the topic of climate change, the Credibility Project, organized by the Center for Inquiry, a nonprofit educational organization promoting science and freedom in inquiry, found that of nearly 700 experts who provided opinions to the United States Senate Minority Report on Global Warming (denying the existence of anthropogenic climate change), 80 percent had no peer reviewed published work on climate science and lacked any scientific expertise on the subject. Ibid., pp. 2–3.

[46] See the U.S. arguments in *Japan – Measures Affecting the Importation of Apples*, Complaint by the United States, WT/DS245, Report of the Panel DSR 2003:IX, paras. 8.90; see also the WTO Appellate Body discussion of scientific evidence in *Canada – Continued Suspension of Obligations in the EC – Hormones Dispute*, WT/DS320 (2008), paras. 278, 315–16, 581, 590–1.

[47] *Whaling in the Antarctic (Australia* v. *Japan: New Zealand intervening)*, Judgment, [2014] ICJ Rep. 226.

[48] In particular, Article VIII provides that

> Notwithstanding anything contained in this Convention any Contracting Government may grant to any of its nationals a special permit authorizing that national to kill, take and treat whales for purposes of scientific research subject to such restrictions as to number and subject to such other conditions as the Contracting Government thinks fit, and the killing, taking, and treating of whales in accordance with the provisions of this Article shall be exempt from the operation of this Convention.

and Japan proffered experts with similar theories about what constitutes scientific research. Australia's experts maintained that scientific research in the context of the Convention has four essential characteristics: defined and achievable relevant objectives (questions or hypotheses); "appropriate methods," including the use of lethal methods only where the objectives of the research cannot be achieved by any other means; peer review; and the avoidance of adverse effects on whale stocks. Japan's expert differed on some points, but agreed generally on these elements. The Court observed the experts' broad agreement, but as to the criterion of peer review, the Court concluded that even if peer review of proposals and results is common practice in the scientific community, the Convention sets up its own alternative review mechanism that could substitute for publication and peer review. The Court then introduced a reasonableness test in its focus on the meaning of the phrase "for the purposes of" in Article VIII. It thus accepted a judicial role in examining how reasonable a state's scientific design is for achieving a specific set of scientific objectives and indicated, at least implicitly, some of the parameters of what constitutes "reasonable" scientific research for the purposes of the Whaling Convention. In doing so, the Court limited the discretion of states to unilaterally decide what constitutes permissible scientific research and preserved a role for judicial review of scientific claims.

PROVING ALLEGATIONS

Generally, the proponent of a fact has the burden of proof. The ICJ has been clear that this applies to cases before it: "in accordance with the well-established principle of *onus probandi incumbit actori*, it is the duty of the party which asserts certain facts to establish the existence of such facts."[49] This burden may be discharged not only by direct evidence, but by presumptions, inferences, and circumstantial evidence. Moreover, in international cases, where the evidence may be within the sovereign control of the other party, the opposing party should cooperate in the provision of such evidence as may be in its possession.[50] The court in turn determines which facts are relevant, assesses the probative value of the evidence and draws conclusions as appropriate. Like the ICJ, other international tribunals overtly avoid rigid rules of evidence, preferring to admit all proffered material and decide on its relevance and weight.

To prevail in a case alleging injury from environmental harm, it is usually necessary to establish the factual origin of the harm and that it was the proximate

The Schedule that forms an integral part of the Convention further provides that decisions taken "shall be such as are necessary to carry out the objectives and purposes of this Convention and to provide for the conservation, development, and optimum utilization of the whale resources" and "shall be based on scientific findings." Art. V, para. 2.

49 *Pulp Mills on the River Uruguay (Argentina v. Uruguay)*, [2010] ICJ Rep. 83.

50 Ibid., para. 163.

cause of the injury. Often cause-and-effect is obvious in litigation, but can be difficult to prove in environmental cases. Health consequences of pollution may arise only after decades of slow exposure or remain latent for many years. Questions of intervening or contributing causes arise, particularly when an illness is present in the general unexposed population. Demonstrating the exact cause of harm also may be difficult when there are diffuse contributing sources. The seemingly unending development of new compounds and products, which may interact with preexisting substances in the environment, may lead to unpredicted synergies and widespread harm difficult to evaluate. Courts may be led into error by not realizing that scientific certainty and legal certainty are different. Scientists pronounce a causal connection only when the probability of a link between exposure and injury is at least 95 percent. Direct causal connections thus may be accepted in science only after large numbers of injuries occur.[51] The legal standard of proof in civil cases is far lower, but judges may be influenced to deny relief when scientists are unable to pronounce causality based on the scientific standard.

Courts are often asked to weigh evidence in environmental cases based on probabilities.[52] Epidemiology, for example, determines the probability of an association between a specified exposure and the occurrence of disease – examining the frequency and distribution of diseases and factors that may explain them, to infer the causes in a group of people, establishing the level of risk of contracting a disease.[53] However, judges must scrutinize the evidence, because studies may be subject to bias in the design, lack a large enough sample to be significant, exclude consideration of contributing factors, or fail to follow the subjects for a sufficiently long time period to accurately reveal the rate of disease. Where information comes from toxicological studies conducted on animals, it must be questioned whether the results can be extrapolated to humans. Other problems arise because data may be subject to different interpretations or different studies may have reached different conclusions.

The need for expert opinions on scientific evidence, and the equally important need to ensure that the evidence submitted is scientific, raise a threshold issue of the admissibility. One national admissibility framework, articulated in the case *R* v. *Turner*,[54] established four requirements:[55] knowledge beyond the understanding

[51] Peter W. Huber, *Galileo's Revenge: Junk Science in the Courtroom* (Basic Books, 1991).

[52] Some courts have adopted a test that looks to the frequency, regularity, and proximity of exposure to decide the probability of causation. See *Lohrmann* v. *Pittsburgh Corning Corp.*, 782 F.2d 1156 (4th Cir. 1986); *James* v. *Bessemer Processing Co.*, 155 N.J. 279 (Supreme Court of New Jersey 1998).

[53] Bert Black and David E. Lilienfeld, "Epidemiologic Proof in Toxic Tort Litigation," *Fordham Law Review* 52(5) (1984), pp. 732–785.

[54] R v. *Turner*, QB 834 (England, 1975).

[55] The Law Commission, *The Admissibility of Expert Evidence in Criminal Proceedings in England and Wales: A New Approach to the Determination of Evidentiary Reliability* (2009), www.lawcom.gov.uk/wp-content/uploads/2015/03/cp190_Expert_Evidence_Consultation.pdf.

of the fact-finder, relevant expertise, impartiality, and evidentiary reliability. U.S. federal courts apply a test articulated by the Supreme Court in *Daubert* v. *Merrell Dow Pharmaceuticals, Inc.*,[56] which requires that "the party presenting the expert must show that the expert's findings are based on sound science."[57] This requires "some objective, independent validation of the expert's methodology,"[58] such as scientific scrutiny through peer review and publication;[59] alternatively, the "experts must explain precisely how they went about reaching their conclusions and point to some objective source . . . to show that they have followed the scientific method, as it is practiced by (at least) a recognized minority of scientists in their field."[60] Following the *Daubert* judgment, the Federal Judicial Center published a Reference Manual on Scientific Evidence (1994), providing both procedural and substantive information on scientific methodologies.[61]

International tribunals may resort to experts, even when there is no express provision in their governing rules allowing appointment.[62] The International Court of Justice relies on the parties to produce evidence, but also may act independently to appoint an expert or arrange for the testimony of witnesses.[63] Witnesses and experts are called by the party that named them and may be cross-examined. It is often the case, however, that the experts in the pay of each side produce "dueling narratives" or contradictory views of the relevant facts. It has been argued that in such instances a tribunal's task "should not simply be to choose between two competing conceptions of the facts presented in adversarial fashion."[64] Instead, if resources allow, international courts and tribunals should appoint and consult their own independent experts.[65]

Other commentators and judges caution, however, that there is some danger that experts may be drawn into treaty interpretation in environment cases and into

56 *Daubert* v. *Merrell Dow Pharmaceuticals, Inc.*, 509 U.S. 579, 590 (1993).
57 Ibid.
58 *Daubert* v. *Merrell Dow Pharmaceuticals, Inc.* (*Daubert II*), 43 F.3d 131, 1316 (9th Cir. 1995).
59 Ibid., p. 1318.
60 Ibid., p. 1319.
61 See also Committee on Identifying the Needs of the Forensic Scientific Community of the National Research Council, *Strengthening the Forensic Sciences in the United States: A Path Forward* (National Academies Press, 2009).
62 Article 50 of the ICJ Statute, Article 289 of the UN Convention on the Law of the Sea, and Article 13.2 of the WTO Dispute Settlement Understanding all allow for the appointment of scientific or technical experts. The International Centre for Settlement of Investor Disputes (ICSID) has no specific provision, but it does use experts. See, e.g., *S.A.R.L. Benvenuti & Bonfant* v. *Congo*, ARB 77/2, Award (ICSID, 1981); *Liberian Eastern Timber Corporation (LETCO)* v. *Liberia*, ARB 83/2, Award (ICSID, 1986).
63 Rules of the Court, art. 62 (1978).
64 Caroline E. Foster, "The Consultation of Independent Experts by International Courts and Tribunals in Health and Environment Cases," *Finnish Yearbook of International Law* 20 (2009), pp. 391–418, 392, citing Mirjan Damaška, *Evidence Law Adrift* (Yale University Press, 1997), p. 100.
65 Foster, "Consultation of Independent Experts," pp. 393–4, 400–4.

deciding mixed questions of law and fact, such as whether an activity poses a "serious" or "irreversible" risk to the environment or whether and to what extent there is scientific uncertainty. In WTO cases, the question often arises as to whether the measures taken by the responding state were "necessary" to protect human, animal, or plant life and health, an issue that generally involves mixed questions of law and science. In the *Pulp Mills* case, the dissenting opinion of Judges Al-Khasawneh and Simma commented that "[t]he conclusions of scientific experts might be indispensable in distilling the essence of what legal concepts such as 'significance' of damage, 'sufficiency,' 'reasonable threshold' or 'necessity' come to mean in a given case."[66] Judge Yusef then queried whether the use of experts might reduce or eliminate the role of the judge in deciding facts, but ultimately concluded that it would not negatively affect the judicial function.[67] The concern remains, however, about the respective roles of experts and judges.

Human rights courts and tribunals have less recourse to experts, because often they can rely on domestic court findings of fact showing violation of the law and resulting environmental harm. *Taşkin and Others* v. *Turkey*, at the European Court of Human Rights, involved challenges to the development and operation of a gold mine, which the applicants alleged could cause environmental damage to the detriment of people in the region in violation of Article 8 of the European Convention. The European Court was able to rely on findings of the Turkish Supreme Administrative Court, which repeatedly had concluded that the operating permit in issue did not serve the public interest and that the safety measures that the company had taken did not suffice to eliminate the risks involved in such an activity, in breach of the law.[68] The European Court thus found a violation despite the absence of any accidents or incidents at the mine, because it was deemed to present an unacceptable risk.

In *Fadayeva* v. *Russia*,[69] concerning pollution from a steel mill, the findings of domestic and international agencies with expertise on pollution assisted the European Court. A government decree had recited statistics on the increases in respiratory and blood diseases linked to air pollution, as well as the increased number of deaths from cancer.[70] The government had also determined by legislation the safe levels of various polluting substances, many of which were exceeded in the security zone where the applicant lived. The mayor of the city said the steel plant was responsible for more than 95 percent of industrial emissions into the town's air,

66 *Pulp Mills*, [2010] ICJ Rep. 108 (joint dissenting opinion of Judges Al-Khasawneh and Simma). Judges Cançado Trindade, Yusuf, and Vinuesa also considered that the Court should have appointed independent experts in the case. Ibid., pp. 135, 216, 266.

67 *Pulp Mills*, [2010] ICJ Rep. 216, 219 (declaration of Judge Yusuf), para. 10.

68 *Taşkin*, paras. 112, 117, 133.

69 See also *Ledyayeva, Dobrokhotova, Zolotareva and Romashina* v. *Russia*, Nos. 53157/99, 53247/99, 53695/00 and 56850/00 (European Court of Human Rights, 2006), involving the same steel plant built during the Soviet era.

70 *Fadeyeva*, para. 16.

while a State Report on the Environment indicated that the plant in question was the largest contributor to air pollution of all metallurgical plants in Russia.[71]

The applicant still faced the problem of causality. Her medical records indicated problems, but did not attribute them to any specific causes. The doctors stated, however, that her problems would be exacerbated by working in conditions of vibration, toxic pollution, and an unfavorable climate.[72] The applicant also submitted an expert report that linked the plant specifically to increased adverse health conditions of persons residing nearby.[73] The Court found that the medical evidence did not establish a causal link between the pollution at her residence and her illnesses, but accepted that the evidence, including submissions by the government, was clear about the unsafe, excessive pollution around her home. The Court also made reference to the expert report and the findings of the domestic courts. The Court noted that Russian legislation defined the maximum permissible concentrations as "safe concentrations of toxic elements."[74] Therefore, exceeding these limits produced a presumption of unsafe conditions potentially harmful to health and well-being. This presumption, together with the evidence submitted, led the court to conclude that the applicant's health deteriorated as a result of her prolonged exposure to the industrial emissions from the steel plant. Alternatively, even if that harm could not be quantified, the pollution "inevitably made the applicant more vulnerable to various illnesses" and affected her quality of life.[75]

The Court's analysis raises the question of what evidence is sufficient to raise the presumption of harm it refers to in the *Fadayeva* case. It should not be limited to domestic legislative or administrative findings, because these may be changed to accommodate economic interests without necessarily being based on sound science. The World Health Organization (WHO) and other scientific bodies have determined through epidemiological studies what constitutes safe levels of concentration of toxic, carcinogenic, mutagenic, and other hazardous substances.[76] Courts may accept such reliable evidence to demonstrate presumed harm when the indicated levels are exceeded, even if local legislation permits higher concentrations. A petition admitted by the Inter-American Commission relied on WHO standards to assert that the average sulfur dioxide levels from a metallurgical complex are

[71] Ibid., para. 19. The Court noted that this made the case different from and more easily definable than other air pollution cases where multiple minor sources cumulate to produce the problem. Ibid., para. 91.

[72] Ibid., para. 45.

[73] The Court made it a point to recite the qualifications of the expert when discussing the report. Ibid., para. 46 n. 1.

[74] Ibid., para. 87.

[75] Ibid., para. 88.

[76] See, e.g., World Health Organization, *Guidelines for Drinking Water Quality* (3d ed.) (2004). Independent surveillance of water quality, quantity, accessibility, affordability, and long-term availability are part of the WHO framework.

detrimental to the lives and health of the nearby community in Peru.[77] In *Tătar* v. *Romania*, the European Court relied on UNEP findings about the causes and consequences of a mining accident, as well as WHO determinations about the health consequences of exposure to sodium cyanide, placing heavy reliance on them in the absence of adequate domestic fact-finding.[78]

In the case of *Fägerskiöld* v. *Sweden*, the Court cited WHO guidelines on noise pollution in rejecting the admissibility of an application concerning wind turbines constructed and operating near the applicants' property.[79] The Court noted that the WHO guidelines were set at the level of the lowest adverse health effect associated with noise exposure. The Court also referred to even lower maximum levels adopted by most European countries. Applying these standards to the noise level tests submitted in the case, the Court found that the levels of noise did not exceed the WHO guidelines and were minimally above the recommended maximum level in Sweden. Therefore, the environmental nuisance could not be found to reach the level of environmental pollution sufficient to constitute a human rights violation.

Standards of proof in civil litigation, including human rights cases, vary among legal systems and international human rights tribunals. The common law generally looks to a preponderance of the evidence, while civil law systems seek a moral conviction of the truth of the allegations. The Inter-American Court appears to have a varying scale depending on the seriousness of the alleged violations, while the European Court of Human Rights calls for proof beyond a reasonable doubt.[80] Although the European Court's standard of proof is high,[81] it has been called flexible and takes into account the fact that governments often are the sole repository of relevant evidence. Like other international courts, it makes use of presumptions and inferences.

SCIENTIFIC UNCERTAINTY AND THE ROLE OF THE PRECAUTIONARY PRINCIPLE

Science has moved toward observing and predicting more long-term consequences of environmental harm and the likelihood that it will occur. In response, most laws now require identifying environmental risks in advance so that mitigating action can be taken. Law also expressly or by implication allows for judicial review

77 *Community of La Oroya, Peru*, Inter-Am. Comm'n H.R, Case 12.718, Admissibility Report No. 76/09, OAS/Ser/L/V/II.135, doc. 23 (2009).

78 *Tătar*, paras. 9, 25, 31, 32, 66, 91, 104.

79 *Fägerskiöld* v. *Sweden*, No. 37664/04 (admissibility), (European Court of Human Rights, 2008).

80 *Matthews* v. *United Kingdom*, No. 24833/94 (European Court of Human Rights, 1999).

81 The standard of "proof beyond reasonable doubt" can follow from the coexistence of sufficiently strong, clear, and concordant inferences or of similar unrebutted presumptions of fact. *Fadayeva*, para. 79.

of regulations and decisions to ensure that they have considered "any risks that could reasonably be surmised on the basis of available scientific evidence."[82]

Precaution is intrinsically linked to risk, based on informed speculation as to what consequences will flow in the future from actions today. Some risks are attractive to participants and produce rewards of one type or another, including profits from investment in new technologies and enterprises, and pleasure from sports and leisure activities such as skiing and sky diving. Daily risks are encountered in all human activities from cooking to walking, even sleeping. Some contingencies, however, are considered to be unacceptably harmful if they occur.

Risk is the high or low chance of harm occurring from a specific event. If scientific methodology proves a causal link between an activity and significant damage, even without knowing when the damage might occur, the risk is high and the principle of prevention calls for action to eliminate the damage. When the existence or probability of harm has not been established by science, however, decisions about allowing the activity to go forward must be based on precaution, considering both the gravity of the potential harm and the probability of it occurring.[83]

Gravity may be evaluated by the seriousness of injury to a few or widespread but lesser harm to many. In the absence of consensus about what risk levels are appropriate in society, political bodies or administrative agencies make policy decisions that may be challenged by those unwilling to bear the risk of harm the government has approved. Human rights law and laws for environmental protection may very well shift the balance toward imposing fewer risks than governments would favor based on the desire for economic betterment.

Lack of knowledge about the dangers or hazards involved in a particular enterprise or activity poses a considerable problem, because without knowledge of such dangers there can be no complete assessment of risk. Precaution aims to overcome the problem of lack of information (scientific uncertainty) by presuming that a risk exists. Based on this, decision makers decide whether to ban the activity, impose strict liability for the actor should loss or injury result from the activity, or require mitigating actions to reduce the assumed risk. This approach involves an evaluation of risk, a weighing of the gravity of the harm threatened against the utility of the actor's conduct.

Although scientific uncertainty was an issue in the *Gabčíkovo-Nagymaros* and *Pulp Mills* cases, the ICJ declined to take a strong view of the precautionary

[82] Sheila Jasanoff, *Science at the Bar* (Harvard University Press, 1995), p. 39. Jasanoff cites two landmark cases in the development of a precautionary approach. In *Reserve Mining* v. *EPA*, 514 F.2d 492 (8th Cir. 1975) and *Ethyl Corp.* v. *EPA*, 541 F2d 1 (D.C. Cir. 1976), federal appellate courts held that conclusive evidence of harm is not needed for regulatory action, but could be based on the reciprocal elements of risk/probability and harm/severity.

[83] *Cambridge Water Co Ltd* v. *Eastern Counties Leather plc*, [1994] 2AC 264, [1993] UKHL.

principle or make adjustments in the burden of proof.[84] In the *Gabčíkovo* case, dealing with the 1977 bilateral Treaty on the Construction and Operation of the Gabčíkovo-Nagymaros Barrage System, the Court stated only that it "is mindful that, in the field of environmental protection, vigilance and prevention are required on account of the often irreversible character of damage to the environment and of the limitations inherent in the very mechanism of reparation of this type of damage."[85] In the *Pulp Mills* case, the Court considered that "a precautionary approach may be relevant in the interpretation and application of the provisions of [the 1975 Statute of the River Uruguay]."[86] The Court, however, expressly refused to reverse the burden of proof in the case based on the precautionary principle.

In contrast, the precautionary principle has become part of EU law and is often applied in the context of consumer protection, particularly in regard to food.[87] It has also had a reception in decisions of dispute settlement and appellate bodies of the World Trade Organization. In the *Beef Hormones* case, the Appellate Body held that member states are not restricted in their risk assessments to those hazards to human health that can be proved by scientific means.[88] A trade-restrictive measure can be based on a risk assessment if it is reasonably supported by the results of scientific studies – i.e., there is a rational relationship between the measure and the risk assessment, even if the scientific study utilized does not represent mainstream opinion in the relevant scientific community. Thus, even respectable minority views among scientists may constitute a sufficient justification for preventive measures.

In *Tâtar* v. *Romania*, the European Court of Human Rights for the first time discussed the precautionary principle. The Court found that current scientific knowledge was not sufficiently certain to demonstrate a causal link between exposure to sodium cyanide and asthma. It nonetheless concluded that the applicants had demonstrated the existence of a serious and material risk for their health and well-being; this risk engendered, in turn, a duty on the part of the state to undertake an assessment, both at the time that it granted the operating permit and subsequent to the accident, and a duty to take appropriate measures to mitigate the risks revealed.[89] The Court noted the fact that the company had been able to continue its industrial operations by obtaining further authorizations after the January 2000 accident and held that this constituted a breach of the precautionary principle, according to which the absence of certainty with regard to current scientific and technical

[84] For a critique of the Court's approach to the scientific evidence, see *Pulp Mills*, [2010] ICJ Rep. 108 (dissenting opinion of Judges Al-Khasawneh and Simma), para. 28.

[85] *Gabčíkovo-Nagymaros*, [1997] ICJ Rep. 7, para. 140.

[86] *Pulp Mills*, [2010] ICJ Rep. 83, para. 164.

[87] See Rudolf Streinz, "Risk decisions in cases of persisting scientific uncertainty: the precautionary principle in European Food Law," in Gordon R. Woodman and Diethelm Klippel (eds.), *Risk and the Law* (Routledge 2009), pp. 53–81.

[88] *EC Measures concerning Meat and Meat Products (Hormones)*, WT/DS 26/AB/R and WT/DS 48/AB/R (WTO Appellate Body, 1998).

[89] *Tâtar*, paras. 104–7.

knowledge could not be used to justify any delay by the state in adopting effective and proportionate measures in response to the risks.[90]

On the national level, the Constitutional Court of South Africa determined that the National Environmental Management Act requires application of the precautionary approach, "a risk averse and cautious approach" that takes into account the limitation on present knowledge about the consequences of an environmental decision.[91] This precautionary approach was seen to be especially important in that NEMA requires authorities to investigate and address the cumulative impact of a development on the environmental and socioeconomic conditions.[92] The authorities thus had to insist on adequate precautionary measures to safeguard against the contamination of underground water in the face of scientific uncertainty as to the future impact of the proposed development. In the absence of such measures, the Court set aside the decision of the environmental authorities and required reconsideration consistent with the judgment. In doing so, it addressed the role of the judiciary:

> The role of the courts is especially important in the context of the protection of the environment and giving effect to the principle of sustainable development. The importance of the protection of the environment cannot be gainsaid. Its protection is vital to the enjoyment of the other rights contained in the Bill of Rights; indeed, it is vital to life itself. It must therefore be protected for the benefit of the present and future generations. The present generation holds the earth in trust for the next generation. This trusteeship position carries with it the responsibility to look after the environment. It is the duty of the court to ensure that this responsibility is carried out.[93]

If this is the case, and if the gravity of the potential harm as well as its likelihood of occurring are important in conducting a precautionary assessment, then the potential that a project or activity could harm human rights should impose even greater caution in decisions about approval, rejection, or mitigation, as well as stricter judicial review. It is not surprising that environmental texts like Rio Principle 15 and the UNFCCC call for taking precautionary measures despite scientific uncertainty "where there are threats of serious or irreversible damage," without specifying the object of the damage; it seems implicit that it is damage to the environment that is being considered, but there is no reason why the impact on

90 See ibid., paras. 66, 104.

91 *Fuel Retailers*, Case No. CCT 67/06 (South Africa, 2007). The case arose out of a decision by a provincial government agency to grant private parties permission to construct a filling station.

92 Section 24(7)(b) of NEMA provides "Procedures for the investigation, assessment and communication of the potential impact of activities must, as a minimum, ensure . . . investigation of the potential impact, including cumulative effects, of the activity and its alternatives on the environment, socio-economic conditions and cultural heritage, and assessment of the significance of that potential impact."

93 *Fuel Retailers*, para. 102.

human rights should not also be included in the evaluation. Application of the precautionary principle may also be reinforced when human rights are involved by reference to the extensive jurisprudence on the positive obligation of states to prevent infringement of human rights. Although human rights treaties generally do not mention the environment, case law has detailed the obligations of states to prevent environmental harm that would limit the ability to enjoy internationally-guaranteed human rights.[94]

Application of the precautionary principle may allow the applicant to make out a prima facie case of illegality, requiring the responding party to come forward with adequate contrary evidence to overcome the prima facie case. In disputes involving scientific uncertainty about potential future harm, judicial bodies will have to make decisions even though potentially decisive facts are unavailable at the time of adjudication.

SETTING ASIDE DECISIONS, LAWS, AND REGULATIONS: WHAT LEVEL OF SCRUTINY?

Both national and international courts have used environmental law and science to give content to the level of environmental protection required by human rights law. At the national level, *Montana Environmental Information Center* v. *Department of Environmental Quality* provides an example of strict judicial scrutiny of actions taken by other authorities.[95] Plaintiffs in the case asserted that specific groundwater discharges degraded high-quality waters, as shown by the government's water quality standards. The Court concluded that:

> . . . the right to a clean and healthful environment is a fundamental right because it is guaranteed by the Declaration of Rights found at Article II, Section 3 of Montana's Constitution, and that any statute or rule which implicates that right must be strictly scrutinized and can only survive scrutiny if the state establishes a compelling state interest and that its action is closely tailored to effectuate that interest and is the least onerous path that can be taken to achieve the state's objective.[96]

The Court concluded that the delegates who adopted the provision intended to provide protections that were both anticipatory and preventive.

The European Court, to the contrary, affords a high degree of deference to substantive decisions of governments. Beyond ensuring that any domestic environmental rights are enforced, the European Court examines the domestic law to see if the state has ensured a fair balance between the interests of the community and the rights of those affected. The Court accords each state a wide margin of appreciation in this respect, because national authorities "are in principle better placed than an

[94] See, e.g., *Oneryildiz*, *Fadayeva*.
[95] *Montana Environmental Information Center*, 988 P.2d 1236 (1999).
[96] Ibid., p. 1246.

international court to assess the requirements" in a particular local context and to determine the most appropriate environmental policies and individual measures while taking into account the needs of the local community.[97]

The wide margin of appreciation afforded governments means that the Court will only find a violation if there is a "manifest error of appreciation" by the national authorities in striking a fair balance between the competing interests of the different private actors.[98] The final evaluation as to whether the justification given by the state is relevant and sufficient remains subject to review by the Court, but "only in exceptional circumstances" will the court look beyond the procedures followed to disallow the conclusions reached by domestic authorities on the environmental protection measures to be taken on the projects and activities allowed to proceed.[99] Even if it finds that the state decided wrongly, the Court will not determine exactly what should have been done to reduce the pollution in a more efficient way.[100]

In *Budayeva* v. *Russia*, looking at the substantive aspect of the government's obligations respecting dangerous activities, the Court placed special emphasis on the adoption of regulations geared to the special features of the activity in question, particularly with regard to the level of the potential risk to human life.[101] Such regulations must govern the licensing, setting up, operation, security, and supervision of the activity and must make it compulsory for all those concerned to take practical measures to ensure the effective protection of citizens whose lives might be endangered by the inherent risks.[102] Supervision and monitoring are also required. The choice of particular practical measures is in principle a matter within the state's margin of appreciation and the Court will seek to avoid placing an impossible or disproportionate burden on authorities.[103] The wide margin of appreciation afforded in environmental matters, due to their technical complexity and the variations in state priorities and resources, is given even greater weight in the sphere of emergency relief after the fact, in responding to weather events. The Court held that the state's positive obligation is less in the context of natural disasters, "which are as such beyond human control," than in the sphere of dangerous activities of a man-made nature. The right to peaceful enjoyment of possessions, which is not absolute,

97 *Giacomelli* v. *Italy*, No. 59909/00 (European Court of Human Rights, 2007), para. 80.

98 *Fadayev*, para. 105.

99 Ibid., paras. 102, 105.

100 In particular, the Court said it would be going too far to assert that the state or the polluting undertaking was under an obligation to provide the applicant with free housing. Ibid., para. 133. It is enough to say that the situation called for a special treatment of those living near the plant.

101 *Budayeva and Others* v. *Russia*, Nos. 15339/02, 21166/02, 20058/02, 11673/02 and 15343/02 (European Court of Human Rights, 2008), para. 132.

102 Ibid.

103 Ibid., para. 135.

requires only that the state do what is reasonable in the circumstances.[104] The standard of care is different and higher when the risk involves potential loss of life.

As the *Tătar* case illustrates, the European Court has increasingly relied on international environmental law as a basis for determining the adequacy of measures taken by the respondent government. For Article 8 to be an effective guarantee, as consistent jurisprudence requires, the Court cannot defer entirely to decisions of states parties concerning the permissibility or conduct of industrial activities.[105] The solution increasingly adopted by the Court is to insist that each government comply with the state's own environmental laws and constitutional guarantees, its international treaty obligations, and accepted norms and principles of international environmental law. Although the Court does not refer to these norms and principles as customary international law, it does refer to Stockholm Principle 21 and Rio Principle 14 in recalling the general obligation of authorities to discourage and prevent transboundary environmental harm.[106] In this case, the Court explicitly stated that Romanian authorities should have applied, apart from national legislation, existing international environmental norms, including the precautionary principle, which the Court found had become binding European law, citing ECJ judgments that call the precautionary principle one of the foundations of the EU policy favoring a high level of environmental protection.[107]

Noise pollution cases often turn on compliance with local environmental laws. Where the state conducts inspections and finds that the activities do not exceed permissible noise levels established for the area, at least in the absence of evidence of serious and long-term health problems, the European Court is unlikely to find that the state failed to take reasonable measures to ensure the enjoyment of Article 8 rights. In other words, where no specific environmental quality is guaranteed by the constitution or applicable human rights instrument, the courts accord considerable deference to the level of protection enacted by state or local authorities.

Adjudicating cases under broadly-worded standards is not new for judges, however, nor is it uncommon for them to be faced with adjudicating highly technical matters. Courts must regularly, and on a case-by-case basis, define what constitutes "reasonable," "fair," or "equitable" conduct. With the adoption of constitutional environmental rights provisions and increasing acceptance of the links between environmental degradation and the violation of other human rights, national and international tribunals struggle to give substance to environmental rights without

[104] Ibid., para. 174. While the Court found that the measures taken by the state were negligent, it found the causal link was not well established. The mudslide of 2000 being exceptionally strong, the Court said it was unclear whether a functioning warning system or proper maintenance of the defense infrastructure would have mitigated the damage.

[105] See *Tâtar*, para. 108, in which the Court described its inability to substitute its judgment for that of local authorities regarding environmental and industrial policy, with the consequence that it affords a wide margin of appreciation to governments on such matters.

[106] Ibid., para. 111.

[107] Ibid., paras. 69(h), 112.

overstepping the judicial function. In general, courts have taken the view that such enactments serve to place environmental protection in a position superior to ordinary legislation and it is the role of the courts to enforce the protections.

REMEDIES

From applying the law to the facts, where the judge may act as fact-finder, interpreter, or developer of the law, the case moves to the fashioning of remedies, where environmental cases arguably reveal a growth in judicial power.[108] This is particularly true when a judge or tribunal enjoins actions approved by political or administrative bodies, from banning the release of genetically-modified organisms to enjoining construction of a hydroelectric project. Claims of judicial overreach sometimes follow.

Although interim or precautionary measures are not technically a remedy, they can serve to prevent harm. In the International Tribunal for the Law of the Sea (ITLOS), the *Bluefin Tuna Cases* involved a request for interim measures to limit the taking of fish to ensure that the parties' annual catches did not exceed the agreed annual national allocations.[109] The Tribunal declared that the "conservation of the living resources of the sea is an element in the protection and preservation of the marine environment,"[110] and there was a need to prevent serious harm to the southern bluefin tuna, but given the lack of scientific certainty regarding measures to be taken to conserve the stock of the fish or whether the stock was improving, the court concluded that "the parties should in the circumstances act with prudence and caution to ensure that effective conservation measures were taken to prevent serious harm to the stock, as a matter of urgency."[111] Although the Tribunal avoided mentioning the precautionary principle, the need to protect and preserve the environment clearly led to preventive measures being adopted.

International courts have generally avoided requiring the dismantling of structures or projects that have been constructed, even if violations of environmental or human rights law is proved. There is, no doubt, concern about non-compliance with any judgment that would issue such an order. In addition, the harm caused by removal of a major dam could itself be considerable. Litigants thus are more likely to prevail when they take anticipatory action to prevent a project or activity from going forward, even though the available evidence may be less compelling than after the

[108] See generally Olivier Lecucq and Sandrine Maljean-Dubois (eds.), *Le Rôle du Juge dans le Développement du Droit de l'Environnement* (Bruylant, 2008).

[109] *Southern Bluefin Tuna Cases (New Zealand* v. *Japan; Australia* v. *Japan), Provisional Measures*, ITLOS Rep. 1999, 280–336 (ITLOS, 1999). The *Bluefin Tuna* cases were initiated separately by Australia and New Zealand against Japan, but joined by the Court.

[110] Ibid., para. 70.

[111] Ibid., para. 77.

harm has occurred. The dilemma for judges is when to override governmental decisions taken in accordance with the law, on the grounds that the environmental and human rights consequences are too serious to defer to the legislative or administrative bodies. Each case will present its own set of circumstances, but there should be a greater role for precaution when both human rights and the environment are at stake.

7

Reasoning Up

Environmental Rights as Customary International Law

Rebecca M. Bratspies[*]

For nearly a half century, the international community has embraced the goal of "defend[ing] and improv[ing] the human environment for present and future generations."[1] Over that time period, there has been a veritable explosion of international treaty-making concerning state environmental obligations.[2] Agreements like the Law of Sea Convention, the Convention on Biological Diversity, and the UN Framework Convention on Climate Change, which have near-universal membership, articulate a series of generalized state obligations vis-à-vis the environment. Even as the tally of multinational environmental agreements grows, however, the actual condition of the environment continues to deteriorate precipitously.[3] We are now at the point where planetary boundaries are being crossed, and many thinkers have taken to announcing the arrival of the Anthropocene – a global epoch in which human activity is the primary driver of planetary conditions.[4]

The struggle to generate positive environmental changes within states has prompted a search for new legal tools and approaches. Increasingly, scholars, activists, and policymakers turn to international human rights law as a potentially transformative framework for promoting environmental protection. The common-sense proposition that enjoyment of basic human rights hinges on adequate environmental

* Professor of Law and Director of the CUNY Center for Urban Environmental Reform.

1 Declaration of the UN Conference on the Human Environment, UN Doc. A/CONF.48/14/Rev.1 (June 5–16, 1972).

2 See Governing Council of the UN Environment Programme, *Background Paper for the Ministerial Consultations: Global Environment Outlook and Emerging Issues: Setting Effective Global Environmental Goals: Discussion Paper by the Executive Director*, UN Doc. UNEP/GCSS.XII/13 (January 5, 2012).

3 For details, see UN Environment Programme, *Keeping Track of Our Changing Environment: From Rio to Rio+20 (1992–2012)* (2011).

4 See, e.g., Jan Zalasiewicz et al., "The New World of the Anthropocene," *Environmental Science and Technology* 2228 (2010), p. 44.

protection enjoys wide support. Indeed, it has been roughly two decades since Judge Weeramantry characterized protection of the environment as "the *sine qua non* for numerous human rights such as the right to health and the right to life itself."[5] There is broad consensus that "environmental degradation can and does interfere with the enjoyment of a wide range of human rights."[6] There is also broad agreement that considering environmental protection through a human rights lens leads states toward choices that promote human dignity, equality, and freedom, while simultaneously improving environmental policies.[7]

Yet, even as environmental protection and human rights discourses increasingly converge, fundamental questions remain about where and how claims about environmental rights fit into the framework of international law of human rights. To date there is no clear answer. Some theories focus on ways that environmental degradation impacts various well-established human rights like the right to life or the right to food.[8] Others theorize directly about a free-standing human right to a healthy environment.[9] This latter group faces the challenge of establishing that the growing body of environmental norms has actually crystallized into a legal obligation under customary international law.

Traditionally, the inquiry around customary law focuses on the international level, either reasoning inductively to derive custom from the course of interstate interactions, or reasoning deductively[10] from multilateral treaties and other international instruments, such as declarations from the UN General Assembly and UN treaty bodies.[11] This top-down analysis considers whether international conduct has crystallized into customary international law that binds states. This approach allows one to "reason down" to principles of customary law from the growing body of international soft law. For example, much will undoubtedly be made of the Paris

5 *Gabcikovo-Nagymaros Case (Hungary* v. *Slovakia)*, [1997] ICJ Rep. 91 (separate opinion of Judge Weeramantry).

6 John H. Knox, *Report of the Independent Expert on the Issue of Human Rights Obligations Relating to the Enjoyment of a Safe, Clean, Healthy and Sustainable Environment: Mapping Report*, UN Doc. A/HRC/25/53 (December 30, 2013).

7 John H. Knox, *Report of the Special Rapporteur on the Issue of Human Rights Obligations Relating to the Enjoyment of a Safe, Clean, Healthy and Sustainable Environment: Implementation Report*, UN Doc. A/HRC/31/53 (December 28, 2015), para. 12.

8 In other places, I have described this approach in detail. See Rebecca Bratspies, "Do We Need a Human Right to a Healthy Environment?," *Santa Clara Journal of International Law* 13(1) (2015), pp. 31–69, at 51–7.

9 Ibid., pp. 57–61.

10 See Anthea Elizabeth Roberts, "Traditional and Modern Approaches to Customary International Law: A Reconciliation," *American Journal of International Law* 95(4) (2001), pp. 757–91, at 762–3.

11 See e.g., *Military and Paramilitary Activities in and Against Nicaragua (Nicaragua* v. *United States of America), Merits*, [1986] ICJ Rep. 14 (deriving customary law from General Assembly resolutions).

Agreement's acknowledgement, albeit in its preamble, of the state obligation to consider human rights in responding to climate change.[12]

This chapter takes a different approach to locating environmental human rights norms within the framework of international law. Using the development of the obligation to conduct an environmental impact assessment (EIA) as an example, this chapter posits that customary international law of environmental rights can emerge from the near-universal environmental obligations states impose on themselves through their own municipal law. Under such an approach, the consistency of environmental principles enshrined across state regulatory law becomes evidence of both state practice and *opinio juris* in the form of the environmental obligations that states consider themselves bound to respect and uphold. Analytically, this approach bears some resemblance to a more common form of "reasoning up" – which involves staking a claim that environmental rights have become customary international law on the ubiquity of environmental provisions in state constitutions.[13] In short, this chapter argues that "reasoning up" from state municipal law demonstrates that key principles have crystallized into customary law about the nature of state obligations in the environmental context.

CUSTOM AS A SOURCE OF LAW

Custom as a source of law has been subject to extensive scholarly interrogation.[14] Article 38 of the ICJ Statute explicitly directs the International Court of Justice to look to customary law in deciding international legal disputes. In particular, Article 38(1) further specifies that custom is "evidence that a practice is to be considered legally binding under international law."[15] However, the ICJ Statute nowhere

[12] Paris Agreement, December 12, 2015, in force November 4, 2016, UN Doc. FCCC/CP/2015/19. In this volume, see Lavanya Rajamani, Chapter 13; Sumudu Atapattu, Chapter 14.

[13] See, e.g., David R. Boyd, *The Environmental Rights Revolution: A Global Study of Constitutions, Human Rights, and the Environment* (University of British Columbia Press, 2012); James R. May and Erin Daly, *Global Environmental Constitutionalism* (Cambridge University Press, 2015).

[14] Indeed, scholarly opinions run the gamut. Where some view custom as "enjoy[ing] privileged status in the international order" and "even more central than the treaty," see, e.g., Brigitte Stern, "Custom at the Heart of International Law," *Duke Journal of Comparative and International Law* 11(1) (2001), pp. 89–108, at 89, others see a legal fiction that does not influence state behavior. See, e.g., Jack L. Goldsmith and Eric Posner, *The Limits of International Law* (Oxford University Press, 2005). See also W. Michael Reisman, "The Cult of Custom in the Late 20th Century," *California Western International Law Journal* 17 (1987), pp. 133, 136 (criticizing custom as a "vague term" telling little more than that the rule in question "did not derive from a legislative process.")

[15] In relevant part, Article 38(1)(b) provides that: "The Court, whose function is to decide in accordance with international law such disputes as are submitted to it, shall apply: . . . international custom, as evidence of a general practice accepted as law . . ." Statute of the International Court of Justice, June 26, 1945, 33 UNTS 993, art. 38(1). Section 102(1)(b) of the *Restatement (Third) of Foreign Relations Law* parallels this construction, stating in relevant

specifies when a practice should be considered a custom for purposes of this analysis. Nor is the term "custom" defined. Nevertheless, the ICJ, assisted by "the most highly qualified publicists of the various nations,"[16] has fleshed out a working definition of custom as "evidence of a general practice accepted as law."

To be considered customary law, a candidate rule proposition must satisfy two elements: state practice and *opinio juris*.[17] State practice means an observed pattern of activity generally and consistently adhered to by states. *Opinio juris* means that states accept the practice as a legal obligation. Custom is thus based on empirically-observed interstate interactions, combined with subjective state belief about the content of legal obligations.[18]

Much ink has been spilled over the proper balance between state practice and state belief in assessing customary law. Based on the assertion that environmental protection presents unique challenges under international law, some "highly qualified jurists" have advocated relaxing the requirement of state belief (or consent).[19] Others suggest that state practice is not as central as this definition suggests.[20] Although the precise contours for the definition of customary law remain contested,[21] there is at least a general consensus that the relevant inquiry includes an assessment of whether international actors have consistently followed a rule, and whether they observe that rule out of a sense of legal obligation.[22]

In determining whether a candidate rule has matured into a custom recognized by Article 38 as a source of international law, the ICJ considers the uniformity,

part: "(1) A rule of international law is one that has been accepted as such by the international community of states … in the form of customary law …" *Restatement (Third) of the Foreign Relations Law of the United States*, §102 (1987).

[16] Statute of the International Court of Justice, art. 38(1)(d).

[17] *North Sea Continental Shelf Cases (Federal Republic of Germany/Denmark/Netherlands)*, [1969] ICJ Rep. 3, 44.

[18] *Restatement (Third)*, §102(2); see also Ian Brownlie, *Principles of Public International Law*, 5th ed. (Oxford University Press, 1998), pp. 4–11; Michael Byers, *Custom, Power and the Power of Rules* (Cambridge University Press, 1999), p. 130.

[19] See, e.g., Jonathan Charney, "Universal International Law," *American Journal of International Law* 87(4) (1993), pp. 529, 551 (proposing that declarations from multilateral forums can be considered binding customary law, even in the absence of state consent); see also Anthony D'Amato, "Trashing Customary International Law," *American Journal of International Law* 87 (1) (1987), pp. 101, 102 (asserting more generally that customary law should be derived from what states actually do).

[20] See, e.g., Andrew T. Guzman, "Saving Customary International Law," *Michigan Journal of International Law* 115 (2005), pp. 115, 122 (claiming that state practice does not contribute to the existence of customary international law).

[21] Marti Koskenniemi, *From Apology to Utopia* (Cambridge University Press 1989), p. 355 (noting that custom as a source of law can be "an apology" for power because custom often privileges wealthy European and imperialist powers at the expense of new states or former colonies).

[22] See *Asylum Case (Colombia* v. *Peru)*, [1950] ICJ Rep. 266, 277 (describing custom as a "constant and uniform usage, accepted as law"); Frederic L. Kirgis, "Custom as a Sliding Scale," *American Journal of International Law* 81 (1987), pp. 146, 149.

consistency, and longevity of the rule in question.[23] There is no precise formula to indicate how widespread a practice must be before it will be considered uniform enough to qualify, but it is clear that uniformity need not be perfect.[24] In the *Lotus* case, for example, the Court found customary international law based on the actions of six western states.[25] Similarly, state conduct need not always be in conformity with the rule, so long as inconsistencies are treated as a breach of legal obligation rather than evidence of an alternative norm.[26] And, under the appropriate circumstances, relatively recent legal developments can rapidly become customary law.[27] For example, it took less than two decades for state claims to offshore oil and gas deposits based on sovereignty over the continental shelf to become customary law.[28]

The question of whether a rule should be considered customary international law has far-reaching ramifications. Something becomes international custom "not because it was prescribed by any superior power, but because it has been generally accepted as a rule of conduct."[29]

Unlike treaties, where affirmative state action is required before a state is bound, silence is treated as consent in the context of custom. Unless a state persistently and clearly objects,[30] it will be bound by a customary rule.

CUSTOM AND HUMAN RIGHTS

Human rights occupy a curious place in the pantheon of international law. At the same time that thinkers like Theodor Meron have viewed custom as an important source of human rights,[31] others have characterized human rights as a radical break from what had traditionally been considered customary law.[32] Either way, there is

[23] *North Sea Continental Shelf Cases*, p. 73.

[24] *Anglo Norwegian Fisheries Case (United Kingdom* v. *Norway)*, [1951] ICJ Rep. 116, 138; see also *Restatement (Third)*, §102, comment b (noting that a practice can be considered general even if it is not universally followed).

[25] *Case of the S. S. Lotus (France* v. *Turkey)*, [1927] P.C.I.J. (ser. A) No. 10, at 29.

[26] *Asylum Case*, pp. 276–7; *Military and Paramilitary Activities*, p. 98.

[27] See *North Sea Continental Shelf Cases*, p. 73 ("even without the passage of any considerable period of time, a very widespread and representative participation in [a] convention might suffice of itself [to crystallize customary international law], provided it included that of States whose interests were specially affected").

[28] Ibid., p. 44.

[29] *The Paquete Habana*, 175 U.S. 677, 711 (1900).

[30] *Anglo Norwegian Fisheries Case*, p. 131.

[31] See generally Theodor Meron, *Human Rights and Humanitarian Norms as Customary Law* (Oxford University Press, 1989); see also Myres S. McDougal et al., *Human Rights and the World Public Order: The Basic Politics of an International Order of Human Dignity* (Yale University Press, 1980).

[32] Louis Henkin, "Human Rights and State Sovereignty," *Georgia Journal of International and Comparative Law* 25 (1995–6), pp. 31, 37, 40.

no doubt that in the decades since Nuremberg,[33] human rights have become core principles of international law. As a result of what Anthony D'Amato calls this "human rights revolution," traditional notions of sovereignty no longer shield a state from international scrutiny vis-à-vis its treatment of individuals and groups within the state.[34] The scope of international law now extends to the welfare of individuals within their state at the hand of their state, with even the core principle of non-intervention into the internal affairs of sovereign states[35] yielding in the face of large-scale violations of human rights.[36] Indeed, nothing in the UN Charter permanently divides state actions between the purely domestic and the legitimately international. Instead, Article 13 carves out space for the progressive development of international law and the realization of human rights, allowing the scope of issues considered to be of international concern to evolve with changing circumstances.[37]

Climate change, loss of biodiversity, deforestation, and the spread of toxic pollutants, among other problems, make it increasingly clear that the enjoyment of basic human rights hinges on adequate protection for the environment.[38] Thus, environmental protection has become a vital part of human rights discourse. Putting aside the question of whether there is, or should be, a free-standing human right to a healthy environment, there can be no question that environmental degradation increasingly poses an obstacle to "the enjoyment of a wide range of human rights."[39] Perhaps for that reason, advocates are increasingly urging decision makers to consider environmental protection through a human rights lens. The recognition that environmental and human rights problems are frequently entwined has the potential to guide decision makers toward better, more

33 The U.S. Supreme Court has identified the Nuremberg tribunal as a critical source for examining the scope of customary international law concerning human rights. *Kiobel v. Royal Dutch Petroleum*, 133 S. Ct. 1659 (2013).

34 Anthony D'Amato, "Human Rights as Part of Customary International Law: A Plea for Change of Paradigms," *Georgia Journal of International and Comparative Law* 25 (1995–6), p. 47.

35 Charter of the United Nations, June 26, 1945, in force October 24, 1945, 1 UNTS 16, art. 2(7) ("Nothing contained in the present Charter shall authorize the United Nations to intervene in matters which are essentially within the domestic jurisdiction of any state . . . .").

36 The clearest example is perhaps the Responsibility to Protect (R2P) doctrine that emerged from the 2005 UN World Summit. See General Assembly res. 60/1 (October 24, 2005), paras. 138, 139. The Security Council has invoked R2P in multiple resolutions. See www.responsibilitytoprotect.org/index.php/component/content/article/136-latest-news/5221–references-to-the-responsibility-to-protect-in-security-council-resolutions.

37 Charter of the United Nations, art. 13(1).

38 See, e.g., Aarhus Convention on Access to Information, Public Participation in Decision-Making and Access to Justice in Environmental Matters, June 25, 1998, in force October 21, 2001, 2161 UNTS 447, pmbl.

39 John H. Knox, *Report of the Independent Expert on the Issue of Human Rights Obligations Relating to the Enjoyment of a Safe, Clean, Healthy and Sustainable Environment: Preliminary Report*, UN Doc. A/HRC/22/43 (December 24, 2012), para. 34.

sustainable environmental choices that improve the quality of the environment while simultaneously promoting human dignity and equality.[40]

While the synergistic effects of protecting the environment and promoting human rights seem clear, the relationship between international legal principles concerning human rights and environmental protection remain somewhat murky. Given the complexity of these bodies of international law, not to mention the rapidity with which both have developed, it is not surprising that there is no clear consensus about how their intersection might form customary international law. What we are talking about, after all, is nothing less than the formation of unwritten yet universally binding rules between nations about environmental protection as a human right.

Nevertheless, there are clear signs that a consensus is emerging. In March 2014, the Independent Expert on human rights and the environment submitted a mapping report to the Human Rights Council indicating burgeoning agreement about an emerging set of norms related to the environment, focused on both procedural and substantive obligations.[41] On the procedural side, these emerging norms include a state obligation to make environmental information publicly available, to facilitate public participation in environmental decision making, and to provide access to legal remedies.[42] The substantive obligations involve the state duty to adopt an institutional framework capable of protecting against environmental harm that may infringe on enjoyment of human rights and to regulate private actors to protect against environmental harms.[43] This chapter suggests that "reasoning up" – looking to state practice in the form of domestic regulation – supports the conclusion that at least the procedural environmental rights have crystallized into customary international law.

"REASONING UP" TO CUSTOMARY LAW

Using obligations identified in state-based regimes to establish international legal obligations of states, "reasoning up" is not the most typical analysis for identifying international customary law. The more common practice involves reasoning down – using state practices in state-to-state interactions to identify those obligations that bind a state's behaviors, both beyond and within its borders. This "reasoning down" approach focuses on the language of multilateral treaties, and on the diplomatic practices of states in the international sphere. Often, this approach relies on the decisions of international tribunals interpreting state actions and intentions.

[40] See, e.g., Knox, *Implementation Report*, para. 12.
[41] Knox, *Mapping Report*.
[42] Ibid., para. 29.
[43] Ibid., para. 46.

Generally, discussions of customary law focus on the way that states behave vis-à-vis each other. This vision of customary law focuses on how states navigate those points where state sovereignties intersect. Traditionally, when a state acted entirely internally, there was no other state "interested" in the action and therefore no role for customary international law. Human rights law changed that. Today it is clear that actions a government takes vis-à-vis its own citizens, within its own territory, are actions to which international customary law might apply. As such, human rights law reveals that customary law can be about the inherent obligations and contours of sovereignty within the state as well as externally with regard to other states. Even with this modification, legal experts still typically deploy "reasoning down" strategies to discern the content of this customary law of human rights. For example, the reports of the Independent Expert on human rights and the environment direct attention to international treaties and soft-law declarations in their discussion of customary international law. Similarly, many scholars have pointed to the spread of environmental rights in state constitutions, together with the growing multiplicity of environmental treaties and soft law agreements, as grounds for recognizing environmental rights under customary international law.[44] Others go so far as to characterize soft-law instruments as a means of identifying custom through "the solidifying of indicators for a documentation of the opinio juris" of States.[45]

While "reasoning down" may be the more conventional approach, it is not the sole criterion for establishing customary international law. A less-frequently employed strategy, but one still solidly within the accepted approaches to identifying customary law involves "reasoning up" – recognizing how states view their own obligations within their own territorial borders, and then using that information to construct a theory of the obligations that bind a state under international law.[46] Indeed, for nearly two centuries, "reasoning up" from municipal law has played a role in making assessments about what constitutes customary international law.[47]

[44] See, e.g., Boyd, *The Environmental Rights Revolution*, pp. 88, 91, 111, 113; Lynda Collins, "Are We There Yet? The Right to Environment in International and Environmental Law," *McGill International Journal of Sustainable Development Law and Policy* 3 (2007), pp. 119, 129, 136; John Lee, "The Underlying Legal Theory to Support a Well-Defined Human Right to a Healthy Environment as a Principle of Customary International Law," *Columbia Journal of Environmental Law* 25 (2000), pp. 283, 339.

[45] Harald Hohmann, *Precautionary Legal Duties and Principles of Modern International Environmental Law* (Graham & Trotman/Martinus Nijhoff, 1994), p. 337.

[46] The U.S. Department of State has long highlighted the relationship between municipal regulations and customary law. See Arthur Rovine (ed.), 1974 *Digest of United States Practice in International Law*, 1973 at 3 (Government Printing Office, 1974). State municipal law is almost always included as a state practice that can be used as evidence of custom. See, e.g., Michael Akehurst, "Custom as a Source of International Law," *British Yearbook of International Law* 47 (1977), pp. 1, 4–10 (asserting that "the mere enactment of a law is a form of State practice").

[47] See, e.g., *Paquete Habana* (looking to domestic law of key European seafaring states in deciding the content of customary international law with regard to ship seizures.).

This "reasoning up" approach focuses on the commonalities in how states use their own lawmaking powers to discern customary international law. To that end, "reasoning up" draws heavily on shared legal principles in state constitutions, state court decisions, and state municipal law. For all its seeming unconventionality, this approach has some significant advantages.[48] Because it draws on how states actually define their own powers in their own constitutive documents, "reasoning up" responds to critics who disparage customary law as a tool for reinforcing global power disparities under the guise of law.[49] And because it focuses on how states actually exercise these powers, "reasoning up" also responds to those critics who deride customary law as aspirational and idealized standards with little relation to actual state conduct.[50] Thus, "reasoning up" can be a way to identify both elements of customary international law: state practice and *opinio juris*. While human rights law aspires to be more than the lowest common denominator of state practices, surely that lowest common denominator creates a floor for the minimum conduct that international law expects of states.

"REASONING UP" ABOUT ENVIRONMENTAL PROCESS AS CUSTOMARY INTERNATIONAL LAW

Climate change, loss of biodiversity, and the spread of toxic pollutants, among other environmental challenges, make it abundantly clear that the environmental consequences of state decisions affect a state's ability to realize and protect human rights within its territory. This insight has prompted calls to recognize state environmental decisions as implicating human rights and to identify international legal principles that govern state environmental conduct. The Special Rapporteur on human rights and the environment has done an excellent job of collecting and sifting international law and international declarations on this point. Yet the challenge of articulating a theory for why and how these soft-law statements might create binding legal obligations remains. For example, in the *Pulp Mills* case, the ICJ characterized environmental impact assessment (EIA) as having "gained so much acceptance among States that it may now be considered a requirement under general international law."[51] Yet the ICJ offered no support for this assertion, and

48 This approach also has disadvantages, particularly because human rights law aspires to be more than the lowest common denominator of state domestic legal practice.

49 See generally Shawkat Alam et al. (eds.), *International Environmental Law and the Global South* (Cambridge University Press, 2015).

50 J. Shand Watson, *Theory and Reality in the International Protection of Human Rights* (Transnational Publishers, 1999), pp. 85–9; Daniel Bodansky, "Customary (And Not So Customary) International Environmental Law," *Indiana Journal of Global Legal Studies* 3(1) (1995), pp. 105–19, 110–11.

51 *Pulp Mills on the River Uruguay (Argentina* v. *Uruguay)*, [2010] ICJ Rep. 83, para. 204.

limited this requirement to situations in which the proposed industrial activity poses a significant risk of transboundary harm.[52]

Using "reasoning down" tactics alone to root this obligation in international law can be problematic. Conventions articulating enforceable state environmental process obligations, like the Aarhus or Espoo Convention,[53] are certainly very important to the progressive development of international law. Indeed, many of the innovations from these conventions were incorporated into the International Law Commission's Draft Articles on Prevention of Transboundary Harm from Hazardous Activities.[54] However, the Draft Articles have not been embraced as grounds for a new, binding treaty, and the Aarhus and Espoo treaties are binding only on state parties. Moreover, membership in both treaty regimes is limited to a self-selected group of (mostly) European countries.[55] Extrapolating from those narrow, Eurocentric treaties to a principle of customary international law that would be binding on all states has unpleasant echoes of colonialism.

Indeed, when Argentina argued that principles from the Espoo Convention should govern the *Pulp Mills* dispute, the ICJ rejected this contention on the ground that neither state in the case was party to the treaty. The ICJ made it very clear that its process of "reasoning down" to an EIA obligation did not rest on these treaties, at least not alone. Instead, the ICJ directed attention to many widely-subscribed soft-law documents embracing EIAs. The Court also tied the obligation to conduct an EIA to the state obligation to ensure that activities within a state's jurisdiction and control respect the environment of other states or of areas beyond national control.[56] Thus, the ICJ squarely situated the obligation to conduct an EIA to the *sic utere* norm stated in Principle 21 of the Stockholm Declaration.[57]

In terms of the specific procedures and content to be included in those EIAs, however, the Court was more circumspect, refusing to find that either Principle 5 of the 1987 Goals and Principles of Environmental Impact Assessment of the United

[52] Ibid. Assertions that EIAs have become customary international law date back to at least the early 1990s. See, e.g., Nicholas A. Robinson, "International Trends in Environmental Impact," *Boston College Environmental Affairs Law* Review 19 (1991), pp. 591, 602.

[53] Espoo Convention on Environmental Impact Assessment in a Transboundary Context, February 25, 1991, in force September 10, 1997, 1989 UNTS 310.

[54] See "Draft Articles on Prevention of Transboundary Harm from Hazardous Activities," in *Report of the International Law Commission on the Work of Its Fifty-Third Session*, UN Doc. A/56/10 (2001), pp. 370–7.

[55] As of June 2016, the Espoo Convention had forty-five parties, while the Aarhus Convention had forty-seven. With the exception of Canada, all were European or former Soviet-bloc countries.

[56] *Pulp Mills*, para. 193.

[57] Declaration of the UN Conference on the Human Environment, UN Doc. A/Conf.48/14/Rev.1 (June 5–16, 1972), Principle 21 ("States have, in accordance with the Charter of the United Nations and the principles of international law, the sovereign right to exploit their own resources pursuant to their own environmental policies, and the responsibility to ensure that activities within their jurisdiction or control do not cause damage to the environment of other States or of areas beyond the limits of national jurisdiction.").

Nations Environment Programme or the Draft Articles on Prevention of Transboundary Harm from Hazardous Activities imposed specific legal obligations on the conduct of that EIA.[58] Indeed, the only substantive components the ICJ recognized as part of this international law duty to conduct an EIA were the obligation to conduct the EIA prior to implementation of the project, and a duty to continually monitor environmental effects once the project commences.[59] Beyond those minima, the ICJ stated that "it is for each State to determine in its domestic legislation or in the authorization process for the project, the specific content of the environmental impact assessment required in each case."[60]

Like the ICJ in the *Pulp Mills* case, Stockholm Principle 21 focuses on transboundary environmental effects. Principle 17 of the Rio Declaration, by contrast, provides that signatory nations must undertake an EIA "for proposed activities that are likely to have a significant adverse impact on the environment and are subject to a decision of a competent national authority."[61] Thus, the Rio Declaration does not premise the obligation to conduct an EIA on the potential for transnational harm. Together, these two articulations of state obligation have become a cornerstone of international environmental legal theory and are widely cited as evidence that the requirement to conduct EIAs amounts to *opinio juris* – what states believe they are obligated to do. Yet this kind of "reasoning down" to custom is vulnerable to the critique that it blurs the lines between customary international law and aspirational statements of international policy. After all, as critics are apt to point out, neither the Stockholm nor the Rio Declaration is legally binding, and by their own terms they do not create any obligations under international law. In light of the notable state reluctance to negotiate international agreements with binding environmental obligations,[62] these critics do have a point.

That is where "reasoning up" comes in. Support for the proposition that EIAs have become customary international law can be found in widespread state practices under municipal law. Focusing on what states actually do – how states use law to construct their own environmental decision-making authority – reveals striking, near-universal commonalities that bolster the customary law status of the EIA norm encoded in Principle 17.[63] Virtually every government has enacted EIA requirements as explicit legal principles governing their environmental decision making within its borders, with regard to choices about the environment. Given the entwined nature of environmental decision making, and the frequently

[58] *Pulp Mills*, paras 205, 210, 216.

[59] Ibid., para. 205.

[60] Ibid., para. 205.

[61] Rio Declaration on Environment and Development, UN Doc. A/CONF.151/26/Rev.1, annex I (June 14, 1992), Principle 17.

[62] See Louis J. Kotzé, "Arguing Global Environmental Constitutionalism," *Transnational Environmental Law* 1(1) (2012), pp. 199, 202.

[63] There is also an argument that these commonalities signal that EIAs have become a general principle of international law under Article 38(1)(c) of the ICJ Statute.

transboundary consequences of so many environmental decisions, there is an argument that these common practices amount to a general state practice affecting other states significantly enough to implicate international law.[64] The fact that these are legal enactments created by the states themselves supports a contention that they are state practice, and the legally-binding nature of these practices supports a claim of *opinio juris*.

This approach must address the question of whether the practice has been prevalent enough, for long enough, to have crystallized into international law. EIAs do have a relatively short history. The first formal legislative enactment mandating an environmental assessment process was the groundbreaking 1969 National Environmental Policy Act adopted in the United States.[65] In other contexts, however, this has been more than enough time for a practice to crystallize into customary international law.[66]

Moreover, state conduct over five decades since EIAs first appeared on the scene only underscores the claim that EIAs have become customary international law. Over that time period, more and more states began requiring environmental impact assessments. Institutions like the World Bank have incorporated EIA procedures into their lending decisions, effectively requiring states to adopt EIA in order to qualify for World Bank loans.[67] Today, EIA processes are routinely required in virtually every corner of the globe. Indeed, according to a 2011 report, 191 of the United Nation's 193 member states had a legal obligation to conduct environmental impact assessments, under either domestic or international law.[68] The two lone holdouts were South Sudan (which had just achieved independence and been admitted to the United Nations) and North Korea. Of the other 191, the overwhelming majority (181 states) had national legislation requiring some form of EIA in decision making.[69] The other ten states were parties to a regional or international legal instrument mandating the use of EIAs. Subsequently, South Sudan adopted a new constitution, which like the overwhelming majority of modern state constitutions, provided for environmental rights.[70] To implement the new constitution,

[64] For example, John Knox has argued that transboundary EIAs embody the principle of non-discrimination within international law – requiring states to accord the same participation and voice to potentially affected parties regardless of whether the effects will be manifest internally or externally to a state. John H. Knox, "The Myth and Reality of Transboundary Environmental Impact Assessment," *American Journal of International Law* 96(2) (2002), pp. 291–319, 300–1.

[65] National Environmental Policy Act of 1969, 42 U.S.C. §§ 4321–27 (2016).

[66] See *North Sea Continental Shelf Cases*, p. 73.

[67] See World Bank, Operational Policy 4.01, Environmental Assessment (2013).

[68] See Richard K. Morgan, "Environmental Impact Assessment: The State of the Art," *Impact Assessment and Project Appraisals* 30 (2012), pp. 5, 9–14.

[69] Ibid., p. 6.

[70] Article 44 of the Transitional Constitution of the Republic of South Sudan provides that "every person or community shall have the right to a clean and healthy environment."

South Sudan has been adopting a slew of statutes requiring environmental planning and assessments.[71] As of 2016, all the members of the United Nations save North Korea had legally bound themselves to require environmental impact assessments. This universality is strong evidence that EIAs have become integrated into the very fabric of statehood as "the way" that states make environmental decisions. Thus, claims about the customary law status of EIAs are significantly strengthened when the kind of "reasoning down" the ICJ employed in the *Pulp Mills Case* is buttressed by evidentiary support derived from "reasoning up."

Yet using "reasoning up" to buttress the claim that the requirement that States conduct EIAs has become customary international law only goes so far. Near universal embrace of the *principle* of EIAs does not answer the question of what customary international law *requires* from that EIA. Indeed, in *Pulp Mills*, after finding that EIAs were part of general international law, the ICJ went on to conclude that there was no international law governing the content of those EIAs. Instead, that was to be determined individually by the relevant state, on the basis of domestic law. The level and rigor of implementation in state-mandated EIAs continues to vary widely. That creates a strange situation in which the content of an international legal obligation varies based on municipal law. Given the wide diversity of state requirements,[72] more work needs to be done to develop a consistent set of EIA obligations that can form the basis of a "reasoned up" EIA requirement. Fortunately, there seems to be a growing convergence in state law on this point as well, with states increasingly requiring disclosure of information and a participation period as part of an EIA, and creating an institutional structure that separates the responsibility for EIA preparation from the responsibility of approving the adequacy of the impact assessment.

CONCLUSION

Too often, international law and domestic law are treated as independent spheres developing in parallel rather than in dialectical tension. Looking to how states consistently bind themselves through their domestic laws can provide valuable information about how states view their own obligations *qua* states. Examining the development of EIA requirements in international law against a backdrop of municipal law underscores the point that state municipal law offers valuable insights about the kinds of evidence available to support a claim that a practice should be considered legally binding under international law. While the EIA context may be the clearest such example, there are other developing international law obligations

[71] Nhial Tiitmamer, *Assessment of Policy and Institutional Responses to Climate Change and Environmental Disaster Risks in South Sudan* (Sudd Institute, 2015).

[72] See John H. Knox, "Assessing the Candidates for a Global Treaty on Transboundary Environmental Impact Assessment," *New York University Environmental Law Journal* 12 (2003), p. 153.

that might benefit from a similar analysis. Two likely candidates include the emerging international obligation to provide for public participation in environmental decision making, and the obligation to afford access to effective remedies.

To be clear, the conclusion that the requirements to prepare EIAs are part of customary international law, important as it is, merely identifies a state obligation to engage in a process; it does not require a substantive outcome. EIA processes do not impose specific environmental standards and rarely require that States select environmentally protective outcomes. Instead, EIAs are procedural mechanisms to provide information to both the decision maker and the general public. To borrow a phrase from the U.S. Supreme Court, an EIA "does not mandate particular results, but simply prescribes the necessary process," or, in other words, it "merely prohibits uninformed – rather than unwise – agency action."[73] The broader challenge for the progressive development of international law is to ensure that these environmental decision processes actually produce decisions that protect the environment and respect substantive human rights.[74]

[73] *Robertson* v. *Methow Valley Citizens Council*, 490 U.S. 332, 351 (1989).

[74] See generally Matthew Baird and Richard Frankel, *Environmental Impact Assessment: Comparative Analysis in the Lower Mekong Delta* (Mekong Partnership for the Environment 2015) (comparing and critiquing effectiveness of EIA procedures in the countries of the Lower Mekong Delta); Jennifer C. Li, *Environmental Impact Assessments in Developing Countries: An Opportunity for Greater Environmental Security?* (Foundation for Environmental Stability and Security and U.S. Agency for International Development, 2008) (critiquing EIA laws by region); Neil Craik, *The International Law of Environmental Impact Assessment: Process, Substance and Integration* (Cambridge University Press, 2010) (describing both universality of EIA procedures and a lack of effectiveness).

8

In Search of a Right to a Healthy Environment in International Law

Jus Cogens *Norms*

*Louis J. Kotzé**

A right is generally taken to mean an entitlement (usually juridically embedded at an apex constitutional level) to which morality or valid rules of law give people a claim.[1] Although there is disagreement on its exact formulation, the right to a healthy environment could be understood to mean in trite terms the right to an ecologically balanced, sustainable, healthy, clean, or satisfactory environment that permits healthy living for human (and sometimes non-human) entities on Earth. An example of such a formulation is found in the Constitution of the Republic of South Africa of 1996;[2] numerous other domestic constitutions also currently provide for such a right.[3] To this end, the right to a healthy environment has arguably become "global" in the sense that it has spread transnationally,[4] and it continues to infiltrate domestic legal orders, creating a transnational environmental constitutional constellation or normative web that spans the globe and that increasingly shares common characteristics.[5]

* Research Professor, North-West University, South Africa; Visiting Professor of Environmental Law, University of Lincoln, United Kingdom. Sections 4 and 5 of this chapter are based in part on Louis Kotzé, "Constitutional Conversations in the Anthropocene: In Search of *Jus Cogens* Environmental Norms," in Maarten en Heijer and Harmen van der Wilt (eds.), *Netherlands Yearbook of International Law* (Springer, 2015), pp. 241–71.

[1] John Merrills, "Environmental Rights," in Daniel Bodansky, Jutta Brunnée, and Ellen Hey (eds.), *Oxford Handbook of International Environmental Law* (Oxford University Press, 2007), p. 665.

[2] Section 24 states: "Everyone has the right to an environment that is not harmful to their health or well-being . . ."

[3] See David R. Boyd, Chapter 2, and Erin Daly and James R. May, Chapter 3.

[4] Louis Kotzé and Caiphas Soyapi, "Transnational Environmental Law: The Birth of a Contemporary Analytical Perspective," in Douglas Fisher (ed.), *Research Handbook on Fundamental Concepts of Environmental Law* (Edward Elgar, 2016), pp. 82–110.

[5] See generally James R. May and Erin Daly, *Global Environmental Constitutionalism* (Cambridge University Press, 2015); David R. Boyd, *The Environmental Rights Revolution: A Global Study of Constitutions, Human Rights, and the Environment* (University of British Columbia Press, 2012); David R. Boyd, "Constitutions, Human Rights, and the Environment: National

One peculiar aspect of this right's domestic emergence is not that it is being adopted, or even its increasing popularity, but the way in which it is evolving domestically vis-à-vis the supra-national legal order. Some regional human rights instruments provide for a right to a healthy environment,[6] and while some of these regional instruments are binding and others not, the emergence and maturation of their environmental rights are encouraging and helpful to the extent that they cater for unique regional needs and circumstances. But because these regional efforts are fragmented and have different compliance and enforcement mechanisms, they do not create a uniform global standard. The reality then is that no universally binding international instrument has included such a right, despite calls for its adoption.[7]

Whereas domestic human rights are located in domestic sources of law and regional human rights in regional instruments, "[i]nternational human rights are those human needs that have received formal recognition as rights through the sources of international law."[8] An international right to a healthy environment, broadly conceived, is therefore a formally recognized moral entitlement to a particular quality of environment that states, and by implication their citizens, could claim through a source of international law that would hold states to account in the international regulatory domain vis-à-vis one another *and* in relation to their citizens. Somewhat counter-intuitively then, unlike the majority of social and political rights in many constitutions, the domestic codification of human rights to a healthy environment has not occurred on the back of international law that has foregrounded their domestic emergence. If one of the objectives of providing for such a right in international law is to encourage states to adopt a right to a healthy environment in domestic constitutions, it could be said that this objective has mostly

Approaches," in Anna Grear and Louis Kotzé (eds.), *Research Handbook on Human Rights and the Environment* (Edward Elgar, 2015), pp. 171–5; and the reports by the United Nations Special Rapporteur on human rights and the environment, available at www.srenvironment.org and www.ohchr.org/EN/Issues/Environment/SREnvironment/Pages/SRenvironmentIndex.aspx.

6 E.g., African Charter on Human and Peoples' Rights, June 27, 1981, in force October 21, 1986, 1520 UNTS 217, art. 24; Additional Protocol to the American Convention on Human Rights in the Area of Economic, Social and Cultural Rights: Protocol of San Salvador, November 17, 1988, in force November 16, 1999, 28 ILM 161, art. 11; Arab Charter on Human Rights, May 22, 2004, in force March 15, 2008, 12 IHRR 893 (2005), art. 38; Association of Southeast Asian Nations (ASEAN) Human Rights Declaration, November 18, 2012, art. 28(f). See generally Lilian Chenwi, Chapter 4, and Ole W. Pedersen, Chapter 5.

7 See, e.g., Laura Horn, "The Implications of the Concept of a Common Concern of Human Kind on a Human Right to a Healthy Environment," *Macquarie Journal of International and Comparative Environmental Law* 1 (2004), pp. 233–68; and more comprehensively, Stephen J. Turner, A *Global Environmental Right* (Routledge, 2014).

8 Stephen Marks, "Emerging Human Rights: A New Generation for the 1980s?," *Rutgers Law Review* 33 (1981), pp. 435–52 at 436.

been achieved, even in the absence of a single universally binding source of international law entrenching such a right.[9]

Is it then useful to continue the debate on an "international right to a healthy environment" if we accept its transnational domestic emergence and the unlikelihood of its emergence in the international law milieu? And if it is useful to continue the debate, how could we proceed? This chapter seeks to answer these questions by investigating alternative avenues for the possible existence or future emergence of an international right to a healthy environment. While Rebecca M. Bratspies, in Chapter 7, reflects on the place of such a right in customary international law, and Lilian Chenwi and Ole W. Pedersen, in Chapters 4 and 5, on its emergence in regional human rights instruments, the present chapter focuses on the existence or the possible emergence of this right in the realm of *jus cogens* or peremptory norms, which are those norms in international law from which no derogation is allowed and which bind all states regardless of their consent. As we shall see subsequently, *jus cogens* is an alternative, but potentially powerful, source of binding international law to entrench an international right to a healthy environment and/or at the very least, to bolster the myriad aspects that such a right would typically seek to protect.

In pursuit of an expanded exploration of a right to a healthy environment in international law, I commence by briefly showing the extent to which it could be said that such a right exists in international treaty law. I then elaborate on why we need to expand our search for an international right to a healthy environment to the myriad sources of international law. I next discuss in general terms what is meant by *jus cogens* norms and its *erga omnes* (universally applicable) obligations, including reference to the place of these norms in the normative hierarchy of international law. Finally, the chapter critically interrogates whether an international right to a healthy environment currently exists as part of *jus cogens* norms, and if not, what its potential is to become part of these norms.

AN INTERNATIONAL RIGHT TO A HEALTHY ENVIRONMENT: THE *LEX LATA*

To date, the United Nations General Assembly (which is considered the final arbiter on the formal creation and inclusion of international human rights into the body of international law), has not yet seen its way open to proclaiming a binding international right to a healthy environment.[10] One consequence is that the many domestic human rights to a healthy environment are some of the few rights widely

[9] The jury, however, is still out on whether such broad-based domestic constitutional entrenchment of the right could be said to satisfy the requirements of *usus* and *opinio juris* for the right to a healthy environment to be considered customary international law. See Chapters 1, 2, and 3.

[10] See Philip Alston, "Conjuring up New Human Rights: A Proposal for Quality Control," *American Journal of International Law* 78(3) (1984), pp. 607–21 at 609.

recognized in constitutions today that have no ancestral claim in the so-called "International Bill of Rights," composed of the Universal Declaration of Human Rights, the International Covenant on Economic, Social and Cultural Rights, and the International Covenant on Civil and Political Rights.[11] For example, the provision in Article 25 of the Universal Declaration that "Everyone has the right to a standard of living adequate for the health and well-being of himself and of his family" does not equate to a right to a healthy environment.

In 1968, the General Assembly expressed its concern "about the consequent effects [of environmental degradation] on the condition of man, his physical, mental and social well-being, his dignity and his enjoyment of basic human rights, in developing as well as developed countries."[12] The General Assembly consequently endorsed the Stockholm Declaration, which was the outcome of the foregoing resolution following the United Nations Conference on the Human Environment in Stockholm in 1972. This non-binding soft law declaration provided the first, albeit vague, parameters of an international right to a healthy environment.[13]

From an ecological integrity perspective that recognizes the importance of environmental protection as a critical concern in and of itself, and as a *sine qua non* for human existence, the Rio Declaration of 1992 could be considered a retrogressive step when compared to the Stockholm Declaration. The Rio Declaration emphasized in pure anthropocentric developmental and domestic-focused terms that "States have ... the sovereign right to exploit their own resources pursuant to their own environmental and developmental policies" and that "[t]he right to development must be fulfilled so as to equitably meet developmental and environmental needs of present and future generations."[14] Its articulation of a right to development for the satisfaction of human needs is far removed from what a right to a healthy environment arguably should ideally provide, i.e., socioeconomic well-being that is subject to ecological limits. So too, its inward-looking, state-bound focus and reaffirmation of sovereignty are contrary to the type of multilateralism that international law generally and global environmental governance specifically require.

The 2002 Johannesburg Declaration on Sustainable Development did not include human rights commitments in any of its provisions, although it did recognize the importance of international law and multilateralism in confronting global

[11] See May and Daly, *Global Environmental Constitutionalism*.

[12] General Assembly res. 2398 (December 3, 1968).

[13] Declaration of the UN Conference on the Human Environment, UN Doc. A/Conf.48/14/Rev.1 (June 5–16, 1972). Principle 1 states: "Man has the fundamental right to freedom, equality and adequate conditions of life, in an environment of a quality that permits a life of dignity and well-being, and he bears a solemn responsibility to protect and improve the environment for present and future generations."

[14] Rio Declaration on Environment and Development, UN Doc. A/CONF.151/26/Rev.1, annex I (June 14, 1992), Principles 2 and 3.

environmental degradation, in more pronounced terms than the former two declarations.[15] The accompanying Plan of Implementation of the World Summit on Sustainable Development of 2002 was more explicit in linking human rights and environmental concerns, although it also stopped well short of recognizing an international right to a healthy environment.[16]

More recently, in 2012, Rio+20's outcome document, The Future We Want, reaffirmed "respect for all human rights, including the right to development and the right to an adequate standard of living," and recognized "the importance of the Universal Declaration of Human Rights, as well as other international instruments relating to human rights and international law."[17] Signaling a possible turn away from the resolutely state-focused anthropocentric rights orientation of the earlier declarations, this outcome document also confirmed that rights of nature could play a role in the promotion of sustainable development, although it did not endorse such rights in any explicit terms.[18] Yet, as with the previous declarations, it did not recognize an international right to a healthy environment.

In sum, as far as all these foundational environmental declarations that have played such a crucial role in the current design of environmental law the world over are concerned, it seems that the imprecisely formulated international right to a healthy environment only has the status of soft law, which can only provide non-binding guidance to states in their relations to one another and in their internal affairs.[19]

The closest that any binding international environmental instrument has come to explicitly recognizing a right to a healthy environment is the Aarhus Convention on Access to Information, Public Participation in Decision-making, and Access to Justice in Environmental Matters of 1998. Although the Convention is exclusively aimed at promoting environmental protection through procedural environmental rights, as its name suggests, it recognizes in its preamble "that every person has the

[15] Johannesburg Declaration on Sustainable Development, UN Doc. A/CONF.199/20 (2002), para. 32 (reaffirming "commitment to the principles and purposes of the Charter of the United Nations and international law, as well as to the strengthening of multilateralism").

[16] For example, states acknowledged in paragraph 169 of the Plan of Implementation "the consideration being given to the possible relationship between environment and human rights, including the right to development."

[17] General Assembly res. 66/288, The Future We Want (July 27, 2012), paras. 8, 9.

[18] See, e.g., ibid., para. 39 ("We are convinced that in order to achieve a just balance among the economic, social and environmental needs of present and future generations, it is necessary to promote harmony with nature.").

[19] Another soft law instrument that provides in broad terms for an international right to a healthy environment is the Hague Declaration on the Environment, signed by representatives of twenty-four states in 1989, which provides, *inter alia*, that "remedies to be sought involve not only the fundamental duty to preserve the ecosystem, but also the right to live in dignity in a viable global environment, and the consequent duty of the community of nations vis-a-vis present and future generations to do all that can be done to preserve the quality of the atmosphere."

right to live in an environment adequate to his or her health and well-being, and the duty, both individually and in association with others, to protect and improve the environment for the benefit of present and future generations."[20] While this is a laudable provision in every way, the Convention is not a product of the United Nations General Assembly, but rather the regionally focused United Nations Economic Commission for Europe (UNECE), which is an international organization set up by Eastern and Western European states during the Cold War. Although it is open for ratification to all members of the United Nations, it is generally considered to operate mostly in the "European 'Aarhus space,'" which means it still has a more limited binding effect geographically speaking.[21]

Also from a global constitutionalism perspective, i.e., an analytical endeavor that seeks the emergence of constitutional type norms in the international legal order, there is general agreement that no global (environmental) constitution or clear, self-standing international environmental right exists.[22] Global "constitutional" environmental provisions, including the right to a healthy environment, rather lie scattered across the global regulatory domain, manifesting as they do in transnational legal regimes, regional human rights instruments, and soft law.[23] It can therefore be concluded, in the words of May and Daly, that "[i]nternational environmental law is especially soft. The congress of international environmental accords has fallen short of expectations for protecting environmental rights. Despite the abundance of treaties and conventions, there is no independent international environmental rights treaty."[24]

WHY CONTINUE THE DEBATE ON THE EXISTENCE AND STATUS OF AN INTERNATIONAL RIGHT TO A HEALTHY ENVIRONMENT?

Considering the foregoing conclusion, is it worthwhile to continue the debate on the emergence of a right to a healthy environment in international law? I would suggest that it is, for several reasons.

First, in a general justificatory sense, international human rights are higher order juridical means by which to mobilize state and public support and instill compliance with minimum guarantees through the invocation of high moral principles in any given cause or struggle, of which the environment has arguably become the most

[20] See also the provision in its Article 1 to the same effect.

[21] Ellen Hey, "The Interaction between Human Rights and the Environment in the European 'Aarhus Space,'" in Anna Grear and Louis Kotzé (eds.), *Research Handbook on Human Rights and the Environment* (Edward Elgar, 2015), pp. 353–76 at 354–5.

[22] Louis Kotzé, "Arguing Global Environmental Constitutionalism," *Transnational Environmental Law* 1(1) (2012), pp. 199–233.

[23] For a comprehensive discussion, see Louis Kotzé, *Global Environmental Constitutionalism in the Anthropocene* (Hart Publishing, 2016).

[24] May and Daly, *Global Environmental Constitutionalism*, p. 21.

recent and critically pertinent.[25] Recognizing the social and morally justified objective of environmental protection as an international right could be a critically important means of establishing regulatory priorities in global environmental governance:

> [T]he incorporation of environmental rights into national constitutions or their adoption into international treaties does not guarantee that the holder of such rights will always be successful when they come into conflict with other rights, but it certainly means that environmental rights must always be taken into account and also that good reasons will be needed for denying them effect.[26]

Prioritizing environmental protection at the international level is now more urgent than ever before, with scientists speculating that we are possibly entering a new geological epoch called the Anthropocene, or the epoch of humans.[27] In stark contrast to the relatively harmonious Holocene epoch (still viewed as being "current"), the imagery of the Anthropocene explicates global socio-ecological disorder at an unprecedented scale, where humans are changing Earth and its system for the worse. We are crossing planetary boundaries and entering an unsafe "operating space" where the very continuation of life on Earth is uncertain.[28] Accepting the dire state of global ecological integrity and the severity of the global socio-ecological crisis, the intuitive response of a lawyer is that we need the strongest possible intervention to counter this crisis through authoritative, legitimate, far-reaching, and, ultimately, effective juridical measures.[29]

Naturally, these could be embedded in the constitutionalism paradigm, including its associated constructs of rights. Constitutions and human rights, arguably more than any other "level" or type of law, have been able to change human behavior and the destiny of many polities for the better. They have provided a familiar language of good rule and order by acting as a logical "go to" solution to attempt wholesale reforms in the aftermath of wars, or in the political transitions of countries from pariah states to global participative democracies.[30] Internationally, the canon of

[25] Alston, "Conjuring Up New Human Rights," p. 608.

[26] Merrills, "Environmental Rights," p. 666. Or as Horn states: "If international environmental law is failing to achieve its objectives then a human right to a healthy environment which gains strong international support could draw attention to the need for environmental protection." Horn, "Common Concern," p. 268.

[27] Paul Crutzen and Eugene Stoermer, "The 'Anthropocene,'" *IGBP Global Change Newsletter* 41 (2000), pp. 17–18.

[28] Johan Rockström et al., "Planetary Boundaries: Exploring the Safe Operating Space for Humanity," *Ecology and Society* 14(2) (2009), pp. 1–24.

[29] The argument is carried by the belief that "as threats to sustainability increase [as they do in the Anthropocene], norms for behavior toward the global environment are also likely to become part of the *jus cogens* set." Brian Walker et al., "Looming Global-Scale Failures and Missing Institutions," *Science* 325 (2009), pp. 1345–6 at 1346.

[30] The adoption of the Charter of the United Nations and the equally important Universal Declaration of Human Rights, as well as many domestic constitutions, such as the Constitution of the Republic of South Africa in 1996, are examples of constitution-type innovations that

universally recognized and binding political and social rights in the International Bill of Rights are means to respond to myriad global social and political disasters, and they have managed to create a global minimum human rights standard to which states must aspire and which they cannot transgress without incurring liability or at the very least the scorn of their peers.

In the environmental context, the Anthropocene and its markers are symbolic, but highly persuasive, motivations for critical reformative action. They act to overcome the traction of existing assumptions and epistemic closures in parochially limited international (environmental) law by providing a highly current cognitive framework or approach to global environmental governance that assumes *urgency* as a point of departure. Within this alternative cognitive framework, the global socio-ecological crisis of the Anthropocene provides a convincing normative justification to strive toward the urgent development of an international right to a healthy environment within the cadre of binding international human rights and environmental law.

Second, at a more practical level, we require binding international law norms, which include rights, to hold states accountable in the international regulatory domain for their environment-related actions vis-à-vis one another and those actions directed at their citizens. If we accept that states as the primary subjects of international law will remain the principal (if admittedly decreasingly exclusive) actors in global environmental law and governance, then we must continue to have the discussion about an international right to a healthy environment as a hitherto nonexistent, but potentially evolving and possibly binding, obligation that could create protective guarantees for environmental protection and associated obligations for states at the international level. To this end, an international right to a healthy environment could usefully restrict unimpeded free will of states to act as they please in relation to the environment, and it could open up the full gamut of international law's compliance and enforcement machinery. Some domestic and regional rights to a healthy environment already provide such limitations on state power for the purpose of domestic and regional regulation, and where they remain absent, a universally binding international environmental right could spur domestic and subsequent regional legal reforms and the adoption of such rights, in tandem with providing a minimum "constitutional" standard or threshold for state conduct in the international regulatory domain.[31] While one could argue that incidental environment-related rights, such as those recognized in the International Bill of

resulted from "constitutional moments" that sought to counter injustice, oppression, political mayhem and societal instability. See Louis Kotzé, "The Anthropocene's Global Environmental Constitutional Moment," *Yearbook of International Environmental Law* 25(1) (2015), pp. 24–60.

[31] After all, international and domestic laws are (often dialectical) spaces of juridical contention that are intimately intertwined and dependent on one another for their existence, legitimacy, further refinement, and implementation.

Rights, already play an important role in "greening" the international environmental protection legal order, having an explicit right to a healthy environment enshrined in a global multilateral agreement might establish clearer rights-based duties of states with respect to the environment, while providing a more uniform and universally standardized minimum level of obligation and associated duties of care for states. It may also provide greater juridical leverage to state and non-state parties that pursue compliance with such an international right against a transgressor state.

Third, if we accept that the realization of all human rights, domestically, regionally, and internationally, is conditional on a healthy environment, discussions about an international right to a healthy environment must continue, considering the multiple implications of a healthy environment for other mutually dependent human rights such as the rights to life, dignity, and equality. This critical consideration has already been acknowledged by the United Nations Human Rights Council and the General Assembly.[32] It is highly likely that we will only be able to advance the international human rights agenda in a comprehensively holistic, and ultimately effective and sustainable way, if we elevate environmental concerns to be incorporated more explicitly into the canon of binding international human rights.

Finally, it is not only treaty law that provides binding and enforceable human rights norms at the international level; human rights could innovatively evolve through other primary sources of international law. For example, in the normative hierarchy of international law (a debate that is embedded in the broader global constitutionalism paradigm) treaties rank below *jus cogens* or peremptory norms. These higher-order norms are perceived to create a normative hierarchy in international law to the extent that they have a "constitutional" character that is elevated above other norms in the international law domain.[33] International law therefore has a "layered texture"[34] that instills some degree of superiority among its norms.[35] If environmental concerns could be encapsulated by these apex global "constitutional" norms that are situated at the top end of this normative hierarchy, it could ultimately be easier to ensure that states respect, protect, and fulfill their environment-related human rights and associated international environmental law obligations. The final parts of this chapter investigate whether it is possible for an international right to a healthy environment to be located in the *jus cogens* paradigm.

32 See Human Rights Council resolutions 16/11 (March 24, 2011), 19/10 (March 22, 2012), 25/21 (March 28, 2014), and 28/11 (March 26, 2015) on human rights and the environment.

33 Evan Criddle and Evan Fox-Decent, "A Fiduciary Theory of *Jus Cogens*," *Yale Journal of International Law* 34 (2009), pp. 331–87 at 332.

34 Erika de Wet, "The International Constitutional Order," *International and Comparative Law Quarterly* 55(1) (2006), pp. 51–76 at 62. See also, for a definitive account on hierarchy in international law, Erika de Wet and Jure Vidmar (eds.), *Hierarchy in International Law: The Place of Human Rights* (Oxford University Press, 2012).

35 Dinah Shelton, "Normative Hierarchy in International Law," *American Journal of International Law* 100(2) (2006), pp. 291–323.

JUS COGENS NORMS

Article 53 of the Vienna Convention of the Law of Treaties (VCLT) positivized *jus cogens* norms in 1969 by stating that:

> A treaty is void if, at the time of its conclusion, it conflicts with a peremptory norm of general international law. For the purposes of the present Convention, a peremptory norm of general international law is a norm accepted and recognized by the international community of States as a whole as a norm from which no derogation is permitted and which can be modified only by a subsequent norm of general international law having the same character.

Article 64 of the VCLT adds that "[i]f a new peremptory norm of general international law emerges, any existing treaty which is in conflict with that norm becomes void and terminates." Within the ambit of these provisions, *jus cogens* is understood as universally imperative, compelling, and obligatory law (or *jus strictum*) that sharply contrasts with *jus dispositivum* (voluntary law that yields to the will of the parties).[36] *Jus cogens* norms are compelling to the extent that they are mandatory, do not permit derogation, and can be modified only by general international norms of equivalent authority: i.e., other *jus cogens* norms.[37] They are universal in that they are seen to have *erga omnes* effect, meaning that they apply to all members of the international community of states, even if a state does not consent to a peremptory norm's mandatory application.[38] They are obligatory to the extent that they create negative obligations on states to refrain from doing something.[39]

The originally intended purpose of *jus cogens* norms lies in their function to resolve norm conflicts. Article 53 of the VCLT is titled "Treaties conflicting with a peremptory norm of general international law" and is included under section 2 of the VCLT which, in turn, carries the general heading "Invalidity of treaties." This wording suggests that *jus cogens* has to do with those instances where treaties, including the conclusion of treaties and treaty-related acts, may be declared invalid

36 Dissenting opinion of Judge Tanaka in *South-West Africa Cases (Ethiopia* v. *South Africa; Liberia* v. *South Africa)*, Second Phase, Judgment [1966] ICJ Rep 298.

37 Criddle and Fox-Decent, "A Fiduciary Theory of *Jus Cogens*," p. 332.

38 A point that was confirmed by the International Court of Justice (ICJ) in *Barcelona Traction, Light and Power Company Ltd (Belgium* v. *Spain)*, Second Phase, [1970] ICJ Rep 32. See de Wet, "The International Constitutional Order," p. 61. However, not all *erga omnes* obligations necessarily have *jus cogens* status.

39 *Jus cogens* does not create positive obligations that compel states to do something, e.g., to make good human rights abuses. They only compel states not to embark on human rights abuses. This is often seen as one of the greatest drawbacks of *jus cogens* rules. Jure Vidmar, "Norm Conflicts and Hierarchy in International Law: Towards a Vertical International Legal System?" in de Wet and Vidmar, *Hierarchy in International Law*, p. 33.

if they conflict with a peremptory norm. However, no international court has to date declared invalid a treaty that allegedly transgressed a peremptory norm.[40]

Outside the treaty-based normative conflict arena, *jus cogens* has since evolved in the context of the law of state responsibility to mean the creation of a non-derogable universal standard against which to measure state conduct, supposedly by providing weight to arguments that allege one or the other transgression of some minimum standard in international law.[41] By this reading, *jus cogens* is situated at the apex of the hierarchy of international law norms, surpassing all other sources of international law. In the words of the International Criminal Tribunal for the former Yugoslavia, *jus cogens:*

> enjoys a higher rank in the international hierarchy than treaty law and even "ordinary" customary rules. The most conspicuous consequence of this higher rank is that the principle at issue cannot be derogated from by States through international treaties or local or special customs or even general customary rules not endowed with the same normative force.[42]

Harking back to their natural law roots, the extent to which *jus cogens* norms act as "an important element of [a] certain moral order in international relations"[43] within this normative hierarchy is evident from the generally accepted belief that all states are considered bound by peremptory norms in arbitrary legal acts and in their actual day-to-day conduct.[44] Where peremptory norms that protect the interest of the international community of states are transgressed, certain qualified legal effects arise that seek to rectify the transgression.[45]

The potential allure of *jus cogens* norms for the global environmental cause clearly emerges from the foregoing: If environmental protection could be elevated to a non-derogable peremptory state obligation with *erga omnes* effect, one that also trumps other sources of international law situated lower in its normative hierarchy, a much higher standard of care, and the potential to unequivocally impose liability in

[40] Władysław Czapliński, "*Jus Cogens* and the Law of Treaties," in Christian Tomuschat and Jean-Marc Thouvenin (eds.), *The Fundamental Rules of the International Legal Order:* Jus Cogens *and Obligations* Erga Omnes (Martinus Nijhoff, 2006), p. 89.

[41] Eva Kornicker Uhlmann, "State Community Interests, *Jus Cogens* and Protection of the Global Environment: Developing Criteria for Peremptory Norms," *Georgetown International Environmental Law Review* 11(1) (1998), pp. 101–35 at 101.

[42] *Prosecutor* v. *Anto Furundžija*, Case No. IT-95–17/1-T (International Criminal Tribunal for the former Yugoslavia, 1998).

[43] Czapliński, "*Jus Cogens* and the Law of Treaties," p. 97.

[44] Eva Kornicker, *Ius Cogens und Umweltvölkerrecht: Kriterien, Quellen und Rechtsfolgen zwingender Völkerrechtsnormen und deren Anwendung auf das Umweltvölkerrecht* (Helbing & Lichtenhahn, 1997), p. 8.

[45] See Vienna Convention on the Law of Treaties (VCLT), May 23, 1969, in force January 27, 1980, 1155 UNTS 331, art. 71 (parties to the treaty shall "(a) Eliminate as far as possible the consequences of any act performed in reliance on any provision which conflicts with the peremptory norm of general international law; and (b) Bring their mutual relations into conformity with the peremptory norm of general international law.").

the case of contravention, could be established. In essence, where state actions do harm the environment and affect people, and where states affect the sustainability of the Earth system or upset ecological balance, *jus cogens* environmental norms would take state discretion out of the equation by placing a peremptory negative obligation on states not to cause such harm. This would occur even in the absence of an explicit treaty or other international law provision recognizing a right to a healthy environment.

It remains unclear which norms have attained peremptory status and consequent upon a lack of guidance in the relevant treaty provisions, the identification and elaboration of specific *jus cogens* norms have been left to states, courts, and epistemic communities such as the International Law Commission (ILC) and scholars. Although there is no universal agreement, the rules of international law that are currently accepted as having *jus cogens* status include prohibitions of: the aggressive use of force; genocide; torture; crimes against humanity; slavery and the slave trade; piracy; racial discrimination and apartheid; and hostilities or force directed at a civilian population.[46] Two initial issues are evident from the foregoing list: (a) strongly influenced as they are by natural law principles, the majority of these norms are directly or indirectly related to human rights concerns (a leading commentator even suggests they are pure human rights norms);[47] and (b) this is not a closed list. What are perceived to be *jus cogens* rules today may very well change in future, thus providing the opportunity to expand the repertoire of peremptory norms.[48] Whiteman reminds us in this respect that:

> A listing, that is to say, identification in a general way of certain peremptory norms of rules of international law (*jus cogens*) existing at any period of time cannot be done with complete precision, enveloped as such rules of *jus cogens* or peremptory norms are bound to be in word symbols definable by more precise interpretations with the passage of time. Also, because of changes and developments as civilization moves on, such listing can never be completely invariable or exhaustive.[49]

Accepting that *jus cogens* norms are embedded in the human rights paradigm, and that it is possible to extend the current list of *jus cogens* norms, is it possible for these norms to also envelop environmental concerns and ultimately, to provide for an international right to a healthy environment?

[46] Erika de Wet, "*Jus Cogens* and Obligations *Erga Omnes*," in Dinah Shelton (ed.), *Oxford Handbook on International Human Rights Law* (Oxford University Press, 2015), p. 543.

[47] De Wet, "The International Constitutional Order," pp. 58–9.

[48] See also Criddle and Fox-Decent, "A Fiduciary Theory of *Jus Cogens*," pp. 331–2.

[49] Marjorie Whiteman, "Jus Cogens in International Law, with a Projected List," *Georgia Journal of International and Comparative Law* 7(2), pp. 609–26 at 625.

DEVELOPING AN INTERNATIONAL HUMAN RIGHT TO A HEALTHY ENVIRONMENT AS A *JUS COGENS* NORM?

To answer this question, it must first be determined if environmental *jus cogens* norms currently form part of the generally accepted canon of *jus cogens* norms. A prohibition on environmental harm is not usually included in the repertoire of *jus cogens* norms. Singleton-Cambage believes that:

> Currently, environmental rights and responsibilities are not recognized as having this legal status, despite the fact that global environmental preservation represents an essential interest of all individuals within the entire international society. Sufficient time has not yet passed to enable environmental issues to evolve to this status of international law. The establishment of peremptory norms must develop from a specific practice for an extended period of time by the general majority of states.[50]

Beyerlin and Marauhn have also expressed their doubts about the recognition of environmental *jus cogens* norms. With reference to Article 19 of the 1980 Draft Articles on State Responsibility,[51] which introduced the notion of an international crime that is seen as a violation of *jus cogens*, they argue that environmental pollution cannot at this stage be considered an international crime.[52] The authors conclude: "only very few rules can actually be considered as peremptory norms and . . . hardly any of them is part of international environmental law."[53]

Moving from the doctrine to international adjudicatory practice, while conflict does arise in the global environmental law and governance domain as a result of the inherently opposing goals of socioeconomic development on the one hand and the concomitant need for environmental protection on the other, such conflicts "have not led international courts to employ the concept of *ius cogens* or to give human rights, environmental protection or economic development automatic priority."[54] No international court or tribunal has explicitly identified any norm that has peremptory status in the environmental domain; nor has any international court or tribunal invoked Articles 53 and 64 of the VCLT to settle an environment-related treaty dispute. The closest that the International Court of Justice (ICJ) came in doing so was in its *Gabčikovo-Nagymaros* judgment, where it accepted by implication Slovakia's contention that none of the norms on which Hungary relied was of a

[50] Krista Singleton-Cambage, "International Legal Sources and Global Environmental Crises: The Inadequacy of Principles, Treaties and Custom," *ILSA Journal of International and Comparative Law* 2 (1995), pp. 171–87 at 185.

[51] International Law Commission, *Report of the International Law Commission on the Work of Its 32nd Session* (May 25, 1980), UN Doc. A/35/10, p. 32.

[52] Ulrich Beyerlin and Thilo Marauhn, *International Environmental Law* (Hart Publishing, 2011), p. 287.

[53] Ibid., p. 362.

[54] Patricia Birnie, Alan Boyle, and Catherine Redgwell, *International Law and the Environment*, 3d ed. (Oxford University Press, 2009), p. 115.

peremptory nature.[55] The Court, however, did not rule out the possibility that environmental norms may develop in future and that whenever they do, they must be considered by the parties. The Court pointed out that:

> . . . newly developed norms of environmental law are relevant for the implementation of the Treaty and . . . the parties could, by agreement, incorporate them through the application of Articles 15, 19 and 20 of the Treaty.[[56]] These articles do not contain specific obligations of performance but require the parties, in carrying out their obligations to ensure that the quality of water in the Danube is not impaired and that nature is protected, to take new environmental norms into consideration when agreeing upon the means to be specified in the Joint Contractual Plan.[57]

Whether the ICJ actually meant to include *jus cogens* norms specifically under "newly developed norms of environmental law" is unclear. Equally unclear are Judge Weeramantry's preliminary remarks in his dissenting opinion in the *Nuclear Weapons* Advisory Opinion, where he seems to accept, without detailed engagement, that certain environmental *jus cogens* norms exist:

> The global environment constitutes a huge, intricate, delicate and interconnected web in which a touch here or palpitation there sends tremors throughout the whole system. Obligations *erga omnes*, rules *jus cogens*, and international crimes respond to this state of affairs by permitting environmental wrongs to be guarded against by all nations.[58]

For all practical purposes, the present discussion can easily be concluded here, considering that on the foregoing account, the possibility of environmental norms currently having *jus cogens* status seems slim. But the normative implications of ending the debate could potentially mute the prospects of creating apex peremptory norms at the top of international law's normative hierarchy that could force states to observe better environmental care in the Anthropocene.

The maintenance, improvement, and safeguarding of socio-ecological security in the Anthropocene is (to borrow from Article 53 of the VCLT) arguably becoming an issue that concerns the "international community of States as a whole." The international community is not only the sum of its parts, but also a sense of a community of states where, as Kritsiotis suggests, "The idea is to conceive the community beyond its discursive incarnation toward a system of shared ideals, policies, [and] values,"[59] which must also be expressed through the constitutional

[55] *Gabčikovo-Nagymaros Case (Hungary* v. *Slovakia)*, [1997] ICJ Rep. 91, para. 97.

[56] The relevant treaty is the bilateral Treaty Concerning the Construction and Operation of the Gabčikovo-Nagymaros System of Locks of 1977.

[57] *Gabčikovo-Nagymaros Case*, para. 112.

[58] [1996] ICJ Rep. 429.

[59] Dino Kritsiotis, "Imagining the International Community," *European Journal of International Law* 12 (2002), pp. 961–91 at 980.

elements of a shared legal system, such as international law and its peremptory norms that govern the global polity. To be sure, the gradual Anthropocene-induced epistemological shift is redirecting our attention away from territorially limited and individual state-bound environmental concerns to a more globally collective conception of Earth system changes, their impacts on the international community of states, and the collective responsibility of states in this respect. This much is evident from the tentative steps by the ICJ in the *Nuclear Weapons* Advisory Opinion to more directly connect *jus cogens*, *erga omnes* obligations and the common heritage of mankind in the context of a globalized community of states that should be seeking urgent collective responses to shared environmental problems. Mohammed Bedjaoui, the President of the Court, noted that we are witnessing:

> . . . the gradual substitution of an international law of co-operation for the traditional law of co-existence, the emergence of the concept of "international community" and its sometimes successful attempts at subjectivization. A token of all these developments is the place which international law now accords to concepts such as obligations *erga omnes*, rules of *jus cogens*, or the common heritage of mankind. The resolutely positivist, voluntarist approach of international law still current at the beginning of the [twentieth] century has been replaced by an objective conception of international law, a law more readily seeking to reflect a collective juridical conscience and respond to the social necessities of states organised as a community.[60]

Even more pertinent are the words of Judge Weeramantry in his separate opinion in *Gabčikovo-Nagymaros*:

> When we enter the arena of obligations which operate *erga omnes* rather than *inter partes*, rules based on individual fairness and procedural compliance may be inadequate. The great ecological questions now surfacing will call for thought upon this matter. International environmental law will need to proceed beyond weighing the rights and obligations of parties within a closed compartment of individual State self-interest, unrelated to the global concerns of humanity as a whole.[61]

The international judiciary's open stance toward accepting the urgency of the global socio-ecological crisis, its recognition of the need for universal action by the international community of states, and the need to impose universal ecological obligations through higher-order international law norms, auger well for the potential development of *jus cogens* environmental norms. Accepting then that environmental *jus cogens* norms could in principle be created, how could this happen?

[60] [1996] ICJ Rep. 268, 270–1.

[61] *Gabčikovo-Nagymaros Case*, Separate Opinion of Vice-President Weeramantry, [1997] ICJ Rep. 88, 118.

While many existing *jus cogens* norms are intimately related to human rights concerns, they are typically not formulated in trite rights terms; i.e., *jus cogens* norms aim to prohibit certain actions by states by placing a negative obligation on them not to infringe those interests that are often also protected by human rights, but they do not entrench rights as such. For example, the prohibition against genocide protects the right to life, and the prohibition against discrimination and apartheid protects the rights to equality and human dignity, among others. It is therefore unlikely that a right to an ecologically balanced, sustainable, healthy, clean, or satisfactory environment that permits healthy living for human and non-human entities on Earth will evolve in these exact terms as a *jus cogens* norm. It is more likely that an environmental *jus cogens* norm would seek to prohibit states from transgressing the considerations or aspects that a right to healthy environment would typically guarantee. An environmental *jus cogens* norm could thus seek to prohibit states from harming an environment that people depend on, or upsetting an ecologically balanced environment through their actions.

Admittedly it will be difficult to determine the minimum threshold of transgression, which is arguably one of the reasons why an environmental *jus cogens* norm has not been accepted yet. Following the jurisprudence of the ICJ as described earlier, it could be that environmental harm has to be so serious that it negatively impacts the "global concerns of humanity as a whole." Determination of the norm will also be significantly complicated by the general challenges surrounding the identification and development of *jus cogens* norms. For example, Article 53 of the VCLT does not specify the process by which a norm of general international law is identified or when it rises to the level of being peremptory.[62] These challenges are likewise set to arise when states eventually decide to contemplate what they deem to be an environmental norm that is "accepted and recognized by the international community of States as a whole as a norm from which no derogation is permitted."[63]

Presumably the easiest way to circumvent challenges surrounding the declaration of an environmental *jus cogens* norm would be to develop peremptory norms from existing customary environmental law. De Wet suggests that Article 53 of the VCLT provides states sufficient freedom to determine themselves what are peremptory norms and what are not.[64] In practice, this would occur through a process that first identifies a norm as customary international law and then an agreement on whether derogation is permitted from that customary norm or not. This form of "double acceptance" therefore not only requires proof of *usus* and *opinio juris* (the first stage of acceptance); but also acceptance of the special character of the norm in question (the second stage) that is seen to be embedded in the natural law-derived

[62] Gennady Danilenko, "International Jus Cogens: Issues of Law-Making," *European Journal of International Law* 2(1) (1991), pp. 42–65; International Law Commision, *Report of the International Law Commission, 66th Session*, UN Doc. A/69/10 (2014), p. 277.

[63] VCLT, art. 53.

[64] De Wet, "*Jus Cogens* and Obligations *Erga Omnes*," p. 542.

"universally accepted strong ethical underpinning of these norms,"[65] and that affords them their peremptory character. Despite some controversy, the no-harm rule (*sic utere tuo ut alienum non laedas*), which imposes a negative obligation on states (as *jus cogens* norms typically do) not to cause environmental harm to another state, is generally accepted to have the status of customary international law.[66] Although there are no hard and fast rules in this respect, it is now generally accepted that the harm that occurs as a result of activities in a particular state must be "serious" and must be at least more than *de minimis*.[67] A state causing environmental harm does not need to do so with the intent to injure. The duty not to cause harm is rather associated with a duty to exercise due diligence, which incidentally does not detract from the nature of the obligation imposed by the norm, i.e., a negative one.[68]

Today, the no harm principle "has been so widely accepted in international treaty practice, numerous declarations of international organisations, the codification work of the ILC, and in the jurisprudence of the ICJ that it can be considered to be a customary substantive rule at the universal level."[69] It should thus easily satisfy the VCLT peremptory requirement of being "a norm accepted and recognized by the international community of States as a whole" (the first stage of acceptance).[70] Whether it has attained the status of a norm "from which no derogation is permitted"[71] (the second stage of acceptance) is, however, debatable. It is still unlikely that states have universally accepted any universally binding and "strong ethical [ecological] underpinning"[72] that should be associated with the no harm principle. Yet, because of its customary status, its application at an interstate level to environmental resources within state territories as well as to the global environmental commons, and its imposition of negative obligations, suggest that at least theoretically, the no harm principle has the potential to become a peremptory norm in the future that would also be able to protect some of the concerns that a right to a healthy environment typically seeks to protect. If it does, the no harm rule could aim to hold states accountable when their actions cause, for example,

65 Vidmar, "Norm Conflicts and Hierarchy in International Law," p. 26.

66 While the principle of sustainable development, the polluter pays principle, and the precautionary principle frequently surface in debates as possible contenders for achieving customary status in international law, there is little agreement among international courts and scholars whether they have achieved customary status. While the element of *usus* is usually easier to prove and mostly present, it is far more difficult to show that *opinio juris* is sufficiently present to conclusively state the customary status of these principles. See Beyerlin and Marauhn, *International Environmental Law*, pp. 47–84.

67 Ibid., p. 4. See also *Pulp Mills on the River Uruguay (Argentina* v. *Uruguay)*, [2010] ICJ Rep. 83.

68 Beyerlin and Marauhn, *International Environmental Law*, p. 42.

69 Ibid., p. 44.

70 VCLT, art. 53.

71 Ibid.

72 Vidmar, "Norm Conflicts and Hierarchy in International Law," p. 26.

seriously devastating and widespread environmental harm and associated human rights abuses in one or more countries.

Another possibility is to include aspects of a right to a healthy environment into the ambit of concerns that the existing set of *jus cogens* norms currently seeks to address. The regulatory issues that arise from a broadly conceived "environment" are numerous and difficult to circumscribe:

> The boundaries of what constitutes an "environmental" issue have already become blurred ... our understanding of what constitutes an environmental issue must grow to encompass economic, social, and trade policy. Indeed, if, as some claim, everything is interconnected, then everything becomes an environmental problem.[73]

For example, it could consequently be possible to argue that the prohibition against apartheid (which includes human rights issues such as the rights to life, dignity, and equality) also affects environmental interests. According to the United Nations Special Rapporteur on human rights and the environment, "Human rights are grounded in respect for fundamental human attributes such as dignity, equality and liberty. The realization of these attributes depends on an environment that allows them to flourish."[74] This point on the interrelatedness of rights was also made by Judge Weeramantry in his separate opinion in the *Gabčikovo-Nagymaros* judgment. He explained that:

> The protection of the environment is likewise a vital part of contemporary human rights doctrine, for it is a *sine qua non* for numerous human rights such as the right to health and the right to life itself. It is scarcely necessary to elaborate on this, as damage to the environment can impair and undermine all the human rights spoken of in the Universal Declaration and other human rights instruments.[75]

A classic environmental justice example illustrating the deeply intertwined relationship between the environment and other human rights concerns is a situation where disenfranchised societies living in poverty with restricted access to housing, water, and food, as a result of racial and/or gender discriminatory policies of a country, often bear the brunt of environmental impacts which could affect their dignity and livelihoods. Apartheid South Africa is a case in point where a racist minority government deliberately marginalized the majority of the country's citizens for many years by restricting their access to life-sustaining resources, such as water.[76]

[73] Daniel Bodansky, *The Art and Craft of International Environmental Law* (Harvard University Press, 2010), pp. 10–11.

[74] John H. Knox, *Report of the Independent Expert on the Issue of Human Rights Obligations Relating to the Enjoyment of a Safe, Clean, Healthy and Sustainable Environment: Preliminary Report*, UN Doc. A/HRC/22/43 (December 24, 2012), p. 4.

[75] *Gabčikovo-Nagymaros Case*, Separate Opinion of Vice-President Weeramantry, pp. 91–2.

[76] See South Africa Department of Water Affairs, *National Water Resource Strategy: Managing Water for an Equitable and Sustainable Future* (2004).

By depriving people of material conditions that are necessary to sustain their health and well-being, apartheid has succeeded in also impacting on their human dignity, equality, and quality of life.

An approach that derives environmental obligations from existing *jus cogens* norms might entail that the environment could be protected through the application of, for example, the prohibition of racial discrimination and apartheid where such discrimination has a direct correlation to environmental aspects. Thus, for example, if people suffer undue environmental injustice as a result of apartheid laws and practices, such laws and practices would be violating a *jus cogens* norm; i.e., prohibition against racial discrimination and apartheid. Conversely, where the environment is harmed to promote racial discriminatory practices, or where the environment is used as a tool to marginalize a community on racial grounds, such a practice could also be in potential violation of the aforementioned peremptory norm.

CONCLUSION

Humanity seems to be in a situation where we need to run before we can walk. The Anthropocene epoch requires us to think far more urgently about reforming existing international (environmental) and human rights law, and to develop binding international standards to hold states to account where they do impact the environmental foundations necessary to sustain life on Earth. Plainly, our legal institutions must play a crucial role in changing the type and severity of human and state actions that are leading to the present and predicted encroachments on the Earth system. This would entail a drastic rethink of international (environmental) law's composition, purpose, and scope. Thus, if *jus cogens* is accepted to constitute the minimum threshold of an international value system that belongs to the international community of states,[77] then this international value system will have to be expanded to include notions of environmental care that are also situated at the "constitutional" apex of international law's hierarchy. To this end, the foregoing analysis illustrates both the urgent need to continue the debate on developing environmental *jus cogens* norms, and the potential of the right to a healthy environment to form a crucial part of the nascent and continuously evolving paradigm of such higher-order constitutional peremptory norms.

77 Vidmar, "Norm Conflicts and Hierarchy in International Law," p. 38.

9

A Human Right to a Healthy Environment?

Moral, Legal, and Empirical Considerations

*César Rodríguez-Garavito**

Should there be a human right to a healthy environment? In this chapter, I aim to analytically and empirically unpack this question. Analytically, I draw on moral and legal theory in order to examine the premises of the question, reframe it, and offer an answer to it. Empirically, building on socio-legal studies of rights, I explore the potential benefits and costs of using "rights talk"[1] in environmental debates in general, and of adopting the right to a healthy environment in an international legal instrument in particular.

My argument is threefold. First, I posit that the terms of the question seem to assume a theory of human rights that views legal recognition as a constitutive component of rights. Implicit in the question of whether the time has come to consider a right to a healthy environment is the claim that the status of the latter as a right hinges on it being incorporated into a formal legal instrument. In line with Amartya Sen's criticism of such a "legally parasitic" view of rights, I argue that a strong case can be made that the aspiration to live in a healthy environment already *is* a human right. Second, I contend that, even from a narrower, purely legal perspective, it can be said that a global right to a healthy environment is already in existence within customary international law. Third, I therefore argue that it is useful to reframe the question in the following terms: Should the right to a healthy environment be formally adopted in an international legal instrument? Thus restated, the question raises a host of issues regarding efficacy and impact that are common to efforts to turn moral and political claims into legal claims in general, and into international legal claims in particular. Based on an overview of these issues, I answer the question in the affirmative.

* Executive Director, Center for Law, Justice and Society (Dejusticia); Associate Professor, University of los Andes Law School. I gratefully acknowledge Helena Durán's and Celeste Kauffman's research assistance for this article.

[1] Mary Ann Glendon, *Rights Talk: The Impoverishment of Political Discourse* (Free Press, 1991).

This chapter is divided into three sections, each related to one of the arguments, followed by a conclusion. In the first section, I briefly discuss Sen's objection to "legally parasitic" theories of rights in order to substantiate my claim that, understood as a moral right, a right to a healthy environment already exists. In the second section, I succinctly review the legal evidence and arguments in favor of the existence of such a right in customary international law. In the third section, I examine the trade-offs involved in the potential recognition of the right in an international legal instrument, whether a global treaty or an instrument of soft law. In the concluding section, I summarize the argument and wrap up my case for an international right to a healthy environment.

A MORAL CASE FOR THE RIGHT TO A HEALTHY ENVIRONMENT

Before considering the issue of whether the right to a healthy environment is an idea whose time has come, it is worth pondering the premises of the question. Is it possible that such a right is already an idea of our time, and has been with us for longer than our legalistic view of rights would suggest? What is the current status of the demand for a healthy environment? Is formal legal recognition in an international hard- or soft-law document necessary for it to have the status of a human right?

These queries evoke the classic jurisprudential debate between legal and moral theories of rights.[2] Jeremy Bentham offered the canonical formulation of the former when he provocatively wrote: "*Right*, the substantive *right*, is the child of law; from *real* laws come *real* rights; but from *imaginary* laws, from 'law of nature' [can come only] *imaginary* rights."[3] Against the American and French revolutions' conception of rights, he famously insisted that "natural rights is simple nonsense: natural and imprescriptible rights (an American phrase), rhetorical nonsense, nonsense upon stilts."[4]

Bentham is not alone. Indeed, his law-centered theory of rights has thoroughly permeated the discourse and the practice of human rights actors, from advocates and judges to policy makers and international regulators. Further, the dominance of lawyers and legal discourse in human rights practice and scholarship has contributed to mainstreaming the Benthamite conception in this field. However, legal theories of rights, Bentham's among them, suffer from conceptual and empirical drawbacks. Conceptually, as powerfully vindicated by the revolutionary tradition that Bentham criticizes, rights are fundamentally moral claims about the intrinsic worth of every human being, and of the importance of the prerogatives they protect

[2] See generally Jeremy Waldron (ed.), *Theories of Rights* (Oxford University Press, 1984).

[3] Jeremy Bentham, *Anarchical Fallacies; Being an Examination of the Declaration of Rights Issued during the French Revolution* (1792), republished in John Bowring (ed.), *The Works of Jeremy Bentham*, vol. II (William Tait, 1843), p. 523.

[4] Ibid., p. 501.

to a dignified human life. As Sen has argued, just as in Bentham's utilitarianism, human rights must be seen as an approach to ethics, which asserts the intrinsic ethical importance of certain basic human entitlements (which stand in contrast, for instance, to the ethical importance of Benthamite "utilities").[5]

For example, invoking a right to a healthy environment entails making a strong ethical assertion about the central importance of a livable natural environment to a dignified human existence. In addition to its essential role in the enjoyment of other human rights, the right has an intrinsic ethical significance. It specifically protects basic conditions of individual and communal existence that are increasingly under threat due to growing ecological stress: human beings' relationship to their lived environment, the possibility to remain in one's habitat and develop a sustainable relationship with nature, the entitlements of future generations to enjoy a livable planet, and even the potential recognition of certain rights to non-human animals and natural entities.[6]

This ethical approach also means granting special consideration to the right to a healthy environment in concrete cases and situations in which claims based on other ethical approaches may point in the opposite direction (for instance, utilitarian arguments about the priority of short-term economic growth). Thus, the moral right to a healthy environment updates the human rights approach to the conditions of the Anthropocene, just as emerging forms of "new Earth politics" are revising political thought and action in light of the conditions of our epoch.[7]

Law-centered conceptions of rights also fail to hold up to empirical scrutiny. In practice, activists, courts, and even governments oftentimes make rights-based demands long before the respective entitlement has been acknowledged in a formal legal document. Women's movements and courts around the world invoked women's right to be free from domestic violence long before national constitutions recognized it and the United Nations adopted the 1993 Declaration on the Elimination of Violence Against Women.[8] Socioeconomic rights advocacy and litigation preceded the adoption of the 1966 International Covenant on Economic, Social, and Cultural Rights by several decades.[9] The fact that the 2007 UN Declaration on the Rights of Indigenous Peoples required over twenty years of international negotiations for its adoption did not prevent indigenous peoples' movements from

5 Amartya Sen, "Human Rights and the Limits of Law," *Cardozo Law Review* 27(6) (2006), pp. 2913–27.

6 Christopher D. Stone, *Should Trees Have Standing? Law, Morality and the Environment* (Oxford University Press, 2010).

7 Simon Nicholson and Sikina Jinnah (eds.), *New Earth Politics: Essays from the Anthropocene* (MIT Press, 2016).

8 Sally Engle Merry, *Human Rights and Gender Violence: Translating International Law into Local Justice* (Chicago University Press, 2006).

9 Malcolm Langford (ed.), *Social Rights Jurisprudence: Emerging Trends in International and Comparative Law* (Cambridge University Press, 2008).

effectively using the language of human rights in the meantime, as a means to demand the protection of their territories, cultures, and livelihoods.[10]

Similarly, at least since the 1972 Stockholm Declaration of the UN Conference on the Human Environment, civil society and state actors have invoked the right to a healthy environment regardless of the fact that it has not been formally incorporated into an international legal instrument. Theretofore, as one constitution after another has incorporated the right into national law, it has become a standard component of bills of rights, policy making, and litigation in more than half of the world's countries.[11]

The moral view of human rights also reminds us that law-centered strategies such as litigation are just one alternative in a wide range of enforcement strategies. As literature about the use of social movements' use of rights discourse abundantly documents,[12] naming and shaming strategies, information politics, documentation of rights violations, ethical tribunals, and other mechanisms are often the strategies of choice of individuals and organizations seeking to uphold human rights standards, regardless of the latter's formal legal status. This has certainly been the case in the field of environmental advocacy, where activists ranging from Chico Mendes in Brazil to Ken Saro-Wiwa in Nigeria to Greenpeace members worldwide were using the language of rights to support their causes and campaigns even before national constitutions acknowledged the right.[13]

If not formal legal recognition, what conditions would the ethical demand for a healthy environment need to meet in order to qualify as a human right? This is not the place for a thorough examination of this question, which would lead to different answers depending on the moral theory used. For the purposes of this chapter, it suffices to note that the right to a healthy environment would clearly meet the threshold conditions that Sen proposes. Indeed, the freedom under study (i.e., the freedom to enjoy a healthy environment) is (1) widely recognized in the public sphere as having a special importance (increasingly so in the face of the risk of environmental disaster) and (2) socially influenceable, insomuch as its realization depends to a large extent on the decisions of other human beings and human-controlled entities such as governments, corporations, and civil society organizations.[14]

[10] César Rodríguez-Garavito, "Ethnicity.gov: Global Governance, Indigenous Peoples and the Right to Prior Consultation in Social Minefields," *Indiana Journal of Global Legal Studies* 18(1) (2011), pp. 263–305.

[11] David R. Boyd, The Environmental Rights Revolution: A Global Study of Constitutions, Human Rights, and the Environment (University of British Columbia Press, 2012).

[12] Michael McCann, "Law and Social Movements: Contemporary Perspectives," *Annual Review of Law and Social Science* 2 (2006), pp. 17–38.

[13] See, e.g., Kathryn Hochstetler and Margaret E. Keck, *Greening Brazil: Environmental Activism in State and Society* (Duke University Press, 2007).

[14] Amartya Sen, "Elements of a Theory of Human Rights," *Philosophy and Public Affairs* 32(4) (2004), pp. 315–56, 319. In line with Sen's view of rights, the combination of the two threshold

We can thus conclude that the entitlement to a healthy environment already is a human right. Why is this conclusion relevant in the context of a volume largely focused on the possibility of enshrining the right in international positive law? In addition to providing a conceptual corrective to the mainstream legal views of rights, this conclusion has a practical implication: If the effort to formalize the right in international law fails to overcome the considerable institutional obstacles that it would encounter (which I discuss later in this chapter), this outcome would not detract from the status of the right as a human right, or the ability of human rights actors to invoke it.

In reality, the right already has a stronger practical foundation than its moral status alone would warrant. Indeed, the right is grounded in comparative constitutional law and international practice, to the point of reaching, to my mind, the status of customary international law. To this issue I now turn.

THE LEGAL CASE FOR THE RIGHT TO A HEALTHY ENVIRONMENT

Having conceptually uncoupled human rights from legal rights, it is important to acknowledge the connection between them. H. L. A. Hart cogently characterized the link:

> There is of course no simple identification to be made between moral and legal rights, but there is an intimate connection between the two, and this itself is one feature which distinguishes a moral right from other fundamental moral concepts. It is not merely that as a matter of fact men speak of their moral rights mainly when advocating their incorporation in a legal system, but that the concept of a right belongs to that branch of morality which is specifically concerned to determine when one person's freedom may be limited by another's and so to determine what actions may appropriately be made the subject of coercive legal rules.[15]

There is of course additional value in enshrining a human right in a legally enforceable rule. As we will see in the following section, such an action tends to endow a moral claim with additional material and symbolic power. In addition to providing greater precision, certainty, and enforceability, it sends an authoritative institutional message about the importance of the entitlement in question, which may in turn energize movements and coalitions advocating for the right. These additional powers explain why human rights actors spend a considerable part of their

conditions sets the right to a healthy environment and other rights apart from other individually and socially desirable freedoms, such as tranquility or happiness. The latter would meet the first condition but not the second, due to the "the difficulty of guaranteeing [them] through social help." Ibid., p. 330.

[15] H. L. A. Hart, "Are There Any Natural Rights?," *Philosophical Review* 64(2) (1955), pp. 175–91, 177.

efforts trying to enshrine rights in legal texts, whether national constitutions, domestic legislations, regional treaties, or international hard- or soft-law instruments.[16]

In the environmental realm, this has no doubt been part of the motivation for the drive to include the right in global declarations, regional treaties, and national constitutions over the last four decades. The wealth of hard- and soft-law instruments that already incorporate this right raises the following question: Has the right attained legally binding international status, despite the fact that it has yet to be recognized in a global treaty? Although other contributions to this volume focus on this question, for the purposes of the logical sequence of my argument, at least a cursory treatment of it is in order before discussing the merits of an explicit adoption of the right to a healthy environment in international hard law.

Just as there is a strong moral case for the existence of a right to a healthy environment, the development of international law and doctrine supports the claim that the right is already part of customary international law. Indeed, the aforementioned conception of human rights fits well with modern doctrines of customary international law, which, unlike traditional ones, tend to prioritize *opinio juris* (the widespread sense of legal obligation across the globe) over the uniformity of interstate practice as the defining feature of a rule forming part of customary international law.[17] Put differently, in interpreting Article 38 of the ICJ statute – according to which international custom entails "evidence of a general practice accepted by law" – modern approaches argue that "state practice is less important in forming modern custom because these customs prescribe ideal standards of conduct rather than describe existing practice,"[18] and that "the reduced focus on state practice in the modern approach is generally explained by its use to create generally binding laws on moral issues."[19]

The priority of *opinio juris* as "generally binding laws on moral issues" resonates with the moral view of human rights outlined in the previous section. The convergence of the moral and the legal case for the existence of an international right to a healthy environment is further supported by current understandings of state practice, the second component of customary international law. Indeed, contemporary international law doctrine suggests that the practices that constitute human rights customary law may be different from those that are required to generate other types

[16] For an authoritative review of relevant global and regional sources, see John H. Knox, *Report of the Independent Expert on the Issue of Human Rights Obligations Relating to the Enjoyment of a Safe, Clean, Healthy and Sustainable Environment: Mapping Report*, UN Doc. A/HRC/25/53 (December 30, 2013).

[17] On the debate between traditional and modern approaches to customary international law, see the *First Report on Formation and Evidence of Customary International Law*, prepared by Special Rapporteur Michael Wood for the International Law Commission, UN Doc. A/CN.4/663 (May 17, 2013), pp. 45–56.

[18] Anthea Elizabeth Roberts, "Traditional and Modern Approaches to Customary International Law: A Reconciliation," *American Journal of International Law* 95(4) (2001), pp. 757–91, 764.

[19] Ibid., p. 766.

of customary law. As the *Third Restatement on Foreign Relations* of the American Law Institute posits, "the practice of states that is accepted as building customary law of human rights includes some forms of conduct different from those that build customary international law generally."[20] An important sector of international law scholarship has embraced and developed this distinction.[21] As John Lee concludes, "from that distinction, a form of state practice that uniquely acts to create customary human rights law is the incorporation of human rights provisions in national constitutions and laws."[22] Hence, the fact that more than half of the world's nations have recognized the right is highly significant.

Global and regional legal developments also support the conclusion that the right forms part of customary international law. At the global scale, at the UN Conference on the Environment and Development held in Rio de Janeiro in 1992, almost every nation accepted without reservation Principle 1 of the Rio Declaration, according to which: "Human beings are ... entitled to a healthy and productive life in harmony with nature." Although this principle does not explicitly refer to a right to a healthy environment, its language is consistent with the moral theory of human rights outlined earlier in this chapter. The terms of Principle 1 have been reaffirmed in various international declarations, such as those resulting from the 1994 UN Conference on Population and Development, the 1995 World Summit for Social Development, and the 1996 Second Conference on Human Settlements. I concur with Lee that "while each of these reaffirmations is legally non-binding, the fact that almost every nation made this reaffirmation without reservation – at least three times – is evidence of a widespread and consistent state practice."[23]

At the regional scale, the right to a healthy environment has attained recognition in four binding treaties. First, Article 24 of the African Charter, also known as the Banjul Charter, states: "All peoples shall have the right to a general satisfactory environment favorable to their development." Second, Article 38 of the Arab

[20] *Restatement (Third) of the Foreign Relations Law of the United States* § 701, note 2 (1987).

[21] *See, e.g.*, C. M. Chinkin, "The Challenge of Soft Law: Development and Change in International Law," *International and Comparative Law Quarterly* 38(4) (1989), pp. 850–66; Vojin Dimitrijevic, "Customary Law as an Instrument for the Protection of Human Rights," ISPI Working Paper 7 (2006); Louis Henkin, "Human Rights and State Sovereignty," *Georgia Journal of International and Comparative Law* 25(1) (1995/96), pp. 31–45; Richard B. Lillich, "The Growing Importance of Customary International Human Rights Law," *Georgia Journal of International and Comparative Law* 25(1) (1995/1996), pp. 1–30; Theodor Meron, *Human Rights and Humanitarian Norms as Customary Law* (Oxford University Press, 1989); Niles Petersen, "Customary Law without Custom? Rules, Principles, and the Role of State Practice in International Norm Creation," *American University International Law Review* 23(2) (2007), pp. 275–310, 305; Roberts, "Traditional and Modern Approaches," p. 777; Oscar Schachter, "International Law in Theory and Practice," *Recueil des Cours* 178 (1982), p. 334.

[22] John Lee, "The Underlying Legal Theory to Support a Well-Defined Human Right to a Healthy Environment as a Principle of Customary International Law," *Columbia Journal of Environmental Law* 25 (2000), pp. 283–339, 313.

[23] Ibid., p. 309.

Charter on Human Rights acknowledges that "every person has the right to . . . a healthy environment." Third, in Europe, the right is importantly acknowledged in the Aarhus Convention on Access to Information, Public Participation in Decision-Making and Access to Justice in Environmental Matters, Article 1 of which refers to the right of "every person of present and future generations to live in an environment adequate to his or her health and well-being."[24] And, finally, Article 11 of the San Salvador Protocol (the Additional Protocol to the American Convention on Human Rights), states that "everyone shall have the right to live in a healthy environment." Significantly, in 2017, the Inter-American Court of Human Rights interpreted this article as (i.) protecting not only individuals, but also the the right of collectivities (such as future generations) to a healthy environment, and (ii.) holding states responsible for cross-border violations of such rights.[25]

In sum, legal trends at the global, regional, and national levels all point to the recognition of the right in customary international law. This conclusion, however, is far from unanimous. Government representatives from countries that have not incorporated the right in their constitutions (such as the United States, China, Japan, Canada, and Australia), as well as international scholars who embrace the traditional conception of customary law, argue that because the right has been adopted internationally only in soft-law instruments, such a recognition cannot be seen as state practice constitutive of customary international law. According to Prosper Weil, for instance, there is no justification for considering that "by dint of repetition, non-normative resolutions can be transmuted into positive law through a sort of incantory effect: the accumulation of non-law or pre-law is no more sufficient to create law than is thrice of nothing to make something."[26]

In response to the traditionalist view, one could point to the fact that, in an increasing multipolar and legally fragmented world, soft-law instruments will probably be the dominant modality of international lawmaking.[27] This explains why soft-law instruments have proliferated in new global regulatory arenas, from business

[24] African Charter on Human and Peoples' Rights, June 27, 1981, in force October 21, 1986, 1520 UNTS 217; Additional Protocol to the American Convention on Human Rights in the Area of Economic, Social and Cultural Rights: Protocol of San Salvador, November 17, 1988, in force November 16, 1999, 28 ILM 161; Arab Charter on Human Rights, May 22, 2004, in force March 15, 2008, 12 IHRR 893 (2005); Aarhus Convention on Access to Information, Public Participation in Decision-Making and Access to Justice in Environmental Matters, June 25, 1998, in force October 21, 2001, 2161 UNTS 447.

[25] Inter-American Court of Human Rights, Advisory Opinion OC-23-17 of November 15, 2017.

[26] Prosper Weil, "Towards Relative Normativity in International Law?," *American Journal of International Law* 77(3) (1983), pp. 413–42.

[27] See Gráinne de Búrca, Robert O. Keohane, and Charles Sabel, "New Modes of Pluralist Global Governance," *NYU Journal of International Law and Politics* 45(1) (2013), pp. 723–86; Alan E. Boyle, "Some Reflections on the Relationship of Treaties and Soft Law," *International and Comparative Law Quarterly* 48(4) (1999), pp. 901–13.

and human rights[28] to climate change.[29] It could further be shown "that countries under some circumstances may comply with legally nonbinding instruments as well as they do with binding ones,"[30] as the global impact of the Universal Declaration of Human Rights has shown.[31]

Given the specific goals of this chapter, I cannot compose a complete reply to objections to granting customary international law status to the right. For my purposes, the fact that state practice (both intrastate and interstate) and *opinio juris* provide strong support for such a status adds legal ammunition to the aforementioned moral case for the existence of the right to a healthy environment as a human right.

Legal and moral reasons notwithstanding, the absence of explicit recognition of the right in positive international law undoubtedly limits its impact. In the next section, I reflect on the benefits and costs of moving in that direction.

AN EMPIRICAL CASE FOR AN INTERNATIONAL RIGHT TO A HEALTHY ENVIRONMENT

In considering the advantages and disadvantages of an international right to a healthy environment, it is necessary to go beyond the moral and legal reasons outlined in the previous sections. Instead, the focus should shift to an examination of the potential social and political benefits and costs of the adoption of the right in international positive law, so as to gauge the overall desirability and feasibility of such a possibility. This is the realm of empirical socio-legal studies of rights, which focus on the impact of rights in practice.

The benefits and costs of the introduction of the right in international positive law can be understood through this lens. As for the *benefits*, the most immediate would be those stemming from the greater certainty, precision, and coercive power that a new legal instrument would give to those seeking the protection of their entitlement to a healthy environment. As has been the case in other areas, such as socio-economic rights, global standards would provide additional procedural and substantive grounding for national and international litigation, thus potentially altering the distribution of resources and power between victims and perpetrators of violations of the right to a healthy environment.

28 See César Rodríguez-Garavito (ed.), *Business and Human Rights: Beyond the End of the Beginning* (Cambridge University Press, 2017).

29 Robert Keohane and David Victor, "The Regime Complex for Climate Change," *Perspectives on Politics* 9(1) (2011), pp. 7–23.

30 Edith Brown Weiss, "Introduction," in Edith Brown Weiss (ed.), *International Compliance with Nonbinding Accords* (American Society of International Law, 1997), p. 1.

31 Michèle Olivier, "The Relevance of 'Soft Law' as Source of International Human Rights," *Comparative and International Law Journal of Southern Africa* 35(3) (2002), pp. 289–307, 299.

As, by definition, the right is a common good (in that it cannot be enjoyed by one person without also being enjoyed by others), the proliferation of pro-environment litigation would have a multiplier effect, as individual cases would probably have beneficial collective impacts. For instance, litigation against the pollution of rivers and water sources, which currently must overcome strict class-action requirements in order to proceed in most jurisdictions, could be potentially facilitated by an international right that grants individuals the possibility of requesting redress for pollution insomuch as it violates their right. Depending on the wording and interpretation of the international right to a healthy environment, it might even be possible for such a right to be invoked in order to counter environmental degradation per se, regardless of its impact on humans.

At the international scale, the right could also play a similar role to that it has played in domestic jurisdictions that recognize this right, to wit, serving as a source of countervailing arguments and power vis-à-vis other legally protected goals, such as the exigencies of economic development.[32] Finally, in order to be meaningful, an internationally recognized right would require an enforcement mechanism, such as a UN committee, working group, or special mandate. Thus, the right would provide an additional venue for the enforcement and development of standards regarding human rights and the environment.

In producing these effects, the international right to a healthy environment should complement, rather than replace, constitutional norms and jurisprudence at the domestic level. Again, developments in the field of socioeconomic rights provide a useful comparison. For decades, global, regional, and national bodies – from the UN Committee on Economic, Social and Cultural Rights and UN special rapporteurships, to regional human rights courts and national constitutional courts – have explicitly drawn from each other's work to give greater precision to and develop enforcement mechanisms for such rights. If a similar multi-scalar virtuous circle could be developed in the field of human rights and the environment, the overall outcome would be a qualitative improvement from the status quo, which is largely focused on the national scale.

Adoption of the right could also produce political benefits. The use of a human rights framework could be a potent mobilizing tool, as such a framework endows advocates with a morally resonant discourse based on entitlements, as opposed to preferences. As has been the case with countless other movements,[33] framing ecological issues in terms of rights creates the possibility of catalyzing and unifying the efforts of environmental advocates and victims of violations by providing a

[32] Alan Boyle, "Human Rights and the Environment: Where Next?" *European Journal of International Law* 23(3) (2012), pp. 613–42; Rebecca Bratspies, "Do We Need a Human Right to a Healthy Environment?" *Santa Clara Journal of International Law* 13(1) (2015), pp. 31–69.

[33] See McCann, "Law and Social Movements."

common language and linking these efforts to a well-established social justice framework and enforcement infrastructure.

Finally, an international right to a healthy environment can be expected to amplify the positive effects that domestic constitutional environmental rights have produced, and to generate them in countries whose constitutions do not explicitly protect it. As Boyd has documented in his empirical study of the impact of constitutional environmental rights, those effects include higher environmental standards in legislation, jurisprudence and policy; greater governmental accountability with regards to environmental policy; prevention of retrogressive laws and policies; greater citizen participation in environmental decision making; and possibly improved environmental performance.[34]

These potential gains would not come without *costs*. As critics of the rights framework have argued, using "rights talk" may have an atomizing effect, as collective demands for justice become fragmented into individual litigation and claims.[35] For instance, the growing global consciousness about the planetary, existential challenges posed by climate change (and the need for a global regulatory response) might be displaced by myriad litigation efforts at the national level, leading to widely differing outcomes in each case.

Similarly, the ascendance of the rights approach to environmental issues could deepen the dominance of professional organizations (as opposed to affected communities) in the field.[36] As has been the case in other human rights issue areas, this could also give lawyers and legal discourse a disproportionate influence vis-à-vis other relevant forms of expertise. As Scheingold put it in his classic study on "the myth of rights":

> Legal frames of reference tunnel the vision of both activists and analysts leading to an oversimplified approach to social processes – an approach that grossly exaggerates the role that lawyers and litigation can play in a strategy for change. The assumption is that litigation can evoke a declaration of rights from courts; that it can, further, be used to assure the realization of these rights; and, finally, that realization is tantamount to meaningful change.[37]

Another potential disadvantage that is worth considering is the cost of obtaining the recognition of the right in international law in the first place. As demonstrated by the recent debate in the business and human rights field between supporters of the existing soft-law approach based on the UN Guiding Principles and supporters of a hard-law approach that would lead to a binding treaty,[38] both routes involve

34 Boyd, *The Environmental Rights Revolution*.

35 Glendon, *Rights Talk*.

36 On the dominance of professional environmental organizations, see Sarah Hansen, *Cultivating the Grassroots: A Winning Approach for Environment and Climate Funders* (NCPR, 2016).

37 Stuart A. Scheingold, *The Politics of Rights: Lawyers, Public Policy and Political Change* (University of Michigan Press, 1974), p. 5.

38 See Rodríguez-Garavito (ed.), *Business and Human Rights*.

considerable political and institutional costs. Crafting and adopting international human rights, treaties face daunting and enduring obstacles in a geopolitical context marked by increasingly fragmented global governance. Even soft-law instruments, such as UN declarations or guiding principles, demand considerable political and institutional capital. Although these obstacles are by no means a definitive ground to decide against promoting the adoption of an international right to a healthy environment, proponents of this strategy must keep them in mind when gauging the inevitable trade-offs associated with such an effort.

Finally, any new right inevitably falls short of its transformational promises, as the language of rights tends to be more definitive than the complications of implementation warrant. This had led rights skeptics to warn about potential disappointment. With regard to the right to a healthy environment, Watson has cautioned that "the resulting mismatch between expectation and accomplishment might diminish the significance of the right to a healthy environment and erode confidence in human rights more generally."[39] This risk may be increased by the fact that, in terms of rights theory, the corresponding duties of the right to a healthy environment are "imperfect": Unlike other rights (such as the right not to be tortured), the duty-bearers of the right and the actions expected of them would need further clarification through practice, doctrine, and jurisprudence. Some of the difficult questions that would need to be resolved over time include the following: Given the transnational nature of many forms of environmental damage, such as global warming, are perpetrators accountable for violations they committed outside their jurisdictions? Could corporations qualify as duty-bearers? Would lack of resources and the priority of economic development constitute valid arguments for a low-income state not to protect the right?[40]

It should be noted that objections regarding limited implementation and imperfect obligations are common to many other types of human rights. Again, the parallel with socioeconomic rights helps to put these objections in perspective and offers useful lessons for a potential right to a healthy environment. As international and domestic doctrine and jurisprudence on socioeconomic rights have established, rights can be progressively realized. The progressive realization standard could be also applied to this right, so that states would fulfill their obligations under the right as long as they make progress toward its realization in accordance with their maximum available resources. Further, empirical studies of socioeconomic rights implementation show that courts have developed jurisprudence and enforcement mechanisms that, while acknowledging the imperfect nature of the obligations

39 J. Shand Watson, *Theory and Reality in the International Protection of Human Rights* (Transnational Publishers, 1999).

40 An important step toward answering some of these questions is the report by John H. Knox, the then Independent Expert on the issue of human rights obligations relating to the enjoyment of a safe, clean, healthy and sustainable environment, compiling good practices, UN Doc. A/HRC/28/61 (February 3, 2015).

associated with socioeconomic rights, effectively prompt state authorities to progressively realize them.[41] As Scheppele observes, "courts know how to specify what states must do to realize their imperfect obligations – to do as much as they can, when they can. Courts can stay on top of these issues, monitoring state compliance with imperfect obligations and giving new pushes when the state fails."[42] Courts could certainly do the same in enforcing an international right to a healthy environment, just as they are already doing in applying constitutional environmental rights.

CONCLUSION

In this chapter, I offered a moral, legal, and empirical case for the international right to a healthy environment. From the viewpoint of moral theory, based on Sen's conception of rights, I argued that human rights should be understood as moral claims, rather than legal claims. I further posited that the right meets the threshold conditions of a human right, inasmuch as it protects essential components of a human life with dignity in times of increasing environmental stress. I thus concluded that the right to a healthy environment is already a human right.

From a legal perspective, I contended that the right would qualify as part of binding international law under a contemporary understanding of the customary international law. The recognition of the right in most national constitutions and four regional human rights instruments, together with numerous soft-law international instruments, offers solid evidence of both the relevant state practice and *opino juris* necessary to grant the right the status of customary international law.

Finally, based on empirical studies of the impact of the rights framework, I suggested that the adoption of the right in a formal international law instrument would entail both benefits and costs. Among the benefits are greater certainty, precision, and coercive power of the demand to a healthy environment. This may further encourage pro-environment litigation, create a mutually beneficial feedback loop between international and national environmental law, energize environmental movements, and promote higher environmental standards in domestic legislation, jurisprudence, and policy. However, it may also produce costs, including the atomization of environmental activism, the dominance of lawyers and legal discourse in environmental movements, the potential frustration of some of the

[41] César Rodríguez-Garavito, "Beyond the Courtroom: The Impact of Judicial Activism on Socioeconomic Rights in Latin America," *Texas Law Review* 89(7) (2011), pp. 1669–98; César Rodríguez-Garavito and Diana Rodríguez-Franco, *Radical Deprivation of Trial: The Impact of Judicial Activism on Socioeconomic Rights in the Global South* (Cambridge University Press, 2015).

[42] Kim Lane Scheppele, "Amartya Sen's Vision for Human Rights – and Why He Needs the Law," *American University International Law Review* 27(1) (2011–12), pp. 17–35, at 30.

expectations raised by the adoption of the right, and the concentration of scarce resources in difficult and potentially protracted international negotiations of a treaty or declaration.

Overall, I believe that the benefits of recognizing an international right to a healthy environment would outweigh the costs, and the empirical record also supports the case for this right. In conclusion, the right is indeed an idea whose time has come.

Since the outcome of the effort to create an international right to a healthy environment is uncertain, it is important to recall, in closing, the implication of the conception of human rights that served as my point of departure. Even if such an effort were to fail, the right is an already-existing human right, whose clearly imperfect realization is but a call to action. As Sen has put it, "the understanding that some rights are not fully realized, and may not even be fully *realizable* under present circumstances, does not, in itself, entail anything like the conclusion that these are, therefore, not rights at all. Rather, this ethical understanding suggests ... the need to work toward changing the prevailing circumstances to make the unrealized rights realizable, and ultimately, realized."[43]

[43] Sen, "Elements of a Theory of Human Rights," p. 348.

10

Quality Control of the Right to a Healthy Environment

*Marcos Orellana**

Writing in 1984, Philip Alston concluded that "a more orderly and considered procedure should be followed before the United Nations accords the highly prized status of a human right to any additional claims."[1] Alston's proposal for quality control was based not on the articulation of substantive criteria, which he concluded was "an unworkable approach," but on "procedural safeguards to govern the proclamation of new human rights within the UN system."[2] Two years later, the UN General Assembly adopted a resolution setting international standards in the field of human rights.[3] What is not devoid of irony is that the General Assembly heeded Alston's call for quality control, but articulated substantive rather than strictly procedural guidelines.

This issue of quality control is directly relevant to the proclamation of the right to a healthy environment at the global level by either the Human Rights Council or the General Assembly. Would the proclamation of the right to a healthy environment satisfy the guidelines established by the General Assembly? Would it satisfy the essence of the procedural safeguards proposed by Alston? In addition to these two questions, there is also the issue of powers and legitimacy within the UN system. More specifically, the question arises whether the UN Human Rights Council could authoritatively proclaim new human rights, or whether that role is

* Marcos A Orellana is the Director of the Environment and Human Rights Program at Human Rights Watch. This chapter was prepared while he was with the Center for International Environmental Law (CIEL).

1 Philip Alston, "Conjuring Up New Human Rights: A Proposal for Quality Control," *American Journal of International Law* 78(3) (1984) pp. 607–21, 614.

2 Ibid., p. 618.

3 General Assembly res. 41/120 (December 4, 1986).

reserved for the General Assembly. This chapter examines these three questions as they apply to a right to a healthy environment.[4]

THE UN GENERAL ASSEMBLY GUIDELINES ON INTERNATIONAL HUMAN RIGHTS STANDARD-SETTING

The guidelines adopted by the UN General Assembly in 1986 state that international instruments in the field of human rights should, *inter alia*:

> "(a) Be consistent with the existing body of international human rights law;
> (b) Be of fundamental character and derive from the inherent dignity and worth of the human person;
> (c) Be sufficiently precise to give rise to identifiable and practicable rights and obligations;
> (d) Provide, where appropriate, realistic and effective implementation machinery, including reporting systems; [and]
> (e) Attract broad international support."[5]

In the elaboration of these guidelines, the General Assembly sought to strike a balance between the "fundamental importance" of the effective implementation of the International Bill of Rights and other international human rights standards, on the one hand, and the inherent dynamism and evolving character of the human rights field, on the other. By striking a balance, the General Assembly recognized the value of both the implementation and standard-setting functions of the UN human rights system, thereby dismissing calls for the elimination of one or the other.

While the General Assembly recognized the critical importance of both elements of the implementation vs. standard-setting equation, it called upon Member States and UN bodies "to accord priority to the implementation of existing international standards in the field of human rights."[6] At the same time, the General Assembly recognized "the value of continuing efforts to identify specific areas where further international action is required to develop the existing international legal framework in the field of human rights pursuant to Article 13, paragraph 1 a, of the Charter of the United Nations."[7] The acknowledgment of the importance of both the implementation and standard-setting functions, while accompanied by a statement of

[4] This chapter uses the terminology of a right to a healthy environment as an umbrella formulation that encompasses the various terminological variations of this right in national constitutions and international instruments, including terms such as "adequate," "clean," "productive," "harmonious," and "sustainable." See James R. May and Erin Daly, *Global Environmental Constitutionalism* (Cambridge University Press, 2015), p. 64.

[5] General Assembly res. 41/120, para. 4.

[6] Ibid., para. 1.

[7] Ibid., pmbl.

priority for implementation, would also have influenced the swinging of the pendulum of institutional direction (and budgets) within the UN system.

Once the general point of principle reaffirmed by the guidelines in regard to the importance of standard setting in the field of human rights was established, more mundane operational questions surfaced. In particular, should the General Assembly articulate guidelines based on substantive or procedural criteria? That was then the question addressed by Member States. And it was answered largely in favor of substantive criteria, despite Alston's observation that it was "an artificial and unrewarding task to seek to distill from the broad range of human rights already proclaimed by the General Assembly any scientifically valid criteria that would be capable of practical application in respect of new claims."[8]

There are certain angles that may explain the General Assembly's preference for more substantive guidelines. For one, there is the institutional powers question, alongside the possible distinction between guidelines and requirements. Regulating a procedure involving requirements for the then Commission on Human Rights would have called for a potentially complex exchange with the Economic and Social Council, the then parent body of the Commission. Instead of dealing with the myriad traps that could surface in the articulation by the General Assembly of procedural requirements involving another Charter body and its subsidiary bodies, it was simpler for the General Assembly to articulate open-textured substantive guidelines.

Another consideration that could explain the General Assembly's preference is that substantive guidelines set the stage for a debate among UN Member States, thereby underscoring that the proclamation of new rights is a political issue. Alston had already made this point in 1984 precisely in respect of the right to a healthy environment, noting that "it is clear that the issue of whether to proclaim some form of environmental rights cannot realistically be resolved through the application of standardized criteria; it is, after all, a quintessentially political issue."[9] The point can be framed in a slightly more subtle way, as underscoring that substantive guidelines would not set a benchmark of mathematical legality, but a frame of reference for the key issues and parameters of the political debate.

The UN record regarding the debate on this resolution further supports the view that it set a frame of reference for a more structured process regarding the political debates on standard-setting. Australia introduced the draft resolution in the General Assembly on behalf of its sponsors,[10] noting that it "was aimed at improving the process of standard-setting in the field of human rights."[11] The discussions at the Third Committee included a revision of the operative paragraph containing

[8] Alston, "Quality Control," p. 616.

[9] Ibid., p. 617.

[10] The resolution was sponsored by Australia, Canada, Costa Rica, Morocco, Netherlands, New Zealand, and Philippines.

[11] UN Doc. A/C.3/41/L.71.

the guidelines, which changed from the formulation, “Such instruments should be:,” to the formulation, “Such instruments should inter alia:.”[12] While the distinction is subtle and could even be considered merely editorial, it does suggest that the guidelines are not a closed list of legal benchmarks or criteria, but instead guidelines that can be used to structure and guide a political and technical debate with a view to strengthening the process of standard-setting.

APPLICATION OF THE UN GENERAL ASSEMBLY GUIDELINES TO THE GLOBAL RECOGNITION OF THE RIGHT TO A HEALTHY ENVIRONMENT

The General Assembly resolution on setting international human rights standards identifies the key elements and parameters of the debate over the recognition of new human rights. How does the right to a healthy environment fare when assessed against the General Assembly's guidelines? The answer to this question is explored next in relation to each of the guidelines and with the benefit of decades of discussion on the environmental dimensions of human rights law.

Consistency with Existing Body of International Human Rights Law

If at some point in time the question of how the environment relates to human rights law was a novel one, that is hardly the situation today. After decades of discussion about the interface between environmental protection and human rights, the consistency and synergy between a healthy environment and the existing body of international human rights law have been underscored by treaty bodies, special rapporteurs, and regional human rights courts.[13] These institutions and mechanisms have expanded on the interrelations between environmental issues and the rights to life, health, water, food, housing, standard of living, property, privacy, participation, information, self-determination, and culture, among other internationally recognized rights. They have looked at cross-cutting environmental threats to human rights, such as hazardous wastes, natural resources, and climate change, and they have also applied a rights-based approach to the protection of particular groups, including indigenous peoples, environmental defenders, and children. What has emerged from this decades-long work is the recognition by the UN Human Rights Council that the protection of the environment can contribute to human well-being

[12] UN Doc. A/41/878.

[13] United Nations Environment Programme and Center for International Environmental Law, *Compendium on Human Rights and the Environment* (2014). See also the fourteen reports that inform and accompany the *Report of the Independent Expert on the Issue of Human Rights Obligations Relating to the Enjoyment of a Safe, Clean, Healthy and Sustainable Environment: Mapping Report*, UN Doc. A/HRC/25/53 (December 30, 2013), which are available at www.srenvironment.org.

and to the enjoyment of human rights, and conversely that environmental damage can have negative implications, both direct and indirect, for the effective enjoyment of all human rights.[14]

The Male' Declaration on the Human Dimension of Global Climate Change, adopted by representatives of Small Island Developing States in 2007, underscores this central point of principle.[15] The first preambular paragraph of the Male' Declaration states its awareness "that the environment provides the infrastructure for human civilization and that life depends on the uninterrupted functioning of natural systems."[16] And a subsequent preambular paragraph highlights the consistency between the environment and human rights law by noting that "the fundamental right to an environment capable of supporting human society and the full enjoyment of human rights is recognized, in varying formulations, in the constitutions of over one hundred states and directly or indirectly in several international instruments."

Consistency does not mean or imply the lack of tensions between the right to a healthy environment and other protected rights. For example, tensions may arise in the implementation of the right to housing where programs disregard a rights-based approach to the urban environment. Tensions may also arise with the right to development where this right is interpreted as a right to pollute and to increase emissions of greenhouse gases into the atmosphere. Tensions between rights are not unknown in human rights law. Few human rights are absolute: e.g., the rights to be free from torture, enforced disappearances, or racial discrimination. Instead, the human rights regime contains tools and methods to deal with tensions among rights, to balance the interests of the individual and the community, and to address trade-offs between competing societal priorities. Therefore, tensions that may arise between the right to a healthy environment and other rights do not reveal inconsistency, but instead can be constructively addressed and resolved by the well-known application of the tools and methods available in the body of human rights law.

Consistency between the right to a healthy environment and the existing body of international law is also apparent in regard to the obligations arising from the right. While this issue is further elaborated subsequently, suffice it here to note that these obligations are not different in kind from obligations attaching to other rights. The environmental quality, or substantive, dimensions of the right to a healthy environment, for example, are similar to the obligations attaching to economic, social, and cultural rights. Similarly, the societal dialogue, or procedural, dimensions of the right are comparable to the obligations attaching to civil and political rights. In other words, the obligations attached to the right to a healthy environment

[14] Human Rights Council res. 25/21 (March 28, 2014).

[15] See Daniel Magraw and Kristina Wienhöfer, Chapter 12.

[16] Malé Declaration on the Human Dimension of Global Climate Change, November 14, 2007, available at www.ciel.org/Publications/Male_Declaration_Nov07.pdf.

are not qualitatively different from that of other rights, thereby underscoring the consistency criterion in this particular guideline. In fact, this qualitative similarity of the obligations is emphasized by how many human rights sources essentially derive the right to a healthy environment from other existing rights, such as the right to life, the right to health, and the right to an adequate standard of living. For example, the Arab Charter and the ASEAN Declaration both include the right as one of the components of the right to an adequate standard of living.[17]

The Human Rights Council has further articulated the notions of consistency, synergies, and mutual support in its resolutions on human rights and the environment, all adopted by consensus. The Council has repeatedly recognized "that sustainable development and the protection of the environment can contribute to human well-being and to the enjoyment of human rights," and "also, conversely, that climate change, unsustainable management and use of natural resources and the unsound management of chemicals and wastes may interfere with the enjoyment of a safe, clean, healthy and sustainable environment, and that environmental damage can have negative implications, both direct and indirect, for the effective enjoyment of all human rights."[18]

Fundamental Character: Deriving From the Inherent Dignity of the Human Person

The fundamental character of the right to a healthy environment and its indissoluble linkage with human dignity can be traced back to the UN Conference on the Human Environment held in Stockholm in 1972. The Stockholm conference and its resulting declaration were able to place a narrative in the collective imagination of humanity at a time when the environment was only peripheral to policy making.[19] This narrative led to the incubation of the right to a healthy environment in national constitutions (addressed in Chapters 2 and 3). It also marked the inception of the notion that the environment is a precondition for the enjoyment of human rights. The Stockholm Declaration's first preambular paragraph states, "Both aspects of man's environment, the natural and the man-made, are essential to his well-being and to the enjoyment of basic human rights – even the right to life itself."[20] Not only does this proclamation affirm the fundamental character of

[17] Arab Charter on Human Rights, May 22, 2004, in force March 15, 2008, 12 IHRR 893 (2005), art. 38; Association of Southeast Asian Nations Human Rights Declaration, November 18, 2012, art. 28(f).

[18] Human Rights Council res. 25/21 (March 28, 2014), 28/11 (March 26, 2015), 31/8 (March 23, 2016).

[19] Marcos Orellana, "Keynote Address: Habitat for Human Rights," *Vermont Law Review* 40 (2016), p. 417.

[20] Declaration of the UN Conference on the Human Environment, UN Doc. A/CONF.48/14/Rev.1 (June 5–16, 1972).

the right to a healthy environment, but it also underlines the consistency of the right with the whole body of human rights.

Moreover, the very first Principle of the Stockholm Declaration on the Human Environment expressly recognizes the linkage between the environment and a life of dignity. Principle 1 proclaims that:

> Man has the fundamental right to freedom, equality and adequate conditions of life, in an environment of a quality that permits a life of dignity and well-being, and he bears a solemn responsibility to protect and improve the environment for present and future generations. In this respect, policies promoting or perpetuating apartheid, racial segregation, discrimination, colonial and other forms of oppression and foreign domination stand condemned and must be eliminated.[21]

This proclamation of principle cannot be overstated or dismissed. The rights-based approach to environmental protection brought about by the Stockholm Declaration narrative has provided a solid foundation for the emergence of a whole body of international law on human rights and the environment. This body of law has identified concrete, practicable and far-reaching rights and obligations, as examined next.

Precision: Giving Rise to Identifiable and Practicable Rights and Obligations

The question of the normative content of the right to a healthy environment has been perhaps one of the most contested issues in the debate over its recognition. Besides its strong symbolic and discursive strength in expanding human awareness and recasting human identity, what does the right to a healthy environment actually require in legal terms? Answering this question involves an assessment of the state of the law on human rights and the environment as it exists today as well as a prognosis of potential developments in the field. These two angles are relevant to the right to a healthy environment because normative reality is not static but in constant flux, owing to greater human understanding, evolving societal needs, changing interactions, novel technologies, and urgent environmental threats.

As to the first angle regarding existing rights and obligations, the Special Rapporteur on human rights and the environment has undertaken the task of mapping the vast normative *acquis* concerning human rights and the environment. This task has involved looking at the judgments of human rights courts, the pronouncements of treaty bodies, the specialized reports of special rapporteurs, and the decisions of human rights bodies, among other authoritative sources of law. In furtherance of his mandate, the Special Rapporteur has clarified the nature, scope, and content of

[21] Ibid.

human rights obligations in respect of a safe, clean, healthy, and sustainable environment.[22] Specifically, the Special Rapporteur has identified rights threatened by environmental harm, including the rights to life, health, food, and water, and has mapped procedural and substantive obligations, including obligations to protect against environmental harm from private actors and obligations relating to transboundary environmental harm. Moreover, the Special Rapporteur has identified particular duties in respect of vulnerable groups and has articulated the implications of fundamental principles such as non-discrimination and non-regression.

Despite the diversity of sources, there is a remarkable commonality among them in outlining the character of obligations pertaining to a healthy environment. Two main dimensions stand out: one procedural and another substantive. Procedural obligations sustain a society's ability to engage in civil dialogue to foster effective environmental policy. This procedural dimension of the right to a healthy environment involves critical issues for the social exchange of ideas and debate such as access to information, meaningful participation, access to justice, and freedom of assembly, association, and expression. At the same time, substantive obligations sustain an environmental quality conducive to a life of dignity. This substantive dimension of the right to a healthy environment links directly with the conditions that enable a healthy planet; such as clean water, air, and soils; a balanced climate system; and healthy and diverse ecosystems.

This normative *acquis*, as derived from the environmental dimensions of existing protected rights and fundamental human rights principles, would be brought together under the umbrella of the right to a healthy environment. The normative content of human rights in respect of the environment would thus no longer be dispersed or fragmented across a range of rights, but would come together under a single normative frame. This normative content comprises identifiable and practicable rights and obligations that, when under a single frame, would further help in implementation and progressive development.

As to the second angle regarding new developments, the experience of domestic courts in the implementation of constitutional rights to a healthy environment reveals the potential for the right to enable normative development.[23] In that regard, a certain level of indeterminacy in the content of the right may be considered not only acceptable but even desirable, so that national courts as well as international tribunals may continue to strengthen the tools available in the body of human rights law.

The potential of the right to a healthy environment to enable normative development cannot be overstated, in light of the serious environmental and social crisis

[22] See Knox, *Mapping Report*.

[23] See Dinah Shelton, "Developing Substantive Environmental Rights," *Journal of Human Rights and the Environment* 1(1) (2010), pp. 89, 90; May and Daly, *Global Environmental Constitutionalism*.

facing the planet, where its continued ecological viability has been placed into question by scientists worldwide.[24] The need for new and robust legal tools to preserve the integrity of the planet, to restore degraded ecosystems, to foster a balanced interaction between humans and nature, and to secure global environment justice has been consistently voiced by civil society organizations in their statements to the Human Rights Council.[25] It can be expected that global recognition of the right to a healthy environment would thus enable new ways of thinking and using the law to enhance and achieve the protection of the environment and human rights.

Realistic and Effective Implementation Machinery

Implementation is key to actualizing the transformative potential of the global proclamation of the right to a healthy environment. Some preliminary observations can help situate the assessment of the implementation machinery. First, the question of whether the existing human rights implementation machinery is realistic and effective remains open for virtually all human rights. Second, the implementation of the right to a healthy environment would largely take place at the national level, owing to existing governance structures resting on the nation-state and the characteristic of international human rights law as complementary to national laws and measures. Third, the implementation machinery is not static but can and should be strengthened in order to capture the transformative potential of the law. Fourth, while the right to a healthy environment involves distinctive tools from other rights, such as the use of data on chemicals or biology to establish impacts, its implementation can also be advanced by the traditional means of the human rights machinery. Last, the right to a healthy environment cannot (and should not) be implemented in isolation, but in regard to its linkages with other civil, cultural, economic, political, and social rights and to fundamental human rights principles.

The machinery for implementation at the national level for the right to a healthy environment would include normative, programmatic, and institutional dimensions that incorporate a rights-based approach. Examples of good practices in this regard have been identified by the Special Rapporteur on human rights and the environment.[26] For example, the important role of national human rights institutions in monitoring implementation of the right to a healthy environment was explored at a side event held during the March 2016 session of the Human Rights Council,

[24] See e.g., Will Steffen et al., "Planetary Boundaries: Guiding Human Development on a Changing Planet," *Science* 347(6223) (2015), p. 746.

[25] Marcos Orellana, "Reflections on the Right to a Healthy Environment," *Santa Clara Journal of International Law* 13(1) (2015), pp. 71–9, 77–8.

[26] John H. Knox, *Report of the Independent Expert on the Issue of Human Rights Obligations Relating to the Enjoyment of a Safe, Clean, Healthy and Sustainable Environment: Compilation of Good Practices*, UN Doc. A/HRC/28/61 (February 3, 2015).

including concrete experiences in Mexico, Chile, and other countries. Accordingly, there is already a wealth of knowledge on good practices regarding effective and realistic implementation of the right to a healthy environment.

Implementation at the international level would involve existing as well as new monitoring mechanisms. As to new mechanisms, implementation at the international level would depend on how the right to a healthy environment is incorporated into the body of international human rights law. If it is included in an optional protocol to an existing treaty that is supervised by a treaty body, then the implementation of the right would be monitored by the respective treaty body machinery. As to existing mechanisms, the Universal Period Review, for example, could be used in relation to the right to a healthy environment. At the regional level, mechanisms are already in place in the Americas and Africa that can address implementation of the right to a healthy environment. For example, under the Organization of American States, specific indicators on the right to a healthy environment have been prepared and adopted to guide and assess the performance of States Parties to the Protocol of San Salvador to the American Convention on Human Rights.[27] Similarly, the Special Rapporteur on human rights and the environment is uniquely placed to carry out a monitoring role and has already begun to receive communications from individuals and communities. In order to carry out this monitoring role effectively, however, the mandate would need far greater resources than are currently available.

While the existing human rights machinery can advance implementation of the right to a healthy environment, and while in many instances this machinery already has encompassed this right, effective implementation would nevertheless benefit from focused capacity-building efforts at various levels. The efforts by the Office of the High Commissioner for Human Rights and the UN Environment Programme, described by Marc Limon in Chapter 11, are of direct relevance to introducing a rights-based approach to environmental policy making, at the national level as well as in multilateral environmental agreements. The reports, country visits, consultations, and other activities of the Special Rapporteur on human rights and the environment have also greatly contributed to advancing knowledge and building capacity. The expertise of specialized non-governmental organizations has also helped to illuminate the field. These efforts lay the foundation for more progressive efforts toward the full implementation and realization of the right to a healthy environment.

Attracting Broad International Support

Since the Stockholm Conference on the Human Environment in 1972, there has been a rich debate on whether the right to a healthy environment has attracted

[27] See Organization of American States, *Progress Indicators for Measuring Rights under the Protocol of San Salvador* (2d ed.), Doc. OEA/Ser.D/XXVI.11 (2015).

broad international support. The Stockholm Declaration, as quoted, was noted with satisfaction by the UN General Assembly in a resolution adopted without dissent.[28] The Stockholm Declaration was also expressly reaffirmed by the UN Conference on Environment and Development in Rio de Janeiro, Brazil, in 1992.[29] The Human Rights Council resolutions on human rights and environment, as referenced, were adopted by consensus, without a vote.

While these pronouncements by the General Assembly and the Human Rights Council have been adopted by consensus, their language has been crafted to accommodate states that have voiced concerns regarding the recognition of a new right to a healthy environment. These concerns have dealt with certain elements or characteristics of the right, including the questions of its justiciability and universality as well as its collective and/or individual character. These concerns may have been warranted in the early stages of the debate regarding the environmental dimensions of human rights law in the 1970s and 1980s, but today, significant developments in international human rights law have rendered them baseless. As to collective rights, the UN Declaration on the rights of indigenous peoples clearly articulates both individual and collective environmental rights, including in relation to land and territories.[30] As to universality, after decades of discussion on the interaction between cultural specificities and universal claims, it is increasingly clear that the process of translation and acquisition of meaning of a general and abstract right into a defined historical societal setting does not negate the universality of the right. As to justiciability, the conclusion and operation of the Optional Protocol to the International Covenant on Economic, Social and Cultural Rights[31] does away with the idea that the substantive dimension of the right to a healthy environment is not justiciable.

Accordingly, there is a clear opportunity to take fresh stock of developments in the field and hold a focused political and technical dialogue on the application of the General Assembly's guidelines to the right to a healthy environment. The quality of this dialogue would benefit from the wealth of expert knowledge that has been produced in the process of discussion on the interface between human rights and the environment.

[28] General Assembly res. 2994 (XXVII) (December 15, 1972).

[29] Rio Declaration on Environment and Development, UN Doc. A/CONF.151/26/Rev.1, annex I (June 14, 1992).

[30] UN Declaration on the Rights of Indigenous Peoples, UN Doc. A/RES/61/295 (September 13, 2007). See also *Kichwa Indigenous People of Sarayaku* v. *Ecuador*, Inter-Am. Ct. H.R. (ser. C) No. 245 (June 27, 2012) (declaring that the community as such is entitled to protection, not just its individual members).

[31] Optional Protocol to the International Covenant on Economic, Social and Cultural Rights, December 10, 2008, in force May 5, 2013, UN Doc. A/RES/63/117.

ASSESSMENT OF THE PROCESS CONCERNING GLOBAL RECOGNITION OF THE RIGHT TO A HEALTHY ENVIRONMENT

Alston's proposal for established procedures to be used to scrutinize candidates for new rights was motivated by the shortcomings of the process by which new rights were being proclaimed. As he summarized these shortcomings,

> "there has been no prior discussion, not to mention analysis, of the major implications of the proposed innovation; there has been no attempt to seek comments from governments, specialized agencies or nongovernmental organizations; there has been no request to the Secretariat or to any other expert group for advice on technical matters relating either to the general principles involved or to the specific formulations proposed; there has been no explicit recognition of the fact that a new human right was being proclaimed; and there has been insufficient debate on the basis of which to ascertain, with some degree of precision, the real intentions underlying the affirmative votes of states."[32]

In addition to these process deficiencies, Alston also observed that new rights were being proclaimed without an initial "incubation" phase involving the recognition of rights in national constitutions and national legislation. In consequence, he argued, said claims for endorsement as rights were much closer to "general social values than to legal principles."[33]

While Alston's critique did not lead the General Assembly toward the establishment of procedural safeguards, the shortcomings that he identified in relation to the process of proclamation of new rights nevertheless enable an assessment of the state of play regarding the process of recognition of the right to a healthy environment. Given the dynamism of the current dialogue at the Human Rights Council on the theme of human rights and environment, this assessment not only provides a scorecard, but also guidance on additional steps that can be taken to strengthen the debate over the right to a healthy environment.

Incubation at the National Level

The lack of experience at the national level with claims asserted as rights directly in international forums can lead to serious problems regarding content and precision as well as legitimacy. That is not a concern with the right to a healthy environment, however, given the advent of what scholars have termed "the environmental rights revolution."[34]

32 Alston, "Quality Control," p. 613.
33 Ibid., p. 614.
34 David R. Boyd, *The Environmental Rights Revolution: A Global Study of Constitutions, Human Rights, and the Environment* (University of British Columbia Press, 2012), p. 3.

Since the 1972 Stockholm Conference on the Human Environment, the environment began to be seen as an issue of priority in many states, and this new perspective on the fundamental importance of the environment in policy making led to unprecedented normative and institutional developments. Environmental ministries and commissions were created around the world, and so were environmental laws, including framework laws and environmental assessment laws.[35]

Perhaps the most important legal development is that many states amended their national constitutions – the framing of the basic social contract and the values enabling society – to incorporate environmental considerations. These references to the environment in national constitutions were often formulated as a duty of the state for environmental protection or as an individual or collective right enforceable in court.[36] Back in 1994, the Special Rapporteur on human rights and the environment of the Sub-Commission on the Prevention of Discrimination identified over sixty countries devoting constitutional provisions to the environment.[37] In 2011, the Office of the High Commissioner prepared a detailed analytical study on human rights and environment that identified about 140 countries devoting constitutional provisions to the environment.[38]

State practice as reflected in the constitutional environmental rights revolution invites a renewed inquiry on the question of whether the right to a healthy environment has entered the realm of international customary law, including on account of its fundamentally norm-creating character.[39] More generally, the High Commissioner's aforementioned study concluded that "The increasing constitutional recognition of environmental rights and responsibilities globally reflects growing awareness of the importance of environmental values and greater acceptance of a right to a healthy environment."[40]

Discussion and Analysis of the Implications of Recognition

Since the Stockholm Conference there has been significant discussion and analysis of the relationship between human rights and the environment. This debate has also addressed the implications of recognition of the right to a healthy environment. For example, the Special Rapporteur of the Human Rights Council held an expert consultation on constitutional environmental rights in 2014.[41] Twenty years earlier, the then Special Rapporteur of the Sub-Commission on the Prevention of

35 Ibid., pp. 495–6.

36 Fatma Zohra Ksentini, *Final Report*, UN Doc. E/CN.4/Sub.2/1994/9, annex III (July 6, 1994).

37 Ibid., para. 241.

38 *Analytical Study on the Relationship between Human Rights and the Environment*, UN Doc. A/HRC/19/34, (December 16, 2011), para. 30. See David R. Boyd, Chapter 2.

39 See Rebecca Bratspies, Chapter 7, and Louis J. Kotzé, Chapter 8.

40 *Analytical Study*, para. 31.

41 The report on the consultation is available at www.srenvironment.org.

Discrimination largely devoted her final report in 1994 to the right to a healthy environment.[42] That report was informed by expert consultations involving governmental and non-governmental experts. On its part, academia has produced a wealth of knowledge on human rights and the environment, including specialized conferences, journal articles, and books, including this very volume.[43] This decades-long discussion has shed light on key implications of recognition of the right to a healthy environment, including normative content, interaction with other rights, justiciability, and implementation.

Attempts to Seek Comments from Governments, Specialized Agencies, and Nongovernmental Organizations

In 2011, the Human Rights Council adopted resolution 16/11 whereby it requested the Office of the High Commissioner to prepare a detailed study on human rights and the environment. According to the terms of resolution 16/11, the study was to be conducted "in consultation with and taking into account the views of States Members of the United Nations, relevant international organizations and intergovernmental bodies, including the United Nations Environment Programme and relevant multilateral environmental agreements, special procedures, treaty bodies and other stakeholders."[44]

This experience shows how the Council mandated the Office to seek comments from a range of actors as an integral element of the process leading to its analytical study. Since numerous comments and submissions from governments, specialized agencies, and non-governmental organizations were received, the experience also shows the extended opportunity for deliberation regarding the key issues in the human rights and environment interface, including the recognition of the right to a healthy environment.

The Special Rapporteur on human rights and the environment has also sought and received comments to inform consultations on various themes relevant to its mandate, including the right to a healthy environment. This practice of fostering a conversation with a wide range of actors underscores the quality of deliberation and the strength of the process concerning the global recognition of the right to a healthy environment.

Expert Advice on Technical Matters

The UN Environment Programme and the Office of the High Commissioner for Human Rights have partnered for more than a decade in providing expert advice on

[42] Ksentini, *Final Report.*

[43] A comprehensive bibliography up to 2015 is available at www.srenvironment.org/academic-research.

[44] Human Rights Council res. 16/11 (March 24, 2011).

technical matters relating to human rights and the environment, including the right to a healthy environment. For example, these UN bodies co-organized an expert seminar in 2002, a high-level meeting in 2009, and several side events at important international policy making forums, including the UN Conference on Sustainable Development, the UN Environment Assembly, and sessions of the Human Rights Council. The UN Environment Programme and the Office of the High Commissioner have also produced high-quality publications that have contributed to clarifying the contours and elements of the human rights and environment field.[45]

The expert advice provided by the Special Rapporteur on human rights and the environment to the international community must also be regarded as an important element of the process concerning the global recognition of the right to a healthy environment. At times, this advice has been tailored to specific situations, such as the interaction with government officials and civil society organizations in official country visits to Costa Rica, France, and Madagascar.[46] More generally, this expert advice has covered a broad range of good practices regarding rights-based approaches to environmental protection, as detailed.[47]

Sufficient Intergovernmental Debate

The creation in 2012 of a special procedure on the issue of human rights obligations relating to the enjoyment of a safe, clean, healthy, and suitable environment by the Human Rights Council has provided an institutional platform for a rich intergovernmental debate on the topic. This debate has addressed a range of important issues in the human rights and environment nexus, including procedural obligations on access to information, participation, and justice that are central to environmental democracy, as well as substantive obligations regarding the adequacy of the environmental legal framework. While this debate has also included references to the right to a healthy environment, they have not (yet) focused on applying the General Assembly guidelines examined earlier. In that sense, the special procedure on human rights and environment offers an institutional vehicle to inform a focused intergovernmental debate on the recognition of the right to a healthy environment.

[45] See, e.g., UNEP and CIEL, *Compendium on Human Rights and Environment*.

[46] John H. Knox, *Report of the Independent Expert on the Issue of Human Rights Obligations Relating to the Enjoyment of a Safe, Clean, Healthy and Sustainable Environment: Mission to Costa Rica*, UN Doc. A/HRC/25/53/Add.1 (March 21, 2014); John H Knox, *Report of the Independent Expert on the Issue of Human Rights Obligations Relating to the Enjoyment of a Safe, Clean, Healthy and Sustainable Environment: Mission to France*, UN Doc. A/HRC/28/61/Add.1 (March 6, 2015); John H. Knox, *Report of the Special Rapporteur on the Issue of Human Rights Obligations Relating to the Enjoyment of a Safe, Clean, Healthy and Sustainable Environment: Mission to Madagascar*, UN Doc. A/HRC/34/49/Add.1 (April 26, 2017).

[47] See note 26 and accompanying text.

Preliminary Conclusion on the Process

The assessment of the discussion on the right to a healthy environment over the last four decades reveals significant analysis of its substantive elements, scope, and implications. Specialized technical studies have significantly advanced knowledge on this right, and expert consultations have engaged UN bodies, governments, and non-governmental organizations in a rich debate. Moreover, decades of experience with constitutional environmental rights at the national level dispel doubts as to the legitimacy of the recognition of the right at the global level. Therefore, the process of recognition of the right to a healthy environment cannot be said to suffer from the process shortcomings identified by Alston in his *Quality Control* article. At the same time, the body of knowledge resulting from the decades-long discussion has set the stage for a focused debate at the Human Rights Council on the application of the General Assembly guidelines to the right to a healthy environment.

THE ROLE OF THE HUMAN RIGHTS COUNCIL IN THE PROCLAMATION OF NEW HUMAN RIGHTS

One important underlying point in Alston's *Quality Control* was that the General Assembly's authoritative role as final arbiter in transforming rhetoric into rights was in serious danger of being undermined. This threat to the General Assembly's primacy was in large measure due to the "growing tendency on the part of a range of United Nations and other international bodies, including in particular the UN Commission on Human Rights, to proceed to the proclamation of new human rights without reference to the Assembly."[48]

Should the General Assembly still be regarded as sole, final arbiter in these matters? Does the demise of the Human Rights Commission and the creation of the Human Rights Council, as a subsidiary body of the General Assembly, alter the landscape in some material respect?

There is likely to be common ground in the recognition of the authority of the General Assembly in proclaiming human rights. From a historical perspective, the adoption by the General Assembly of the three key instruments comprising the International Bill of Human Rights is clear testament of its role and authority. More recent history confirms this role: In 2010 the General Assembly recognized "the right to safe and clean drinking water and sanitation as a human right that is essential for the full enjoyment of life and all human rights."[49] From a legal perspective, Article 13 of the UN Charter explicitly mandates the General Assembly to "initiate studies and make recommendations for the purpose of . . . assisting in the realization of human rights and fundamental freedoms for all . . ." From a political

[48] Alston, "Quality Control," p. 607.
[49] General Assembly res. 64/292 (July 28, 2010).

perspective, the General Assembly is the arena that brings together all UN Member States and therefore its human rights proclamations reflect universal character.

Under the light of these historical, legal, and political perspectives, the authority of the General Assembly to proclaim new rights is not in serious question. Rather, the issue concerns the role of the Human Rights Council in regard to the recognition of new human rights, such as the right to a healthy environment. In a more pointed formulation, the question arises whether the authority and hierarchy of the General Assembly exclude the possibility that the Human Rights Council may affirm new rights.

Looking back at the concerns that had been expressed regarding the priorities, structure, and position of the Commission on Human Rights in the UN system could shed initial light on the role of the Human Rights Council in proclaiming new rights. In prior decades, concerns with standard-setting activities by the then Commission on Human Rights had been expressed by those who wanted to see a greater focus on implementation, promotion, and monitoring of human rights. While there is much to show in the Commission's standard-setting work, including nine core treaties and more than ninety other standard-setting documents,[50] concerns with this function were also code for broader critiques regarding structural challenges facing the Commission, particularly its composition and the fact that it was populated by some states with dismal human rights records. Yet another concern was more institutionally grounded: The Commission reported to the Economic and Social Council, which does not have universal membership. The creation of the Human Rights Council as a subsidiary body of the General Assembly was meant to address these and other concerns, and therefore its role on the proclamation of new human rights is not encumbered by the baggage of the Commission.

There is another angle worth considering on this question of powers and authority, which is implicated in the language of the General Assembly resolution setting international human rights standards. This resolution "invites Member States and UN bodies to bear in mind" the guidelines. This language plainly does not exclude other UN bodies from standard-setting. Moreover, operational paragraph three of this resolution "reaffirms the important role of the Commission on Human Rights, among other appropriate United Nations bodies, in the development of international instruments in the field of human rights." Thus, the General Assembly did not seek to establish a monopoly in the field of human rights standard-setting.

The creation of the Human Rights Council in 2006 gives concrete expression to the mandate of the General Assembly in respect of human rights, as established in the Charter (as referenced). The standard-setting work of the Human Rights Council, therefore, should be seen as reinforcing, and not as undermining, the work of its

[50] *See* Donald Anton and Dinah Shelton, *Environmental Protection and Human Rights* (Cambridge University Press, 2011), p. 290.

parent body. In that light, for example, the recognition by the Human Rights Council in 2010 of the human right to safe drinking water and sanitation, as derived from the right to an adequate standard of living,[51] contributes to strengthening the General Assembly's proclamation of the right to water. Accordingly, a proclamation by the Human Rights Council of new rights would serve to further the General Assembly's mandate in the field.

While this preliminary analysis sustains the Human Rights Council's power to proclaim new human rights, the General Assembly resolution establishing the Council introduces a degree of nuance on this point. Said resolution specifies the functions of the subsidiary body, mandating it to, *inter alia*, "serve as a forum for dialogue on thematic issues on all human rights," and "make recommendations to the General Assembly for the further development of international law in the field of human rights."[52]

The terms of the Council's functions as quoted raise certain questions of interpretation. It could be argued that by expressly tasking the Council with making recommendations to the General Assembly, the resolution sought to reserve to the General Assembly the role of making final determinations on the further development of international law in the field of human rights. On the other hand, it could be argued that including within the Council's powers the possibility of making recommendations to the General Assembly does not negate its own ability to clarify existing human rights law, including through the proclamation of new human rights, and thereby contribute to standard-setting in the field. This interpretation has the added advantage of opening further possibilities for intergovernmental decision making, allowing the Council to better gauge political temperatures regarding normative developments in international human rights law.

A distinct question of interpretation also arises on the scope and meaning of the phrase "further development of international law." Specifically, would the proclamation of a new human right qualify as "further development of international law"? It could be argued that proclamation of a new right implicates the articulation of legal responsibilities, and thus constitutes "further development of international law." Under this reading, the Council's function could be argued to be limited to making recommendations to the General Assembly. But this reading misses an important nuance resting on the distinction between clarification of existing law and elaboration of new law.

The adoption of a resolution *proclaiming new law* would appear prima facie to constitute "further development of international law." By contrast, the adoption of a resolution *proclaiming a new right based on existing law* would appear to not impermissibly extend beyond the Council's mandate. This conclusion finds support on the notion that standard-setting is a key function in human rights policy, and it

[51] Human Rights Council res. 15/9 (September 30, 2010).
[52] General Assembly res. 60/251 (April 3, 2006).

would lead to absurd results if the Council were unable to carry out its standard-setting work just because said work contributed to the further development of international law.

Actual practice supports the conclusion that the Human Rights Council is empowered to proclaim a new human right based on existing law. For example, as noted, the Council recognized in 2010 the human right to safe drinking water and sanitation, *as derived from the right to an adequate standard of living*. This formulation is instructive of how the Council approached the recognition of a new right based on existing law, and therefore operational paragraph three of the Council's resolution is quoted in full:

> *[The Human Rights Council] Affirms* that the human right to safe drinking water and sanitation is derived from the right to an adequate standard of living and inextricably related to the right to the highest attainable standard of physical and mental health, as well as the right to life and human dignity.[53]

Therefore, the Council could exercise its powers to proclaim the existence of the right to a healthy environment as an umbrella right that brings together the existing rights and obligations in human rights law pertaining to a clean, safe, healthy, and sustainable environment. That said, a proclamation by the General Assembly of the right to a healthy environment would be more authoritative because of the prominent position of the Assembly in the governance structure of the United Nations.

What is plain is that the resolution establishing the Human Rights Council affirms the power of the Council to engage in a substantive dialogue on the recognition of the right to a healthy environment. That debate would be guided by the key issues and parameters established in the General Assembly resolution setting international human rights standards, as discussed. That debate would also be informed by the work of the Special Rapporteur on human rights and the environment in clarifying human rights obligations with respect to a safe, clean, healthy, and sustainable environment.

CONCLUSION

This chapter assessed the process and substantive discussions relating to the recognition of the right to a healthy environment, in light of the guidelines established by the UN General Assembly for the setting of international human rights standards and of Philip Alston's proposed procedural safeguards in his *Quality Control* article. In regard to the substantive guidelines, the chapter shows, *inter alia*, how the right to a healthy environment has a fundamental character that derives from the inherent dignity and worth of the human person and is otherwise consistent with the body of international human rights law. In regard to the process, the record shows evidence

[53] Res. 15/9, para. 3.

of extensive technical and political discussions involving governments, intergovernmental organizations, and global civil society over key issues relevant to the articulation of the symbolic and legal dimensions of the right to a healthy environment. Therefore, on both procedural and substantive grounds, the right to a healthy environment is ripe for a focused and renewed debate regarding its global recognition.

This focused and fresh debate concerning the global proclamation of the right to a healthy environment may appropriately take place at the Human Rights Council, in light of the Council's mandate and authority. The General Assembly's guidelines on standard-setting establish the parameters to structure and guide this political and technical debate at the Council. The debate would intensely benefit from the expert contributions of the Special Rapporteur on human rights and the environment, the Office of the High Commissioner for Human Rights, the UN Environment Programme, and specialized civil society organizations. As a result of this debate, the Human Rights Council could proclaim the right to a healthy environment or recommend its proclamation to the General Assembly.

11

The Politics of Human Rights, the Environment, and Climate Change at the Human Rights Council

Toward a Universal Right to a Healthy Environment?

Marc Limon

International efforts to draw attention to, understand, clarify, and leverage the relationship between human rights and the environment have made remarkable progress since the establishment of the UN Human Rights Council in 2006. As is recounted elsewhere in this book,[1] environmental concerns were entirely absent during UN discussions on the Universal Declaration of Human Rights and, by extension, during the negotiation of the two international human rights covenants. This can be explained by the fact that the instruments were negotiated before the advent of the modern environmental movement in the late 1960s. In the mid-1990s, a group of states led by Costa Rica, South Africa, and Switzerland tabled the first of three resolutions at the UN Commission on Human Rights, the predecessor to the Human Rights Council, on "human rights and the environment."[2] However, from the very start, these states faced considerable opposition from some large UN Member States (developed and developing), with the result that the resolutions were relatively unambitious and were eventually discontinued.

This remained the situation until 2006, when the Commission was replaced by the Council, and a small island state, the Maldives, took it upon itself to revive international efforts to draw links between human rights and environmental harm. It acted first through a series of resolutions on human rights and climate change and then, from 2011 onwards, through annual resolutions on human rights and the environment. It was the unspoken hope of the Maldives that the norm-setting exercise initiated by these texts, clearly important in of itself, might also represent a first step toward open and informed intergovernmental reflections on the relative merits of declaring a new universal right to a clean and healthy environment.

[1] See John H. Knox and Ramin Pejan, Chapter 1.

[2] Human Rights Commission res. 1994/65 (March 9, 1994); res. 1995/14 (Feb. 24, 1995); res. 1996/13 (April 11, 1996).

In pursuing this effort, the Maldives was confronted by the same alignment of states that had opposed the Costa Rica-led initiative over a decade earlier.

This chapter will begin by describing why large developing and developed states have consistently opposed steps toward strengthened links between human rights and the environment. The chapter then explains how the Maldives and its allies, through their initiatives on human rights and climate change, and then on human rights and the environment, circumvented this political opposition, bringing the international community to within touching distance of the elaboration and declaration of a new universal right to a clean and healthy environment.

POLITICAL OPPOSITION TO ENVIRONMENTAL RIGHTS AT THE UNITED NATIONS

Throughout the 1990s and the first decade of the twenty-first century, the default position of many powerful UN Member States (developed and developing) was a *de facto* belief that the promotion and protection of human rights and the preservation and protection of the environment were, and should remain, two completely separate areas of UN policy. Drawing links between the two was not only unnecessary; it was, from the viewpoint of many states, deeply unwelcome.

Why was this the case? As described in Chapters 2 and 3 in this volume, many states have adopted a notably progressive position on human rights and the environment at the national level, even going so far as to recognize a constitutional right to a safe and healthy environment. Yet at the international level, despite some small steps forward such as the 1972 Stockholm Declaration of the United Nations Conference on the Human Environment and, to a lesser extent, the 1992 Rio Declaration on Environment and Development, those same states would generally reject the notion that environmental harm had any implications for fundamental rights, or that promoting human rights norms could help protect against environmental damage.

The basic reason for this apparent schizophrenia can be understood through reference to attempts by some states (and resistance thereto on the part of others) from 1994 onwards to move the international human rights community toward a more progressive understanding of the links between human rights and the environment.

Building on reports submitted to the Sub-Commission on Prevention of Discrimination and Protection of Minorities by its Special Rapporteur on human rights and the environment, Fatma Zohra Ksentini,[3] in 1994 a group of states, led by Costa Rica, South Africa, and Switzerland, began tabling resolutions at the

[3] See, e.g., Fatma Zohra Ksentini, *Human Rights and the Environment*, UN Doc. E/CN.4/Sub.2/1992/7 and Add.1 (July 2, 1992); *Human Rights and the Environment*, UN Doc. E/CN.4/Sub.2/1993/7 (July 26, 1993); *Final Report*, UN Doc. E/CN.4/Sub.2/1994/9, annex III (July 6, 1994).

Commission on Human Rights on "human rights and the environment."[4] These early resolutions were interesting for two main (interconnected) reasons. First, they were notably unambitious – a result of difficult negotiations between the global North and the global South. Second, a reading of the texts gives the strong sense of the latter's determination to "balance" environmental concerns with a linked (and overriding) determination not, under any circumstances, to put their national socioeconomic development at risk. This determination can be most obviously seen in the repeated references, in the final texts, to the concept of the "right to development."[5]

Before proceeding, therefore, it is worth considering the right to development, and how it came to claim such a predominant position in the mindsets and negotiating positions of developing countries. The 1986 Declaration on the Right to Development declares that the right is built on two main pillars: the national and the international. At the national level, the right makes clear that everyone is "entitled to participate in, contribute to, and enjoy economic, social, cultural and political development, in which all human rights and fundamental freedoms can be fully realized."[6] At the international level, the Declaration confirms that "States have the duty to cooperate with each other in ensuring development and eliminating obstacles to development."[7]

Since the adoption of the 1986 Declaration, the right to development has been cited – always at the insistence of influential developing states – in numerous important international agreements, especially those dealing with sustainable development. For example, Principle 3 of the 1992 Rio Declaration on environment and development states that "the right to development must be fulfilled so as to equitably meet developmental and environmental needs of present and future generations"; the 2015 Paris Agreement on climate change calls on Parties to the UNFCCC to "respect, promote and consider their respective obligations on human rights ... and the right to development"; while the 2030 Sustainable Development Agenda and the Sustainable Development Goals (SDGs) are, according to the Agenda, specifically informed by ..."the Declaration on the Right to Development."[8]

Unfortunately, the seemingly (at first glance) benign nature of the Declaration on the Right to Development masks deep political tensions over the concept of the

4 Human Rights Commission res. 1994/65; res. 1995/14; res. 1996/13.

5 Taken from the title of the 1986 Declaration on the Right to Development, UN Doc. A/RES/41/128 (December 4, 1986). It is important to note that, despite its title, the Declaration asserts a human rights-based approach to development, rather than a new stand-alone right.

6 Ibid., art. 1.

7 Ibid., art. 3(3).

8 Rio Declaration on Environment and Development, UN Doc. A/CONF.151/26/Rev.1, annex I (June 14, 1992), Principle 3; Paris Agreement, December 12, 2015, in force November 4, 2016, UN Doc. FCCC/CP/2015/19, pmbl.; General Assembly res. 70/1, *Transforming our World: the 2030 Agenda for Sustainable Development* (September 25, 2015), para. 10.

right to development. Broadly speaking, states are divided between, on the one side, proponents of the right (generally countries of the global South), which assert its relevance or even pre-eminence, and argue that the realization of the right to development is heavily dependent on international cooperation; and, on the other, skeptics or rejectionists (some countries of the global North), which deny that there is an internationally recognized right to development, argue that a certain level of development is not a precondition for the protection of human rights, and disagree that the enjoyment of human rights is in any way dependent on international cooperation between states (e.g., the provision of overseas development assistance, or the avoidance of causing transboundary pollution). On the last point, developed countries regularly make the point that states themselves cannot be holders of human rights.

This is partly a question of semantics. Perhaps if the 1986 Declaration had been called the "declaration of a rights-based approach to development" or the "declaration on human rights and development," then it would not be the source of so much disagreement three decades later. But it is also a question of substance: of disagreements between developed and (some but certainly not all) developing countries as to the relationship between civil and political rights, on the one hand, and economic, social, and cultural rights on the other, and over who/what is responsible for promoting development and protecting human rights. Is it the state only, or is it the (developing) state together with the wider international community (which should create an enabling environment for development)?

This apparently separate debate over the right to development is essential to any understanding of the politics around human rights and the environment and, eventually, of the politics around the right to a healthy environment. That is because (some) developing countries see civil and political rights and environmental protection as Western or "rich world" preoccupations. Developing countries, they argue, must prioritize socioeconomic development over such "distractions" – until such a time as they have reached similar levels of development to their more developed peers. (It goes without saying that diplomatic representatives of these countries will only ever say this implicitly.)

Linked with this argument, the developing countries tend to emphasize the notion that the socioeconomic development of rich countries took place at the expense of the environment and frequently in the absence of concerns over human rights. This notion is reflected most clearly in the principles of "historic responsibility" and "common but differentiated responsibilities," first recognized in Principle 7 of the 1992 Rio Declaration on environment and development. On the other side, developed countries see the promotion of the right to development as an attempt by some developing states to create a preemptive justification for their failure to abide by their international human rights and environmental obligations. Developed states likewise see any attempt to introduce the notion of "common but differentiated responsibilities" into human rights law as a dangerous exercise in suggesting that states have differentiated responsibilities (or obligations) to respect human rights, depending on their levels of development and/or their vulnerability to environmental harm (e.g., linked to climate change) caused by the historic actions of developed states.

This debate can be clearly seen playing out in the evolution of the Commission's various resolutions on human rights and the environment from 1994 to 1996. For example, resolution 1994/65, while recognizing in one operative paragraph that "environmental damage has potentially negative effects on human rights," nevertheless reiterates in another paragraph that "the right to development must be fulfilled so as to meet equitably the developmental and environmental needs of present and future generations," and that (in a preambular paragraph) states have "in accordance with the Charter of the United Nations and the principles of international law, the sovereign right to exploit their own resources pursuant to their own environmental and developmental policies."[9]

Further developing this theme, while acknowledging that "the promotion of an environmentally healthy world contributes to the protection of the human rights to life and health of everyone," the resolution nonetheless makes clear that "in this connection States shall act in accordance with their common but differentiated responsibilities and respective capabilities," and that, in order to protect the environment, developing countries will need "access to and the transfer of environmentally sound technologies ... on favourable terms," and "new and additional financial resources ... to achieve sustainable development."[10]

After 1996, the resolutions (which continued to include language such as "common but differentiated responsibilities" and "additional financing") were discontinued. The issue of human rights and the environment would be largely absent from the Commission's agenda for the next five years.

In April 2001, the Commission adopted decision 2001/111, which called for an expert seminar on human rights and the environment to be convened jointly by the Office of the High Commissioner for Human Rights (OHCHR) and the UN Environment Programme (UNEP).[11] The seminar was eventually held in January 2002 in Geneva.

Later that year, which was also the year of the World Summit on Sustainable Development, the initiative on human rights and the environment returned in earnest, but with draft resolutions now called: "Human rights and the environment as part of sustainable development."[12] This was a small but highly symbolic shift. According to a Costa Rican diplomat involved in the negotiations, the name change was one of a number of concessions extracted from the main sponsors by large

9 Human Rights Commission res. 1994/65.

10 Ibid.

11 Human Rights Commission dec. 2001/111 (April 25, 2001).

12 Human Rights Commission res. 2002/75 (April 25, 2002); see also Human Rights Commission res. 2003/71 (April 25, 2003); res. 2005/60 (April 20, 2005).

developing states. The goal of these countries, in 2002 as in 1994–6, was to place the mutually dependent goals of promoting human rights and protecting the environment within the wider framework of (sustainable) development.

Asserting the right to development, these states worked to block any attempt (real or imagined) by Western states to push an environmental or human rights agenda as a way of holding back the socioeconomic development of poorer countries. At the same time, these states sought to assert the principles of common but differentiated responsibilities, respective capabilities, and historical responsibility to make the case that any downward pressure on human rights in the developing world caused by environmental harm was not (wholly or even principally) their responsibility, but rather the responsibility of developed states. Thus, unless the global North were to create an enabling environment (e.g., through international cooperation to mitigate transboundary environmental harm, or through financial support or technology transfers) then they could not be held responsible for the human rights consequences of such harm.

The following year, the Commission adopted another resolution: 2003/71. After opening with a piece of historical revisionism, "recalling the extensive work, reports and resolutions [of] the Commission on Human Rights on issues relevant to *environmental protection and sustainable development* " (emphasis added), and the underwhelming assertion that "environmental damage can have *potentially* negative effects on the enjoyment of *some* human rights,"[13] the resolution sets out many of the positions common in earlier texts.

The now preeminent position of development is clearly reflected in the first operative paragraph of the new resolution, which (despite being a resolution of the Commission on *Human Rights*) is not focused on human rights at all, but on sustainable development. It reaffirms that "peace, security, stability and respect for human rights and fundamental freedoms, including the right to development, as well as respect for cultural diversity are essential for achieving sustainable development and ensuring that sustainable development benefits all, as set forth in the Plan of Implementation of the World Summit on Sustainable Development."[14]

The following operative paragraphs then present a rather confusing mix of issues and concerns related to sustainable development, some of which explicitly mention human rights, and others that do not. For example, the resolution reaffirms the rights of freedom of association and assembly "when promoting environmental protection and sustainable development,"[15] but then sets down a number of other paragraphs that appear to be lifted from UN resolutions on sustainable development and that make only oblique reference to human rights. Through the resolution, the Commission: "stresses the importance for States, when developing their environmental

[13] Res. 2003/71, paras. 2, 3.

[14] Ibid., para. 1.

[15] Ibid., para. 4.

policies, to take into account how environmental degradation may affect disadvantaged members of society, including individuals and groups of individuals who are victims of or subject to racism"; "encourages all efforts towards the implementation of the principles of the Rio Declaration, in particular principle 10, in order to contribute, *inter alia*, to effective access to judicial and administrative proceedings, including redress and remedy"; "reaffirms that good governance within each country and at the international level is essential for sustainable development"; "welcomes the Ministerial Declaration ... on the occasion of the Third World Water Forum, held in Kyoto, Japan, which points out the importance of good governance with a stronger focus on household and neighbourhood community-based approaches by addressing equity in sharing benefits, with due regard to pro-poor and gender perspectives in water policies"; "welcomes actions taken by States, such as legal measures and public awareness activities, that promote and protect human rights and that also assist in the promotion of environmental protection and sustainable development"; and "requests the United Nations High Commissioner for Human Rights and UNEP ... to continue to coordinate their efforts in capacity-building activities for the judiciary."[16]

Toward the end of the text, in the eleventh operative paragraph, Member States of the Commission do acknowledge what an impartial observer might see as a crux of the issue (and thus as the main focus of any resolution): the "relationship between the environment and human rights." However, the Commission explicitly qualifies the text by making clear that it is only a "possible relationship."[17]

HUMAN RIGHTS AND CLIMATE CHANGE

This was the situation when the Member States of the new Human Rights Council took their seats for the first time in June 2006. By this point, UN-level efforts to clarify and leverage the relationship between human rights and the environment had ground to a halt. As a Costa Rican diplomat who had been involved in the last resolutions of the Commission noted: "we [the main sponsors of the resolutions] had been tied in so many knots, from so many sides, that the resolutions had become incomprehensible and the initiative had lost any sense of purpose."[18]

The key to overcoming the impasse would not be (for the time being) further resolutions on human rights and the environment, but rather a completely new initiative, focused on human rights and climate change. This initiative was significant because it reflected a new determination on the part of small, vulnerable developing countries to question and then openly oppose the "development first" paradigm, presented by their larger, more powerful partners in the Global South, as

[16] Ibid., paras. 5–10.
[17] Ibid., para. 11.
[18] Personal Communication, Costa Rican diplomat.

the basic position of the developing world. For these environmentally vulnerable states, it was unthinkable that the prioritization of economic growth or development (often presented by large developing countries through the lens of the right to development) could be used as a justification or an excuse to harm the natural environment, especially in a globalized world in which such harm is increasingly transboundary in nature. Similarly, it was unthinkable that the international community could ignore the real and present threat posed by environmental harm (especially harm linked to climate change) to internationally recognized human rights (e.g., the rights to life, health, water, food, and an adequate standard of living).

From 2006 onwards, climate change and its relationship with human rights became the issue within which these vulnerable country concerns were distilled and projected. The links between human rights and climate change first began to be drawn – at the intergovernmental level – during the seventh session of the Council in March 2008. Prompted by the Malé Declaration of November 2007,[19] a number of countries, including the Maldives and Philippines, noted the serious consequences of climate change for the full enjoyment of human rights and called on the Council to address the human rights dimension.[20] Then, on March 28, 2008, a core group of states, including Bangladesh, Germany, Ghana, Maldives, Philippines, Switzerland, United Kingdom, Uruguay, and Zambia, secured the adoption by consensus of Council resolution 7/23 on "human rights and climate change."[21]

Resolution 7/23 was the first UN resolution to state explicitly that climate change poses "an immediate and far-reaching threat to people and communities around the world and has implications for the full enjoyment of human rights."[22] The resolution also asked OHCHR to prepare a study on the nature and extent of those implications. That study, published the following January, details the adverse impacts of global warming on a spectrum of human rights, including the rights to life, food, water, the highest attainable standard of health, housing, and self-determination; describes the effects on specific groups, including women, children, and indigenous peoples; and presents a survey of possible state obligations related to climate change.[23]

[19] Malé Declaration on the Human Dimension of Global Climate Change, November 14, 2007, available at www.ciel.org/Publications/Male_Declaration_Nov07.pdf.

[20] See Daniel Magraw and Kristina Wienhöfer, Chapter 12.

[21] Human Rights Council res. 7/23 (March 28, 2008).

[22] Ibid., pmbl. para. 1.

[23] OHCHR, *Report on the Relationship between Climate Change and Human Rights*, UN Doc. A/HRC/10/61 (January 15, 2009). Scholars have also paid increasing attention to the topic. See Lavanya Rajamani, Chapter 13; Sumudu Atapattu, Chapter 14. See also Sumudu Atapattu, *Human Rights Approaches to Climate Change: Challenges and Opportunities* (Routledge, 2016); Jane McAdam and Marc Limon, *Human Rights, Climate Change and Cross-Border Displacement* (Universal Rights Group, 2015); Edward Cameron and Marc Limon, "Restoring the Climate by Realizing Rights: The Role of the International Human Rights System," *Review of European Community and International Environmental Law* 21(3) (2012), pp. 204–19;

A second Council resolution (10/4), adopted in March 2009, echoes the findings of the OHCHR report and affirms that "human rights obligations and commitments have the potential to inform and strengthen international and national policy making in the area of climate change, promoting policy coherence, legitimacy and sustainable outcomes."[24]

Although the final texts of resolutions 7/23 and 10/4 are more coherent and focused on the principal issue at hand (i.e., the relationship between human rights and climate change/environment) than the earlier Commission resolutions, the negotiations leading up to their adoption were not straightforward. The Commission may have been replaced by the Council, but the old political fault lines remained firmly in place, especially over the relative emphasis placed on human rights, environmental protection, and socioeconomic development, and over the relative emphasis given to individual state responsibility and obligation on the one hand, and the responsibility of the international community on the other.

In particular, during the negotiations, large emerging economies (e.g., China, Egypt, India, Iran, Nigeria, Saudi Arabia) insisted on the inclusion of strong and repeated references to the right to development (especially as a collective right), as well as to the (state-centric rather than individual-centric) principles of historic responsibility, respective capabilities, and common but differentiated responsibilities. According to the emerging economies, if these concepts and principles (or, as their diplomats referred to them, "safeguards") could not be included, then the resolution(s) should be withdrawn by the main sponsors.

Western European states opposed the inclusion of such language, arguing that these references risked creating the impression (and precedent) that developing countries could only guarantee the enjoyment of human rights if they were provided with a conducive international environment in which to do so: Namely, an environment wherein they are left to pursue their collective right to development, wherein rich countries would provide development assistance to support such efforts, and wherein rich countries would take responsibility for mitigating transboundary environmental harm (e.g., climate change) and pay for vulnerable states to undertake necessary adaption measures.

Stephen Humphreys (ed.), *Human Rights and Climate Change* (Cambridge University Press, 2010); International Council on Human Rights Policy, *Climate Change and Human Rights: A Rough Guide* (2008); Daniel Bodansky, "Introduction: Climate Change and Human Rights: Unpacking the Issues," *Georgia Journal of International and Comparative Law* 38(3) (2010), pp. 511–24; John H. Knox, "Climate Change and Human Rights Law," *Virginia Journal of International Law* 50(1) (2009), p. 163; Ole W. Pedersen, "The Janus-Head of Human Rights and Climate Change: Adaptation and Mitigation," *Nordic Journal of International Law* 80(4) (2011), pp. 403–23; Pamela J. Stephens, "Applying Human Rights Norms to Climate Change: The Elusive Remedy," *Colorado Journal of International Environmental Law and Policy* 21(1) (2010), pp. 49–83.

[24] Human Rights Council res. 10/4 (March 25, 2009), pmbl. para. 10.

In the end, a compromise was reached whereby the core group of main sponsors agreed to include two carefully worded preambular paragraphs in resolution 7/23 (the text of the second paragraph also appeared in resolution 10/4):

> *Recalling* that the Vienna Declaration and Programme of Action reaffirmed the right to development, as established in the Declaration on the Right to Development, as a universal and inalienable right and as an integral part of fundamental human rights,
>
> *Recognizing* that human beings are at the centre of concerns for sustainable development and that the right to development must be fulfilled so as to equitably meet the development and environmental needs of present and future generations.[25]

The main sponsors refused to include any explicit reference to common but differentiated responsibilities, respective capabilities, or historic responsibilities, on the grounds that these (albeit) important principles of sustainable development and climate change diplomacy had no place in a human rights text.

Notwithstanding this clear position, latent Western European (especially UK) concerns over any suggestion that there might be a hierarchy of rights, with the right to development at the top, led them, during negotiations on resolution 10/4, to call for the aforementioned paragraphs to be immediately followed by a further one:

> *Reaffirming further* that all human rights are universal, indivisible, interdependent and interrelated and that they must be treated in a fair and equal manner, on the same footing and with the same emphasis.[26]

Other Western states, notably Canada (a Council member) and the United States (at the time an observer), also expressed concern about including concepts such as the right to development in the text, or incorporating principles of international climate change and sustainable development policy into (soft) human rights law. But these states were also worried about setting two other interconnected precedents: first, that individual harm caused by environmental degradation could be considered a human rights violation; and second, that polluting (or "high emitting") countries (i.e., industrialized or emerging economies) could be held accountable for resulting human harm in a third country, such as Bangladesh, Maldives, or the Philippines.

These concerns led Canada and the United States to repeatedly disavow the idea, during the negotiations over the resolution, that there was any relationship between human rights and climate change. They proposed an important amendment to operative paragraph 1, replacing "has consequences" with "may have consequences," so that the language would read:

[25] Res. 7/23 (March 28, 2008), pmbl. paras. 6, 7. The language in the preambular paragraph 7 is taken from Principles 1 and 3 of the Rio Declaration.

[26] Res. 10/4, pmbl. para. 4.

> *Concerned* that climate change may have consequences, both direct and indirect, for the full enjoyment of human rights.[27]

Canada and the United States also insisted on the deletion of a paragraph, in the draft text that would become resolution 10/4, that listed a number of human rights particularly affected by global warming.

Nevertheless, after the OHCHR report made clear that climate change does have implications for human rights, and also identified those rights that are particularly at risk, Canada and the United States agreed to stronger wording in a preambular paragraph of resolution 10/4:

> *Noting* that climate change-related impacts have a range of implications, both direct and indirect, for the effective enjoyment of human rights including, inter alia, the right to life, the right to adequate food, the right to the highest attainable standard of health, the right to adequate housing, the right to self-determination and human rights obligations related to access to safe drinking water and sanitation, and recalling that in no case may a people be deprived of its own means of subsistence.[28]

Despite these compromises, Canada and the United States – principally reflecting their concern about being accused (due to their "historic responsibility" for climate change) of violating human rights in vulnerable developing states – joined large emerging economies in calling on the main sponsors to consider withdrawing the resolutions. The main sponsors refused. As an interesting aside, this situation led the German Ambassador, during one open informal negotiation, to congratulate the Maldives for creating an "unlikely human rights alliance" between Canada, the United States, Egypt, Iran, and Saudi Arabia.

THE OHCHR REPORT

The OHCHR report on the relationship between human rights and climate change, called for by resolution 7/23, identifies three key legal questions:

- Is there a relationship between climate change and human rights, and if so, what is the nature of that relationship?
- Does climate change constitute a violation of human rights, especially the rights of vulnerable people?
- Irrespective of whether climate change represents a human rights violation, what are states' national-level and international-level human rights obligations pertaining to climate change?

[27] U.S. and Canadian efforts to delete the words "both direct and indirect" were unsuccessful.

[28] Ibid., pmbl. para. 7.

Regarding the first question, the OHCHR report concludes that:

> Climate change-related impacts ... have a range of implications for the effective enjoyment of human rights. The effects on human rights can be of a direct nature, such as the threat extreme weather events may pose to the right to life, but will often have an indirect and gradual effect on human rights, such as increasing stress on health systems and vulnerabilities related to climate change-induced migration.[29]

After clearly stating that there is an important connection between climate change and the enjoyment of human rights, OHCHR then provides its views on the exact nature of the relationship. It draws four broad conclusions:

1. Certain specific rights are most directly affected: the right to life, the right to adequate food, the right to water, the right to health, the right to adequate housing, and the right to self-determination.
2. The human rights impacts of climate change will be felt unevenly both between and within nations.
3. Climate change is very likely to lead to large-scale human rights crises with horizontal impacts across the aforementioned specific rights and across the aforementioned vulnerable population groups.
4. As well as the direct and indirect impacts of climate change itself, measures taken to mitigate and adapt to global warming can also have adverse secondary effects on human rights.

Regarding the second question, OHCHR states:

> While climate change has obvious implications for the enjoyment of human rights, it is less obvious whether, and to what extent, such effects can be qualified as human rights violations in a strict legal sense.[30]

On the third question, OHCHR argues that although "the physical impacts of global warming cannot easily be classified as human rights violations ... addressing that harm remains a critical human rights concern and obligation under international law,"[31] and those obligations exist at both the national level and the international level. This last point is extremely important. OHCHR is, in effect, balancing its judgment on the absolute and inalienable nature of national-level obligations with an equally forceful conclusion on the existence of parallel, mutually inclusive obligations held at the international level.

In a summary of a number of different General Comments by the Committee on Economic, Social and Cultural Rights, OHCHR in its report proposes four distinct types of international or extraterritorial human rights obligations. The OHCHR argues that states have legal obligations to:

[29] OHCHR, *Climate Change and Human Rights*, para. 92.
[30] Ibid., para. 70.
[31] Ibid., para. 96.

- refrain from interfering with the enjoyment of human rights in other countries;
- take measures to prevent third parties (e.g. private companies) over which they hold influence from interfering with the enjoyment of human rights in other countries;
- take steps through international assistance and cooperation, depending on the availability of resources, to facilitate the fulfillment of human rights in other countries; and
- ensure that human rights are given due attention in international agreements and that such agreements do not adversely impact upon human rights.[32]

In its conclusions, OHCHR builds on this analysis and states that: "International human rights law complements the UNFCCC [United Nations Framework Convention on Climate Change] by underlining that international cooperation is not only expedient but also a human rights obligation and that its central objective is the realization of human rights."[33]

JUNE 2009 PANEL DEBATE

In its resolution 10/4, the Council decided "to hold a panel discussion on the relationship between climate change and human rights at its eleventh session."[34] The panel took place three months later, on June 15, 2009.[35]

During the June debate, no delegation argued with the notion that climate change has implications for a wide range of explicitly identified, internationally protected human rights; that already vulnerable "climate frontline" countries are most at risk (and the least able to adapt); and that the human rights impacts do not fall evenly across a given population, but rather have disproportionate effect on marginalized or vulnerable groups, such as women and children.[36]

Despite progress in forming a consensus on the broad parameters of the relationship between climate change and human rights, significant differences in emphasis persisted in 2009, especially regarding the legal implications of the relationship.

[32] Ibid., para. 86.

[33] Ibid., para. 99. For a detailed analysis of the report, and the debate at the Council when the report was presented by OHCHR, see Marc Limon, "Human Rights Obligations and Accountability in the Face of Climate Change," *Georgia Journal of International and Comparative Law* 38(3) (2010), pp. 543–92.

[34] Res. 10/4, para. 1.

[35] For the concept note and a summary of the panel debate, see www.ohchr.org/EN/Issues/HRAndClimateChange/Pages/Panel.aspx.

[36] The detailed summary of the panel debate, including an analysis of the statements of key states, is taken from Limon, "Human Rights Obligations and Accountability in the Face of Climate Change."

In particular, while many developing and vulnerable states argued that human rights law creates legal obligations that are applicable to international action on the issue of climate change, developed countries by and large continued to insist that climate change and human rights inhabit two separate and very different bodies of law with no formal connection between the two. For example, during the debate, the U.S. delegation agreed that "climate change . . . has implications for the full enjoyment of human rights," but at the same time noted that "there is no direct formal relationship between climate change and human rights as a legal matter." Similarly, Canada argued that situations may occur in which environmental degradation amplified by climate change may set conditions that impact on the effective enjoyment of human rights but went on to make clear that there is no legal link between the UNFCCC and the international human rights conventions.

These differences in emphasis were amplified in the context of the other two key questions posed by the OHCHR report, namely whether climate change impacts constitute a human rights violation, and what human rights obligations exist, at national and international levels, in relation to climate change.

On the first point, a few (though not many) states used the June panel debate to question the assertion made by OHCHR that "the physical impacts of global warming cannot easily be classified as human rights violations, not least because climate change-related harm often cannot clearly be attributed to acts or omissions of specific States."[37] The strongest opponent of this reading of the situation was Pakistan. Pakistan argued that it is possible to establish responsibility for climate change and to link this responsibility to human rights harm, stating, "we believe it is important and possible to 'disentangle' [the] basics of this causal relationship."[38] According to Pakistan, responsibility for climate change can be easily determined at two levels: developed countries' historical responsibility for climate change, and their failure to comply with international legal obligations.

India also questioned the idea that it is difficult to assign responsibility and, like Pakistan, posited that responsibility can be determined on the basis of both historic emissions and of failure to abide by legal (UNFCCC) obligations on contemporary emissions:

> The present crisis that we are now discussing is the result of activity over the past two centuries, where the contribution of developing countries had been minimal. . . . It is a matter of concern that despite the targets for reductions in emissions that [developed] countries assumed under the Kyoto Protocol, there are few signs that these will be met. The question of accountability for failure

[37] OHCHR, *Climate Change and Human Rights*, para. 96.

[38] Marghoob Saleem Butt, Counselor, Permanent Mission of Pakistan to the United Nations at Geneva, United Nations Human Rights Council, Panel on Human Rights and Climate Change at the Eleventh Session of the Human Rights Council (June 15, 2009) (on file with the *Georgia Journal of International and Comparative Law*).

> to implement legally binding and internationally agreed provisions relating to emissions reduction targets needs to be looked at closely.[39]

Notwithstanding the importance of these differences, the main division between states at the June 2009 panel debate was on the question of the relative weight of national human rights obligations in the context of the climate crisis as against extraterritorial obligations. As has been the case throughout the history of UN debates on human rights and the environment, the fault line between states ran roughly along developed-developing country lines.

For their part, most (but not all) developed countries insisted that while the climate crisis may be international in scope, human rights promotion and protection is the sole purview of national governments vis-à-vis their citizens and others within their jurisdiction. It is therefore up to individual states to promote and protect the human rights of their people in the face of such crises, irrespective of the additional burden placed upon them.

On the other hand, the importance of recognizing and enforcing *extraterritorial* human rights obligations in the face of climate change was made, in varying formulae, by almost all developing country delegations that took part in the debate, as well as by some more progressive developed country representations. Most vocal were environmentally vulnerable states. Bangladesh offered the most frank rebuttal of the state-centric assessment offered by industrialized countries:

> It is often said that human rights protection is the responsibility of the national authorities—basically downgrading international cooperation. Even in dealing with climate change, which is a global issue, too much emphasis is put on national responsibility. As has been said by the Deputy High Commissioner [in her introductory remarks], Least Developed Countries and Small Island States will be the worst affected by climate change although they have contributed least to global greenhouse gas emissions. It is not only unfair but also unjustified to hold these countries responsible fully for protecting their people.[40]

Many vulnerable states were quick to emphasize that the need to give greater emphasis to international-level obligations should not be seen as commensurate with a reluctance to accept and honor national-level obligations. Rather, while accepting the importance of domestic action, developing states were nonetheless robust in their defense of the idea that in order to effectively protect human rights in the face of climate change, observance of national-level commitments must

[39] Rajiv Kumar Chander, Permanent Representative of India to the United Nations at Geneva, United Nations Human Rights Council, Panel on Human Rights and Climate Change at the Eleventh Session of the Human Rights Council (June 15, 2009) (on file with the *Georgia Journal of International and Comparative Law*).

[40] Webcast: Mustafizur Rahman, *Chargé d'affaires*, Permanent Mission of Bangladesh to the United Nations, Panel on Human Rights and Climate Change at the Eleventh Session of the Human Rights Council (United Nations Human Rights Council, June 15, 2009), www.un.org/webcast/unhrc/archive.asp?go-090615.

necessarily be combined with respect, on the part of the international community, for extraterritorial human rights obligations – most particularly the obligation "to refrain from taking action which interferes with the enjoyment of human rights in other countries, and to take steps through international cooperation to facilitate the fulfillment of those rights."[41]

For example, the Maldives, speaking on behalf of twelve small island developing states, emphasized that while they were committed through domestic policies to address the human rights implications of climate change,

> with emission levels continuing to rise and considering the barriers preventing direct and simplified access to adaptation funding, as well as the current inadequacy of new and additional adaptation funding, the fact is that it will become increasingly difficult for us [acting alone] to fully safeguard the fundamental freedoms and rights of our island populations. This then raises the issue of international cooperation. . . . We believe that such cooperation is not only desirable; it is vital and, moreover, is a legal obligation under the core international human rights instruments. Under these agreements there is a clear extraterritorial obligation beholden on State Parties to refrain from acting in such a way as knowingly undermines human rights in other countries; a fact reinforced by reference to Principle 2 of the Rio Declaration. There is also an extraterritorial legal obligation to take steps through international assistance to facilitate the fulfilment of human rights in other countries.[42]

A FORK IN THE ROAD

After the conclusion of the June 2009 panel, the main sponsors of the Council's resolutions on human rights and climate change (Bangladesh, Germany, Ghana, Maldives, Philippines, Switzerland, UK, Uruguay, and Zambia) faced two questions.

The first was how to leverage the emerging consensus on the human rights impacts of climate change, by feeding into and helping to promote ambition in the UNFCCC climate change negotiations, and promoting a rights-based approach to (international and domestic) climate policy. On this question, the Council had already decided, with resolutions 7/23 and 10/4, to transmit its deliberations and conclusions on the relationship between human rights and climate change to the

[41] Office of the U.N. High Commissioner for Human Rights [OHCHR], *Report of the Office of the U.N. High Commissioner for Human Rights on the Relationship between Human Rights and Climate Change*, U.N. Doc. A/HRC/10/61 (Jan. 15, 2009).

[42] Shazra Abdul Sattar, First Secretary, Maldives Permanent Mission to the United Nations, Statement on Behalf of Twelve Small Island Developing States, United Nations Human Rights Council, Panel on Human Rights and Climate Change at the Eleventh Session of the Human Rights Council (June 15, 2009) (on file with the *Georgia Journal of International and Comparative Law*).

Conference of Parties (COP) to the UNFCCC. This decision, together with intensive lobbying by the Maldivian and Swiss delegations to the Conference of Parties to the UNFCCC – especially in the run-up to COP15 in Copenhagen and COP16 in Cancun, and a late intervention at COP16 by Ambassador Luis Alfonso de Alba (previously the first President of the Human Rights Council and, by the time of COP16, Mexico's Special Envoy on climate change) – eventually resulted in the inclusion of human rights language in the Cancun Agreements (a non-binding COP "decision," rather than a treaty).

Preambular paragraph 7 of the decision taken at the Cancun COP (decision 1/COP.16) notes:

> Resolution 10/4 of the United Nations Human Rights Council on human rights and climate change, which recognizes that the adverse effects of climate change have a range of direct and indirect implications for the effective enjoyment of human rights and that the effects of climate change will be felt most acutely by those segments of the population that are already vulnerable owing to geography, gender, age, indigenous or minority status, or disability.[43]

Building on this, operative paragraph 8 (under "a shared vision for long-term cooperative action") affirms that: "Parties should, in all climate change related actions, fully respect human rights." This was the first inclusion of human rights language in a multilateral climate change agreement, while the text used in operative paragraph 8 would be closely reflected, five years later, in the wording of preambular paragraph 7 of the Paris Agreement.[44]

The second question facing the main sponsors of Council resolutions 7/23 and 10/4 was: how to usefully continue their work at the Council to further clarify human rights norms as they pertain to climate change, and do so in a manner that would maintain consensus? This was a not insignificant challenge.

The boundary of consensus was clearly marked by, broadly speaking, the same issues that had divided countries during negotiations of the Commission resolutions on human rights and environment. Large emerging countries continued to hold that it was unfair to expect them to make significant progress in the areas of human rights and environmental protection in the absence of socioeconomic development, and that international cooperation must form an important part of facilitating such development. These countries, therefore, emphasized the concepts of the right to development, international cooperation, and common but differentiated responsibilities. Developed countries, on the other hand, argued that human rights promotion and protection are solely the concern of national governments, and that concepts such as the right to development should not be used as an excuse for the failure of developing countries to respect human rights. Some, such as the United

[43] UNFCCC, *Report on the Conference of the Parties on Its Sixteenth Session, Held in Cancun from 29 November to 10 December 2010*, UN Doc. FCCC/CP/2010/7/Add. 1 (March 15, 2011).

[44] See Lavanya Rajamani, Chapter 13.

States and Canada, were also concerned that the initiative on human rights and climate change should not encourage litigation on the part of climate-vulnerable communities. There was, in short, a real risk, as the main sponsors of resolutions 7/23 and 10/4 surveyed the politics of the Council in 2011, that the initiative on human rights and climate change might be seized by one side of this divide and used as a political tool to attack the other.

A STEP SIDEWAYS: THE RETURN OF HUMAN RIGHTS AND ENVIRONMENT

Against this background, the Maldives approached Costa Rica and Switzerland, two of the three former main sponsors of the Commission's resolutions on human rights and the environment (Switzerland was also a member of the core group on human rights and climate change), to discuss their interest in restarting that initiative at the Council.

The thinking of these countries was that further meaningful, useful, and consensus-based progress at the Council on human rights and climate change was highly unlikely. Yes, it was possible to put forward further resolutions on climate change, but if those resolutions did not achieve anything substantively useful, then there was a real risk of the initiative either treading water, or being hijacked and used to push political agendas.

At the same time, the Maldives, Costa Rica, and Switzerland rejected the argument of certain civil society organizations (e.g., CIEL, Earthjustice, FES) and some members of the human rights and climate change core group (principally Bangladesh and the Philippines – countries that had always been inclined to sway toward the position of the large emerging economies), that the Council should establish a new Special Procedures mandate on human rights and climate change.

According to the Maldives, Costa Rica, and Switzerland, the Council's initiative on human rights and climate change had fulfilled its purpose – to generate awareness and understanding about the impacts of global warming on human rights, to show how human rights principles could be leveraged to improve global climate change policy, and to transfer that understanding to the main UN forum for addressing climate change: the UNFCCC COP. A common refrain of these states was that the problem of climate change would never, in the final analysis, be resolved by the Human Rights Council; it would be resolved, if at all, by the UNFCCC climate negotiations. Thus, for example, a new Special Procedures mandate might generate interesting debates at the Council, but he or she would be unlikely to play a useful role in driving more ambitious and more just international climate policy responses, especially when considering the heavily intergovernmental nature of negotiations at the UNFCCC COP.

What was needed, rather, was a norm-clarifying and norm-defining effort, at the Council, to understand more precisely how human rights principles and commitments might be applied to international and national environmental policy, including climate change policy. In other words, the main sponsors wanted to move beyond general debates between states on the presence and nature of the relationship between human rights and environment, to a more practical exercise premised on setting out the norms and, ultimately, working with all relevant stakeholders to apply those norms internationally and domestically.

Crucially, such an exercise would be more feasible and would achieve better results within the overall context of human rights and the environment than if the focus were to remain centered on climate change. Climate change, at the time (and so it remains), was an issue of high politics. With so much at stake internationally, with such impassioned positions among countries of the global South, the global North, and civil society, and with such differences of opinion over questions of responsibility, it was unlikely that states at the Human Rights Council would be able to come to a common understanding on whether and how to apply human rights principles and commitments. Questions of environmental conservation and protection more broadly, on the other hand, were unlikely to generate the same level of political reaction, thus providing an opportunity for more objective reflection. Even in the wider context of environmental (not just climate change) policy, further progress would be difficult were it to be left to interstate negotiation. Far better would be for the Council to appoint an independent expert to clarify and set down relevant norms, in an objective manner and free from political influence.

With this in mind, in March 2011, at the 16th session of the Council, Maldives, Costa Rica, and Switzerland, together with a wider core group that included Morocco, New Zealand, Slovenia, and Uruguay, began consultations on a new draft resolution on human rights and the environment – the first text on the subject in eight years.

The eventual result, Council resolution 16/11, represents a fine balancing act between the needs and concerns of large emerging economies and those of large developed countries. The preamble recalls relevant principles of sustainable development (e.g., common but differentiated responsibilities), but, crucially, it does so by directly citing relevant international instruments (e.g., Principle 7 of the Rio Declaration) rather than by asserting the principles in their own right (in a human rights text), and repeats the paragraph found in Council resolutions 7/23 and 10/4 regarding the right to development. At the same time, the preamble also contains reassurances for developed states, with the paragraphs referencing principles of sustainable development juxtaposed with paragraphs such as:

> *Reaffirming* that all human rights are universal, indivisible, interdependent and interrelated ... [and]
> *Reaffirming also* that good governance, within each country and at the international level, is essential for sustainable development.[45]

[45] Human Rights Council res. 16/11 (March 24, 2011), pmbl. paras. 7, 10.

Further preambular paragraphs then recall the broad parameters of the common ground agreed on by states in the context of the Council's two resolutions on climate change, the OHCHR report and the 2009 panel debate. For example, in resolution 16/11, the Council recalls that:

- Sustainable development and the protection of the environment can contribute to human well-being and the enjoyment of human rights.
- Environmental damage can have negative implications, both direct and indirect, for the effective enjoyment of human rights.
- While these implications affect individuals and communities around the world, environmental damage is felt most acutely by those segments of the population already in vulnerable situations.
- Human rights obligations and commitments have the potential to inform and strengthen international, regional, and national policy making in the area of environmental protection and promoting policy coherence, legitimacy, and sustainable outcomes. (The resolution's preamble ends with a call on states to take human rights into consideration when developing their environmental policies.)
- Many forms of environmental damage are transnational in character, and effective international cooperation to address such damage is important in order to support national efforts for the realization of human rights.[46] (This last point represented a carefully negotiated compromise between developed countries, which emphasized the primary responsibility of the home state to promote and protect human rights, and developing countries, which emphasized the importance of international cooperation.)

Finally, despite opposition from both developing and developed countries that did not want the new resolution to mention climate change, the text does refer to both of the Council's earlier resolutions on the subject, and to relevant paragraphs of the Cancun Agreements.

The aim of all these paragraphs was to define the existing common ground around human rights and climate change / human rights and environment – to clarify, and set down in an intergovernmental resolution, the contours of contemporary consensus.

The operative paragraphs then put in place the first step through which the main sponsors of the resolution would seek to further expand the contours of that consensus. Most importantly, the Council asked OHCHR to prepare an assessment of the current situation vis-à-vis the relationship between human rights and environment,

[46] Ibid., pmbl. paras. 13–17.

internationally, regionally, and nationally.[47] The aim here was threefold: to set down in an official UN document (an OHCHR report) the current state of international agreement around the relationship; in so doing, to identify gaps and areas where further norm clarification and norm setting would be needed or useful; and to demonstrate that many states had gone much further at national level (e.g., by agreeing to constitutional provisions on environmental rights) than they were currently willing to do at international level. The resolution asked OHCHR to prepare this "scoping" report for consideration at the Council's 19th session one year later, in March 2012.[48]

THE EMERGENCE OF TWO "DISTINCT AND PARALLEL TRACKS"

Not everyone agreed with the aforementioned "sideways step." Bangladesh and the Philippines had not supported the switch to address human rights and the environment because, they felt, it suggested a diminished interest in the issue of climate change. They therefore declined to join the core group on human rights and environment. At the same time, key civil society organizations, especially CIEL, Earthjustice, FES, and Nord-Sud, continued to lobby for the establishment of a Special Rapporteur on climate change. In late 2011, these organizations persuaded Bangladesh and the Philippines (with the latter playing the lead role) to restart the Council's initiative on human rights and climate change, but this time without the Maldives, Switzerland, and Costa Rica. The assumption of the organizations was that Bangladesh and Philippines would support the rapid deployment of a new Special Procedures mandate on climate change. In practice, however, the Council saw the development of two distinct and parallel tracks, which at times seemed to compete against one another.

Thus, in September 2011, at the Council's 17th session, Bangladesh and Philippines tabled a new text on human rights and climate change. Much of the final language, which became Council resolution 18/22, is a repeat of paragraphs of resolution 7/23 and 10/4. However, beyond those paragraphs, the resolution is interesting for two reasons.

First, the new main sponsors abandoned any effort to walk a middle line between the demands of large developing states and the demands of their rich world counterparts. The new text very clearly and very explicitly favors the former. Many of the preambular paragraphs focus on the effects of climate change on development, poverty eradication, and hunger, and do not mention human rights at all, except in the context of the right to development. For example, one paragraph notes that "responses to climate change should be coordinated with social and economic development in an integrated manner with a view to avoiding adverse impacts on

[47] Ibid., para. 1.
[48] Ibid., para. 2.

the latter, taking into full account the legitimate priority needs of developing countries for the achievement of sustained economic growth and the eradication of poverty."[49] The text also emphasizes international cooperation "in accordance with [states'] common but differentiated responsibilities and respective capabilities and their social and economic conditions."[50]

Second, the main sponsors, pressed by civil society organizations, worked to include in the resolution an ambitious timetable for future steps that would leave open the possibility of establishing a new Special Procedures mandate on climate change at the same time as the sponsors of the Council initiative on human rights and environment were expected to move to establish a mandate on that subject (i.e., March 2012). Under normal circumstances, a Council resolution will request OHCHR to prepare a report or to organize an event (e.g., a panel discussion or an inter-sessional seminar/workshop) in time to present that report/outcome of the event to the Council one year later, for further consideration. On this occasion, however, the Philippines and Bangladesh used the September 2011 resolution to ask OHCHR to convene a seminar "prior to the 19th session of the Council" (i.e., before March 2012). In initial drafts of the text, the sponsors also requested OHCHR to submit a summary report of the seminar for the March 2012 session. This timetable was designed to safeguard the option of creating a new mandate on climate change in March.

During open informal consultations on the draft, Costa Rica, Maldives, and Switzerland argued that this timeframe was unrealistic and would not provide space for proper consideration of the issues, or sufficient time for the OHCHR to organize the seminar and prepare the summary report. (A representative from OHCHR also attended the informal consultations to make the same point, but was initially refused the opportunity to speak). In the end, Bangladesh and Philippines insisted that the seminar should be held before March (it was eventually held on February 23, 2012), but agreed to delay, slightly, Council consideration of the summary report, which eventually took place during the 20th session, in June 2012.

Ahead of and during the February 23 seminar, some civil society organizations held a strong expectation that Bangladesh and the Philippines would call for the creation of a new Special Procedures mandate. For example, in a speech during session four of the seminar, on "The Way Forward," David Azoulay of CIEL referred to a joint CIEL–Earthjustice–FES paper that called for distinct mandates on climate change and on the environment, or for some form of joint mandate covering both issues. However, in the event, the opening statement of H.E. Ms. Dipu Moni, the Foreign Minister of Bangladesh, failed to offer any concrete suggestions on possible mechanisms to take forward the issue of human rights and climate change. According to Bangladesh and Philippine diplomats, this was

[49] Human Rights Council res. 18/22 (September 30, 2011), pmbl. para. 10.
[50] Ibid., pmbl. para. 9.

because leading countries of the global South, including China, Egypt, and India, did not support the creation of a mandate on climate change. In other words, by abandoning the middle ground between developed and developing states, the main sponsors had, as one consequence, made themselves and their initiative beholden to the interests of large emerging economies. (In a further sign of the difficult position this placed them in, Bangladesh and Philippines did not table another text on human rights and climate change until June 2014.)

In March 2012, during the first week of the 19th session of the Council, the Maldives, together with Costa Rica, Switzerland, and other members of the core group, tabled a new draft resolution that welcomed the analytical study on human rights and environment, prepared by OHCHR, yet recognized, nonetheless, "that certain aspects of human rights obligations relating to the enjoyment of a safe, clean, healthy and sustainable environment require further study and clarification."[51]

With that normative gap in mind, the text therefore called for the establishment of "an independent expert on the issue of human rights obligations relating to the enjoyment of a safe, clean, healthy and sustainable environment." As an Independent Expert (rather than a Special Rapporteur), the new three-year mandate-holder would focus mainly on studying and clarifying human rights norms relating to the enjoyment of a clean and healthy environment. As noted earlier in this chapter, the Council had already reached the outer limits of intergovernmental consensus on issues of human rights, climate change, and the environment; the aim of this new independent, objective, and expert mechanism would be to work through inclusive dialogue and consultation "to study ... the human rights obligations, including non-discrimination obligations, relating to the enjoyment of a safe, clean, healthy and sustainable environment." In other words, the Independent Expert would further clarify and codify the human rights normative framework related to the environment.

It was the unspoken hope of the main sponsors that such a norm-clarifying and norm-setting exercise, undertaken in consultation with, and with the consent of, all states, would represent important progress in of itself, and that it would also represent a first step toward open and informed intergovernmental reflections on the relative merits of declaring a new universal right to a clean and healthy environment. (In this regard, it is interesting to note that the approach adopted by the main sponsors of the Council's initiative on human rights and environment was very similar to the approach adopted, earlier in the life of the Council, by the main sponsors of the initiative on human rights, drinking water, and sanitation – an initiative that eventually led to the declaration of a human right to water and sanitation.)

Chapter 1 of this volume describes the work of the Independent Expert to clarify the human rights obligations relating to the enjoyment of a safe, clean, healthy, and

[51] United Nations Human Rights Council, Draft Resolution on Human Rights and the Environment. UN Doc. A/HRC/19/L.8/Rev.1 (March 20, 2012), pmbl. para. 12.

sustainable environment, and to identify best practices in the use of these obligations. At the conclusion of the mandate, in March 2015, in resolution 28/11, the Council (based on a text negotiated by Costa Rica on behalf of the core group) decided to renew the mandate on human rights and environment for a further three years – but this time as a Special Rapporteur, meaning the mandate-holder would be expected to switch his emphasis from working with states and other stakeholders to clarify and set down relevant norms, to working with states and other stakeholders to see those norms implemented and realized at national level.[52]

The most recent Council text on human rights and environment (at the time of drafting this chapter) is resolution 31/8, adopted in March 2016.[53] This remarkably ambitious resolution, adopted by consensus on the basis of a draft prepared by Slovenia as the lead negotiator for the core group, sets out, in many cases for the first time in an intergovernmental text, a range of newly clarified human rights norms relating to the environment. Resolution 31/8 is significant both as an indicator of how far the Council has come, in five years, in understanding and setting such norms, and because much of the text could be used, in the future, to provide the substantive content of a future international right to a clean and healthy environment.

In resolution 31/8, the Council calls on or encourages states to:

- Respect, protect, and fulfill human rights obligations when taking actions to address environmental challenges, and when developing environmental laws and policies.
- Adopt and implement laws ensuring, among other things, the rights to information, participation, and access to justice in the field of the environment.
- Facilitate public awareness and participation in environmental decision making, including on the part of civil society and vulnerable population groups, by protecting all human rights, including the rights to freedom of expression and to freedom of peaceful assembly and association.
- Ensure non-discrimination when undertaking environmental action, including climate action, to ensure that laws and policies are responsive to the needs of persons and communities in vulnerable situations.
- Promote a safe and enabling environment for civil society and environmental human rights defenders, so that they may operate free from threats, hindrance and insecurity.
- Provide for effective remedies for human rights violations and abuses, including those relating to the enjoyment of a safe, clean, healthy, and

[52] See Human Rights Council res. 28/11 (March 26, 2015).
[53] Human Rights Council res. 31/8 (March 23, 2016).

sustainable environment, in accordance with their international obligations and commitments.
- Take into account human rights obligations and commitments relating to the enjoyment of a safe, clean, healthy, and sustainable environment in the implementation and monitoring of the Sustainable Development Goals.
- Facilitate the exchange of knowledge and experiences between national experts in the environmental and human rights fields, in order to promote coherence between different policy areas.
- Collect disaggregated data on the effects of environmental harm on vulnerable groups, as appropriate.
- Explore ways to incorporate information on human rights and the environment, including climate change, in school curricula.
- Build capacity for the judicial sector to understand the relationship between human rights and the environment.
- Foster a responsible private business sector and encourage corporate sustainability reporting in accordance with relevant international standards and initiatives.
- Address compliance with human rights obligations and commitments relating to the enjoyment of a safe, clean, healthy, and sustainable environment in the framework of their interaction with the international human rights mechanisms (e.g. UPR, treaty bodies, special procedures).
- Ensure that projects supported by environmental finance mechanisms respect all human rights.[54]

As well as providing possible substantive content for a future international right to a clean and healthy environment, the resolution repeatedly uses a formulation, first seen in resolution 16/11, designed to provide a potential stepping-stone to such a right: namely "the promotion and protection of human rights as they relate to the *enjoyment of* a safe, clean, healthy and sustainable environment." As was noted by observers at the time of the adoption of resolution 16/11, this wording (especially the inclusion of the phrase "enjoyment of") seemed designed to enable proponents, at some point in the future, to add the words "... the right to ..." so that the United Nations would consider "the enjoyment of [the right to] a safe, clean, healthy and sustainable environment." Indeed, paragraph 5(a) of resolution 31/8 gives a clear indication that this is the ultimate objective of the main sponsors. Paragraph 5(a) encourages states:

> To adopt an effective normative framework for the enjoyment of a safe, clean, healthy and sustainable environment.

***

[54] Ibid., paras. 4, 5.

With these historic steps, UN Member States including Costa Rica, the Maldives, Slovenia, and Switzerland, together with the first UN Special Rapporteur on human rights and environment, and supportive NGOs such as CIEL and Earthjustice, have moved the international community to within touching distance of what would be the capstone of their decades-long endeavor: to elaborate, negotiate, and declare a new universal right to a safe, clean, healthy, and sustainable environment.

12

The Malé Formulation of the Overarching Environmental Human Right

Daniel Magraw and Kristina Wienhöfer***

This chapter focuses on the formulation of the right to an overarching environmental human right agreed to by small island developing states in the 2007 Malé Declaration on the Human Dimension of Global Climate Change: the "fundamental right to an environment capable of supporting human society and the full enjoyment of human rights."[1] It describes the process leading up to the drafting of the Malé formulation, including the Inuit petition on climate change to the Inter-American Commission on Human Rights which catalyzed a series of actions leading to the human rights language in the 2015 Paris Agreement. Both the Inuit petition and the Republic of the Maldives' initiative occurred in the face of existential threats to the communities involved, and both were intended to put a human face on climate change. The chapter then analyzes the substance and value of the Malé formulation and compares it with other formulations of the overarching environmental right, concluding that the Malé formulation provides functional content and definitional clarity absent in other formulations.

The first part of this chapter describes the conceptual provenance and drafting history of the Malé formulation. The chapter then examines the content and meaning of that formulation, including the value of its being an overarching environmental right, and contrasts it with other ways of expressing the overarching environmental right. Although much of the discussion herein refers to climate change, the discussion also relates to other causes of environmental harm and to environmental degradation generally.

* Professorial Lecturer and Senior Fellow, Foreign Policy Institute, Johns Hopkins University School of Advanced International Studies (SAIS).

** Associate, International Justice Initiative, SAIS.

1 Malé Declaration on the Human Dimension of Global Climate Change, November 14, 2007, available at www.ciel.org/Publications/Male_Declaration_Nov07.pdf, and reproduced in Appendix A at the end of this chapter.

MALÉ DECLARATION: CONCEPTUAL BACKGROUND AND ROAD TO THE FORMULATION

The successful decades-long effort to establish a relationship between environmental harm and human rights led inevitably to claims that climate change implicates human rights.[2] Over time, it has become clear that this relationship has three primary aspects. First, substantive and procedural rights must be respected, protected, and fulfilled whenever governments take action relating to climate change, just as they must regarding government actions relating to other issues. Second, climate change can directly affect the realization of human rights by virtue of its effects on the environment, as is evident from the situations facing vulnerable communities such as the Inuit and residents of the Maldives. Third, climate change can cause migration, which in turn can affect the human rights of both climate migrants and local populations in areas receiving climate migrants.[3]

The application of human rights, including of an overarching environmental right, to these three types of situations varies according to the specific factual contexts and in particular because climate change involves transboundary causes and impacts. A thorough analysis of the extent to which human rights may apply in a transboundary context (which is unfortunately and inaccurately usually referred to by the term "extraterritorial") is beyond the scope of this chapter, but the possibility that the overarching environmental human right does not apply in a transboundary context is referred to in the following section.

The understanding that climate change implicates human rights has now been set forth in many individual and joint statements by UN human rights special procedures[4] and vindicated by the UN Human Rights Council,[5] the UN Development Programme,[6] the Conference of the Parties[7] to the United Nations Framework

[2] See Marc Limon, "Human Rights and Climate Change: Constructing a Case for Political Action," *Harvard Environmental Law Review* 33 (2009), pp. 439–76, at 450–75.

[3] For a more detailed exposition, see Daniel Magraw et al., "Human Rights, Labour and the Paris Agreement on Climate Change," *Environmental Policy and Law* 46 (2016), pp. 313–20.

[4] See, e.g., Joint Statement of the Special Procedure Mandate Holders of the Human Rights Council on the UN Climate Change Conference (December 7, 2009) (issued by twenty UN special procedure mandate holders), available at www.ohchr.org/EN/NewsEvents/Pages/DisplayNews.aspx?NewsID=9667&LangID=E; John H. Knox, *Report of the Independent Expert on the Issue of Human Rights Obligations Relating to the Enjoyment of a Safe, Clean, Healthy and Sustainable Environment: Mapping Report*, UN Doc. A/HRC/25/53 (December 30, 2013).

[5] See, e.g., Human Rights Council res. 18/22 (September 30, 2011) ("climate change poses an immediate and far-reaching threat to people and communities around the world and has adverse implications for the full enjoyment of human rights."); res. 28/11 (March 26, 2015); res. 29/15 (July 2, 2015).

[6] United Nations Development Programme, *Human Development Report 2007/08: Fighting Climate Change - Solidarity in a Divided World* (2007).

[7] United Nations Framework Convention on Climate Change, *Report on the Conference of the Parties on Its Sixteenth Session, Held in Cancun from 29 November to 10 December* 2010, UN Doc. FCCC/CP/2010/7/Add. 1 (March 15, 2011), pmbl. ("climate change represents an urgent

Convention on Climate Change (UNFCCC),[8] the United Nations Environment Programme,[9] and most recently in the Paris Agreement adopted by the Conference of the Parties in December 2015,[10] each of which recognized that there is an important relationship between climate change and human rights. However, achieving this recognition was not easy. It involved a sustained effort by many individuals, nongovernmental organizations, inter-governmental organizations, UN Human Rights Council special procedure mandate holders, and governments.[11] Two early milestones along the path to recognizing the relationship between climate change and human rights were the Inuit petition against the United States, brought to the Inter-American Commission on Human Rights in 2005,[12] and the Malé Declaration on the Human Dimension of Climate Change, adopted in 2007 by a conference of small island states. The Malé Declaration is also significant because it is the instrument in which the formulation of an overarching environmental human right that is the subject of this chapter first appears.

The Inuit Petition in the Inter-American Commission on Human Rights

In 2005, Sheila Watt-Cloutier, then Chair of the Inuit Circumpolar Conference, presented a petition to the Inter-American Commission on Human Rights (IACHR), on behalf of herself, sixty-two other named individuals, and all other affected Inuit populations of the American and Canadian Arctic. The Inuit are an indigenous group that descended from the Thule people. Traditionally, they inhabited four countries: the northern and western parts of Alaska in the United States, northern Canada, Greenland, and Chukotka in Russia. "Inuit" describes an expansive ethnic group with certain differences but characterized by a common culture of, for instance, a reliance on subsistence harvesting for food and an ability to adapt to Artic conditions. As indigenous people, the Inuit have adapted over time their knowledge and techniques of living to their arctic environment. Their identity, culture and living conditions thus depend on this environment. The Inuit Petition, titled "Violations Resulting from Global Warming Caused by the United States," asserted that climate change was violating their human rights and that the United

and potentially irreversible threat to human societies and the planet, and thus requires to be urgently addressed by all Parties").

[8] United Nations Framework Convention on Climate Change, May 9, 1992, in force March 21, 1994, 1771 UNTS 107.

[9] United Nations Environment Programme, *Climate Change and Human Rights* (December 2015).

[10] Paris Agreement, December 12, 2015, in force November 4, 2016, UN Doc. FCCC/CP/2015/19. For a discussion of the Paris Agreement and human rights, see Lavanya Rajamani, Chapter 13, and Sumudu Atapattu, Chapter 14; Magraw et al., "Human Rights, Labour and the Paris Agreement."

[11] See ibid.

[12] The Inuit Petition is available at www.ciel.org/Publications/ICC_Petition_7Dec05.pdf.

States was responsible for at least a portion of that violation, because it was then the world's largest emitter, was failing to take adequate measures to curb its emissions, and was not even participating in the international community's strongest effort to deal with climate change, i.e., the Kyoto Protocol to the UNFCCC.[13]

The factual basis for the petition was that the Arctic is warming dramatically,[14] which is causing severe disruption and harm to the Inuit, their culture, health, way of life, and society. The Inuit depend on snow and ice in myriad ways. As the Inuit petition stated: "[T]he Inuit rely on the natural environment for their cultural and physical survival. The Inuit and their culture have developed over thousands of years in relationship with, and in response to, the physical environment of the Arctic. . . . The judicious use of plants and game, for everything from food to clothing to lighting, has allowed the Inuit to thrive in the Arctic climate, while developing a complex social structure based upon the harvest."[15]

Among other things, the Inuit rely on being able to traverse enormous ice shelves to hunt, gather food, and communicate. They rely on shore ice to protect their shorelines and villages from erosion. They depend on a specific type of snow to build igloos for shelter while traveling to hunt and for other purposes. Their houses, schools, roads and other built infrastructure often rest directly on permafrost. The warming temperature is resulting in thinning ice shelves, disappearing shore ice, shorter freeze periods, more rapid melt periods, melting permafrost, and an overall decrease in ice surface area. These changes are directly impacting the Inuit's traditional ways of life and posing direct dangers to life (e.g., due to falling through ice, which melts from below), property (e.g., because increased shore erosion has caused buildings to topple into the sea and melting permafrost has left buildings, roads, and airstrips unusable), and culture (e.g., because of reduced ability to travel and hunt). Moreover, Arctic wildlife essential to the Inuit's survival and culture, such as seals, walruses, polar bears and whales, are threatened by destruction as their habitat melts and disappears due to warming.

The Inuit Petition asserted that the IACHR was obligated to act on issues of climate control because, as exemplified in the circumstances of the Inuit people, global warming directly impedes human rights.[16] The Petition was intended to bring

[13] Kyoto Protocol to the United Nations Framework Convention on Climate Change, December 11, 1997, in force February 16, 2005, 2303 UNTS 148.

[14] See, e.g., Thomas Sumner, "Arctic sea ice shrinks to second-lowest low on record," *Science News* (September 19, 2016).

[15] Inuit Petition, p. 74.

[16] The petition requested the IACHR to recommend that the United States adopt mandatory limits to its emissions of greenhouse gases and cooperate with the international community to "prevent dangerous anthropogenic interference with the climate system," the objective of the UNFCCC. The petition also asked the IACHR to declare that the United States has an obligation to cooperate with the Inuit to develop a plan to help the Inuit adapt to impacts of climate change and to take into account the impact of its emissions on the Arctic and Inuit before approving any major government action.

to bear the moral and legal force of international human rights law to cause the United States and, indirectly, other countries to take action to combat climate change, to use the human rights institutional structure to publicize the relationship between human rights and climate change, to bring attention to the plight of the Inuit, and generally to put a human face on climate change.

The Inuit Petition identified ways the effects of climate change violate seven specific human rights of the Inuit. These were the rights: to enjoy the benefits of their culture; to use and enjoy the lands they have traditionally occupied; to use and enjoy their personal and intellectual property; to the preservation of health; to life, physical protection and security; to their own means of subsistence; and to residence and movement and inviolability of the home. Relying partly on the fact that the Inuit are an indigenous people, the Petition also argued that the Inuit have a "right to a healthy environment" that is being violated. Emphasizing the inseparability of indigenous people's human rights and their environment, the petition stated:

> Preservation of the arctic environment is one of the distinct protections required for the Inuit to fully enjoy their human rights on an equal basis with all peoples. States thus have an international obligation not to degrade the environment to an extent that threatens indigenous peoples' culture, health, life, property, or ecological security. Within the Inter-American system, and in the international community generally, indigenous peoples' right to a healthy environment has been repeatedly recognized and enforced.[17]

As support, the petition cited *inter alia* the *Awas Tingni* case, in which the Inter-American Court of Human Rights found that the failure to prevent environmental damage to indigenous lands "causes catastrophic damage" to indigenous peoples because "the possibility of maintaining social unity, of cultural preservation and reproduction, and of surviving physically and culturally, depends on the collective, communitarian existence and maintenance of the land."[18] The Petition also cited the IACHR report on Ecuador, which states that damage to traditional lands "invariably leads to serious loss of life and health and damage to the cultural integrity of indigenous peoples."[19] The report further states that environmental degradation can "give rise to an obligation on the part of a state to take reasonable measures to prevent" the risks to health and life associated with environmental degradation, and that environmental degradation, "which may cause serious physical illness,

[17] Inuit Petition, p. 72. See also United Nations Declaration on the Rights of Indigenous Peoples, UN Doc. A/RES/61/295 (September 13, 2007), art. 29(1) ("Indigenous peoples have the right to the conservation and protection of the environment and the productive capacity of their lands or territories and resources.").

[18] *Mayagna (Sumo) Awas Tingni Community* v. *Nicaragua*, Inter-Am. Ct. H.R. (ser. C.) No. 79 (2001), para. 151.

[19] Inter-American Commission on Human Rights, *Report on the Human Rights Situation in Ecuador*, Doc. No. OEA/Ser.L/V/II.96 (1997), chapter 9.

impairment and suffering on the part of the local populace, [is] inconsistent with the right to be respected as a human being."[20]

The last two of these statements apply to nonindigenous people as well. Indeed, the Inuit Petition went on to assert that the right to a healthy environment is a norm of customary international law with respect to all people, not just indigenous peoples.[21]

As is evident, the Inuit Petition alleges that the vast effects of climate change are essentially altering the Inuit's entire environment, resulting in many violations of separate human rights. Even acknowledging that human rights are interdependent and indivisible, it is obvious that an overarching right to an environment that supports this set of rights would be logical and analytically helpful. Indeed, the Inuit included a claim that a right to a healthy environment was being violated. The Inuit, however, were careful to provide detailed arguments relating to established human rights, believing that too great a reliance on a controversial right such as the right to a healthy environment would distract attention from the issue of whether violations were occurring of well-recognized human rights – such as the right to life – that are beyond cavil.[22]

Ultimately the IACHR decided not to proceed with the Inuit Petition, without providing any reasons.[23] But the petition had important impacts, among which was that the Commission staff simultaneously indicated that the IACHR would welcome a request to hold a hearing on climate change and human rights. Sheila Watt-Cloutier made such a request, which was duly granted. The hearing was held and webcast globally. Before the hearing opened, the IACHR's Chair personally thanked Ms. Watt-Cloutier for "bringing this important human rights issue to the Commission's attention."[24] In addition, the Inuit Petition catalyzed actions by others, including by the Republic of the Maldives.

[20] Ibid., p. 444.

[21] Among other evidence of this, the Petition quoted International Court of Justice Judge Weeramantry:

> The protection of the environment is likewise a vital part of contemporary human rights doctrine, for it is a *sine qua non* for numerous human rights such as the right to health and the right to life itself. It is scarcely necessary to elaborate on this as damage to the environment can impair and undermine all the human rights spoken of in the Universal Declaration and other human rights instruments.

Gabčíkovo-Nagymaros Case (Hungary v. *Slovakia)*, [1997] ICJ 7, p. 88 (separate opinion of Vice-President Weeramantry). This is only a part of the jurisprudence and other support for the existence of an overarching environmental human right, as other chapters of this book explain. That material will not be repeated here.

[22] This and other assertions about the Inuit petition and its handling are based in part on personal knowledge of one of the authors, who participated in the case.

[23] Center for International Environmental Law, "Inuit Petition and the IACHR," at www.ciel.org/project-update/inuit-petition-and-the-iachr.

[24] Observation by one of the authors (Daniel Magraw).

The Malé Declaration on the Human Dimension of Climate Change

The Malé Declaration grew out of the Inuit Petition to the IACHR. Although the IACHR did not proceed with the Inuit Petition, the petition and the response to it caught the attention of the Republic of the Maldives. A representative of the Maldives approached one of the two NGOs that had been involved in the Inuit Petition[25] and requested that it work with the Maldives to provide advice to conceptualize and draft a declaration that would meet the precise needs of the Maldives and other small island developing states. As with the Inuit, the Maldives wanted to focus on the "human dimension" of climate change using a rights-based approach, with the goal of harnessing the legal and moral power of human rights law to force action to combat climate change. As also is true for the Inuit, the situation facing the Maldives is grave.

The Maldives consists of a chain of approximately 1200 tropical low-lying islands southwest of India. About one-third of the Maldives' roughly 400,000 population lives in Malé, the capital. The highest point in the Maldives is 1.8 meters above sea level.[26] Rising sea levels and sea surges have already made some of the outlying islands uninhabitable, for example by flooding land and infiltrating fresh water sources with salt water. The government of the Maldives has begun relocating the populations of some particularly vulnerable islands to safer islands; and the island of Malé is surrounded by concrete barriers in an effort to prevent erosion and flooding. But the Maldives' options to adapt to climate change will run out if sea level continues to rise. The government of the Maldives has reportedly explored the possibility of purchasing land in Australia, India, and Sri Lanka for an eventual home,[27] much as the government of Kiribati has purchased land in Fiji.[28]

It is immediately apparent that in both the Arctic and the Maldives the environment is changing in fundamental ways that threaten myriad human rights. There is an apparent difference in that the land mass of the Maldives on which Maldivians reside will entirely disappear if climate change continues its present course, whereas

[25] A Washington, D.C., representative of the Republic of the Maldives, Ed Cameron, contacted the Center for International Environmental Law (CIEL). That person and the Maldives' then-representative on human rights issues in Geneva, Marc Limon, were integrally involved in bringing the Malé Declaration to fruition, as well as in subsequent efforts to address climate change and human rights. The other NGO involved in the Inuit Petition was Earthjustice, which, like CIEL, has remained a leader in efforts to establish and elaborate the linkage between climate change and human rights.

[26] Central Intelligence Agency, "Maldives," *The World Factbook* (2016).

[27] Randeep Ramesh, "Paradise Almost Lost: Maldives Seek to Buy a New Homeland," *The Guardian* (November 9, 2008).

[28] Laurence Caramel, "Besieged by the rising tides of climate change, Kiribati buys land in Fiji," *The Guardian* (June 30, 2014). Commendably, the president of Fiji has stated that people of Kiribati would be welcome in Fiji. Office of the President of the Republic of Kiribati, "Press Release: Fiji Supports Kiribati On Sea Level Rise" (February 11, 2014).

the ice and land of the Inuits will change (e.g., ice will weaken and thin and permafrost will melt), but most will remain as land or ice. That may be a distinction without a difference, however: shore erosion is causing some of the Inuit's land to wash into the sea, some melted permafrost no longer supports buildings, roads, airstrips, and other infrastructure, and some of the ice on which the Inuit depend is disappearing, at least during summer months.[29] In any event, the existential threat facing the Maldives – that its land mass may entirely disappear into the sea – presents as dire a situation as can be imagined.

The severity of the threat facing the Maldives led to a reexamination of the value of an overarching environmental human right in the context of the Maldives' predicament, i.e., why such a right adds to the amalgam of other human rights in this context, as well as an analysis of what the overarching environmental right actually means, i.e., what does it require, in this context, and in light of both of those, how best can such a right be formulated. Regarding the latter, for example, what would a right to a "clean" or "healthy" environment require when the issue is disappearing land mass? Ultimately, the representatives of the Maldives and other small island developing states that negotiated and signed the Malé Declaration concluded that articulating the overarching environmental right in functional terms best communicates the nature and purpose of the right.

The Malé Declaration defines the overarching environmental right as: "the fundamental right to an environment capable of supporting human society and the full enjoyment of human rights."[30] In addition, the Malé Declaration "stated explicitly (and for the first time in an international agreement) that 'climate change has clear and immediate implications for the full enjoyment of human rights' and called on the United Nations human rights system to address the issue as a matter of urgency."[31] The Declaration made specific requests not only to the Human Rights Council and the Office of the High Commissioner for Human Rights, but also to the Alliance of Small Island States (AOSIS), the Conference of the Parties of the UNFCCC, and the international community as a whole.[32]

The Malé Declaration was presented to the 13th Conference of the Parties of the UNFCCC in Bali, Indonesia, by Maldives President Maumoon Abdul Gayoom. Other speakers, including Kyung-wha Kung, the then-Deputy High Commissioner of Human Rights, also referred to the importance of addressing the human rights dimension of climate change.

[29] Even if all of the Maldives sinks into the sea, the Maldives might retain its rights under the United Nations Convention on the Law of the Sea to the continental shelf and super-adjacent water in the area where its islands used to exist. That does not affect the analysis in this chapter other than perhaps to moderate the extent of damage due to human rights violations.

[30] Malé Declaration, pmbl.

[31] Limon, "Constructing a Case for Political Action," pp. 439–76.

[32] Malé Declaration, paras. 1–5.

THE MALÉ FORMULATION

Content of the Malé Formulation

The Malé formulation of an overarching environmental right (i.e., "the fundamental right to an environment capable of supporting human society and the full enjoyment of human rights") is intentionally straightforward and its meaning is thus relatively self-evident. The following discussion addresses a few aspects of the formulation of particular significance to the present book. At the outset, it is important to note that the Malé formulation is not qualitatively different from other human rights. For example, the obligations arising from the Malé formulation do not differ in kind from the obligations arising from other human rights. This is evident in part from the relation of the overarching environmental right to rights such as the right to life and right to an adequate standard of living.

The Malé formulation states that the right is "fundamental." The intent here is twofold. The first goal is to emphasize that this right is of primary importance. The second is to indicate that this right supports other human rights.[33]

The word "environment" indicates that the right relates to the entire environment. All environmental media, including air, water, soil, temperature, and sound frequencies, are included. Similarly, all ecosystem services are covered.

The language "capable of supporting" is important for several reasons. It relates to the importance of ecosystem services as the infrastructure of human society. It also indicates the essential role of the environment with respect to human rights, i.e., the full realization of human rights depends on environmental factors, not just other factors. Thus this phrasing highlights the mutual supportiveness between human rights and environmental protection and avoids suggesting there is a hierarchy between the two areas, without diminishing the importance of traditional human rights. Furthermore, the broad concept of "support" encompasses differences among various political, economic, and social systems, as well as among differing cultures and stages of development. Especially in light of the fact that climate change will affect people, communities, and nations at different times and in different ways, the scope of "supporting" allows a different approach in various situations and correspondingly requires different actions by different states and other actors.

The dual focus on human society and human rights in the Malé formulation emphasizes the impacts of climate change and other forms of environmental harm on humans, both collectively and individually. As described, a major goal of the drafters was to put a human face on climate change.

[33] This and other assertions about the Malé Declaration and formulation are based in part on personal knowledge of one of the authors, who advised the Republic of the Maldives with respect to the Declaration.

The requirement of "full enjoyment" states clearly that these rights are not subservient to other considerations. This is standard human rights parlance.[34] The inclusion of all human rights makes clear the comprehensive scope of states' obligations with respect to environmental protection.

Finally, the right articulated by Malé formulation is not static or limited to present conditions and needs. It implicitly takes into account the fact that societies change and that inter-generational rights must be considered. As stated by the United Nations Development Programme: Climate change represents "a systematic violation of the human rights of the world's poor and future generations, and a step back from universal values."[35]

Value of the Malé Formulation as an Overarching Right

The Malé formulation is supported by several interrelated considerations. Some stem primarily from the fact that the Malé formulation is an overarching norm and some from its precise wording.

The Malé formulation is more than the sum of its parts. An important benefit of having an overarching environmental right, particularly one such as the Malé formulation that expressly refers broadly to other human rights, is that it encompasses more than the set of separate individual human rights, including even those that otherwise may have only an indirect relation to environmental harm. It both is fundamental to these other rights and is all encompassing with respect to them. Moreover, it serves as a gap filler and a test for measuring the human rights implications of new types or combinations of environmental threats.

In this sense, the Malé formulation is akin to the right to due process.[36] It is well recognized that due process not only encompasses a set of separate procedural rights, such as the right to confront one's accusers, the right to know the charges against oneself, the prohibition against judging one's own case, etc., but also is broader than those particular rights.[37] Due process provides a fundamental basis on which those rights exist and provides a doctrine by which to measure new procedural questions as they arise. For example, in the Shrimp/Turtle case, the Appellate Body of the World

[34] See, e.g., Human Rights Council res. 7/23 (March 28, 2008).

[35] UNDP, *Fighting Climate Change*, p. 4.

[36] Another possible analogue can be found in Article 28 of the Universal Declaration of Human Rights, which states: "everyone is entitled to a social and international order in which the rights and freedoms enlisted in this Declaration can be fully realized." Article 28, whose goal is to ensure that individual rights and freedoms can be "fully realized," is overarching and, like the Malé formulation and due process, greater than the sum of its individual parts. It might be argued that the term "social and international order" includes maintaining an environment sufficient to "fully realize" individual rights and freedoms, thus obviating the need for a separate overarching environmental right. That is a stretch, however, because environmental consciousness was not even beginning to form when Article 28 was adopted in 1948.

[37] See Devika Hovell, "Due Process in the United Nations," *American Journal of International Law* 110(1) (2016), pp. 1–48, at 3.

Trade Organization held that the United States' procedure for determining the permissibility of another country's methodology for protecting sea turtles during shrimp harvesting violated due process because, *inter alia*, it did not provide for informing a state whose methodologies had been rejected the reasons for the rejection.[38]

Just as it encompasses all human rights, the Malé formulation addresses the entire human being, both individually and at the level of human society. As noted, the Maldives were interested, as were the Inuit, in putting a human face on climate change. Maldives President Gayoom said at the Malé Conference, "it is time to put people back at the heart of climate change diplomacy."[39] This approach requires that the full human being be protected and that human society be protected, both of which are endangered by climate change in low-lying nations such as the Maldives. The Malé formulation embodies that approach.

The Malé formulation also encompasses the entire range of threats to the environment, the full range of ecosystem services, and the full range of environmental media. The importance of this scope can perhaps best be understood by considering the human rights impacts of climate change. Seeing climate change through a full human rights lens is vital compared to just looking through the lens of individual issues associated with climate change such as water, food, or land rights. By formulating the right as an overarching environmental right in the way the Malé formulation does, a comprehensive approach is incorporated. The Malé formulation is striking as it implies that all human rights are endangered by climate change, an understanding recognized by many others. The United Nations Human Rights Council noted in 2011 that "climate change poses an immediate and far-reaching threat to people and communities around the world and has adverse implications for the full enjoyment of human rights."[40] This reference to "full enjoyment" – which mirrors the language in the Malé formulation – and the reference to a "far-reaching threat" imply that all human rights are potentially endangered and supports the need for a human right that encompasses and supports all the more specific human rights.

An overarching right serves to overcome another issue encountered in human rights law. Treaty-based human rights law is comprised of a variety of legal texts and obligations to which different states are parties and through which different states recognize diverse human rights. Indeed, states often belong to different treaties; and regional treaties serve only a fraction of the world, a world that is, however, globally affected by environmental threats such as depletion of the ozone layer and climate change. The Malé formulation obviates any need to redefine or qualify rights to adapt to specific circumstances, given its characteristics: It is universal and nuanced

[38] *United States – Import Prohibition of Certain Shrimp and Shrimp Products*, WT/DS58/AB/R (WTO Appellate Body, 1998), paras. 177–81.

[39] Ajay Makan, "Island Nations Plan for Rising Seas, Mass Migration," *Reuters* (November 14, 2007).

[40] Human Rights Council res. 18/22 (September 30, 2011).

in its application. Moreover, climate change in the context of low-lying small island states is not a question of a mere problem with bad air quality or health concerns, it is a question of sheer survival. A right to survival is a truly universal right. The Malé formulation provides the needed scope and universality to fully capture the indispensable environmental and human right protection in the context of climate change for all states and individuals.

A related advantage of the Malé formulation is that it entails taking account of the context in which the right is being applied. This allows a nuanced analysis in terms of what is required of a particular state and is also characteristic of other overarching norms such as due process. For example, what might be required to support human society in one environment may differ from what is required to support society in another one or to support a different society in the same environment.

Because of its contextual nature, the Malé formulation implicitly embodies the principle of common but differentiated responsibilities (CBDR).[41] The UNFCCC includes CBDR,[42] but CBDR is of immense importance to developing countries in all environmental contexts. Small island states, which are vulnerable and struggling for their own physical survival, are taking steps to reduce their own emissions of greenhouse gases. The Malé Declaration highlights that it is even more imperative that all other countries do their share to protect the environment and lessen climate change. The vulnerability of small island states has led to a particular articulation of the overarching environmental right that demonstrates a deep understanding of the issue, an understanding that other articulations of the right do not fully capture, as is discussed in the following section.

The Special Rapporteur on human rights and environment, John Knox, noted, "Human rights are grounded in respect for fundamental human attributes such as dignity, equality and liberty. The realization of these attributes depends on an environment that allows them to flourish."[43] The reference to "an environment that allows them to flourish" provides additional support for the Malé formulation. When Knox describes the essential attributes of human rights, he emphasizes how realizing essential rights transcends individual human rights and that these attributes can only exist in an environment that not only provides support for a particular human right such as the right to clean air, but also allows these essential attributes to flourish, i.e., an environment that is capable of supporting all human rights and society itself.

[41] See Rio Declaration on Environment and Development, UN Doc. A/CONF.151/26/Rev.1, annex I (June 14, 1992), Principle 7. For a discussion of CBDR in the context of the human rights dimension of climate change, see Limon, "Constructing a Case for Political Action," pp. 474–5.

[42] UNFCCC, art. 3(1); *cf.* ibid., art. 3(2).

[43] John H. Knox, *Report of the Independent Expert on the Issue of Human Rights Obligations Relating to the Enjoyment of a Safe, Clean, Healthy and Sustainable Environment: Preliminary Report*, UN Doc. A/HRC/22/43 (December 24, 2012), para. 10.

In a general sense, the value of an overarching environmental right such as the Malé formulation is demonstrated by the existence of such a right in many instruments around the world. Such a right appears, for example, in many national and sub-national constitutions.[44] Over 100 states have guaranteed constitutional protection of such a right.[45] Several sub-national constitutions, such as that of the U.S. state of Pennsylvania, also contain such a right.[46] The formulations of the overarching environmental right vary among these instruments.

The following examples from national constitutions demonstrate the utilization of many phrases to describe an overarching environmental right. The first country to include a right to protect the environment in its Constitution was Portugal in 1976: Article 66 provides that "Everyone shall possess the right to a healthy and ecologically balanced human living environment and the duty to defend it.[47] Chile's Constitution of 1980 utilizes more streamlined language in Article 19: "the right to live in an environment free from contamination."[48] Article 79 in Colombia's constitution of 1991 provides "Every person has the right to enjoy a healthy environment."[49] Norway's Constitution (1992) provides in Article 110(b) that "Every person has a right to an environment that is conducive to health and to natural surroundings whose productivity and diversity are preserved."[50] The French Constitution includes a Charter of the Environment with the right to live in a "balanced environment, favorable to human health."[51] The Constitution of Kenya (2010) includes future generations: "Every person has the right to a clean and healthy environment, which includes the right to have the environment protected for the benefit of present and future generations."[52] Other formulations require "pleasant," "satisfying," and "supportive" environments.[53] Regardless of the exact formulation chosen, and regardless of how each of these fits into its respective legal system with respect to enforceability, these states obviously decided that an overarching environmental right was important.

44 See David R. Boyd, Chapter 2, and Erin Daly and James May, Chapter 3.
45 See Boyd, Chapter 2.
46 Constitution of Pennsylvania, art. 1, sec. 27 (provision added in 1971).
47 Constitution of Portugal (1976), art. 66.
48 Constitution of Chile (1980), art. 19, paras. 1, 8.
49 Constitution of Colombia (1991), art. 79.
50 Constitution of Norway (1992), art. 110(b).
51 Legifrance, Charter of the Environment (2005), art. 1.
52 Constitution of Kenya (2010), art. 42(a).
53 David Boyd, *The Status of Constitutional Protection for the Environment in Other Nations* (David Suzuki Foundation Paper #4, undated), p. 14, available at http://davidsuzuki.org/publications/2014/whitepapers/DSF%20White%20Paper%204.pdf. Boyd analyzed the language used in ninety-eight constitutions to articulate an overarching environmental right. He found that sixty-eight use the wording "healthy" or "an environment that is not harmful to health." A significant number of constitutions (twenty-five) use the term "ecologically balanced environment." "Clean" appeared six times, "natural" three times, and "pleasant" one time, among other formulations. The terms "safe" and "sustainable" are sometimes used in other contexts.

An overarching environmental norm may also appear in the Stockholm Declaration on the Human Environment of 1972. The first sentence of Principle 1 provides:

> Man has the fundamental right to freedom, equality and adequate conditions of life, in an environment of a quality that permits a life of dignity and well-being, and he bears a solemn responsibility to protect and improve the environment for present and future generations.[54]

This language did not reappear in the 1992 Rio Declaration or subsequent similar instruments, however.

Value of the Malé Formulation vis-à-vis Other Formulations of the Overarching Environmental Right

As discussed, the overarching environmental right is expressed in many ways in different instruments and contexts. These include "healthy," "clean," "safe," "secure," "balanced," "sustainable," "free of contamination," "pleasant," "satisfying," "supportive," and combinations of these and other terms. Generally speaking, these formulations, although useful, raise questions because their actual meaning is unclear and can be interpreted narrowly or imply undesirable outcomes. A few examples suffice to demonstrate the difficulties with these terms.

The term "healthy environment" is difficult on its face because in many ways the natural environment is not "healthy" for humans. For example, diseases, natural disasters such as floods and earthquakes, and extreme heat and cold can be fatal, as can encounters with poisonous snakes and large carnivores. Is an environment that includes those elements "healthy"? In addition, a focus on "health" may only be associated with environmental issues such as pollution, thus ignoring issues such as biological diversity, access to open spaces and other resources of central importance to human rights such as the right to enjoy culture, or even the right to a traditional source of food. Similarly, the term "healthy" is ambiguous regarding whether it extends beyond human health to include health of ecosystems and other aspects of nature. These considerations also apply to terms such as "clean," "safe," and "secure," which might not even relate to human health, although that may be implied. In addition, there are no criteria for measuring "healthy" and similar formulations.

The term "balanced" provides almost no guidance to states because it does not explain what is to be balanced and according to what criteria. Adding the modifier "ecologically," as some formulations do, provides a bit more guidance but it does not resolve the questions proposed in previous sections. The term "sustainable" is

[54] Declaration of the UN Conference on the Human Environment, UN Doc. A/Conf.48/14/Rev.1 (June 5–16, 1972), Principle 1.

similarly vague, although one can presumably infer that social and economic considerations are to be taken into consideration. The terms "pleasant" and "satisfying" also provide no guidance and may fall far short of calling for an environment capable of supporting the full enjoyment of human rights. The term "supportive," although at first blush promising because it contains the concept of support, ultimately does not provide useful guidance because it is silent as to what is being supported and for what ends.

The actual wording of these and other similar formulations, therefore, does not provide the clarity and content required of an overarching environmental human right, particularly when compared with the Malé formulation. To be clear, this is not to say that the overarching right when expressed using these terms does not have substance or value. For example, they serve as useful shorthand and, importantly, can serve as norms to be elaborated by tribunals and other mechanisms to provide greater clarity.

The Malé Formulation as a Stepping Stone Toward Progress

The value of any formulation of the overarching environmental right depends primarily on whether it leads to improvements in efforts to protect the environment and human health and other human conditions, including through improving efforts to combat climate change. It is too early to reach a final conclusion in this regard, but there are reasons to think the Malé formulation has contributed to such progress and is likely to continue to do so. This conclusion rests on two aspects of the Malé formulation: the focus on humans and human society, and the requirement that the environment be maintained in a condition that supports both human society and human rights.

As described, a primary goal of the drafters of the Malé formulation – as was the case with the progenitors of the Inuit Petition in the Inter-American Commission on Human Rights – was to put a human face on climate change. That this succeeded at least in part is evident from the adoption of the 2007 Malé Declaration on the Human Dimension of Global Climate Change, which not only contained the formulation but also stated expressly that climate change implicates human rights and called on the UN Human Rights Council and other members of the international community to consider the issue and for "an inclusive process that puts people, their prosperity, homes, survival and rights at the center of the climate change debate."[55] This call was followed by many statements acknowledging the relationship between climate change and human rights, including by the Human Rights Council, the Office of the High Commissioner for Human Rights, human rights mandate holders, the 2010 Conference of the Parties of the UNFCCC, and the preamble to the Paris Agreement on Climate Change. Not all of that progress

[55] Malé Declaration, final paragraph.

can be attributed to the Malé formulation or Declaration, of course. But they were a critical element in establishing momentum and channeling action.

As a specific example, the Malé Declaration created momentum that, over several years, catalyzed the subsequent focus on climate change's impacts on vulnerable individuals, populations, and countries. The 2011 Dhaka Ministerial Declaration of the Climate Vulnerable Forum, for example, describes the Malé Declaration as "the founding document of the Climate Vulnerable Forum."[56] In 2015, countries involved in the Forum formed the so-called V20, the Vulnerable 20, composed of countries from around the world that are most affected by the catastrophes connected with climate change,[57] to serve as a counterpoint to the G-20, the group of industrialized countries.

Another reason that the Malé formulation is likely to be influential in the future is that it provides a succinct description of what the overarching environmental right actually requires of states and other international actors subject to human rights obligations. In comparison, the other formulations of the overarching environmental right do not do that.

An important question is how the overarching environmental right will apply in the case of migration, both external and internal, and whether the Malé formulation will be useful in reaching positive outcomes in those contexts. Climate change will cause migration and resettlement, and other environmental damage will also cause migration to occur. The human rights of both migrants and populations receiving migrants could be imperiled. The concept of what the overarching environment requires offered by the Malé formulation could be helpful in guiding states and other actors to protect those rights, including by advance planning to take account of the virtual certainty that climate migration will occur.

Another question is how the overarching environmental right, however phrased, or indeed any human right, applies to the third aspect of the human rights implications of climate change, i.e., when climate change directly impacts the realization of

[56] Available at http://daraint.org/2011/11/14/2748/climate-vulnerable-forum-declaration-adopted. The Climate Vulnerable Forum is an "international partnership of countries highly vulnerable to a warming planet. The Forum serves as a South-South cooperation platform for participating governments to act together to deal with global climate change" (www.thecvf.org/web/climate-vulnerable-forum). The declaration adopted at the first Climate Vulnerable Forum, *inter alia*, called on the parties to the UNFCCC to "consider and address the health, human rights and security implications of climate change, including the need to prepare communities for relocation, to protect persons displaced across borders due to climate change-related impacts, and the need to create a legal framework to protect the human rights of those left stateless as a result of climate change." Declaration of the Climate Vulnerable Forum (2009), available at www.thecvf.org/wp-content/uploads/2013/08/Declaration-of-the-CVF-2009.pdf.

[57] The V20 consists of: Afghanistan, Bangladesh, Barbados, Bhutan, Costa Rica, Ethiopia, Ghana, Kenya, Kiribati, Madagascar, Maldives, Nepal, Philippines, Rwanda, Saint Lucia, Tanzania, Timor-Leste, Tuvalu, Vanuatu, and Vietnam. The V20 organized the Climate Vulnerable forum, composed of countries who view themselves as disproportionately affected by climate change.

human rights in situations such as those facing the Inuit or residents of the Maldives. The problem they face is not caused by their own state alone but rather by states all over the world. Some experts assert that states would not have transboundary/extraterritorial obligations, such as in the situation of climate change harms in the Maldives. Others disagree, concluding that in situations where a state's transboundary/extraterritorial human rights obligation does not exist or is limited there exists a justice gap arising from global interdependence that calls for a re-conceptualization of human rights in this report.[58] An alternative would be to recognize that the overarching environmental right does entail transboundary/extraterritorial obligations even if other human rights do not. In addition to protecting human dignity and aligning with the societal and environmental interdependence of today's world, this recognition would allow human rights to play a productive role in dealing with existential threats such as climate change.

International environmental law, such as Stockholm Declaration Principle 21 and Rio Declaration Principle 2, does address transboundary issues and thus may be an important part of solutions in this context. For example, it could lead to an obligation of the state in which a transboundary harm originated to assist the affected state in meeting its human right obligations in the context of changing environmental conditions. This would be entirely consistent with the obligation to cooperate with other states in protecting human rights.[59] It may also be important in influencing the development of human rights law in the context of transboundary environmental issues such as climate change, along the lines suggested in the previous paragraph.

CONCLUSIONS

The Malé formulation of the overarching environmental right grew out of two responses to climate change: the 2005 Inuit Petition to the Inter-American Commission on Human Rights and the 2007 Malé Conference of Small Island Developing States. Both the Inuit and the residents of the Republic of the Maldives, of which Malé is the capital, face existential threats to their lives, cultures, and societies from climate change. The 1200 islands in the Maldives, for example, will become uninhabitable and literally disappear if climate change continues unabated. The Malé formulation was intended to clearly explain the nature and goal of the overarching environmental right (which in other contexts is expressed in shorthand by phrases such as the right to a "clean," "healthy," "satisfying," "pleasant,"

[58] See Limon, "Constructing a Case for Political Action," p. 473; International Council on Human Rights Policy, *Climate Change and Human Rights: A Rough Guide* (2008), p. 64. See also Maastricht Principles on Extraterritorial Obligations of States in the Area of Economic, Social and Cultural Rights (2013), pmbl. para. 3.

[59] Office of the High Commissioner for Human Rights, *Report on the Relationship between Climate Change and Human Rights*, UN Doc. A/HRC/10/61 (January 15, 2009), paras. 84–8; Knox, *Mapping Report*, para. 67.

"balanced," or "supportive" environment); and it embodies a functional approach to the right: every person has a "fundamental right to an environment capable of supporting human society and the full enjoyment of human rights." Although the Malé formulation arose in the context of climate change, it applies to all environmental threats.

The Malé formulation is, and was intended to be, straightforward. As its words indicate, it is a fundamental right that underlies and encompasses all other individual human rights. It can serve as a gap filler and is more than the sum of its parts. It is contextual and encompasses all environmental threats and impacts, including with respect to ecosystem services.

The Malé formulation, although bulkier than more widely used phrases, has the advantage of addressing the basic characteristics of an overarching environmental right and of providing a clear statement of a state's obligations in this regard. Shorter articulations of the overarching environmental right such as those just mentioned, although valuable, may raise difficulties because they are less precise and can be interpreted as being too narrow or implying undesirable consequences. The Malé formulation has already been influential, including by contributing to the adoption of the Malé Declaration, which in turn catalyzed action in many different forums, including the 13th Conference of the Parties of the UNFCCC in Bali, the Human Rights Council, the Office of the High Commissioner for Human Rights, many special mandate holders, and the Alliance of Small Island States (AOSIS), and was the foundational document for formation of the Climate Vulnerable Forum and the Vulnerable 20 group. Whether this right continues to serve as a stepping stone to dealing with environmental threats more effectively depends primarily on political will, a hurdle that putting a human face on environmental problems hopefully will help overcome.

The overarching environmental right, in the form of the Malé formulation or however phrased, is presumably subject to the same doctrinal challenges as other human rights. If an overarching environmental right is formally recognized by the international community, that recognition could be accompanied by an acknowledgment that it applies in a transboundary/extraterritorial context. That outcome could also be achieved via progressive development and interpretation of the overarching environmental right. International environmental law, such as Stockholm Principle 21, is helpful in this regard. The human rights law obligation that states must cooperate in protecting human rights also is helpful. If human rights doctrine creates a justice gap in the face of existential environmental threats such as climate change, however, a re-conceptualization of human rights in this respect is in order.

APPENDIX A

Malé Declaration on the Human Dimension of Global Climate Change

We the representatives of the Small Island Developing States having met in Malé from 13 to 14 November 2007,

Aware that the environment provides the infrastructure for human civilization and that life depends on the uninterrupted functioning of natural systems;

Accepting the conclusions of the WMO/UNEP Intergovernmental Panel on Climate Change (IPCC) including, *inter alia*, that climate change is unequivocal and accelerating, and that mitigation of emissions and adaptation to climate change impacts is physically and economically feasible if urgent action is taken;

Persuaded that the impacts of climate change pose the most immediate, fundamental and far-reaching threat to the environment, individuals and communities around the planet, and that these impacts have been observed to be intensifying in frequency and magnitude;

Emphasizing that small island, low-lying coastal, and atoll states are particularly vulnerable to even small changes to the global climate and are already adversely affected by alterations in ecosystems, changes in precipitation, rising sea-levels and increased incidence of natural disasters;

Convinced that immediate and effective action to mitigate and adapt to climate change presents the greatest opportunity to preserve the prospects for future prosperity, and that further delay risks irreparable harm and jeopardizes sustainable development;

Reaffirming the United Nations Charter and the Universal Declaration of Human Rights;

Recalling the relevant provisions of declarations, resolutions and programmes of action adopted by major United Nations conferences, summits and special sessions and their follow-up meetings, in particular the Declaration of the United Nations Conference on the Human Environment of 1972 (Stockholm Declaration), the 1992 Rio Declaration on Environment and Development and Agenda 21, and the 2002 Johannesburg Declaration on Sustainable Development and Plan of Implementation of the World Summit on Sustainable Development;

Noting that the fundamental right to an environment capable of supporting human society and the full enjoyment of human rights is recognized, in varying formulations, in the constitutions of over one hundred states and directly or indirectly in several international instruments;

Recognizing the leadership of the Alliance of Small Island States in promoting and organizing international responses to climate change for the benefit of their citizens and humanity through *inter alia* the Male' Declaration on Sea Level Rises, the Barbados Programme of Action, and the Mauritius Strategy;

Acknowledging the United Nations Framework Convention on Climate Change (UNFCCC) and its Kyoto Protocol as important initial multilateral efforts to address climate change through global legal instruments, and the primacy of the United Nations process as the means to address climate change;

Anticipating the publication of the United Nations Development Programme's (UNDP) Human Development Report and the meeting of Commonwealth Heads of Government in Uganda, both of which will emphasise the human aspects of sustainable development;

Concerned that climate change has clear and immediate implications for the full enjoyment of human rights including *inter alia* the right to life, the right to take part in cultural life, the right to use and enjoy property, the right to an adequate standard of living, the right to food, and the right to the highest attainable standard of physical and mental health;

Do solemnly request:

1. The international community to commit in Bali to a formal process that will ensure a post-2012 consensus to protect people, planet and prosperity by taking urgent action to stabilize the global climate and ensure that temperature rises fall well below 2°C above pre-industrial averages, and that greenhouse gas concentrations are less than 450ppm, consistent with the principles of common but differentiated responsibilities.
2. The members of AOSIS in New York to consider including the human dimension of global climate change as one of the agenda items for the meeting of AOSIS Ministers in Bali, and to explore possible alternatives for advancing this initiative in Bali in order to stress the moral and ethical imperatives for action;.

3. The Conference of the Parties of the United Nations Framework Convention on Climate Change, with the help of the Secretariat, under Article 7.2(l), to seek the cooperation of the Office of the United Nations High Commissioner for Human Rights and the United Nations Human Rights Council in assessing the human rights implications of climate change.
4. The Office of the United Nations High Commissioner for Human Rights to conduct a detailed study into the effects of climate change on the full enjoyment of human rights, which includes relevant conclusions and recommendations thereon, to be submitted prior to the tenth session of the Human Rights Council.
5. The United Nations Human Rights Council to convene, in March 2009, a debate on human rights and climate change.

Committed to an inclusive process that puts people, their prosperity, homes, survival and rights at the centre of the climate change debate, other AOSIS members not present in Malé are invited to endorse this Declaration;

Malé, Republic of Maldives, 14 November 2007

13

Human Rights in the Climate Change Regime

From Rio to Paris and Beyond

Lavanya Rajamani[*]

INTRODUCTION

It is now "beyond debate" that the adverse effects of climate change will, in their severity, threaten a range of human rights, including the rights to life, health, food, and housing.[1] There is also a dawning recognition that measures taken to mitigate and adapt to climate change have the potential to impinge on human rights.[2] Even with nationally determined contributions from 189 states[3] covering over 95 percent of global emissions,[4] the chances of stabilizing temperature increase at 2°C or 1.5°C – at which level the adverse effects of climate change are manageable – are limited.[5] The need to prepare for severe adverse effects, and to recognize and address their impact on threatened human rights, is gathering tremendous

* Professor, Centre for Policy Research, New Delhi.

1 See, e.g., Human Rights Council res. 32/33 (June 28, 2016); Office of the High Commissioner for Human Rights, *Understanding Human Rights and Climate Change: Submission of the Office of the High Commissioner for Human Rights to the 21st Conference of the Parties to the United Nations Framework Convention on Climate Change* (November 26, 2015). The human rights approach to climate change is also discussed in Intergovernmental Panel on Climate Change, *Climate Change 2014: Mitigation of Climate Change* (2014), p. 1027. The phrase "beyond debate" was used by John Knox on December 3, 2015, during the Paris Conference of the Parties to the UN Framework Convention on Climate Change (UNFCCC). See *"COP21: States' human rights obligations encompass climate change" – UN expert* (December 3, 2015), available at www.ohchr.org/EN/NewsEvents/Pages/DisplayNews.aspx?NewsID=16836&LangID=E.

2 See, e.g., Human Rights Council res. 32/33, pmbl. para. 5; Human Rights Council res. 29/15 (June 30, 2015), pmbl. para. 3; Human Rights Council res. 26/27 (June 25, 2014), pmbl. para. 3; Human Rights Council res. 18/22 (September 30, 2011), pmbl. para. 4.

3 The intended nationally determined contributions (INDCs) are available at the UNFCCC website, at: www4.unfccc.int/submissions/indc/Submission%20Pages/submissions.aspx.

4 See World Resource Institute, CAIT Climate Data Explorer, available at: http://cait.wri.org/indc.

5 United Nations Environment Programme, *The Emissions Gap Report 2015* (November 2015), p. 26 (INDCs become most consistent with long-term scenarios that limit global average

momentum. Yet, until recently, no legally binding international climate instrument explicitly recognized the existence of intersections between human rights concerns and climate change. The 2015 Paris Agreement,[6] in a marked departure from earlier climate change instruments, contains an explicit reference, albeit in the preamble, to human rights. In addition, it recognizes special interests and vulnerabilities, and it is implicitly attentive to the need to create enabling socioeconomic conditions for the effective protection of human rights. It stops short, however, of recognizing a right to a healthy environment or by extension to a stable climate.

This chapter aims to chart the increasing currency of human rights discourses and the appetite among states to integrate human rights language in the international climate change regime from the 1992 UN Framework Convention on Climate Change (UNFCCC)[7] to the 2015 Paris Agreement. To do so, the chapter will first examine the references to human rights and interests (albeit not framed in rights language) in the UNFCCC, the 1997 Kyoto Protocol,[8] and the decisions of Conferences of the Parties (COPs) under these instruments, in particular the 2010 Cancun Agreements.[9] It will next explore the discussion and debate on various human rights in the lead-up to and during the Paris Climate Conference, drawing on the submissions of parties in the four-year negotiating process from the Durban COP in 2011 to Paris in 2015.[10] It will also deconstruct the text of the preambular reference to human rights in the Paris Agreement, and identify complementary provisions that have human rights dimensions. Although this text does not explicitly endorse a right to a healthy environment, the inclusion of rights language in relation to climate impacts strengthens the argument that such a right may be closer to acknowledgment at the international level.

temperature increase to below 3–3.5°C by the end of the century with >66 percent chance); UNFCCC, *Synthesis Report on the Aggregate Effect of the Intended Nationally Determined Contributions*, UN Doc. FCCC/CP/2015/7 (October 30, 2015), p. 11 (According to the Fifth Assessment Report of the Intergovernmental Panel on Climate Change, the total global cumulative emissions since 2011 that are consistent with a global average temperature rise of less than 2°C above pre-industrial levels at a likely (>66 percent) probability is 1,000 Gt CO_2. Considering the aggregate effect of the INDCs, global cumulative CO_2 emissions are expected to equal 54 (52–56) percent by 2025 and 75 (72–77) percent by 2030 of that 1,000 Gt CO_2.).

6 Paris Agreement, December 12, 2015, in force November 4, 2016, U.N. Doc. FCCC/CP/2015/19.

7 United Nations Framework Convention on Climate Change (UNFCCC), New York, May 9, 1992, in force March 21, 1994, 1771 UNTS 107.

8 Kyoto Protocol to the United Nations Framework Convention on Climate Change, December 11, 1997, in force February 16, 2005, 2302 UNTS 148.

9 UNFCCC, *Report on the Conference of the Parties on its sixteenth session*, UN Doc. FCCC/CP/2010/7/Add. 1 (March 15, 2011).

10 UNFCCC, *Report on the Conference of the Parties on its seventeenth session*, Decision 1/CP.17, UN Doc. FCCC/CP/2011/9/Add.1 (March 15, 2012).

HUMAN RIGHTS UNDER THE UNFCCC AND THE KYOTO PROTOCOL

The UNFCCC and the Kyoto Protocol do not recognize a right to a healthy environment. Indeed, there is minimal rights language in these instruments and in the decisions taken by parties to these instruments. To the extent that rights are referred to, engaged, or implied by any of the provisions of these instruments, it is in relation to established rights such as the rights to life, health, and food, or contested rights such as the right to development, rather than the right to a healthy environment.

Explicit Rights References

The only explicit reference to a "right" in the UNFCCC is in relation to sustainable development. UNFCCC Article 3(4), in relevant part, reads: "The Parties have a right to, and should, promote sustainable development." The right recognized here is "to promote sustainable development," not a "right to development," which was unpalatable to many developed countries.[11] It was unpalatable not just because of the long-articulated concerns with such a right, but also because in the context of climate change a right to development could translate into a right to emit.

Since the early days of negotiations on climate change, developing countries have advanced an equity perspective on climate change – a perspective that is underpinned by human rights concerns. The crux of their argument rests on an appreciation of differences between countries – differences in contributions to the carbon stock and flow in the atmosphere (historical versus current and future), nature of emissions (survival versus luxury), economic status (poverty versus wealth),[12] and physical impacts, including their ability to cope with them (severe versus adaptable). In their view, these differences in contributions to carbon stock, nature of emissions use, and economic status suggest that developing countries should only be expected to contribute to solving the problem to the extent that they are enabled and supported to do so.[13]

While the UNFCCC does not endorse a right to development, it recognizes the central role that development plays in the climate change regime. UNFCCC Article 2 (objective) specifies that stabilization of greenhouse gases (GHGs) in the atmosphere must be achieved within a time frame sufficient to "enable economic development to proceed in a sustainable manner." The discussions in the climate

[11] See Susan Biniaz, *Comma but Differentiated Responsibilities: Punctuation and 30 other ways negotiators have resolved issues in the international climate regime* (Sabin Centre for Climate Change Law, 2016).

[12] For an early articulation of this perspective, see Anil Agarwal and Sunita Narain, *Global Warming in an Unequal World: A Case of Environmental Colonialism* (Centre for Science and Environment, 1991), p. 3.

[13] UNFCCC, art. 4(7).

negotiations, and on the sidelines of it, on survival and luxury emissions,[14] the contraction and convergence proposal (based on per capita CO_2 emission entitlements),[15] the Greenhouse Development Rights framework (based on the right of all people to reach a dignified level of sustainable human development),[16] equitable access to sustainable development,[17] and the equity reference framework[18] draw on the equity-based right to development. There are numerous provisions in the UNFCCC that reflect these concerns of developing countries. These are discussed later in this chapter.

In the decades since the Convention was negotiated, these concerns with development, and hence perhaps implicitly the conditions for effective protection of human rights, featured prominently in discussions and decisions. And while there are, as we shall see, interests and vulnerabilities recognized and addressed, it is only in the Cancun Agreements in 2010 that parties are explicitly urged to "fully respect human rights" in all climate change related actions.[19] The Cancun Agreements are decisions taken by the Conference of Parties to the UNFCCC and, although not legally binding in a formal sense, they are relevant factors in interpreting the UNFCCC.[20]

[14] See Mark J. Mwandosya, *Survival Emissions: A Perspective from the South on Global Climate Negotiations* (Centre for Energy, Environment, Science and Technology, 1999), p. 74.

[15] Global Commons Institute, "Contraction and Convergence: A Global Solution for a Global Problem" (June 3, 1997). More details available at Global Commons Institute, Contraction and Convergence (C&C) – Climate Truth and Reconciliation, www.gci.org.uk/contconv/cc.html#intro.

[16] Paul Baer et al., *The Greenhouse Development Rights Framework: The Right to Development in a Climate Constrained World* (Heinrich Böll Foundation, Christian Aid, EcoEquity, and Stockholm Environment Institute, 2d ed., 2008).

[17] Cancun Agreements, para. 6; BASIC experts, *Equitable access to sustainable development: Contribution to the body of scientific knowledge* (BASIC expert group: Beijing, Brasilia, Cape Town and Mumbai, 2011).

[18] Submission by Swaziland on behalf of the African Group under Workstream I of the ADP (October 8, 2013), available at https://unfccc.int/files/documentation/submissions_from_parties/adp/application/pdf/adp_african_group_workstream_1_20131008.pdf.

[19] Cancun Agreements, para. 8.

[20] The Cancun Agreements represent decisions taken by Conferences of Parties, and these are not, save in the exception, legally binding in a formal sense. Jutta Brunnée, "COPing with Consent: Law-Making Under Multilateral Environmental Agreements," *Leiden Journal of International Law* 15(1) (2002), pp. 1–52, 15. A COP decision may be considered as a "subsequent agreement between the Parties regarding the interpretation of the treaty or the application of its provisions," under Article 31(3)(a) of the Vienna Convention on the Law of Treaties, May 23, 1969, in force January 27, 1980, 1155 UNTS 331. In *Whaling in the Antarctic (Australia v. Japan; New Zealand intervening)*, [2014] ICJ Rep. 226, the International Court of Justice noted that while recommendations of the Whaling Commission are not binding, "when they are adopted by consensus or by a unanimous vote, they may be relevant for the interpretation of the Convention or its Schedule." Ibid., para. 46. The precise legal status of COP decisions, however, depends on the enabling clause, the language and content of the decisions, and the parties' behavior and legal expectations. All of these are typically prone to varying interpretations. From a formal legal perspective, COP decisions are not, absent explicit authorization, legally binding on parties. And they are not capable of creating substantive new obligations,

Implicit Endorsement of Rights

The UNFCCC implicitly endorses certain procedural rights in relation to the environment. UNFCCC Article 6(a) obliges the parties to promote and facilitate public access to information on climate change and its effects, and public participation in addressing climate change and its effects.[21] Some groups have also read, rather implausibly, the right to food and the right to development into UNFCCC Article 2.[22] The GHG stabilization goal in Article 2 is to be achieved within a timeframe to ensure that "food production is not threatened and to enable economic development to proceed in a sustainable manner."[23]

Recognition of Interests

The UNFCCC recognizes interests that have implications for human rights, and can be interpreted as an endorsement of certain rights, although these are not framed in rights language. For instance, the UNFCCC defines "adverse effects of climate change" as changes that have "significant deleterious effects" on, *inter alia*, "human health and welfare." Both the UNFCCC and its Kyoto Protocol are squarely focused on "combatting climate change and the adverse effects thereof."[24]

Recognition and Protection of Vulnerable Groups

Although the UNFCCC and its Kyoto Protocol do not explicitly recognize and protect groups that suffer from extreme vulnerability, the 2010 Cancun Agreements do. The Cancun Agreements note "that the effects of climate change will be felt most acutely by those segments of the population that are already vulnerable owing to geography, gender, age, indigenous or minority status, or disability."[25] They also recognize the need to engage a broad range of stakeholders at all levels, "including youth and persons with disabilities," and recognize "that gender equality and the effective participation of women and indigenous peoples are

since such obligations would require state consent expressed through conventional means (signature/ratification, etc.). See generally Brunnée, "COPing with Consent."

21 UNFCCC, art. 6(a)(ii) and (iii).

22 Submission of Chile on behalf of AILAC to the ADP on Human Rights and Climate Change, May 31, 2015, www4.unfccc.int/Submissions/Lists/OSPSubmissionUpload/195_99_130775585079215037-Chile%20on%20behalf%20of%20AILAC%20HR%20and%20CC.docx.

23 UNFCCC, art. 2.

24 Ibid., art. 3(1). See generally UNFCCC, pmbl. paras. 1, 2, 16, 17, 19; Kyoto Protocol, arts. 2(3), 3(14), 12(8).

25 Cancun Agreements, pmbl. para. 7.

important for effective action on all aspects of climate change."[26] States are required to engage all relevant stakeholders undertaking measures to reduce emissions from deforestation and forest degradation in developing countries (REDD).[27] The Green Climate Fund, operationalized in 2012, is also required to involve relevant institutions and stakeholders and pursue, *inter alia*, a gender-sensitive approach.[28]

In relation to adaptation, the Cancun Agreements affirm that enhanced action on adaptation should follow a "gender-sensitive, participatory and fully transparent" approach, and that adaptation measures should be guided and based on, as appropriate, traditional and indigenous knowledge.[29] These decisions also urge parties to undertake measures to "enhance understanding, coordination and cooperation with regard to climate change induced displacement, migration and planned relocation . . ."[30]

Conditions for Effective Protection of Human Rights

It is axiomatic that poverty, in particular extreme poverty, and underdevelopment undermine the effective realization of human rights.[31] The UNFCCC is attentive to this concern, albeit it is not articulated in human rights terms. The UNFCCC recognizes in preambular recitals that the share of emissions from developing countries will grow to meet their social and developmental needs,[32] and that developing countries have legitimate priority needs for "sustained economic growth" and "eradication of poverty."[33] UNFCCC Article 4(7) underscores this

[26] Ibid. See also UNFCCC Report of the Conference of the Parties on its twentieth session, Decision 18/CP.20, UN Doc. FCCC/CP/2014/10/Add.3 (February 2, 2015) (Lima work program on gender).

[27] Cancun Agreements, app. 1, para. 2(d).

[28] UNFCCC Report on the Conference of the Parties, Decision 3/CP.17, UN Doc. FCCC/CP/2011/9/Add.1 (March 15, 2012), Annex, para. 3 (launching the Green Climate Fund).

[29] Cancun Agreements, para. 12; see also UNFCCC Report on the Conference of the Parties, Decision 5/CP.17, UN Doc. FCCC/CP/2011/9/Add.1 (March 15, 2012) (National Adaptation Plans).

[30] Cancun Agreements, para. 14(f). For a full discussion of this paragraph, see Koko Warner, "Human Migration and Displacement in the Context of Adaptation to Climate Change: The Cancun Adaptation Framework and Potential for Future Action," *Environment and Planning C: Policy and Space* 1061 (2012), p. 30.

[31] See Magdalena Sepúlveda Carmona, Final Draft of the Guiding Principles on Extreme Poverty and Human Rights, Submitted by the Special Rapporteur on Extreme Poverty and Human Rights, UN Doc. A/HRC/21/39 (July 18, 2012), adopted by Human Rights Council res. 21/11 (September 27, 2012).

[32] UNFCCC, pmbl. para. 3; see also ibid., pmbl. para. 22.

[33] Ibid., pmbl. para. 21; see also ibid., pmbl. para. 10.

recognition in operational text by noting that "economic and social development and poverty eradication are the first and overriding priorities of the developing country Parties."[34]

In an effort, *inter alia*, to support developing countries in pursuing development and eradicating poverty, the UNFCCC and its Kyoto Protocol contain a pervasive form of differential treatment in favor of developing countries, including in relation to central mitigation obligations, implementation, and reporting, and through the provision of support.[35] Such differentiation can be sourced to the principle of common but differentiated responsibilities and respective capabilities.[36] In addition, the UNFCCC recognizes the "specific needs and special situations" of least developed countries[37] and provides them with special treatment.[38] The UNFCCC also recognizes the specific needs of developing country parties that are particularly vulnerable,[39] as well as of those arising from the adverse effects of climate change and/or the impact of the implementation of response measures.[40]

The Kyoto Protocol takes differentiation between developed and developing countries a step further, in that developed countries have GHG mitigation targets while developing countries do not.[41] It also endorses "sustainable development" insofar as the clean development mechanism is premised on the pursuit of sustainable development in developing countries.[42]

THE 2015 PARIS AGREEMENT

In 2015, after a four-year negotiating process, the parties arrived at the Paris Agreement, the third of the three climate treaties. It was signed by a record-breaking 174 states and the European Union on April 22, 2016, Earth Day, and entered into force on November 4, 2016.[43]

34 The language of "overriding priorities" is reiterated in the Cancun Agreements, para. 6 (in the context of "peaking" of global and national greenhouse gas emissions).

35 See generally Lavanya Rajamani, *Differential Treatment in International Environmental Law* (Oxford University Press, 2006).

36 UNFCCC, art. 3(1).

37 Ibid., art. 4(9).

38 See ibid., art. 12(5); UNFCCC Report on the Conference of the Parties on its Seventh Session, Decision 7/CP.7, UN Doc. FCCC/CP/2001/13/Add.12 (January 1, 2002) (funding under the Convention).

39 UNFCCC, art. 3(2).

40 Ibid., pmbl. para. 19, art. 4(8).

41 Kyoto Protocol, art. 3.

42 Ibid., art. 12.

43 It has 160 parties as of September 1, 2017. See Paris Agreement – Status of Ratification, http://unfccc.int/paris_agreement/items/9444.php.

Explicit Rights References

In contrast to earlier phases of the climate negotiations, in the four-year process leading up to Paris many parties,[44] NGOs,[45] and international bodies[46] urged the inclusion of human rights concerns in the Paris Agreement.[47] In this phase, too, the emphasis was not on the right to a healthy environment and its extension to climate protection, but to established human rights such as the rights to life, food, shelter, and health, that could be adversely affected by climate impacts and responses. In an effort to headline human rights, eighteen countries, led by Costa Rica, voluntarily pledged in February 2015 to "enable meaningful collaboration between national representatives in these two processes [UNFCCC and Human Rights Council] to increase our understanding of how human rights obligations inform better climate action."[48] In Paris, many parties sought an explicit human rights reference in an operative part of the Agreement, in particular in Article 2.[49]

[44] See, e.g., *Submission of Chile on behalf of AILAC to the ADP on Human Rights and Climate Change* (May 31, 2015), www4.unfccc.int/Submissions/Lists/OSPSubmissionUpload/195_99_130775585079215037-Chile%20on%20behalf%20of%20AILAC%20HR%20and%20CC.docx; *Proposal of Ecuador, Durban Platform* (March 3, 2013), http://unfccc.int/files/documentation/submissions_from_parties/adp/application/pdf/adp_ecuador_workstream_1_20130301.pdf, p. 2; EIG Surgical edits (October 19, 2015), http://unfccc.int/files/bodies/awg/application/pdf/adp2–11_ws1_eig_19oct2015.pdf; *EU Text Suggestions on Key Issues* (October 19, 2015), http://unfccc.int/files/bodies/awg/application/pdf/151019_eu_proposed_edits_agreement.pdf; *Textual insertions of the Philippines for the Draft Agreement* (October 19, 2015), http://unfccc.int/files/meetings/bonn_oct_2015/application/pdf/textual_insertions_of_the_philippines_for_the_draft_agreement.pdf.

[45] See, e.g., *Civil Society Submission to the Ad Hoc Working Group on the Durban Platform for Enhanced Action Calling for Human Rights Protections in the 2015 Climate Agreement* (February 7, 2015), http://unfccc.int/files/documentation/submissions_from_non-party_stakeholders/application/pdf/489.pdf; Human Rights and Climate Change Working Group, *Submission to the Ad Hoc Working Group on the Durban Platform for Enhanced Action Regarding Information, Views and Proposals Related to the Durban Platform Workplan Under Workstream 1* (March 1, 2013), http://unfccc.int/resource/docs/2013/smsn/ngo/303.pdf; *Submission to the ADP by the Mary Robinson Foundation – Climate Justice* (March 1, 2013), http://unfccc.int/resource/docs/2013/smsn/un/306.pdf.

[46] See, e.g., OHCHR, *An Open Letter from Special Procedures mandate-holders of the Human Rights Council to the State Parties to the UN Framework Convention on Climate Change on the occasion of the meeting of the Ad Hoc Working Group on the Durban Platform for Enhanced Action in Bonn* (20–25 October 2014) (October 17, 2014), www.ohchr.org/Documents/HRBodies/SP/SP_To_UNFCCC.pdf; OHCHR, Special Procedures of the United Nations Human Rights Council, *The Effects of Climate Change on the Full Enjoyment of Human Rights* (April 30, 2015), www.thecvf.org/wp-content/uploads/2015/05/humanrightsSRHRE.pdf.

[47] For a recap of the advocacy movement on human rights in the lead-up to Paris, see Benoit Mayer, "Human Rights in the Paris Agreement," *Climate Law* 109 (2016), p. 6.

[48] *The Geneva Pledge for Human Rights in Climate Action* (February 13, 2015), www.mrfcj.org/resources/geneva-pledge-human-rights.

[49] See, e.g., *Submission of Chile on behalf of AILAC to the ADP on Human Rights and Climate Change*. See also, for media reportage, Human Rights Watch, *UN: Human Rights crucial in addressing climate change - Paris Agreement Should Ensure Transparency, Accountability and*

Article 2 identifies the purpose of the Paris Agreement,[50] sets the long-term temperature goal, and frames the implementation of the Paris Agreement. Early versions of Article 2(2) contained references to human rights.[51] Proponents hoped that a reference to human rights in this provision would have helped promote the protection of human rights in the implementation of the Paris Agreement.[52]

This, however, proved difficult to secure, for several reasons. First and foremost, some parties believed that introducing human rights concerns into the "purpose" of the Paris Agreement would dilute the climate objectives it contained,[53] and argued that other fora would be more appropriate for furtherance of human rights objectives.[54] Next, it was not obvious which rights, if any, should be singled out for protection in the context of implementing the Paris Agreement. There appeared to be broad consensus on rights such as those of women, but others such as the rights of those under occupation provoked fierce debate. The solution mooted was to include a generic reference to human rights, but this proved unpalatable to most parties, as each party or group of parties was invested in one or more specific rights to the exclusion of others.[55] In any case, some argued that a generic reference to rights would lead to greater conceptual fuzziness, and thus less certainty and predictability in implementing the Paris Agreement, as well as protection of the relevant human rights. These reasons, among others, dictated the eventual compromise to reflect

Participation, (December 3, 2015), www.hrw.org/news/2015/12/03/un-human-rights-crucial-addressing-climate-change.

50 Article 3 identifies Article 2 as the "purpose."

51 See *Draft Paris Outcome, Revised draft conclusions proposed by the Co-Chairs of the Ad Hoc Working Group on the Durban Platform for Enhanced Action*, UN Doc. FCCC/ADP/2015/L.6/Rev.1, Annex I (December 5, 2015) (Draft Agreement and Draft Decision). See also *Draft agreement and draft decision on workstreams 1 and 2 of the Ad Hoc Working Group on the Durban Platform for Enhanced Action* (edited version of November 6, 2015, re-issued November 10, 2015), ADP.2015.11. Informal Note.

52 Human rights references are included in Article 2(2) in earlier versions of the negotiating text. See e.g., *Draft Paris Outcome, Proposal by the President*, Version 1 of December 9, 2015 at 15:00, http://unfccc.int/resource/docs/2015/cop21/eng/da01.pdf; and *Draft Paris Outcome, Revised draft conclusions proposed by the Co-Chairs of the Ad Hoc Working Group on the Durban Platform for Enhanced Action*, December 5, 2015, UN Doc. FCCC/ADP/2015/L.6/Rev.1, Annex I (December 5, 2015).

53 See, e.g., Government of Norway, *COP 21: Indigenous Peoples, Human Rights and Climate Change* (December 7, 2015), www.regjeringen.no/no/aktuelt/cop21-indigenous-peoples-human-rights-and-climat-changes/id2466047.

54 See, e.g., *New Zealand Submission to the Ad Hoc Working Group on the Durban Platform for Enhanced Action: Views on options and ways for further increasing the level of global ambition* (March 28, 2012), http://unfccc.int/resource/docs/2012/adp1/eng/misc01.pdf.

55 See Indigenous Rising: An Indigenous Environmental Network Project, *Indigenous Rights on the Chopping Block of UN COP21 Paris Climate Accord* (December 4, 2015), http://indigenousrising.org/indigenous-rights-on-chopping-block-of-un-cop21-paris-climate-accord.

selected human rights in the preamble, which provides context,[56] rather than in an operational provision of the Paris Agreement, which has greater legal gravitas.[57]

Eventually the only explicit reference to human rights agreed to in the Paris Agreement occurs in the preamble. The relevant preambular recital reads:

> Parties should, when taking action to address climate change, respect, promote, and consider their respective obligations on human rights, the right to health, the rights of indigenous peoples, local communities, migrants, children, persons with disabilities and people in vulnerable situations, and the right to development, as well as gender equality, empowerment of women, and intergenerational equity.[58]

This recital carefully circumscribes the impact of an explicit reference to human rights in the Paris Agreement. First, this reference addresses only the human rights aspects of response measures ("when taking action"), not of climate change itself. This is a narrower approach than that advocated by the Office of the High Commissioner of Human Rights (OHCHR), which considers that states are obliged to "take affirmative measures to prevent human rights harms caused by climate change, including foreseeable long-term harms."[59] The Paris Agreement's narrow approach recommends that states should respect, promote, and consider human rights when taking response measures, but is silent with respect to whether they should take human rights considerations into account in determining the ambition, scope, and scale of their mitigation or adaptation actions.

Second, the provision recommends that parties "respect, promote and consider" their human rights obligations, not "respect, protect, promote and fulfill"[60] their obligations, as twenty-eight special rapporteurs and independent experts of the Human Rights Council had urged states to do.[61] In human rights discourses, the terms "respect," "protect," and "fulfill" are terms of art, and the absence of "protect" and "fulfill" is not happenstance. Respecting a right requires states to refrain from interfering with the right, protecting a right requires states to prevent others from interfering with the right, and fulfilling a right requires states to adopt appropriate

56 Vienna Convention, art. 31(2). The preamble is part of the context for purposes of interpretation of the treaty, including its object and purpose. See Anthony Aust, *Modern Treaty Law and Practice*, 2d ed. (Cambridge University Press, 2007), pp. 425–6 (also noting that "the preamble can be the most convenient place to put the leftovers of hopeless causes.").

57 For a discussion of defining elements of legal character, see Lavanya Rajamani, "The 2015 Paris Agreement: Interplay Between Hard, Soft and Non-Obligations," *Journal of Environmental Law* 28 (2016), p. 337, 342–52. See also Daniel Bodansky, "The Legal Character of the Paris Agreement," 25 *Review of European Comparative and International Law* (2016), p. 142.

58 Paris Agreement, pmbl. para. 11.

59 See OHCHR, *Understanding Human Rights and Climate Change*.

60 See ibid. See also OCHCR, Letter from the Special Rapporteur on human rights and the environment (May 4, 2016), http://srenvironment.org/wp-content/uploads/2016/06/Letter-to-SBSTA-UNFCCC-final.pdf.

61 See OHCHR, *An Open Letter from Special Procedures*.

measures toward the full realization of the right.[62] Thus, while the Paris agreement urges states to refrain from taking actions that might interfere with the listed human rights, it does not, by itself, require them to either prevent others from interfering with the right or adopt measures toward full realization. Instead, the Paris Agreement uses the fuzzier terms "promote" and "consider," which do not necessitate specific actions like the terms "protect" and "fulfill" do.

Third, the recital refers to the parties' "respective obligations," thus ensuring that no new human rights obligations are implied for states or argued as applicable as a result of this reference. There were differences of views among parties on the existence (or lack thereof), characterization, relative importance, and boundaries of the listed human rights. Some parties might not have obligations with respect to one or the other human rights listed in this recital. Some parties might have an obligation with respect to one of those listed in the recital but not necessarily consider it a "right," for instance, the right to development. Further, some parties might conceive of a certain right as an "individual right" while others might conceive of it as a "collective right." For example, the Least Developed Countries consider the "right to development" as a right belonging to individuals[63] and Ecuador as a right belonging to developing countries.[64] Additionally, some proposed human rights such as the "rights of people under occupation" proved so controversial that they are only engaged, if at all, by implication. In this instance, "people in vulnerable situations" could arguably include those under occupation. Parties might not wish to subscribe to all the rights listed, in part because of indeterminacy and vagueness, such as "rights of those in vulnerable situations." In the circumstances, deliberate ambiguity about the extent of application of these specific rights to individual parties was considered desirable.

This also forms part of the explanatory context for the comma between the generic reference to human rights and the specific listing of human rights ("... human rights, right to health ...") in this preambular recital. This comma also generates the desired ambiguity, in that it could be argued that the listing that follows limits the generic reference to human rights or that it is illustrative of the rights engaged. Finally, there is further ambiguity generated by the use of the term "on" ("respective obligations on") only before the interests specifically characterized as "rights" rather than again in relation to "gender equality, empowerment of woman and inter generational equity." It could be argued that the latter are not subject to the "respective obligations" qualification, and have wider application.

[62] See, e.g., Committee on Economic, Social and Cultural Rights, *General Comment 12, The right to adequate food (art. 11)*, UN Doc. E/C.12/1999/5 (May 12, 1999), para. 15.

[63] *Submission by Angola on behalf of the Least Developed Countries Group – 'surgical insertions' to co-chairs non-paper (v. 5 October 2015): ARTICLE 2: Purpose* (October 19, 2015), http://unfccc.int/files/bodies/awg/application/pdf/adp2-11_art2_purpose_ldcs_19oct2015.pdf.

[64] *Submission by Ecuador, Views on Options and Ways for further increasing the level of ambition* (March 28, 2012), http://unfccc.int/resource/docs/2012/adp1/eng/misc01.pdf.

It is clear from this discussion that the only explicit reference to human rights in the Paris Agreement is carefully circumscribed. Nevertheless, the very inclusion of an explicit reference to human rights in this Agreement is crucial, and signals enhanced receptivity to rights concerns and discourses. This is reflected throughout the text of the Paris Agreement, albeit not articulated in human rights terms.

Implicit Endorsement of Rights

The Paris Agreement implicitly endorses certain procedural rights in relation to the environment. Article 12 requires parties to cooperate to "enhance climate change education, training, public awareness, public participation and public access to information." The preamble also underlines the importance of these initiatives.[65]

Recognition of Interests

The Paris Agreement recognizes certain interests that "put a human face on climate change impacts" and underscore the importance of protecting human rights. For instance, in preambular recitals it recognizes the "fundamental priority of safeguarding food security and ending hunger," and the imperatives of "just transition of the workforce and the creation of decent work and quality jobs."[66] The agreement also identifies in the context of the adaptation challenge the need "to protect people, livelihoods and ecosystems."[67]

Recognition and Protection of Vulnerable Groups

The Paris Agreement recognizes and seeks to protect various vulnerable groups. There are several vulnerable groups recognized in the preambular recital on human rights, namely indigenous peoples, local communities, migrants, children, persons with disabilities, people in vulnerable situations, and women.[68] In operative provisions, parties acknowledge that adaptation action should follow a "gender-responsive, participatory and fully transparent approach taking into consideration vulnerable groups, communities and ecosystems" and based on and guided by, *inter alia*, "traditional knowledge" and "knowledge of indigenous peoples."[69] In formulating priorities in their adaptation planning, the parties are required to take into account "vulnerable people, places and ecosystems."[70] Further among the potential areas of international cooperation in relation to loss and damage is listed "resilience of

65 Paris Agreement, pmbl. para. 14.
66 Ibid., pmbl. para. 10.
67 Ibid., art. 7(2).
68 Ibid., pmbl. para. 11.
69 Ibid., art. 7(5).
70 Ibid., art. 9(c).

communities, livelihoods and ecosystems."[71] In relation to capacity building, the parties agreed that it should be "participatory, cross-cutting and gender responsive."[72] In the lead-up to Paris, some parties had also proposed prioritized funding to vulnerable groups, but this does not feature in the final text.

Conditions for the Effective Protection of Human Rights

The Paris Agreement, in line with the UNFCCC, is attentive to the concerns of poverty and underdevelopment in the context of addressing climate change. *Inter alia*, in recognition of competing priorities and concerns in developing countries, the Paris Agreement embodies an approach tailored to the national circumstances of each country.[73] It contains differentiation in favor of developing countries, but a more nuanced and muted version of it than in the UNFCCC.[74] It recognizes the "specific needs and special situations" of least developed countries,[75] and thus provides them special treatment in several respects.[76] The Paris Agreement is also attentive to the risks that underdevelopment coupled with extreme vulnerability poses to human rights protection. The Paris Agreement recognizes the "specific needs and special circumstances" of those developing countries that are particularly vulnerable to the adverse effects of climate change,[77] and extends special treatment to them too.[78]

In addition, the Paris Agreement recognizes the importance of poverty eradication, sustainable development, and equity, all of which directly and indirectly contribute to the effective protection of human rights. The Agreement makes numerous references to equity,[79] sustainable development,[80] equitable access to sustainable development,[81] poverty eradication,[82] and climate justice.[83] While these notions are part of the climate change regime and feature in the UNFCCC and decisions taken by the COPs, they are framed differently in the Paris Agreement. References in the UNFCCC to poverty eradication, for instance, recognize it either

71 Ibid., art. 8(4)(h).
72 Ibid., art. 11(2).
73 See e.g., ibid., pmbl. para. 3, arts. 3, 4(3), 4(19).
74 For further details, see Lavanya Rajamani, "Ambition and Differentiation in the 2015 Paris Agreement: Interpretative Possibilities and Underlying Politics," *International and Comparative Law Quarterly* 65 (2016), p. 493.
75 Paris Agreement, pmbl. para. 6.
76 See ibid., arts. 4(6), 9(4), 9(9), 11(1), 13(3).
77 Ibid., pmbl. para. 5.
78 See ibid., arts. 7(2), 7(6), 9(4), 11(1).
79 Ibid., pmbl. para. 3, arts. 2(2), 4(1), 14(1).
80 Ibid., pmbl. para. 8, arts. 2(1), 4(1), 6, 7(1), 8(1), 10(5).
81 Ibid., pmbl. para. 8.
82 Ibid., pmbl. para. 8, arts. 2(1), 4(1), 6(8).
83 Ibid., pmbl. para. 13.

as a "legitimate priority need"[84] or an "overriding priorit[y],"[85] whereas in the Paris Agreement it is recognized as part of the "context" for action.[86] Nevertheless, it is significant that both the "purpose" of the agreement[87] as well as the "net zero" goal[88] in the Paris Agreement recognize the importance of sustainable development and poverty eradication.

Rights of Nature?

Finally, the preamble to the Paris Agreement arguably contains the faintest of acknowledgments of the emerging discourse on the rights of nature. The rights of nature are defined in the Ecuadorian Constitution as nature's "right to exist, persist, maintain and regenerate its vital cycles, structure, functions and its processes in evolution."[89] Bolivia, Ecuador, and other Bolivarian Alliance (ALBA) countries have long argued that the rights of "Mother Earth" should be the benchmark for the global response to climate change.[90] Although there is limited receptivity to this idea outside ALBA, the Paris Agreement does contain a recital recognizing the importance of "ecosystem integrity," with a further recognition that ecosystems are "recognized by some cultures as Mother Earth."[91]

CONCLUSION: FROM RIO TO PARIS AND BEYOND

The UN climate change regime – the UNFCCC, the Kyoto Protocol, the Paris Agreement, and decisions of the parties under these instruments – do not contain any references, explicit or implicit, to an international right to a healthy environment. They do, however, recognize, to varying degrees, that both climate impacts as well as actions to address climate change have serious implications for a range of human rights. This recognition, nascent in the UNFCCC and its Kyoto Protocol, finds full expression in the preambular language of the 2015 Paris Agreement. The preambular language of the Paris Agreement is an effort to ensure that human rights and environmental agreements are implemented in a mutually reinforcing manner. This in turn testifies to the interconnectedness of all human rights – the right to a healthy

84 Ibid., pmbl. para. 21.
85 Ibid., art. 4(7).
86 See, e.g., ibid., arts. 2(1), 4(1), 6(8).
87 Ibid., art. 2.
88 Ibid., art. 4(1).
89 See, e.g., Constitution of the Republic of Ecuador (2008), art. 71.
90 Indeed, Bolivia's INDC contains such a suggestion. *See Intended Nationally Determined Contribution from the Plurinational State of Bolivia* (October 12, 2015), www4.unfccc.int/submissions/INDC/Published%20Documents/Bolivia/1/INDC-Bolivia-english.pdf. See also *Views of the Like-Minded Developing Countries on Climate Change (LMDC) on Workstreams 1 and 2 of the ADP* (September 24, 2013), https://unfccc.int/files/documentation/submissions_from_parties/adp/application/pdf/adp_lmdc_workstream_1_and_2_20130924.pdf.
91 Paris Agreement, pmbl. para. 13.

environment with the rights to health, food, life, etc. The increasing currency of rights language in the climate regime could be interpreted as suggesting that a right to a healthy environment, inextricably linked with other established rights, may be closer to acknowledgment at the international level.

The UN climate regime has come a long way in three decades in relation to the acknowledgment and articulation of rights in relation to climate impacts and actions. The UNFCCC and its Kyoto Protocol, although they did not articulate concerns and interests in the language of human rights, to varying degrees implicitly endorse certain procedural rights, identify interests that have human rights dimensions, recognize and protect vulnerable groups, and are attentive to underlying socioeconomic conditions that enhance effective realization of human rights.

This wariness of explicit human rights framing has various causes. Many negotiators were skeptical of the utility of a human rights approach, given the complex and laden agenda of the climate process, and the limited space for new methodological or conceptual approaches. Human rights approaches, to be effective, they believed, would need to be integrated and mainstreamed. Existing treaties would need to be reinterpreted in a fashion not envisaged at the time they were negotiated. The existing treaties are primarily concerned with interstate burden sharing for a global environmental problem. They are not rights-focused. Any attempt to reinterpret them in a rights-focused manner would of necessity be contrived. Others were concerned that importing a human rights approach to the climate regime would import the chaos and passion that attaches itself to particular causes and rights. And, that it would add further complexity to an already "super wicked" problem. Parties would need to consider which rights should be highlighted, on what basis, how they should be circumscribed, and how conflicts between rights could be dealt with.

In the last decade, however, concerted action by many NGOs, and some states and international bodies, in particular the Human Rights Council, has catapulted the human rights dimensions of climate change to the top of the agenda. The process that led to the Cancun Agreements saw a smattering of submissions from parties on human rights,[92] while the process leading to the Paris Agreement witnessed a dramatic increase both in lobbying as well as in state engagement on these issues. Nevertheless, some of the earlier wariness of incorporating human rights framing in the climate change regime lingered. Parties chose, therefore, to introduce human rights in a targeted and carefully circumscribed way. They resisted efforts to introduce human rights in a central crosscutting operative provision that would have required parties to take human rights into account in their implementation of the Paris Agreement. Instead, they agreed on a delicately crafted preambular recital that ensures that no new rights are created or argued as applicable for

[92] See Lavanya Rajamani, "The Increasing Currency and Relevance of Rights-Based Perspectives in the International Negotiations on Climate Change," *Journal of Environmental Law* 22 (2010), p. 391.

parties, but that parties take their respective human rights obligations into account in their climate change actions. In addition to the explicit reference to human rights in the preamble, the Paris Agreement endorses, implicitly, certain procedural rights, recognizes special interests and vulnerabilities, and is attentive to the need to create enabling socioeconomic conditions for the effective protection of human rights. Together these references, provisions, and hat tips go much farther than earlier instruments – the UNFCCC, Kyoto Protocol, and COP decisions under them – to ensure that climate change and human rights instruments operate in a mutually reinforcing manner. The extent to which these provisions will be developed and operationalized is a work in progress. And the extent to which developments in the UN climate regime will help advance arguments for an international right to a healthy environment, and by extension to a stable climate, remains to be seen.

14

The Right to a Healthy Environment and Climate Change

Mismatch or Harmony?

*Sumudu Atapattu**

The link between human rights and the environment and the right to a healthy environment has received considerable scholarly attention in recent years.[1] Indeed, Mary Robinson has called climate change "the biggest human rights issue of the 21st century."[2] Yet many issues still remain unresolved, particularly in the context of climate change. Regional human rights institutions and national judiciaries have been the foci of many of the developments relating to a right to a healthy environment. Even if a right to a healthy environment is emerging under international law, it is not clear how this right can be used in relation to issues that have multiple contributors and multiple victims with sources located outside state borders.

While the general field of human rights and the environment (or environmental rights) has grown phenomenally in a short period of time, its application to related topics such as climate change received attention only recently. Climate change has the potential to undermine many of the protected rights, including by resulting in forced migration,[3] as the UN Office of the High Commissioner for Human Rights

* Director, Research Centers, and Senior Lecturer, University of Wisconsin Law School and Lead Counsel, Center for International Sustainable Development Law.

[1] This chapter draws from the author's book, *Human Rights Approaches to Climate Change: Challenges and Opportunities* (Routledge, 2015). The extensive scholarship on climate change and human rights includes Stephen Humphreys (ed.), *Human Rights and Climate Change* (Cambridge University Press, 2010); John H. Knox, "Climate Change and Human Rights Law," *Virginia Journal of International Law* 50(1) (2009), p. 163; Pamela J. Stephens, "Applying Human Rights Norms to Climate Change: The Elusive Remedy," *Colorado Journal of International Environmental Law and Policy* 21(1) (2010), p. 49.

[2] Mary Robinson Foundation Climate Justice, "Position Paper: Human Rights and Climate Justice" (2014).

[3] See Michael Gerrard, "What Does Environmental Justice Mean in an Era of Global Climate Change?," *Journal of Environmental and Sustainability Law* 19 (2013), p. 278 ("The single greatest adverse impact of climate change on poor populations around the world is likely to be mass migration.").

(OHCHR) highlighted in 2009.[4] The general consensus is that climate change will displace millions of people as a direct result of sea level rise and severe weather events associated with climate change, as well as indirectly due to conflicts over dwindling natural resources, especially water.[5] Thus, there is a clear link between climate change and protected rights; yet the parameters of this link, the human rights obligations of states with regard to climate change both in relation to mitigation and adaptation, and how the vertical relationship between right holders and duty bearers under international human rights law plays out, are some of the lingering questions that need to be further clarified.[6]

This chapter seeks to discuss the link between climate change and human rights, especially the emerging right to a healthy environment at the international level and what it means in the context of climate change. Does the adoption of a stand-alone, substantive right to a healthy environment help or hinder action in relation to climate change? Are procedural rights more beneficial in this context? How do the human rights obligations of states pan out in relation to mitigation and adaptation measures as states decide how to implement their Nationally Determined Contributions under the Paris Agreement? How do these obligations apply in relation to climate migration, displacement, and vulnerable states and communities?

Against this backdrop, this chapter proceeds in four sections. The first traces the emergence of a right to a healthy environment at the international level, while the second discusses environmental rights in the context of climate change. The chapter then discusses the pros and cons of a distinct right to a healthy environment and concludes that even if states are reluctant to adopt such a right, such a right is emerging under international law as a customary law principle or a general principle. The chapter concludes by proposing recommendations, identifying gaps, and highlighting areas for further research.

EMERGENCE OF A RIGHT TO A HEALTHY ENVIRONMENT AT THE INTERNATIONAL LEVEL

With the convergence of human rights and environmental protection fields in the 1980s, victims of environmental degradation and pollution started resorting to the human rights framework to seek redress. While international human rights law does not recognize a stand-alone substantive right to a healthy environment, regional human rights institutions, especially the European Court of Human Rights and the Inter-American Commission on Human Rights, have developed a detailed

[4] OHCHR, *Report on the Relationship between Climate Change and Human Rights*, UN Doc. A/HRC/10/61 (January 15, 2009).

[5] See Gerrard, "Environmental Justice," p. 287; Atapattu, *Human Rights Approaches to Climate Change*, chapter 6.

[6] See ibid., chapter 3.

jurisprudence applying other human rights to environmental issues.[7] This may support an argument that a human right to a healthy environment is emerging as a principle of customary international law, at least at the regional level.

The convergence between human rights and the environment is even more prominent at the national level. Many judiciaries have articulated environmental rights on the basis of constitutional provisions and even directive principles of state policy.[8] Newer constitutions typically incorporate environmental rights, and many national courts have interpreted existing rights expansively to encompass environmental rights.[9] These developments may be evidence that a general principle of international law on a human right to a healthy environment is emerging.[10] Whether it is called a customary principle or a general principle, one thing is clear: there is an increasing trend toward articulating environmental rights at the international level.

One of the main critiques of recognizing a human right to a healthy environment has been the difficulty in defining the parameters of the right. This issue received attention in the *Ogoniland* case before the African Commission of Human Rights in 2001.[11] The Commission elaborated on the right to a satisfactory environment as embodied in the African Charter on Human and Peoples' Rights as follows:

> The right to a general satisfactory environment, as guaranteed under Article 24 of the African Charter or the right to a healthy environment, as it is widely known, therefore imposes clear obligations upon a government. It requires the State to take reasonable and other measures to prevent pollution and ecological degradation, to promote conservation, and to secure an ecologically sustainable development and use of natural resources. . . .
>
> Government compliance with the spirit of Articles 16 and 24 of the African Charter must also include ordering or at least permitting independent scientific monitoring of threatened environments, requiring and publicising environmental and social impact studies prior to any major industrial development, undertaking appropriate monitoring and providing information to those communities exposed to hazardous materials and activities and providing meaningful opportunities

7 See Lilian Chenwi, Chapter 4, and Ole W. Pedersen, Chapter 5.

8 See David R. Boyd, Chapter 2, and Erin Daly and James R. May, Chapter 3; Sumudu Atapattu, "The Role of Human Rights Law in Protecting Environmental Rights in South Asia," in LaDawn Haglund and Robin Stryker, *Closing the Rights Gap: From Human Rights to Social Transformation* (University of California Press, 2015), p.105.

9 See Svitlana Kravchenko and John E. Bonine, *Human Rights and the Environment: Cases, Law, and Policy* (Carolina Academic Press, 2008), chapter 3.

10 See Philippe Sands and Jacqueline Peel, Principles of International Environmental Law, 3d ed. (Cambridge University Press, 2012), p. 117.

11 *Social and Economic Rights Action Centre (SERAC) and the Centre for Economic and Social Rights (CESR)* v. *Nigeria*, Communication. No. 155/96 (2001).

for individuals to be heard and to participate in the development decisions affecting their communities.[12]

Thus, according to the African Commission, the right to a satisfactory environment need not be indeterminate or vague, as some have contended.[13] As embodied in the African Charter, the right comprises both substantive and procedural components. There are clear obligations that flow from the right, including duties to prevent pollution; to require the preparation of environmental and social impact assessments; to undertake appropriate monitoring and provide information to affected communities; and to give affected communities meaningful opportunities to participate in development decisions affecting them.

The International Court of Justice, likewise, has witnessed the convergence of human rights and the environment, in a case arising from the spraying of herbicide by Colombia to eradicate drug-producing crops along the Colombia/Ecuador border. Ecuador alleged that the actions caused transboundary pollution and significant harm in the territory of Ecuador, including damage to indigenous communities. Although the *Case Concerning Aerial Herbicide Spraying (Ecuador* v. *Colombia)* was settled by the parties before a final judgment was delivered, the memorial submitted by Ecuador in 2009 dealt extensively with the human rights impacts of aerial sprayings by Colombia on those living along the Colombia/Ecuador border. It also alleged the violation of rights of indigenous peoples in Ecuador.[14]

Specifically, Ecuador alleged that by failing to prepare a transboundary EIA and provide information to Ecuador and its people, especially indigenous communities, Colombia had violated its obligations under international law, including under several human rights treaties. Ecuador argued that the relationship between three areas of international law – human rights, environmental protection, and indigenous rights – was at the heart of the case and that their interrelationship had long been recognized.[15] Ecuador stated that "[t]heir interrelationship [in the present case] arises from the fact that the toxic herbicides used by Colombia in aerial spraying of border areas have significantly harmful consequences for the health

[12] Ibid., paras. 52, 53. Article 24 of the African Charter states: "All peoples shall have the right to a general satisfactory environment favourable to their development." Article 16 states: "1. Every individual shall have the right to enjoy the best attainable state of physical and mental health. 2. States parties to the present Charter shall take the necessary measures to protect the health of their people and to ensure that they receive medical attention when they are sick." African Charter on Human and Peoples' Rights, June 27, 1981, in force October 21, 1986, 1520 UNTS 217.

[13] See Alan Boyle, "The Role of International Human Rights Law in the Protection of the Environment," in Alan E. Boyle and Michael R. Anderson (eds.), *Human Rights Approaches to Environmental Protection* (Oxford University Press, 1998), p 51 (noting that "indeterminacy is thus a problem, but not necessarily an insurmountable one").

[14] Memorial of Ecuador, vol. 1 (2009), available at: www.icj-cij.org/docket/files/138/17540.pdf.

[15] Ibid., p. 322.

and well-being of people, natural resources and environment in the affected areas of Ecuador."[16] In particular, Ecuador alleged that the spraying adversely affected the human rights of residents in the border area, including their rights to life, health, food, water, property, information, humane treatment, private life, and a healthy environment. Ecuador noted that the right to a healthy environment is closely related to the enjoyment of several other rights, and stated that what constitutes a healthy environment must be determined by reference to the natural, social, economic, and cultural character of the region in question.[17] It concluded:

> Colombian aerial sprayings over Ecuadorian territory have destroyed peoples' "most basic conditions of survival" and have resulted in a violation by Colombia of the right to a healthy environment as set out in the 1988 Additional Protocol to the American Convention on Human Rights. Colombia's failure to take preventive measures, including mechanisms to facilitate access to information and participation, aggravates its international responsibility.[18]

HUMAN RIGHTS, THE RIGHT TO A HEALTHY ENVIRONMENT, AND CLIMATE CHANGE

This section addresses the link between climate change and human rights and to what extent a rights framework would help victims of climate change. The first attempt to apply human rights to climate change was the petition filed by the Inuit people of the United States and Canada against the United States before the Inter-American Commission on Human Rights in 2005.[19] The petitioners argued that the United States, then the biggest contributor to greenhouse gases, was responsible for the damage caused to the Arctic by climate change which, in turn, was leading to a violation of their protected rights. Although the Commission dismissed the petition

[16] Ibid.

[17] Ibid.

[18] Ibid., p 367. Ecuador also addressed the extraterritorial application of human rights law, which has been a hotly debated issue. Ibid., p. 316 ("It would be unconscionable to so interpret the responsibility under article 2 of the [International] Covenant [on Civil and Political Rights] as to permit a State party to perpetrate violations of the Covenant on the territory of another State, which violations it could not perpetrate on its own territory.") (quoting *Delia Saldias de Lopez* v. *Uruguay*, Comm. No. 52/1979, UN Doc. CCPR/C/OP/1 (Human Rights Committee, 1984), at 88, para. 12.3). Ecuador further alleged that it would be illogical to interpret Article 14(2) of the 1988 Narcotics Convention (which requires each party to "take appropriate measures to prevent illicit cultivation of and to eradicate plants containing narcotic or psychotropic substances ... cultivated illicitly in its territory" and provides that "the measures adopted shall respect fundamental human rights ... as well as the protection of the environment") "as if it required each party only to protect human rights and the environment within its own territory but not in neighbouring countries." Ibid.

[19] See Andrew D. Emhardt, "Climate Change and the Inuit: Bringing an Effective Human Rights Claim to the United Nations," *Indiana International & Comparative Law Review* 24(2) (2014), p. 515.

on the ground that there was insufficient evidence, it did hold a hearing on climate change and human rights and said that it would remain seized of the issue.[20]

Despite its dismissal, or perhaps due to it, this case succeeded in bringing international attention to the plight of the Inuit and the fact that climate change can undermine many of the protected rights of people. This petition was no doubt an impetus for the Human Rights Council to request the UN Office of the High Commissioner for Human Rights to prepare a report on the link between climate change and human rights. The report, published in 2009, explained that climate change threatened the enjoyment of a wide range of human rights, including rights to life and health.[21]

That climate change will lead to the infringement of many protected rights, if not all, is no longer debated. What is debated is the nature of states' human rights obligations in relation to climate change. Climate change is a global issue that has ramifications for communities at the local level. The accumulation of greenhouse gases in the atmosphere over a long period of time emitted by every member of the international community has given rise to global warming and climate change. Thus, identifying a perpetrator and establishing the causal link for damage associated with climate change under traditional principles of state responsibility[22] is an impossible task even though we know who the main contributors are.[23]

Thus, the question is what obligations derive under international human rights law with regard to climate change. The Paris Agreement on Climate Change seems to have addressed the issue somewhat – it calls upon states to "respect, promote and *consider* their respective obligations on human rights" when taking action to address

[20] See Megan S. Chapman, "Climate Change and the Regional Human Rights Systems, *Sustainable Development Law and Policy* 10(2) (2010), p 37; Paul Crowley, "Nobel Prize Nominee Testifies About Global Warming, March 1, 2007," www.ciel.org/Publications/IACHR_WC_Mar07.pdf.

[21] OHCHR, *Report on Climate Change and Human Rights*.

[22] State responsibility principles require the identification of the perpetrator, the establishment of the causal link between the damage in question, and the activity of the perpetrator in question. See International Law Commission, *Draft Articles on Responsibility of States for Internationally Wrongful Acts*, Official Records of the General Assembly, Fifty-Sixth Session, Supplement No. 10, UN Doc. A/56/10 (2001), chapter V. National judiciaries have developed interesting theories, such as the market share liability principle, to address some of these challenges. See Samantha Lawson, "The Conundrum of Climate Change Causation: Using Market Share Liability to Satisfy the Identification Requirement in *Native Village of Kivalina* v. *Exxonmobil Co.*," *Fordham Environmental Law Review* 22(2) (2011), p. 433; Sumudu Atapattu, "Climate Change, Differentiated Responsibilities and State Responsibility: Devising Novel Legal Strategies for Damage Caused by Climate Change," in Benjamin J. Richardson et al. (eds.), *Climate Law and Developing Countries: Legal and Policy Challenges for the World Economy* (Edward Elgar Publishing 2009), p. 37.

[23] Aggregating emissions by States, China is currently the biggest contributor, while the United States is responsible for almost a quarter of all historic emissions. Ninety companies are responsible for almost two-thirds of all greenhouse gas emissions. Suzanne Goldenberg, "Just 90 Companies Caused Two-Thirds of Man-Made Global Warming Emissions," *The Guardian* (November 20, 2013).

climate change.[24] While this language acknowledges the link between climate change and human rights, such an acknowledgment is different from asking what obligations, if any, human rights law imposes on states with regard to climate change. The Paris Agreement has watered down the requirement in human rights treaties that adopt a typology of respect, protect, and *fulfill* with regard to human rights obligations.[25] "Consider" is a much more fluid and soft requirement than "fulfill."

While this dilution of obligations in the context of climate change and the deletion of this obligation from the operative part of the Agreement[26] is unfortunate, the inclusion of human rights in the preamble is a major step forward, as it is the first time that a reference to human rights was explicitly included in a global environmental treaty.[27] As the Special Rapporteur on human rights and the environment noted:

> In an important sense, the Paris Agreement signifies the recognition by the international community that climate change poses unacceptable threats to the full enjoyment of human rights and that actions to address climate change must comply with human rights obligations. *This is a real achievement and, in this respect as in many others, the Paris Agreement is worth celebrating.* In another sense, however, Paris is only the beginning. Now comes the difficult work of implementing and strengthening the commitments made there. In that effort, human rights norms will continue to be of fundamental importance.[28]

In addition, procedural rights have been given a boost in the Paris Agreement. The preamble affirms "the importance of education, training, public awareness, public participation, public access to information and cooperation at all levels on matters addressed in this Agreement." This language reiterates the important role that procedural rights of access to information and public participation, as well as education, training, and cooperation, play in the context of climate change. This ties in well with the obligations identified in the mapping report of the then

[24] Paris Agreement, December 12, 2015, in force November 4, 2016, UN Doc. FCCC/CP/2015/l9, pmbl.

[25] See Olivier De Schutter, *International Human Rights Law* (Cambridge University Press, 2010), p. 242.

[26] An earlier draft of the Paris Agreement contained a reference to human rights in Draft Article 2; ironically, it was deleted on Human Rights Day. See Climate Tracker.Org, "Have Human Rights Died at COP 21?," http://climatetracker.org/have-human-rights-died-at-cop-21 (December 10, 2015).

[27] In the run-up to COP 21, UN Special Procedures called on the negotiators to include a reference to human rights in the climate agreement. See Statement of the United Nations Special Procedures Mandate Holders on the Occasion of the Human Rights Day, Geneva (December 10, 2014), www.ohchr.org/EN/NewsEvents/Pages/DisplayNews.aspx?NewsID=15393&LangID=E.

[28] John H. Knox, *Report of the Special Rapporteur on the Issue of Human Rights Obligations Relating to the Enjoyment of a Safe, Clean, Healthy and Sustainable Environment: Climate Change Report*, UN Doc. A/HRC/31/52 (February 1, 2016), para. 22 (emphasis added).

Independent Expert on human rights and the environment,[29] to which we turn briefly in the context of mitigation, adaptation, and vulnerable communities. If we are to apply the conclusions in the mapping report to climate change, states have substantive obligations and procedural obligations, as well as obligations in relation to vulnerable groups. These obligations must be applied both in relation to mitigation measures and adaptation measures.

Mitigation Measures

Article 4 of the Paris Agreement addresses mitigation measures. It calls upon states to reach global peaking of greenhouse gas emissions as soon as possible to achieve the temperature goal set out in Article 2 (i.e., to limit the temperature increase to below 2 degrees Celsius and to work toward a 1.5 degrees Celsius goal).[30] Developed country parties are encouraged to take the lead by undertaking economy-wide absolute emission reduction targets. Similarly, developing country parties are encouraged to continue enhancing their mitigation efforts and move toward economy-wide emission reductions over time.[31]

Whatever mitigation measures states adopt, they are bound to have an impact on people, whether by reducing sources of greenhouse gases or by enhancing their sinks.[32] While mitigation options will vary with each sector of the economy that produces greenhouse gas (GHG) emissions, many of the alternatives that are adopted could lead to a violation of rights if a rights-based framework is not applied, even if those measures lead to a reduction in GHGs.[33] A good example is the Clean Development Mechanism (CDM), a flexibility mechanism adopted under the Kyoto Protocol.[34] Because the guidelines for CDM projects do not include protection of human rights, several of these projects have resulted in a violation of rights in the host country.[35]

The importance of applying a rights-based approach to climate change mitigation has been brought into sharp focus by the REDD+ (reducing emissions from

[29] John H. Knox, *Report of the Independent Expert on the Issue of Human Rights Obligations Relating to the Enjoyment of a Safe, Clean, Healthy and Sustainable Environment: Mapping Report*, UN Doc. A/HRC/25/53 (December 30, 2013).

[30] Paris Agreement, art. 4.

[31] Ibid.

[32] IPCC defines mitigation as human intervention to reduce the sources of GHGs or enhancing their sinks. Atapattu, *Human Rights Approaches to Climate Change*, p. 128.

[33] For example, several wind energy farms have been sited on the territory of indigenous peoples without their free, prior, and informed consent as required under international law. See Shalanda H. Baker, "Project Finance and Sustainable Development in the Global South," in Shawkat Alam et al. (eds.), *International Environmental Law and the Global South* (Cambridge University Press, 2015), p. 338.

[34] Kyoto Protocol to the UN Framework Convention on Climate Change, December 11, 1997, in force February 16, 2005, 2303 UNTS 162, art. 12.

[35] See Atapattu, *Human Rights Approaches to Climate Change*, p. 134.

deforestation and forest degradation) program, which is aimed at incentivizing countries to achieve emissions reductions by decreasing the conversion of forests to other land uses. Concerns have been raised that REDD+ projects could lead to negative impacts on communities that depend on forests for their daily subsistence, such as indigenous communities,[36] and there are accounts of indigenous peoples being forcibly evicted from their traditional lands to give way for such projects.[37] Thus, applying a rights-based approach to mitigation measures such as the REDD+ program should be mandatory.

As noted earlier, while is it difficult to establish the responsibility of states for damage caused by climate change under current principles, it is possible to hold states accountable under international human rights law for human rights violations associated with mitigation measures. An example of a potential area of conflict associated with mitigation measures is biofuels, which can have an impact on food security of people.[38] Thus, evaluating these projects from a human rights perspective is necessary to ensure that mitigation measures adopted by states do not lead to a violation of human rights. Sustainable development, with its three pillars – environmental protection, economic development and social protection – could also provide a useful framework to minimize such conflicts.[39]

Adaptation Measures

The Intergovernmental Panel on Climate Change (IPCC) defines adaptation as "the process of adjustment to actual or expected climate and its effects."[40] In simple terms, adaptation means learning to cope with the consequences of climate change. While the earlier climate documents referred mainly to mitigation, adaptation has become inevitable because historic emissions are already causing adverse consequences. As a result, there is now an emphasis on adaptation and the need to assist developing countries with adaptation, as they will be disproportionately affected by the adverse consequences and are unable to cope with them. Some scholars have referred to the disproportionate impact on developing countries as "adaptation apartheid."[41] Given that we have locked in a certain level of climate change,

36 Ibid., chapter 7.

37 See ibid., p. 176.

38 See Elisabeth Caesens and Maritere Padilla Rodríguez, *Climate Change and the Right to Food: A Comprehensive Study* (Heinrich Böll Stiftung, 2009), p. 33.

39 Copenhagen Declaration on Social Development (1995), available at: www.un-documents.net/cope-dec.htm.

40 IPCC, *Climate Change 2014: Impacts, Adaptation, and Vulnerability, Summary for Policymakers*, p. 5.

41 Margaux J. Hall and David C. Weiss, "Avoiding Adaptation Apartheid: Climate Change Adaptation and Human Rights Law," *Yale Journal of International Law* 37(2) (2012), p. 309.

adaptation becomes important for the present generation[42] while mitigation efforts will benefit mainly future generations. This has led to a debate on how scarce resources should be allocated – whether for adaptation projects or for mitigation measures.[43] Some contend that financing should be based on the common but differentiated responsibility (CBDR) principle, given the vastly disproportionate contribution of emissions from industrialized countries,[44] while others advocate for the application of a justice framework.[45] Both the CBDR and the justice framework are based on equity and fairness: while the CBDR is based on the disproportionate contribution to the problem, the justice framework places emphasis on the disproportionate impacts on vulnerable states and vulnerable communities whose carbon footprint is minimal.

Article 7 of the Paris Agreement addresses adaptation. This is one area where climate documents have called for a rights-based approach at least since the Cancun Adaptation framework was adopted in 2010.[46] The Paris Agreement reiterated the commitment made to "follow a country-driven, gender-responsive, participatory and fully transparent approach, taking into consideration vulnerable groups, communities and ecosystems."[47] Parties acknowledged the need to be guided by the best available science and traditional knowledge, knowledge of indigenous peoples and local knowledge systems "with a view to integrating adaptation into relevant socioeconomic and environmental policies and actions, where appropriate."[48] The recognition of the need to integrate adaptation into relevant policies and plans is important. Very often development projects and polices are adopted in isolation of adaptation measures and without the participation of the affected communities, leading to a violation of procedural rights. Moreover, these projects and policies run the risk of being redundant in the face of climate change. As the UN Development Programme (UNDP) noted in 2007, climate change is the "defining human

[42] See Chris Wold, David Hunter, and Melissa Powers, *Climate Change and the Law* (LexisNexis, 2009), p. 114.

[43] Ibid., p. 96 ("many observers fear that money and attention spent on adaptation will detract from efforts to mitigation (or prevent) climate change in the first place").

[44] See Paul Baer, "Adaptation: Who Pays Whom?," in W. Neil Adger et al. (eds.), *Fairness in Adaptation to Climate Change* (MIT Press, 2006), p. 131.

See Lavanya Rajamani, *Differential Treatment in International Law* (Oxford University Press, 2006), p. 178 (citing Anil Agarwal and Sunita Narain, *Global Warming in an Unequal World: A Case of Environmental Colonialism* (Centre for Science and Environment, 1991)).

[45] See Zackary L. Stillings, "Human Rights and the New Reality of Climate Change: Adaptation's Limitations in Achieving Climate Justice," *Michigan Journal of International Law* 35 (2014), pp. 637, 640; W. Neil Adger, Jouni Paavola, and Saleemul Huq, "Toward Justice in Adaptation to Climate Change," in W. Neil Adger et al. (eds.), *Fairness in Adaptation to Climate Change*, p. 1.

[46] United Nations Framework Convention on Climate Change, *Report on the Conference of the Parties on its Sixteenth Session, held in Cancun from 29 November to 10 December 2010*, UN Doc. FCCC/CP/2010/7/Add. 1 (March 15, 2011), paras. 11–35.

[47] Paris Agreement, art. 7.

[48] Ibid., art. 7(5).

development issue of our generation,"[49] and, therefore, we need to incorporate adaptation measures into development programs. Not only do we have to prepare these adaptation measures with the participation of the relevant stakeholders, we must also learn from the knowledge of the local and indigenous communities who are most familiar with the local environment. In addition, we need to adopt a rights-based approach to these adaptation measures, including migration. Migration is considered an extreme form of adaptation, although in some instances this may be the only option available.[50] We now turn to a discussion of vulnerable communities, as special measures will be necessary to protect them from the adverse consequences of climate change.

Vulnerable Communities

There is no doubt that climate change is causing a disproportionate impact on developing countries, particularly small island states and low-lying countries.[51] A recent news item that five of the Solomon Islands have disappeared into the Pacific Ocean and six more have experienced a drastic reduction in shorelines[52] highlighted what is in store for small island states across the world, and should have set off alarm bells for even the most vocal climate skeptics. While the fact that small island states face the prospect of obliteration due to sea level rise associated with climate change has been known for some time, the rate at which it is already taking place is alarming. This raises profound justice issues as the contribution of these states and their people to climate change is very small. Yet the impact on them is disproportionately high, as they stand to lose everything they have, including the very nation on which the people rely for their protection. Where will these people go? What will happen to them? Will these states lose their statehood as they lose their territory? What will happen to their maritime boundaries? These are some of the questions facing these communities who are facing a bleak, uncertain future.[53] There is no doubt that adverse effects of climate change will lead to an infringement of protected rights of the inhabitants of small island states.

In addition, it is generally accepted that certain groups within states are also disproportionately affected due to historic marginalization and inequities. Women, children, indigenous peoples, those who are living in poverty, and those who are forced to migrate as a result of climate change (whether internally or across

[49] United Nations Development Programme, *Human Development Report 2007/08: Fighting Climate Change - Solidarity in a Divided World.*

[50] For those who are living on small island states and low lying areas, migration to other countries and higher elevations is the only option available.

[51] See United Nations Framework Convention on Climate Change, May 9, 1992, in force March 21, 1994, 1771 UNTS 107, art. 4(8).

[52] See Michael Hayden, "Five Solomon Islands Disappear into the Pacific Ocean as a Result of Climate Change," *ABC News* (May 9, 2016).

[53] See Atapattu, *Human Rights Approaches to Climate Change*, chapter 9.

borders) are identified as being more vulnerable than others as the adverse consequences of climate change tend to exacerbate their vulnerabilities and inequalities. "A threat multiplier, climate change will exacerbate inequities both between and within communities with the severest impacts being felt by children, the poor and women."[54]

The Paris Agreement identifies several categories of vulnerable people: indigenous peoples, local communities, migrants, children, persons with disabilities, and people in vulnerable situations.[55] While it is unfortunate that women are not specifically identified as a vulnerable group here, despite the success that women's groups have had in getting gender included in climate documents, as well as establishing a women and gender constituency under the purview of the UNFCCC,[56] the Agreement identifies gender equality and empowerment of women as important guidelines that should inform action in relation to climate change.[57] Moreover, the provision on adaptation specifically refers to the need to adopt, *inter alia*, gender-sensitive action.[58] With regard to adaptation plans, states are encouraged to prepare climate change impacts and vulnerability assessments "with a view to formulating nationally determined prioritized actions, taking into account vulnerable people, places and ecosystems."[59] In addition, the reference to climate justice in the preamble, albeit in very vague terms,[60] could be useful to these vulnerable communities to call upon states to take action specifically with regard to them.

The effort to seek justice for vulnerable communities in developing countries must not overlook vulnerable communities in *developed* countries. The village of Kivalina in Alaska is a case in point.[61] Kivalina comprises 403 residents and is situated eighty-three miles above the Arctic Circle.[62] It is slowly being eroded into the sea. In 2006 the Army Corps of Engineers determined that the village must be relocated, but two main questions remain: Who will foot the bill, which is in the range of 50–100 million dollars, and where will they relocate? In the meantime, the villagers live under appalling conditions, with 80 percent of the population lacking toilets.[63] Because the village is to be moved, no money is being invested to improve

54 World Health Organization, *Our Planet, Our Health, Our Future: Human Health and the Rio Conventions* (2012), p. 2.

55 Paris Agreement, pmbl.

56 See http://womengenderclimate.org.

57 Paris Agreement, pmbl.

58 Ibid., art. 7.

59 Ibid., art. 7(9)(c).

60 Ibid., pmbl. ("noting the importance *for some* of the concept of 'climate justice', when taking action to address climate change") (emphasis added).

61 See Marissa Knodel, "Conceptualizing Climate Justice in Kivalina," *Seattle University Law Review* 37(4) (2014), p. 1179.

62 Chris Moony, "The Remote Alaskan Village that Needs to be Relocated Due to Climate Change," Washington Post (February 24, 2015).

63 Ibid.

the living conditions of people. If the wealthiest country in the world cannot address the plight of a mere 400 residents, it is hard to imagine what will happen to vulnerable communities in less affluent parts of the world. Like many other communities that are disproportionately affected by adverse effects of climate change, Kivalina's carbon footprint is very small, thus raising serious justice issues.

One notable omission from the Paris Agreement is a reference to climate displacement. While an earlier draft referred to climate displacement in the context of the loss and damage mechanism,[64] this language was removed from the final version. Perhaps the reference to "migrants" in the preamble was intended to cover climate refugees, but that does not address the plight of those who are forced to move across international borders due to climate change. The international community missed a golden opportunity to address the plight of this vulnerable group of people, especially since there is currently no legal framework to govern those who are forced to move across international borders as a result of climate change. Given the projections of the number of people who will be compelled to move as a result of adverse effects associated with climate change,[65] it is imperative that the international community take steps to design a legal framework to protect this group of people before it is forced to confront the issue. With regard to small island states, the situation is compounded by legal issues relating to statehood and nationality arising out of loss of territory associated with sea level rise. While these issues have received ample attention from scholars,[66] they have yet to receive attention from policy makers in a meaningful manner. Perhaps the universal nature of human rights law, coupled with the principle of cooperation, can be used to protect this category of people, particularly the inhabitants of small island states.[67]

TIME FOR A DISTINCT RIGHT TO A HEALTHY ENVIRONMENT?

The question whether the recognition of a distinct right to a healthy environment would help victims of climate change needs to be evaluated in light of the existing rights that have already been impacted by climate change. It also needs to take into account whether there is political will to adopt such a right. The earlier discussion shows how the human rights framework can (and should) be applied in relation to mitigation, adaptation, and vulnerable communities. It is less useful for establishing responsibility for damage caused by climate change, as current state responsibility

[64] See Draft Paris Outcome, Version 2 of 10 December 2015 at 21:00 (on file with author).

[65] Estimates range widely. See, e.g., Norman Myers, "Environmental Refugees: A Growing Phenomenon of the 21st Century (2002) (20 million to 200 million by 2050); Gerrard, "Environmental Justice," p. 287 (23 million to 62 million per year). But see Jane McAdam, *Climate Change, Forced Migration, and International Law* (Oxford University Press, 2010), p. 16 (arguing that most instances of displacement are likely to be internal and temporary).

[66] See generally McAdam, *Climate Change*; Atapattu, *Human Rights Approaches to Climate Change*, chapter 6, notes 16, 17 (citing authorities).

[67] Ibid., p. 175.

principles do not recognize collective theories of liability. While undoubtedly a stand-alone right to a healthy environment would be an additional benefit to victims of climate change, it will be constrained by the limitations inherent in the human rights framework vis-à-vis environmental issues, particularly climate change.[68] The main limitation stems from the very nature of human rights – the vertical relationship between duty bearers and rights holders and their territorial application – and the recognition of a distinct right to a healthy environment cannot overcome that constraint unless states are willing to recognize extraterritorial human rights obligations with regard to transboundary environmental damage. This would radically change the very nature of human rights law, and the likelihood of its acceptance by states seems highly unlikely.

On the other hand, the recognition of a stand-alone right to a healthy environment would send a clear signal to the international community that environmental rights are important, that such rights are justiciable, and that other protected rights could be jeopardized if a right to a healthy environment is not respected. As the African Commission elaborated on the nature of the right to a healthy environment in the *Ogoniland* case, states will be required to adopt other measures (including legislation), establish institutions, require the preparation of environmental and social impact assessments, carry out monitoring, ensure the availability of effective remedies, and, above all, control the activities of private entities that cause harm to the environment and violate rights of people. In his Mapping Report, the Independent Expert on human rights and the environment also referred to these duties under substantive obligations of human rights that are applicable in relation to the environment.[69]

Thus, far from diluting existing rights, the recognition of a right to environment could strengthen the application of other related rights such as rights to life, health, water, food, privacy, housing, and sanitation. It would give states a useful tool to ensure that activities of multinational companies do not violate environmental rights and give the judiciary the opportunity to articulate the parameters of the right. Many civil and political rights have achieved coherence and refinement because the judiciaries around the world have been given the opportunity to interpret them. So why not leave it to the judiciary to do the same with the right to environment? Above all, it would give an additional avenue to victims of environmental abuse to seek redress at both national and international levels, without having to establish in a roundabout way that one of their rights has been violated due to an environmental issue. Because international human rights law does not yet recognize a distinct right to a healthy environment, victims of environmental abuse have had to rely on existing rights to bring a claim for a violation of their rights (for example, rights to privacy, health, food, and, in extreme situations, life), but sometimes this link cannot

[68] See ibid., chapters 2 and 3.

[69] Knox, *Mapping Report*, paras. 44–57.

be readily established or when it can be established, it may be too late to obtain relief. Once a victim has contracted a deadly disease such as cancer, it is too late to go against the perpetrator to seek a remedy. If, on the other hand, a distinct right to a healthy environment is recognized as a stand-alone, justiciable right, victims may be able to request local authorities or the courts to intervene before a particular issue becomes irreversible. This, probably, is the single most important advantage of adopting a justiciable right to a healthy environment.

The recognition of a right to a healthy environment would not mean the end of investment and industrial activity in countries. As with the adjudication of other rights, this right will have to be balanced against other competing rights, and societal interests and community rights will often trump individual rights. We can draw on the existing environmental rights jurisprudence to provide guidance here and to appease policy makers.

The link between human rights and the environment is no longer disputed and human rights institutions have endorsed this link. As Rebecca Bratspies points out, "Just as a healthy environment can contribute to the enjoyment of human rights, there is a growing sense that environmental degradation and climate change have 'generally negative effects on the realization of human rights.'"[70] Given this close relationship between the two fields, the resistance to recognizing a right to a healthy environment is rather puzzling. Including a right to a healthy environment as part of human rights law would "promote policy coherence and legitimacy."[71]

In addition, if the right were included in an amendment or protocol to an existing human rights treaty, such as the International Covenant on Economic, Social and Cultural Rights, victims could resort to the remedial mechanisms available under that treaty. Moreover, states would have to report on the measures taken to protect the environment in their country reports prepared under the treaty, and these measures would be subject to scrutiny by the relevant treaty body. Currently, some states do report on such measures voluntarily, but there is no legal obligation to do so. These concluding observations can be a useful tool in the hands of civil society groups to demand that states take measures to protect the environment. As noted earlier, states also have a duty to protect people from environmental degradation caused by private actors, even if states did not create those risks,[72] as well as protect especially vulnerable groups such as women, children, and indigenous peoples. The typology of rights adopted by human rights law – the duties to respect, protect, and fulfill – together with duties of equality and non-discrimination become very useful tools vis-à-vis environmental degradation, even in the absence of a distinct right to a healthy environment. As Bratspies points out: "If all human rights are indeed

[70] Rebecca Bratspies, "Do We Need a Human Right to a Healthy Environment?," *Santa Clara Journal of International Law* 13(1) (2015), pp. 31, 35 (quoting OHCHR, *Report on Climate Change and Human Rights*, para. 96).

[71] Ibid.

[72] Ibid., p. 62.

'universal, indivisible, interdependent and interrelated,' then environmental activists have a wealth of tools at their disposal."[73]

CONCLUSION

This chapter discussed the relationship between human rights law and environmental protection and particularly climate change in relation to mitigation, adaptation, and vulnerable groups. It also discussed the emergence of a distinct right to a healthy environment under international law and its pros and cons vis-à-vis climate change.

An issue that will have repercussions for the entire climate legal regime, and in relation to human rights in particular, is the ambition gap between what is promised and what is needed.[74] Although the Paris Agreement was adopted amidst much fanfare and euphoria and was an important milestone in many respects, there is no time for complacency. Much work remains to be done and coordinating activities with the various UN bodies working on climate change, sustainable development, and disaster risk reduction is necessary to ensure that issues such as climate displacement will not continue to fall through the cracks. The legal issues relating to small island states should be addressed separately, as they go to the very core of the international system and relate to a phenomenon hitherto not faced by the international community – the total disappearance of sovereign states. The concept of climate justice, included rather half-heartedly in the Paris Agreement, needs further elucidation, especially regarding what it means for vulnerable communities and states.[75] The relationship between the Sendai Framework for Disaster Risk Reduction and the loss and damage mechanism developed at Warsaw in 2014 and later incorporated into the Paris Agreement also needs to be analyzed.[76]

The recognition of a distinct right to environment would be helpful for victims of environmental abuse and would at least be a symbolic acknowledgment that this right is as important as other rights. However, such a right would be subject to the same limitations that are inherent in the human rights framework vis-à-vis environmental issues. While it is unlikely that the political will exists to adopt a distinct right to a healthy environment at the international level, all is not lost, as regional bodies and national judiciaries will continue to develop this robust body of law and provide relief to victims. These bodies have articulated the parameters of environmental

[73] Ibid., p. 67 (quoting the Vienna Declaration and Programme of Action, adopted by the World Conference on Human Rights in Vienna on June 25, 1993).

[74] See UN Environment Programme, *The Emissions Gap Report 2015*.

[75] See Humphreys, *Human Rights and Climate Change*; Upendra Baxi, "Towards a Climate Change Justice Theory?," *Journal of Human Rights and the Environment* 7(1) (2016), p. 7.

[76] See Stephen Humphreys, "In the Shadow of Paris: Theories of Justice and Principles of Harm," *Journal of Human Rights and the Environment* 7(1) (2016), p. 3 (pointing out the Warsaw mechanism presents a Catch-22 for small island states).

rights and it would be very hard to reverse these positive developments. In addition, the inclusion of environmental rights in over ninety constitutions around the world is strong evidence for the emergence of a general principle of law. Even if opponents argue the contrary, states do have human rights obligations vis-à-vis environmental protection, as clarified by the Independent Expert in his mapping report. They have to fulfill their human rights obligations when taking action in relation to climate change and ensure that a rights-based approach is adopted in relation to mitigation and adaptation, and with regard to vulnerable communities. Neither human rights law nor international environmental law operates in a vacuum. Thus, states are required to fulfill their human rights obligations when taking action in relation to environmental issues and vice versa, whether or not these obligations are specifically mentioned in those treaties.

Ultimately, the well-being of our children and grandchildren will depend on what action we take today to address climate change. In an era where even inanimate objects such as rivers and Mother Nature are accorded rights and legal standing,[77] it is baffling as to why there is so much reluctance to accord *human beings* with a right to a healthy environment.

[77] Bratspies, "Human Right to a Healthy Environment," p. 67; Cole Mellino, "Bolivia and Ecuador Grant Equal Rights to Nature: Is 'Wild Law' a Climate Solution?," *ThinkProgress* (November 21, 2011).

Bibliography

RESOLUTIONS

African Commission on Human and Peoples' Rights res. 148 (November 25, 2009).
African Commission on Human and Peoples' Rights res. 321 (November 18, 2015).
African Commission on Human and Peoples' Rights res. 364 (November 4, 2016).
General Assembly res. 2398 (December 3, 1968).
General Assembly res. 2994 (December 15, 1972).
General Assembly res. 41/120 (December 4, 1986).
General Assembly res. 45/94 (December 14, 1990).
General Assembly res. 55/107 (December 4, 2000).
General Assembly res. 60/1 (October 24, 2005).
General Assembly res. 60/251 (April 3, 2006).
General Assembly res. 64/292 (July 28, 2010).
General Assembly res. 66/288, *The Future We Want* (July 27, 2012).
General Assembly res. 70/1, *Transforming Our World: The 2030 Agenda for Sustainable Development* (September 25, 2015).
Human Rights Commission res. 1994/65 (March 9, 1994).
Human Rights Commission res. 1995/14 (Feb. 24, 1995).
Human Rights Commission res. 1996/13 (April 11, 1996).
Human Rights Commission dec. 2001/111 (April 25, 2001).
Human Rights Commission res. 2002/75 (April 25, 2002).
Human Rights Commission res. 2003/71 (April 25, 2003).
Human Rights Commission res. 2005/60 (April 20, 2005).
Human Rights Council res. 7/23 (March 28, 2008).
Human Rights Council res. 10/4 (March 25, 2009).
Human Rights Council res. 15/9 (September 30, 2010).
Human Rights Council res. 16/11 (March 24, 2011).
Human Rights Council res. 18/22 (September 30, 2011).
Human Rights Council res. 19/10 (March 12, 2012).
Human Rights Council res. 21/11 (September 27, 2012).
Human Rights Council res. 25/21 (March 28, 2014).
Human Rights Council res. 26/27 (June 25, 2014).

Human Rights Council res. 28/11 (March 26, 2015).
Human Rights Council res. 29/15 (July 2, 2015).
Human Rights Council res. 31/8 (March 23, 2016).
Human Rights Council res. 32/33 (June 28, 2016).
Supreme Court of the Philippines, Resolution A.M. No. 09–6–8-SC, Rules of Procedure for Environmental Cases (2010)

REPORTS OF INTERNATIONAL BODIES

African Commission on Human and Peoples' Rights, General Comment No. 3 (2015).

African Commission on Human and Peoples' Rights, *Principles and Guidelines on the Implementation of Economic, Social and Cultural Rights in the African Charter on Human and Peoples' Rights* (2011).

Analytical Study on the Relationship between Human Rights and the Environment, UN Doc. A/HRC/19/34 (December 16, 2011).

Anaya, James, *Report of the Special Rapporteur on the Rights of Indigenous Peoples: Extractive Industries Operating within or Near Indigenous Territories*, UN Doc. A/HRC/18/35 (July 11, 2011).

BASIC Experts, *Equitable Access to Sustainable Development: Contribution to the Body of Scientific Knowledge* (BASIC expert group: Beijing, Brasilia, Cape Town and Mumbai (2011).

Committee on Economic, Social and Cultural Rights, *General Comment 12, The right to adequate food (art. 11)*, UN Doc. E/C.12/1999/5 (May 12, 1999).

Committee on Identifying the Needs of the Forensic Scientific Community of the National Research Council, *Strengthening the Forensic Sciences in the United States: A Path Forward* (National Academies Press, 2009).

Council of Europe, *Manual on Human Rights and the Environment* (2012).

Draft agreement and draft decision on workstreams 1 and 2 of the Ad Hoc Working Group on the Durban Platform for Enhanced Action, (edited version of November 6, 2015, re-issued November 10, 2015).

Draft Articles on Prevention of Transboundary Harm from Hazardous Activities, in *Report of the International Law Commission on the Work of its Fifty-Third Session*, UN GAOR, 56th Sess., Supp. No. 10, at 370–7, UN Doc. A/56/10 (2001).

Draft Paris Outcome, Revised Draft Conclusions Proposed by the Co-Chairs of the Ad Hoc Working Group on the Durban Platform for Enhanced Action, UN Doc. FCCC/ADP/2015/L.6/Rev.1, Annex I (December 5, 2001).

Governing Council of the United Nations Environment Programme, *Background Paper for the Ministerial Consultations: Global Environment Outlook and Emerging Issues: Setting Effective Global Environmental Goals: Discussion Paper by the Executive Director*, UN Doc. UNEP/GCSS.XII/13 (January 5, 2012).

Inter-American Commission on Human Rights, *Report on the Human Rights Situation in Ecuador*, Doc. No. OEA/Ser.L/V/II.96 (1997).

Intergovernmental Panel on Climate Change, *Climate Change 2014: Impacts, Adaptation, and Vulnerability, Summary for Policymakers* (2014).

Intergovernmental Panel on Climate Change, *Climate Change 2014: Mitigation of Climate Change* (2014).

International Law Commission, *Report of the International Law Commission on the Work of its 32nd Session* (May 25, 1980), UN Doc. A/35/10, p. 32.

International Law Commission, *Report of the International Law Commission, 66th Session*, UN Doc. A/69/10 (2014), p. 277.

International Law Commission, *Draft Articles on Responsibility of States for Internationally Wrongful Acts*, Official Records of the General Assembly, Fifty-Sixth Session, Supplement No. 10, UN Doc. A/56/10 (2001), chapter V.

IUCN Environmental Law Programme, *An Introduction to the African Convention on the Conservation of Nature and Natural Resources, IUCN Environmental Policy and Law Paper No. 56* (2008).

Knox, John H., *Report of the Independent Expert on the Issue of Human Rights Obligations Relating to the Enjoyment of a Safe, Clean, Healthy and Sustainable Environment: Preliminary Report*, UN Doc. A/HRC/22/43 (December 24, 2012).

Report of the Independent Expert on the Issue of Human Rights Obligations Relating to the Enjoyment of a Safe, Clean, Healthy and Sustainable Environment: Mapping Report, UN Doc. A/HRC/25/53 (December 30, 2013).

Report of the Independent Expert on the Issue of Human Rights Obligations Relating to the Enjoyment of a Safe, Clean, Healthy and Sustainable Environment: Mission to Costa Rica, UN Doc. A/HRC/25/53/Add.1 (March 21, 2014).

Report of the Independent Expert on the Issue of Human Rights Obligations Relating to the Enjoyment of a Safe, Clean, Healthy and Sustainable Environment: Compilation of Good Practices, UN Doc. A/HRC/28/61 (February 3, 2015).

Report of the Independent Expert on the Issue of Human Rights Obligations Relating to the Enjoyment of a Safe, Clean, Healthy and Sustainable Environment: Mission to France, UN Doc. A/HRC/28/61/Add.1 (March 6, 2015).

Report of the Special Rapporteur on the Issue of Human Rights Obligations Relating to the Enjoyment of a Safe, Clean, Healthy and Sustainable Environment: Implementation Report, UN Doc. A/HRC/31/53 (December 28, 2015).

Report of the Special Rapporteur on the Issue of Human Rights Obligations Relating to the Enjoyment of a Safe, Clean, Healthy and Sustainable Environment: Climate Change Report, UN Doc. A/HRC/31/52 (February 1, 2016).

Report of the Special Rapporteur on the Issue of Human Rights Obligations Relating to the Enjoyment of a Safe, Clean, Healthy and Sustainable Environment: Mission to Madagascar, UN Doc. A/HRC/34/49/Add.1 ((April 26, 2017).

Report of the Special Rapporteur on the Issue of Human Rights Obligations Relating to the Enjoyment of a Safe, Clean, Healthy and Sustainable Environment: Framework Principles, UN Doc. A/HRC/37/59 (January 24, 2018).

Ksentini, Fatma Zohra, *Final Report*, UN Doc. E/CN.4/Sub.2/1994/9, annex III (July 6, 1994).

Human Rights and the Environment, UN Doc. E/CN.4/Sub.2/1992/7 and Add.1 (July 2, 1992).

Human Rights and the Environment, UN Doc. E/CN.4/Sub.2/1993/7 (July 26, 1993).

Maastricht Principles on Extraterritorial Obligations of States in the Area of Economic, Social and Cultural Rights (2013).

New Partnership for Africa's Development (NEPAD), *Review of the Implementation of the Action Plan of the AU/NEPAD Environment* (2012).

New Zealand Constitutional Advisory Panel, *New Zealand's Constitution: A Report on a Conversation* (2013).

Office of the High Commissioner for Human Rights, *Report on the Relationship between Climate Change and Human Rights*, UN Doc. A/HRC/10/61 (January 15, 2009).

Office of the High Commissioner for Human Rights, *Understanding Human Rights and Climate Change: Submission of the Office of the High Commissioner for Human Rights to the 21st Conference of the Parties to the United Nations Framework Convention on Climate Change* (November 26, 2015).

Organization of American States, *Meeting the Challenges: The Role of the OAS in the Americas, 2005–2010* (2010).

Organization of American States, *Progress Indicators for Measuring Rights under the Protocol of San Salvador* (2d ed.), Doc. OEA/Ser.D/XXVI.11 (2015).

Sepúlveda Carmona, Magdalena, Final Draft of the Guiding Principles on Extreme Poverty and Human Rights, Submitted by the Special Rapporteur on Extreme Poverty and Human Rights, UN Doc. A/HRC/21/39 (July 18, 2012).

UK House of Commons and House of Lords Joint Committee on Human Rights, *Twenty-ninth Report* (House of Lords, 2008).

United Nations Human Rights Council, Draft Resolution on Human Rights and the Environment. UN Doc. A/HRC/19/L.8/Rev.1 (March 20, 2012).

United Nations Human Rights Council, Panel on Human Rights and Climate Change at the Eleventh Session of the Human Rights Council (June 15, 2009).

United Nations Development Programme, *Human Development Report 2007/08: Fighting Climate Change - Solidarity in a Divided World (2007).*

United Nations Economic Commission for Latin America and the Caribbean, *The Sustainability of Development in Latin America and the Caribbean: Challenges and Opportunities* (United Nations, 2002), p. 163.

United Nations Environment Programme and Center for International Environmental Law, *Compendium on Human Rights and the Environment* (2014).

United Nations Environment Programme, *Climate Change and Human Rights* (December 2015).

United Nations Environment Programme, *The Emissions Gap Report 2015* (November 2015).

United Nations Environment Programme, *Environmental Assessment of Ogoniland* (2011).

United Nations Environment Programme, *Keeping Track of Our Changing Environment: From Rio to Rio+20 (1992–2012)* (2011).

United Nations Framework Convention on Climate Change, Report on the Conference of the Parties on Its Sixteenth Session, Held in Cancun from 29 November to 10 December 2010, UN Doc. FCCC/CP/2010/7/Add. 1 (March 15, 2011).

United Nations Framework Convention on Climate Change, Report on the Conference of the Parties on Its Seventh Session, Decision 7/CP.7, UN Doc. FCCC/CP/2001/13/Add.12 (January 1, 2012).

United Nations Framework Convention on Climate Change, Report on the Conference of the Parties on Its Seventeenth Session, Decision 1/CP.17, UN Doc. FCCC/CP/2011/9/Add.1 (March 15, 2012).

United Nations Framework Convention on Climate Change, Report on the Conference of the Parties on its Seventeenth Session, Decision 3/CP.17, UN Doc. FCCC/CP/2011/9/Add.1 (March 15, 2012).

United Nations Framework Convention on Climate Change, Report on the Conference of the Parties on Its Twentieth Session, Decision 18/CP.20, UN Doc. FCCC/CP/2014/10/Add.3 (February 2, 2015).

United Nations Framework Convention on Climate Change, Report on the Conference of the Parties on Its Seventeenth Session, Decision 5/CP.17, UN Doc. FCCC/CP/2011/9/Add.1 (March 15, 2012).

United Nations Framework Convention on Climate Change, *Synthesis Report on the Aggregate Effect of the Intended Nationally Determined Contributions*, UN Doc. FCCC/CP/2015/7 (October 30, 2015).

Wood, Michael, *First Report on Formation and Evidence of Customary International Law*, UN Doc. A/CN.4/663 (May 17, 2013).
World Bank, Operational Policy 4.01, Environmental Assessment (2013).
World Health Organization, *Guidelines for Drinking Water Quality*, 3d ed. (2004).
World Health Organization, *Our Planet, Our Health, Our Future: Human Health and the Rio Conventions* (2012).

SCHOLARLY SOURCES: ARTICLES, BOOKS, CHAPTERS

Azu, Miriam, "A Review of the Work of the African Commission's Working Group on Extractive Industries, Environment and Human Rights Violations in Africa," *Africlaw* (2016).
Adger, W. Neil, Jouni Paavola, and Saleemul Huq, "Toward Justice in Adaptation to Climate Change," in W. Neil Adger et al. (eds.), *Fairness in Adaptation to Climate Change* (MIT Press, 2006), p. 1.
Agarwal, Anil and Sunita Narain, *Global Warming in an Unequal World: A Case of Environmental Colonialism* (Centre for Science and Environment, 1991).
Akehurst, Michael, "Custom as a Source of International Law," *British Yearbook of International Law* 47 (1977), pp. 1, 4–10.
Alam, Shawkat et al. (eds.), *International Environmental Law and the Global South* (Cambridge University Press, 2015).
Alley, Kelly D. and Daniel Meadows, "Workers' Rights and Pollution Control in Delhi," *Human Rights Dialogue* 2(11) (2004), pp. 15–17.
Allott, Philip, "The Emerging Universal Legal System," in Janne Nijman and Andre Nollkemper (eds.), *New Perspectives on the Divide between National and International Law* (Oxford University Press, 2007), pp. 63–83.
Alston, Philip, "Conjuring Up New Human Rights: A Proposal for Quality Control," *American Journal of International Law* 78(3) (1984), pp. 607–21.
Amechi, Emeka Polycarp, "Enhancing Environmental Protection and Socio-Economic Development in Africa: A Fresh Look at the Right to a General Satisfactory Environment under the African Charter on Human and Peoples' Rights," *Law, Environment and Development Journal* 5(1) (2009), pp. 58–72.
Anaya, S. James, *Indigenous Peoples in International Law*, 2d ed. (Oxford University Press, 2004).
Anton, Donald and Dinah Shelton, *Environmental Protection and Human Rights* (Cambridge University Press, 2011).
Aristide, Mildred, "A Historical and Dignity-Centred Perspective on Haiti's Struggle for Justice," *International Journal of African Renaissance Studies* 1 (2006), p. 265.
Asamoah, Joe, "The Management of Strategic Resources: The Oil and Gas Find in Ghana," in Timothy Afful-Koomson and Kwabena Awusu Asubonteng (eds.), *Collaborative Governance in Extractive Industries in Africa* (United Nations University Institute for Natural Resources in Africa, 2013), p. 184.
Atapattu, Sumudu, "Climate Change, Differentiated Responsibilities and State Responsibility: Devising Novel Legal Strategies for Damage Caused by Climate Change," in Benjamin J. Richardson et al. (eds.), *Climate Law and Developing Countries: Legal and Policy Challenges for the World Economy* (Edward Elgar Publishing, 2009), p 37.
Human Rights Approaches to Climate Change: Challenges and Opportunities (Routledge, 2015).

"The Role of Human Rights Law in Protecting Environmental Rights in South Asia," in LaDawn Haglund and Robin Stryker (eds.), *Closing the Rights Gap: From Human Rights to Social Transformation* (University of California Press, 2015), p. 105.

Aust, Anthony, *Modern Treaty Law and Practice*, 2d ed. (Cambridge University Press, 2007).

Baer, Paul, "Adaptation: Who Pays Whom?," in W. Neil Adger et al. (eds.), *Fairness in Adaptation to Climate Change* (MIT Press, 2006), p. 131.

et al., *The Greenhouse Development Rights Framework: The Right to Development in a Climate Constrained World* (Heinrich Böll Foundation, Christian Aid, EcoEquity, the Stockholm Environment Institute, 2d ed., 2008).

Baird, Matthew and Richard Frankel, *Environmental Impact Assessment: Comparative Analysis in the Lower Mekong Delta* (Mekong Partnership for the Environment, 2015).

Baker, Shalanda H., "Project Finance and Sustainable Development in the Global South," in Shawkat Alam et al. (eds.), *International Environmental Law and the Global South* (Cambridge University Press, 2015).

Baxi, Upendra, "Towards a Climate Change Justice Theory?," *Journal of Human Rights and the Environment* 7(1) (2016).

Bentham, Jeremy, *Anarchical Fallacies; Being an Examination of the Declaration of Rights Issued during the French Revolution* (1792), republished in John Bowring (ed.), *The Works of Jeremy Bentham*, vol. II (William Tait, 1843), p. 523.

Beyerlin, Ulrich and Thilo Marauhn, *International Environmental Law* (Hart Publishing, 2011).

Biniaz, Susan, *Comma but Differentiated Responsibilities: Punctuation and 30 Other Ways Negotiators Have Resolved Issues in the International Climate Regime* (Sabin Centre for Climate Change Law, 2016).

Birnie, Patricia, Alan Boyle, and Catherine Redgwell, *International Law and the Environment*, 3d ed. (Oxford University Press, 2009).

Black, Bert and David E. Lilienfeld, "Epidemiologic Proof in Toxic Tort Litigation," *Fordham Law Review* 52(5) (1984), pp. 732–85.

Bodansky, Daniel, *The Art and Craft of International Environmental Law* (Harvard University Press, 2010).

"Customary (And Not So Customary) International Environmental Law," *Indiana Journal of Global Legal Studies* 3(1) (1995), p. 105–19.

"Introduction: Climate Change and Human Rights: Unpacking the Issues," *Georgia Journal of International and Comparative Law* 38(3) (2010), pp. 511–24.

"The Legal Character of the Paris Agreement," *Review of European Comparative and International Law* 25 (2016), p. 142.

Boonlai, Kochakorn and Pisit Changplayngam, "Thai Court Halts Many New Plants in Big Industrial Zone," *Reuters*, December 3, 2009.

Bosselmann, Klaus, "Global Environmental Constitutionalism: Mapping the Terrain," *Widener Law Review* 21 (2015), p. 171.

Boyd, David R., "Constitutions, Human Rights, and the Environment: National Approaches," in Anna Grear and Louis Kotzé (eds.), *Research Handbook on Human Rights and the Environment* (Edward Elgar, 2015), pp. 171–5.

The Environmental Rights Revolution: A Global Study of Constitutions, Human Rights, and the Environment (University of British Columbia Press, 2012).

"The Implicit Constitutional Right to a Healthy Environment," *Review of European Community and International Environmental Law* 20(2) (2011), pp. 171–9.

The Right to a Healthy Environment: Revitalizing Canada's Constitution (University of British Columbia Press, 2012).

Boyle, Alan E., "Human Rights and the Environment: Where Next?," *European Journal of International Law* 23(3) (2012), pp. 631–42.

"Human Rights or Environmental Rights? A Reassessment," *Fordham Environmental Law Review* 18 (2007), p. 471.

"Some Reflections on the Relationship of Treaties and Soft Law," *International and Comparative Law Quarterly* 48(4) (1999), pp. 901–13.

"The Role of International Human Rights Law in the Protection of the Environment," in Alan E. Boyle and Michael R. Anderson (eds.), *Human Rights Approaches to Environmental Protection* (Oxford University Press, 1998), p. 51.

Bratspies, Rebecca, "Do We Need a Human Right to a Healthy Environment?," *Santa Clara Journal of International Law* 13(1) (2015), pp. 31–69.

Brownlie, Ian, *Principles of Public International Law*, 5th ed. (Oxford University Press, 1998).

Brunnée, Jutta, "COPing with Consent: Law-Making under Multilateral Environmental Agreements," *Leiden Journal of International Law* 15(1) (2002), pp. 1–52.

de Búrca, Gráinne, Robert O. Keohane, and Charles Sabel, "New Modes of Pluralist Global Governance," *NYU Journal of International Law and Politics* 45(1) (2013), pp. 723–86.

Byers, Michael, *Custom, Power and the Power of Rules* (Cambridge University Press, 1999).

Caesens, Elisabeth and Maritere Padilla Rodríguez, *Climate Change and the Right to Food: A Comprehensive Study* (Heinrich Böll Stiftung, 2009).

Cameron, Edward and Marc Limon, "Restoring the Climate by Realizing Rights: The Role of the International Human Rights System," *Review of European Community and International Environmental Law* 21(3) (2012), pp. 204–19.

Cepeda Espinosa, Manuel José, "The Judicialization of Politics in Colombia: The Old and the New," in Rachel Sieder, Line Schjolden, and Alan Angell (eds.), *The Judicialization of Politics In Latin America* (Palgrave Macmillan, 2005), pp. 67–104.

Chapman, Megan S., "Climate Change and the Regional Human Rights Systems," *Sustainable Development Law and Policy* 10(2) (2010), p. 37.

Charney, Jonathan, "Universal International Law," *American Journal of International Law* 87(4) (1993), p. 529.

Chenwi, Lilian, "Provisional Measures in Rights Protection in Africa: A Comparative Analysis," *South African Yearbook of International Law* 39 (2014), p. 224.

Chinkin, C. M., "The Challenge of Soft Law: Development and Change in International Law," *International and Comparative Law Quarterly* 38 (1989), pp. 850–66.

Chirwa, Danwood Mzikenge, "A Fresh Commitment to Implementing Economic, Social, and Cultural Rights in Africa: Social and Economic Rights Action Center (SERAC) and the Center for Economic and Social Rights v. Nigeria," *ESR Review* 3(2) (2002), pp. 19–21.

Collins, Lynda, "Are We There Yet? The Right to Environment in International and Environmental Law," *McGill International Journal of Sustainable Development Law and Policy* 3 (2007), p. 119.

Cooley, Thomas McIntyre, A *Treatise on the Constitutional Limitations Which Rest upon the Legislative Power of the State of the American Union, Volume 1, 8th ed.* (Little, Brown, and Co., 1927), p. 165.

Craik, Neil, *The International Law of Environmental Impact Assessment: Process, Substance and Integration* (Cambridge University Press, 2010).

Criddle, Evan and Evan Fox-Decent, "A Fiduciary Theory of *Jus Cogens*," *Yale Journal of International Law* 34 (2009), pp. 331–87.

Crutzen, Paul and Eugene Stoermer, "The 'Anthropocene,'" *IGBP Global Change Newsletter* 41 (2000), pp. 17–18.

Cullet, Philippe, *The Sardar Sarovar Dam Project* (Ashgate, 2009).

Cuomo, Kerry Kennedy, "Human Rights and the Environment: Common Ground," *Yale Journal of International Law* 18(1) (1993), pp. 227–33.

Czapliński, Władysław, "*Jus Cogens* and the Law of Treaties," in Christian Tomuschat and Jean-Marc Thouvenin (eds.), The Fundamental Rules of the International Legal Order: *Jus Cogens* and Obligations *Erga Omnes* (Martinus Nijhoff, 2006), p. 89.

Daly, Erin, "*Environmental Human Rights: Paradigm of Indivisibility*" (2011), available at http://works.bepress.com/erin_daly/24.

Daly, Erin and James R. May, "Comparative Environmental Constitutionalism," *Jindal Global Law Review* 6(1) (2015).

Damaška, Mirjan, *Evidence Law Adrift* (Yale University Press, 1997), p. 100.

Danilenko, Gennady, "International Jus Cogens: Issues of Law-Making," *European Journal of International Law* 2(1) (1991), pp. 42–65.

D'Amato, Anthony, "Human Rights as Part of Customary International Law: A Plea for Change of Paradigms," *Georgia Journal of International and Comparative Law* 25 (1995–6), p. 47.

"Trashing Customary International Law," *American Journal of International Law* 87(1) (1987), p. 101.

De Schutter, Olivier, *International Human Rights Law* (Cambridge University Press, 2010).

De Wet, Erika, "The International Constitutional Order," *International and Comparative Law Quarterly* 55(1) (2006), pp. 51–76.

"*Jus Cogens* and Obligations *Erga Omnes*," in Dinah Shelton (ed.), *Oxford Handbook on International Human Rights Law* (Oxford University Press, 2015), p. 543.

De Wet, Erika and Jure Vidmar (eds.), *Hierarchy in International law: The Place of Human Rights* (Oxford University Press, 2012).

Dimitrijevic, Vojin, "Customary Law as an Instrument for the Protection of Human Rights," ISPI Working Paper 7 (2006).

Dupré, Catherine, *The Age of Dignity* (Hart, 2015).

Ebeku, Kaniye S.A., "The Right to a Satisfactory Environment and the African Commission," *African Human Rights Law Journal* 3 (2003), p. 165.

Emhardt, Andrew D., "Climate Change and the Inuit: Bringing an Effective Human Rights Claim to the United Nations," *Indiana International & Comparative Law Review* 24(2) (2014).

Fitzmaurice, Malgosia, "Environmental Degradation," in Daniel Moeckli, Sangeeta Shah, and Sandesh Sivakumaran (eds.), *International Human Rights Law* (2014), p. 593.

Forowicz, Magdalena, *The Reception of International Law in the European Court of Human Rights* (Oxford University Press, 2010).

Foster, Caroline E., "The Consultation of Independent Experts by International Courts and Tribunals in Health and Environment Cases," *Finnish Yearbook of International Law* 20 (2009), pp. 391–418.

Gerrard, Michael, "What Does Environmental Justice Mean in an Era of Global Climate Change?," *Journal of Environmental and Sustainability Law* 19 (2013), p. 278.

Ghertner, David Asher and Matthias Fripp, "Trading Away Damage: Quantifying Environmental Leakage through Consumption-Based Life-Cycle Analysis," *Ecological Economics* 63(2/3) (2006), pp. 563–77.

Glendon, Mary Ann, *Rights Talk: The Impoverishment of Political Discourse* (Free Press, 1991).

Goldsmith, Jack L. and Eric Posner, *The Limits of International Law* (Oxford University Press, 2005).

Grad, Frank P., *Treatise on Environmental Law* (Matthew Bender, 1997).

Guzman, Andrew T., "Saving Customary International Law," *Michigan Journal of International Law* 115 (2005), p. 115.

Hall, Margaux J. and David C. Weiss, "Avoiding Adaptation Apartheid: Climate Change Adaptation and Human Rights Law," *Yale Journal of International Law* 37(2) (2012), p. 309.

Hansen, Sarah, *Cultivating the Grassroots: A Winning Approach for Environment and Climate Funders* (NCPR, 2016).

Hart, H. L. A. "Are There Any Natural Rights?," *Philosophical Review* 64(2) (1955), pp. 175–191.

Hayward, Tim, *Constitutional Environmental Rights* (Oxford University Press, 2005).

Henkin, Louis, "Human Rights and State Sovereignty," *Georgia Journal of International and Comparative Law* 25 (1995–6), pp. 31–45.

Hey, Ellen, "The Interaction between Human Rights and the Environment in the European 'Aarhus Space,'" in Anna Grear and Louis Kotzé (eds.), *Research Handbook on Human Rights and the Environment* (Edward Elgar, 2015), pp. 353–76.

Heyns, Christof, and Magnus Killander, "Africa," in Daniel Moeckli, Sangeeta Shah, and Sandesh Sivakumaran (eds.), *International Human Rights Law* (Oxford University Press, 2014).

Hilson, Christopher, "Risk and the European Convention on Human Rights: Towards a New Approach," in Catherine Barnard and Oke Okudu (eds.), *The Cambridge Yearbook of European Legal Studies 2008–2009* (Hart Publishing, 2009).

Hiskes, Richard P., *The Human Right to a Green Future: Environmental Rights and Intergenerational Justice* (Cambridge University Press, 2008).

Hochstetler, Kathryn and Margaret E. Keck, *Greening Brazil: Environmental Activism in State and Society* (Duke University Press, 2007).

Hohmann, Harald, *Precautionary Legal Duties and Principles of Modern International Environmental Law* (Graham & Trotman/Martinus Nijhoff, 1994).

Horn, Laura, "The Implications of the Concept of a Common Concern of Human Kind on a Human Right to a Healthy Environment," *Macquarie Journal of International and Comparative Environmental Law* 1 (2004), pp. 233–68.

Hovell, Devika, "Due Process in the United Nations," *American Journal of International Law* 110(1) (2016), pp. 1–48.

Huber, Peter W., *Galileo's Revenge: Junk Science in the Courtroom* (Basic Books, 1991).

Humphreys, Stephen (ed.), *Human Rights and Climate Change* (Cambridge University Press, 2010).

Humphreys, Stephen, "In the Shadow of Paris: Theories of Justice and Principles of Harm," *Journal of Human Rights and the Environment* 7(1) (2016).

International Council on Human Rights Policy, *Climate Change and Human Rights: A Rough Guide* (2008).

Jariwala, C. M., "The Directions of Environmental Justice: An Overview," in S. K. Verma and K. Kusum (eds.), *Fifty Years of the Supreme Court of India: Its Grasp and Reach* (Oxford University Press, 2000), pp. 469–94.

Jasanoff, Sheila, *Science at the Bar* (Harvard University Press, 1995).

Jeffords, Christopher, "On the Temporal Effects of Static Constitutional Environmental Rights Provisions on Access to Improved Sanitation Facilities and Water Sources," *Journal of Human Rights and the Environment* 7(1) (2016), pp. 74–110.

Jeffords, Christopher and Lanse Minkler, "Do Constitutions Matter? The Effects of Constitutional Environmental Rights Provisions on Environmental Performance," *Kyklos* 69(2) (2016), pp. 295–334 at 296.

Keohane, Robert and David Victor, "The Regime Complex for Climate Change," *Perspectives on Politics* 9(1) (2011), pp. 7–23.

Kirgis, Frederic L., "Custom as a Sliding Scale," *American Journal of International Law* 81 (1987), p. 146.

Kiss, Alexandre, "The Legal Ordering of Environmental Protection," in Nicholas Tsagourias (ed.), *Toward World Constitutionalism: Issues in the Legal Ordering of the World Community* (Martinus Nijhoff Publishers, 2005).

Knodel, Marissa, "Conceptualizing Climate Justice in Kivalina," *Seattle University Law Review* 37(4) (2014), p. 1179.

Knox, John H., "Assessing the Candidates for a Global Treaty on Transboundary Environmental Impact Assessment," *New York University Environmental Law Journal* 12 (2003), p. 153.

"Climate Change and Human Rights Law," *Virginia Journal of International Law* 50(1) (2009), p. 163.

"The Myth and Reality of Transboundary Environmental Impact Assessment," *American Journal of International Law* 96(2) (2002), pp. 291–319.

Koivurova, Timo, "The Case of Vuotos: Interplay between International, Community, and National Law," *Review of European Community and International Environmental Law* 13(1) (2004), pp. 47–60.

Kornicker, Eva, *Ius Cogens und Umweltvölkerrecht: Kriterien, Quellen und Rechtsfolgen zwingender Völkerrechtsnormen und deren Anwendung auf das Umweltvölkerrecht* (Helbing & Lichtenhahn, 1997).

Koskenniemi, Marti, *From Apology to Utopia* (Cambridge University Press 1989).

Kotzé, Louis, "The Anthropocene's Global Environmental Constitutional Moment," *Yearbook of International Environmental Law* 25(1) (2015), pp. 24–60.

"Arguing Global Environmental Constitutionalism," *Transnational Environmental Law* 1(1) (2012), pp. 199–233.

Global Environmental Constitutionalism in the Anthropocene (Hart Publishing, 2016).

Kotzé, Louis and Caiphas Soyapi, "Transnational Environmental Law: The Birth of a Contemporary Analytical Perspective," in Douglas Fisher (ed.), *Research Handbook on Fundamental Concepts of Environmental Law* (Edward Elgar, 2016), pp. 82–110.

Kravchenko, Svitlana and John E. Bonine, *Human Rights and the Environment: Cases, Law, and Policy* (Carolina Academic Press, 2008).

Kritsiotis, Dino, "Imagining the International Community," *European Journal of International Law* 12 (2002), pp. 961–91.

Langford, Malcolm (ed.), *Social Rights Jurisprudence: Emerging Trends in International and Comparative Law* (Cambridge University Press, 2008).

Lavrysen, Luc, "Belgium," in Louis J. Kotze and Alexander R. Paterson (eds.), *The Role of the Judiciary in Environmental Governance: Comparative Perspectives* (Kluwer Law International, 2009), pp. 85–122.

"Presentation of Aarhus-Related Cases of the Belgian Constitutional Court," *Environmental Law Network International Review* 2 (2007), pp. 5–8.

Law, David S. and Mila Versteeg, "The Evolution and Ideology of Global Constitutionalism," *California Law Review* 99(5) (2011), pp. 1163–257.

Lawson, Samantha, "The Conundrum of Climate Change Causation: Using Market Share Liability to Satisfy the Identification Requirement in *Native Village of Kivalina v. Exxonmobil Co.*," *Fordham Environmental Law Review* 22(2) (2011), p. 433.

Lecucq, Olivier and Sandrine Maljean-Dubois (eds.), *Le Rôle du Juge dans le Développement du Droit de l'Environnement* (Bruylant, 2008).

Ledezma, Rosaly (ed.), *Ministerios Públicos en America Latina* (Asamblea Legislativa Plurinacional de Bolivia Cámara de Diputados, 2011).

Lee, John, "The Underlying Legal Theory to Support a Well-Defined Human Right to a Healthy Environment as a Principle of Customary International Law," *Columbia Journal of Environmental Law* 25 (2000), pp. 283–339.

Li, Jennifer C., *Environmental Impact Assessments in Developing Countries: An Opportunity for Greater Environmental Security?* (Foundation for Environmental Stability and Security and U.S. Agency for International Development, 2008).

Lillich, Richard B., "The Growing Importance of Customary International Human Rights Law," *Georgia Journal of International and Comparative Law* 25(1) (1995/6), pp. 1–30.

Limon, Marc, "Human Rights and Climate Change: Constructing a Case for Political Action," *Harvard Environmental Law Review* 33 (2009), pp. 439–76.

"Human Rights Obligations and Accountability in the Face of Climate Change," *Georgia Journal of International and Comparative Law* 38(3) (2010), pp. 543–92.

van der Linde, Morné, "African Responses to Environmental Protection," *Comparative and International Law Journal of Southern Africa* 35(1) (2002), p. 106.

van der Linde, Morné and Lirette Louw, "Considering the interpretation and implementation of article 24 of the African Charter on Human and Peoples' Rights in light of the *SERAC* communication," *African Human Rights Law Journal* 3 (2003), p. 174.

Magraw, Daniel et al., "Human Rights, Labour and the Paris Agreement on Climate Change," *Environmental Policy and Law* 46 (2016), pp. 313–20.

Marks, Stephen, "Emerging Human Rights: A New Generation for the 1980s?," *Rutgers Law Review* 33 (1981), pp. 435–52.

Marrani, David, "The Second Anniversary of the Constitutionalisation of the French Charter for the Environment: Constitutional and Environmental Implications," *Environmental Law Review* 10(1) (2008), pp. 9–27.

May, James R., "Constituting Fundamental Environmental Rights Worldwide," *Pace Environmental Law Review* 23 (2005/6), pp. 113–29.

"Constitutional Directions in Procedural Environmental Rights," *Journal of Environmental Law and Litigation* 28 (2014), p. 101.

May, James R. and Erin Daly, *Environmental Constitutionalism: A Research Compendium* (Edward Elgar, 2016).

"Environmental Rights and Liabilities," *European Journal of Environmental Liability* 3 (2012), p. 75.

Global Environmental Constitutionalism (Cambridge University Press, 2015).

"New Directions in Earth Rights, Environmental Rights and Human Rights: Six Facets of Constitutionally Embedded Environmental Rights Worldwide," *IUCN Academy of Environmental Law E-Journal* 1 (2011).

"Robinson Township v. Pennsylvania: A Model for Environmental Constitutionalism," *Widener Law Review* 21 (2015), p. 151.

"Vindicating Fundamental Environmental Rights Worldwide," *Oregon Review of International Law* 11 (2010), p. 365.

Mayer, Benoit, "Human Rights in the Paris Agreement," *Climate Law* 109 (2016), p. 6.

McAdam, Jane, *Climate Change, Forced Migration, and International Law* (Oxford University Press, 2012).

McAdam, Jane and Marc Limon, *Human Rights, Climate Change and Cross-Border Displacement* (Universal Rights Group, 2015).

McAllister, Lesley K., *Making Law Matter: Environmental Protection and Legal Institutions in Brazil* (Stanford University Press, 2008).

McCann, Michael, "Law and Social Movements: Contemporary Perspectives," *Annual Review of Law and Social Science* 2 (2006), pp. 17–38.

McDougal, Myres S. et al., *Human Rights and the World Public Order: The Basic Politics of an International Order of Human Dignity* (Yale University Press, 1980).

Meron, Theodor, *Human Rights and Humanitarian Norms as Customary Law* (Oxford University Press, 1989).

Merrills, John, "Environmental Rights," in Daniel Bodansky, Jutta Brunnée, and Ellen Hey (eds.), *Oxford Handbook of International Environmental Law* (Oxford University Press, 2007), p. 665.

Merry, Sally Engle, *Human Rights and Gender Violence: Translating International Law into Local Justice* (Chicago University Press, 2006).

Milanovic, Marko, *Extraterritorial Application of Human Rights Treaties: Law, Principles, and Policy* (Oxford University Press, 2011).

Morgan, Richard K., "Environmental Impact Assessment: The State of the Art," *Impact Assessment and Project Appraisals* 30 (2012), pp. 5–14.

Mwandosya, Mark J., *Survival Emissions: A Perspective from the South on Global Climate Negotiations* (Centre for Energy, Environment, Science and Technology, 1999).

Nicholson, Simon and Sikina Jinnah (eds.), *New Earth Politics: Essays from the Anthropocene* (MIT Press, 2016).

Niehuss, Juliette, "Inuit Circumpolar Conference v. Bush Administration: Why the Arctic Peoples Claim the United States' Role in Climate Change Has Violated Their Fundamental Human Rights and Threatens Their Very Existence," *Sustainable Development Law and Policy* 5(2) (2005).

Nimushakavi, Vasanthi, *Constitutional Policy and Environmental Jurisprudence in India* (Macmillan India, 2006), pp. 23, 156–7.

Ntoubandi, Faustin and Roland Adjouvi, "A Wider Human Rights Spectrum to Fight Climate Change in Africa?," in Ottavio Quirico and Mouloud Boumghar (eds.), *Climate Change and Human Rights: An International and Comparative Law Perspective* (Routledge, 2016), p. 265.

Ogunlade, Adebola, "Can the Bamako Convention Adequately Safeguard Africa's Environment in the Context of Transboundary Movement of Hazardous Wastes?," *University of Dundee* (2010), p. 19.

Olivier, Michèle, "The Relevance of 'Soft Law' as Source of International Human Rights," *Comparative and International Law Journal of Southern Africa* 35(3) (2002), pp. 289–307.

Orellana, Marcos, "Keynote Address: Habitat for Human Rights," *Vermont Law Review* 40 (2016).

"Reflections on the Right to a Healthy Environment," *Santa Clara Journal of International Law* 13(1) (2015), pp. 71–9.

Pallemaerts, Marc, "The Human Right to the Environment as a Substantive Right," in Maguelonne Dejeant-Pons and Marc Pallemaerts (eds.), *Human Rights and the Environment: Compendium of Instruments and Other International Texts on Individual and Collective Rights Relating to the Environment in the International and European Framework* (Council of Europe, 2002).

Passos de Freitas, Vladimir, "The Importance of Environmental Judicial Decisions: The Brazilian Experience," in M. E. Di Paola (ed.), *Symposium of Judges and Prosecutors of Latin America: Environmental Compliance and Enforcement*, pp. 59–64 at 62.

Pedersen, Ole W., "From Abundance to Indeterminacy: The Precautionary Principle and Its Two Camps of Custom," *Transnational Environmental Law* 3 (2014), p. 323.

"Environmental Risks, Rights and Black Swans," *Environmental Law Review* 15 (2003), p. 55.

"European Environmental Human Rights and Environmental Rights: A Long Time Coming?" *Georgetown International Environmental Law Review* 21(1) (2008), p. 73.

"The Janus-Head of Human Rights and Climate Change: Adaptation and Mitigation," *Nordic Journal of International Law* 80(4) (2011), pp. 403–23.

"The Ties that Bind: The Environment, the European Convention on Human Rights and the Rule of Law," *European Public Law* 16(4) (2009), p 571.

Peel, Jacqueline, "Environmental Protection in the Twenty-First Century: The Role of International Law," in Regina S. Axelrod, Stacy D. VanDeever and David Leonard Downie (eds.), *The Global Environment: Institutions, Law, and Policy*, 3d ed. (CQ Press, 2011).

Petersen, Niles, "Customary Law without Custom? Rules, Principles, and the Role of State Practice in International Norm Creation," *American University International Law Review* 23(2) (2007), pp. 275–310.

Pin, Andrea, *The Arab Road to Dignity: The Goal of the Arab Spring* (Kellogg Institute for International Studies, 2016).

Prieur, Michel, "De l'Urgente Nécessité de Reconnaitre le Principe de Non Regression en Droit de l'Environnement," *IUCN Academy of Environmental Law E-Journal* 1 (2011), pp. 26–45.

Rajamani, Lavanya, "The 2015 Paris Agreement: Interplay between Hard, Soft and Non-Obligations," *Journal of Environmental Law* 28 (2016), p. 337.

"Ambition and Differentiation in the 2015 Paris Agreement: Interpretative Possibilities and Underlying Politics," *International and Comparative Law Quarterly* 65 (2016), p. 493.

Differential Treatment in International Law (Oxford University Press, 2006).

"The Increasing Currency and Relevance of Rights-Based Perspectives in the International Negotiations on Climate Change," *Journal of Environmental Law* 22 (2010), p. 391.

Reisman, W. Michael, "The Cult of Custom in the Late 20th Century," *California Western International Law Journal* 17 (1987), p. 133.

Restatement (Third) of the Foreign Relations Law of the United States (1987).

Roberts, Anthea Elizabeth, "Traditional and Modern Approaches to Customary International Law: A Reconciliation," *American Journal of International Law* 95(4) (2001), pp. 757–91.

Mary Robinson Foundation Climate Justice, "Position Paper: Human Rights and Climate Justice" (2014).

Robinson, Nicholas A., "International Trends in Environmental Impact," *Boston College Environmental Affairs Law Review* 19 (1991), p. 591.

Rockström, Johan et al., "Planetary Boundaries: Exploring the Safe Operating Space for Humanity," *Ecology and Society* 14(2) (2009), pp. 1–24.

Rodríguez-Garavito, César, "Beyond the Courtroom: The Impact of Judicial Activism on Socioeconomic Rights in Latin America," *Texas Law Review* 89 (7) (2011), pp. 1669–98.

Rodríguez-Garavito, César (ed.), *Business and Human Rights: Beyond the End of the Beginning* (Cambridge University Press, 2017).

"Ethnicity.gov: Global Governance, Indigenous Peoples and the Right to Prior Consultation in Social Minefields," *Indiana Journal of Global Legal Studies* 18(1) (2011), pp. 263–305.

Rodríguez-Garavito, César and Diana Rodríguez-Franco, *Radical Deprivation of Trial: The Impact of Judicial Activism on Socioeconomic Rights in the Global South* (Cambridge University Press, 2015).

Rovine, Arthur (ed.), 1974 *Digest of United States Practice in International Law, 1973* (Government Printing Office, 1974).

Sabsay, Daniel A., "Constitution and Environment in Relation to Sustainable Development," in Maria Di Paola (ed.), *Symposium of Judges and Prosecutors of Latin America: Environmental Compliance and Enforcement* (Fundacion Ambiente y Recursos Naturales, 2003), pp. 33–43.

de Sadeleer, Nicolas, Gerhard Roller, and Miriam Dross, *Access to Justice in Environmental Matters and the Role of NGOs: Empirical Findings and Legal Appraisal* (Europa Law Publishing, 2005).

Sands, Philippe, *Principles of International Environmental Law*, 2d ed. (Cambridge University Press, 2003).

Sands, Philippe and Jacqueline Peel, *Principles of International Environmental Law*, 3d ed. (Cambridge University Press, 2012).

Sax, Joseph L., "The Public Trust Doctrine in Natural Resource Law: Effective Judicial Intervention," *Michigan Law Review* 68(3) (1970), pp. 471–566.

Schachter, Oscar, "International Law in Theory and Practice," *Recueil des Cours* 178 (1982), p. 334.

Scheingold, Stuart A., *The Politics of Rights: Lawyers, Public Policy and Political Change* (University of Michigan Press, 1974).

Scheppele, Kim Lane, "Amartya Sen's Vision for Human Rights – and Why He Needs the Law," *American University International Law Review* 27(1) (2011–12), pp. 17–35.

Scholtz, Werner, "Human Rights and the Environment in the African Union Context," in Anna Grear and Louis J. Kotzé (eds.), *Research Handbook on Human Rights and the Environment* (Edward Elgar Publishing, 2015), p. 401.

Sen, Amartya, "Elements of a Theory of Human Rights," *Philosophy and Public Affairs* 32(4) (2004), pp. 315–56.

"Human Rights and the Limits of Law," *Cardozo Law Review* 27(6) (2006), pp. 2913–27.

Shelton, Dinah, "Developing Substantive Environmental Rights," *Journal of Human Rights and the Environment* 1(1) (2010), pp. 89–121.

"Normative Hierarchy in International Law," *American Journal of International Law* 100(2) (2006), pp. 291–323.

"What Happened in Rio to Human Rights?" *Yearbook of International Environmental Law* 3(1) (1993), pp. 75–93.

Singleton-Cambage, Krista, "International Legal Sources and Global Environmental Crises: The Inadequacy of Principles, Treaties and Custom," *ILSA Journal of International and Comparative Law* 2 (1995), pp. 171–87.

Staveland-Saeter, Kristi, *Litigating the Right to a Healthy Environment: Assessing the Policy Impact of the Mendoza Case* (Michelson Institute, 2011), p. 48.

Stec, Stephen, "Environmental Justice through Courts in Countries in Economic Transition," in Jonas Ebbesson and Phoebe Okowa (eds.), *Environmental Law and Justice in Context* (Cambridge University Press, 2009), pp. 158–75.

Steffen, Will et al., "Planetary Boundaries: Guiding Human Development on a Changing Planet," *Science* 347(6223) (2015).

Steiner, Achim, *An Introduction to the African Convention on the Conservation of Nature and Natural Resources* (International Union for Conservation of Nature Environmental Law Centre, 2004), p. 1.

Stephens, Pamela J., "Applying Human Rights Norms to Climate Change: The Elusive Remedy," *Colorado Journal of International Environmental Law and Policy* 21(1) (2010), pp. 49–83.

Stern, Brigitte, "Custom at the Heart of International Law," *Duke Journal of Comparative and International Law* 11(1) (2001), pp. 89–108.

Stillings, Zackary L., "Human Rights and the New Reality of Climate Change: Adaptation's Limitations in Achieving Climate Justice," *Michigan Journal of International Law* 35 (2014), pp. 637, 640.

Stone, Christopher D., *Should Trees Have Standing? Law, Morality and the Environment* (Oxford University Press, 2010).

Streinz, Rudolf, "Risk Decisions in Cases of Persisting Scientific Uncertainty: The Precautionary Principle in European Food Law," in Gordon R. Woodman and Diethelm Klippel (eds.), *Risk and the Law* (Routledge 2009), pp. 53–81.

Strydom, Hennie, "Introduction to Regional Environmental Law of the African Union," in Werner Scholtz and Jonathan Verschuuren (eds.), *Regional Environmental Law: Transregional Cooperative Lessons in Pursuit of Sustainable Development* (Edward Elgar Publishing, 2015), p. 34.

"Symposium on Global Environmental Constitutionalism: An Introduction and Overview," *Widener Law Review* 21 (2015).

Thompson, Jr., Barton, "Constitutionalizing the Environment: The History and Future of Montana's Environmental Provisions," *Montana Law Review* 64 (2003), pp. 157–98.

Tiitmamer, Nhial, *Assessment of Policy and Institutional Responses to Climate Change and Environmental Disaster Risks in South Sudan* (Sudd Institute, 2015).

Turner, Stephen J., *A Global Environmental Right* (Routledge, 2014).

A Substantive Environmental Right: An Examination of the Legal Obligations of Decision-Makers towards the Environment (Kluwer Law, 2009).

Uhlmann, Eva Kornicker, "State Community Interests, Jus Cogens and Protection of the Global Environment: Developing Criteria for Peremptory Norms," *Georgetown International Environmental Law Review* 11(1) (1998), pp. 101–35.

Vidmar, Jure, "Norm Conflicts and Hierarchy in International Law: Towards a Vertical International Legal System?," in Erika de Wet and Jure Vidmar (eds.), *Hierarchy in International Law: The Place of Human Rights*, p. 33.

Viljoen, Frans, "Admissibility under the African Charter," in Malcolm Evans and Rachel Murray (eds.), *The African Charter on Human and Peoples' Rights: The System in Practice, 1986–2000* (Cambridge University Press, 2002).

International Human Rights Law in Africa (Oxford University Press, 2012).

"International Protection of Human Rights," in Hennie Strydom (ed.), *International Law* (Oxford University Press, 2016).

Waldron, Jeremy (ed.), *Theories of Rights* (Oxford University Press, 1984).

Walker, Brian et al., "Looming Global-Scale Failures and Missing Institutions," *Science* 325 (2009), pp. 1345–6.

Walsh, Juan Rodrigo, "Argentina's Constitution and General Environmental Law as the Framework for Comprehensive Land Use Regulation," in Nathalie J. Chalifour et al. (eds.), *Land Use Law for Sustainable Development* (Cambridge University Press, 2007), pp. 503–25 at 505.

Warner, Koko, "Human Migration and Displacement in the Context of Adaptation to Climate Change: The Cancun Adaptation Framework and Potential for Future Action," *Environment and Planning C: Policy and Space* 1061 (2012).

Watson, J. Shand, *Theory and Reality in the International Protection of Human Rights* (Transnational Publishers, 1999).

Weil, Prosper, "Towards Relative Normativity in International Law?," *American Journal of International Law* 77(3) (1983), pp. 413–42.

Weiss, Edith Brown (ed.), *International Compliance with Nonbinding Accords* (American Society of International Law, 1997).

Whelan, Daniel J., *Indivisible Human Rights: A History* (University of Pennsylvania Press, 2010).

Whiteman, Marjorie, "Jus Cogens in International Law, with a Projected List," *Georgia Journal of International and Comparative Law* 7(2), pp. 609– 26 at 625.

Wold, Chris, David Hunter, and Melissa Powers, *Climate Change and the Law* (LexisNexis, 2009).

Yang, Tseming and Robert V. Percival, "The Emergence of Global Environmental Law," *Ecology Law Quarterly* 36(3) (2009), pp. 615–64.

Zalasiewicz, Jan et al., "The New World of the Anthropocene," *Environmental Science and Technology* 2228 (2010), p. 44.

Index

CPSIA information can be obtained
at www.ICGtesting.com
Printed in the USA
LVHW081948281222
736059LV00009B/485